Dragon Eye
Volume 6

DEL
REY

Ballantine Books · New York

A Del Rey Manga/Kodansha Trade Paperback Original

Published in the United States by Del Rey Books, an imprint of The Random House Publishing Group, a division of Random House, Inc., New York.

DEL REY is a registered trademark and the Del Rey colophon is a trademark of Random House, Inc.

Publication rights arranged through Kodansha Ltd.

First published in Japan in 2007 by Kodansha Ltd., Tokyo

ISBN 978-0-345-50521-7

Printed in the United States of America

www.delreymanga.com

9 8 7 6 5 4 3 2 1

Translator/Adaptor—Mari Morimoto
Lettering: NMSG

Contents

While pondering what to write in my opening note, I was looking over my illustration for the cover. And then I saw it: a big mistake! I've just gotta get it fixed right away...but can I fix it in time!!?

Oh, no, I've completely forgotten what I was going to write!
—Kairi Fujiyama

Honorifics Explained

Throughout the Del Rey Manga books, you will find Japanese honorifics left intact in the translations. For those not familiar with how the Japanese use honorifics and, more important, how they differ from American honorifics, we present this brief overview.

Politeness has always been a critical facet of Japanese culture. Ever since the feudal era, when Japan was a highly stratified society, use of honorifics—which can be defined as polite speech that indicates relationship or status—has played an essential role in the Japanese language. When you address someone in Japanese, an honorific usually takes the form of a suffix attached to one's name (example: "Asuna-san"), is used as a title at the end of one's name, or appears in place of the name itself (example: "Negi-sensei," or simply "Sensei!").

Honorifics can be expressions of respect or endearment. In the context of manga and anime, honorifics give insight into the nature of the relationship between characters. Many English translations leave out these important honorifics and therefore distort the feel of the original Japanese. Because Japanese honorifics contain nuances that English honorifics lack, it is our policy at Del Rey not to translate them. Here, instead, is a guide to some of the honorifics you may encounter in Del Rey Manga.

-san: This is the most common honorific and is equivalent to Mr., Miss, Ms., or Mrs. It is the all-purpose honorific and can be used in any situation where politeness is required.

-sama: This is one level higher than "-san" and is used to confer great respect.

-dono: This comes from the word "tono," which means "lord." It is an even higher level than "-sama" and confers utmost respect.

-kun: This suffix is used at the end of boys' names to express familiarity or endearment. It is also sometimes used by men among friends, or when addressing someone younger or of a lower station.

-chan: This is used to express endearment, mostly toward girls. It is also used for little boys, pets, and even among lovers. It gives a sense of childish cuteness.

Bozu: This is an informal way to refer to a boy, similar to the English terms "kid" and "squirt."

Sempai/Senpai: This title suggests that the addressee is one's senior in a group or organization. It is most often used in a school setting, where underclassmen refer to their upperclassmen as "sempai." It can also be used in the workplace, such as when a newer employee addresses an employee who has seniority in the company.

Kohai: This is the opposite of "sempai" and is used toward underclassmen in school or newcomers in the workplace. It connotes that the addressee is of a lower station.

Sensei: Literally meaning "one who has come before," this title is used for teachers, doctors, or masters of any profession or art.

-[blank]: This is usually forgotten in these lists, but it is perhaps the most significant difference between Japanese and English. The lack of honorific is known as *yobisute*, and it means that the speaker has permission to address the person in a very intimate way. Usually, only family, spouses, or very close friends have this kind of permission. It can be gratifying when someone who has earned the intimacy starts to call one by one's name without an honorific. But when that intimacy hasn't been earned, it can be very insulting.

Dragon Eye

Kairi Fujiyama

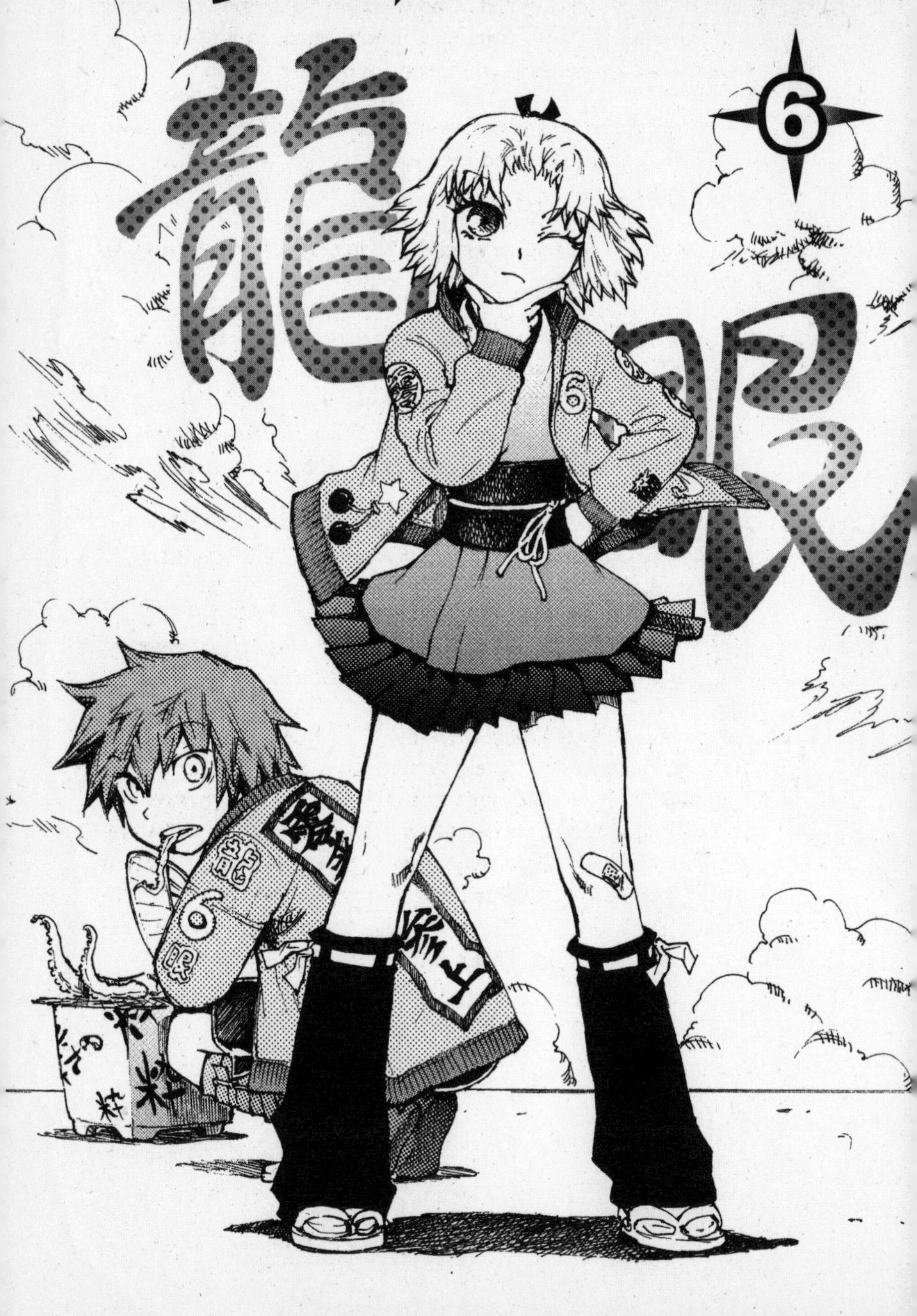

6
龍眼

Story of DRAGON EYE

龍眼物語

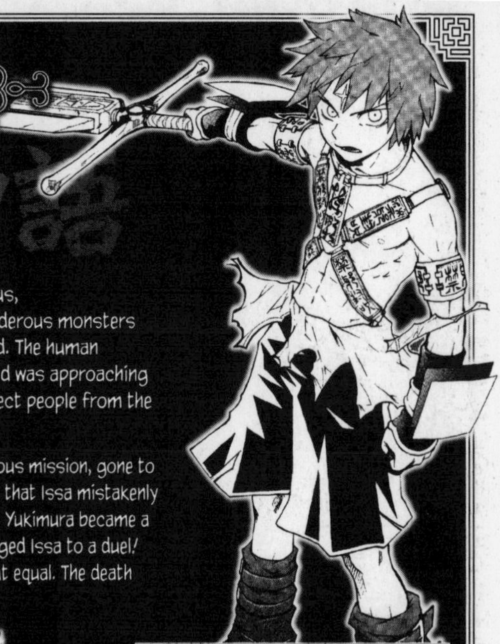

It has been several decades since the D Virus, whose infected victims transform into murderous monsters known as Dracules, spread across the world. The human population plummeted severely and the world was approaching a crisis point....Those who emerged to protect people from the Dracules came to be called the VIUS.

VIUS Squad Zero Captain Issa had, on a previous mission, gone to Yukimu[illegible]s house on a Dracule hunt. It is said that Issa mistakenly killed Y[illegible]mura's twin sister, Futaba, that day. Yukimura became a VIUS i[illegible]rder to avenge his sister, and challenged Issa to a duel! With Issa wounded, their strength is just about equal. The death match between the two is about to begin!!

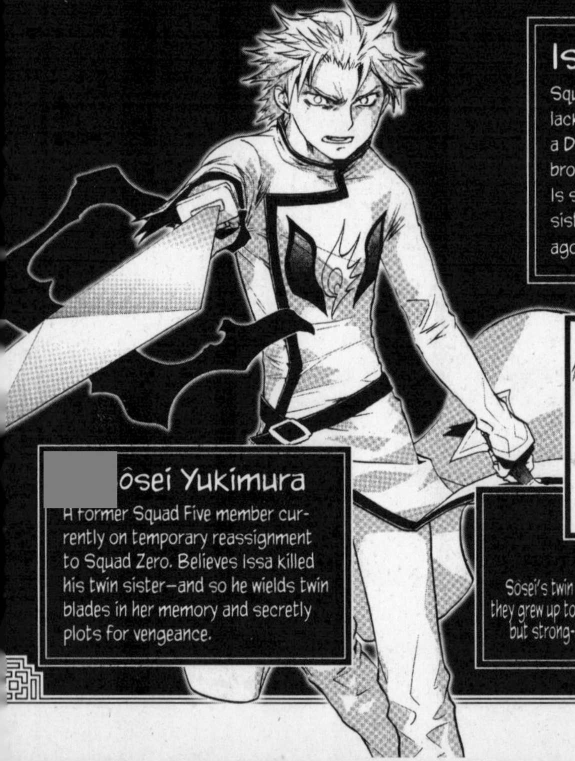

Issa Kazuma

Squad Zero captain. Seems lackadaisical, but possesses a Dragon Eye and wields the broadsword Diamond Sacred Steel. Is said to have killed Yukimura's sister during a mission six years ago, but...?

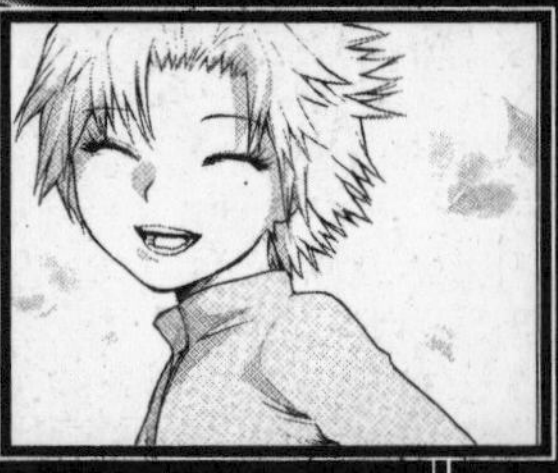

[illegible]ôsei Yukimura

A former Squad Five member currently on temporary reassignment to Squad Zero. Believes Issa killed his twin sister—and so he wields twin blades in her memory and secretly plots for vengeance.

Futaba

Sôsei's twin sister. Having lost both parents, they grew up together and were very close. A sickly but strong-hearted, courageous young girl.

Hyûga

Assigned to the Intelligence Corps. Idolizes Issa because his first mission was with Issa's squad. Supposedly likes Mikuni's pop star NATSUMI★chan.

Leila Mikami

Newly inducted VIUS member. When she was little, both her parents were killed by Dracules, and she alone survived. Her weapon of choice is the *katana* blade, and she is a student of the Shimon School Sacred Blade.

Shizue Aoi

Squad Six captain, said to be Mikuni's number one beauty—everyone gets a crush on her at least once. Because Squad Six is a covert ops unit, is good at undercover investigations.

Sakuraba Shun'ichi

Captain of Squad One, and a good friend of Issa's. Lost one arm in the past, so now seems to be devoted to administrative duties, but is said to be the strongest among all Mikuni VIUS.

Mystery Man

A man who is trying to get Issa exiled from Mikuni by setting Hibiki on him. The reason he hates Issa so much is still a mystery.

Masamune Hibiki

Squad Six member. A young but brilliant and talented warrior. Seems to hold enmity toward Issa, but not for the usual reasons...

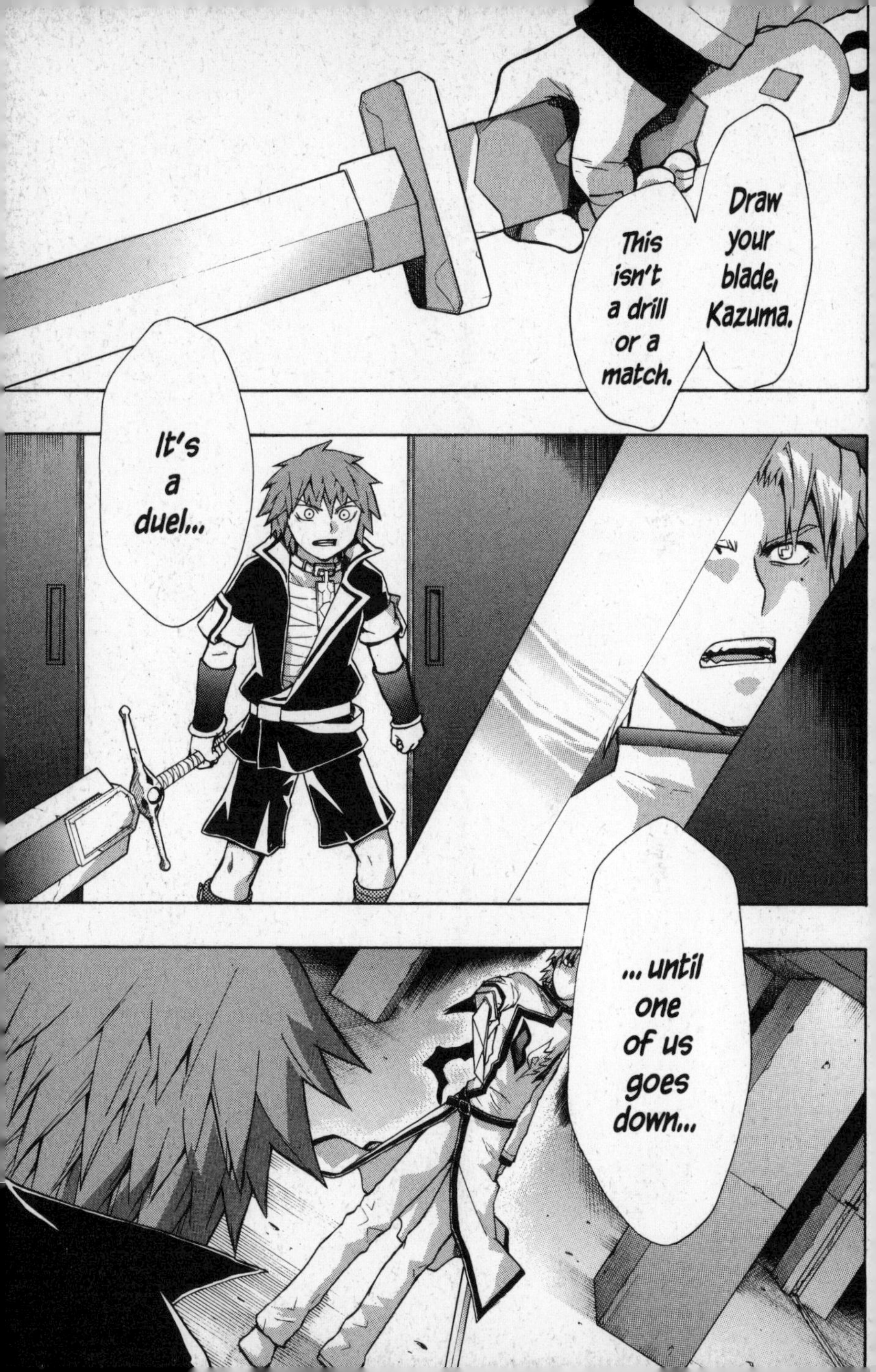
Draw your blade, Kazuma.
This isn't a drill or a match.
It's a duel...
...until one of us goes down...

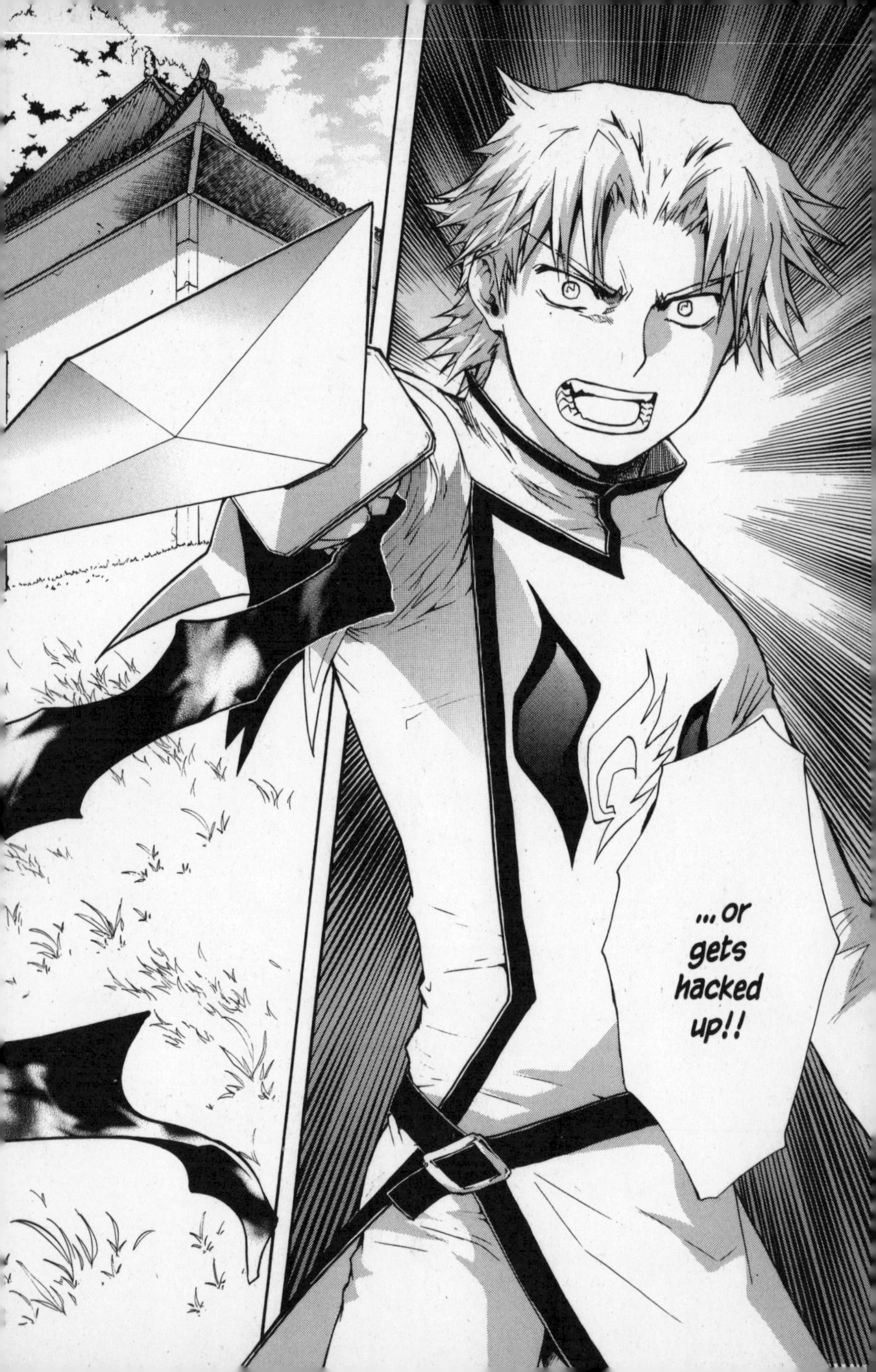
...or gets hacked up!!

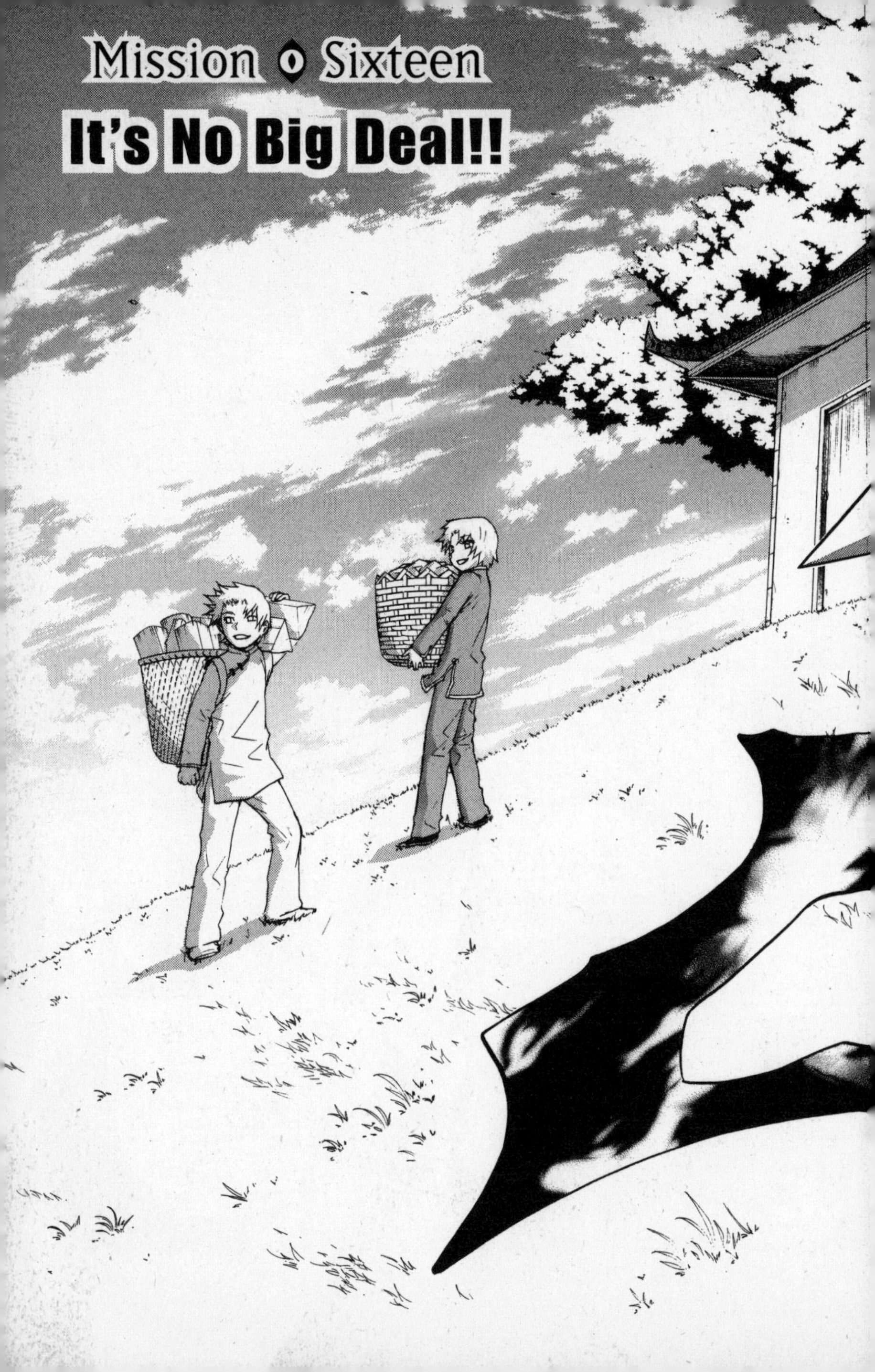
Mission Sixteen
It's No Big Deal!!

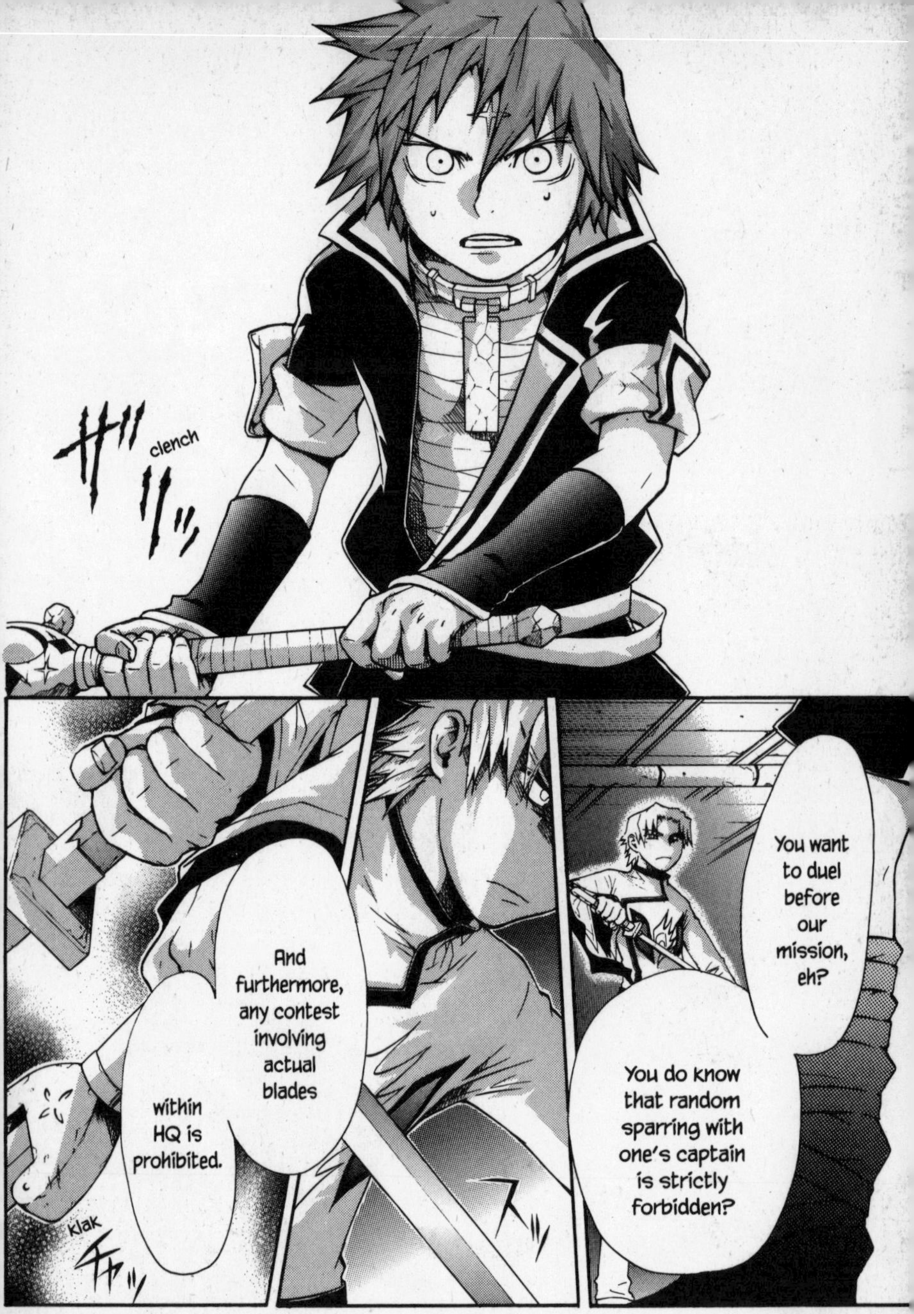
clench
You want to duel before our mission, eh?
You do know that random sparring with one's captain is strictly forbidden?
And furthermore, any contest involving actual blades
within HQ is prohibited.
klak

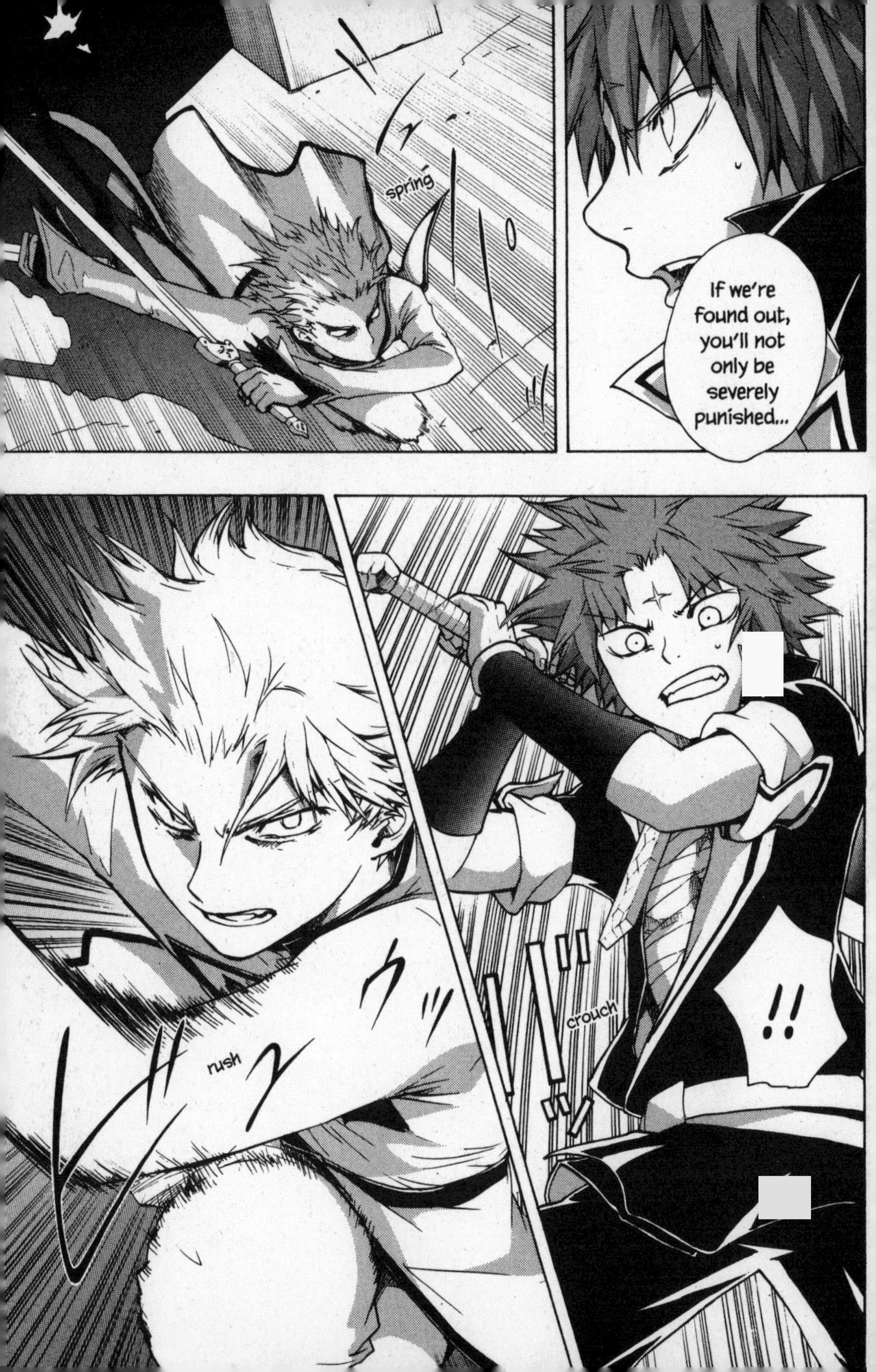
If we're found out, you'll not only be severely punished...
spring
!!
crouch
rush

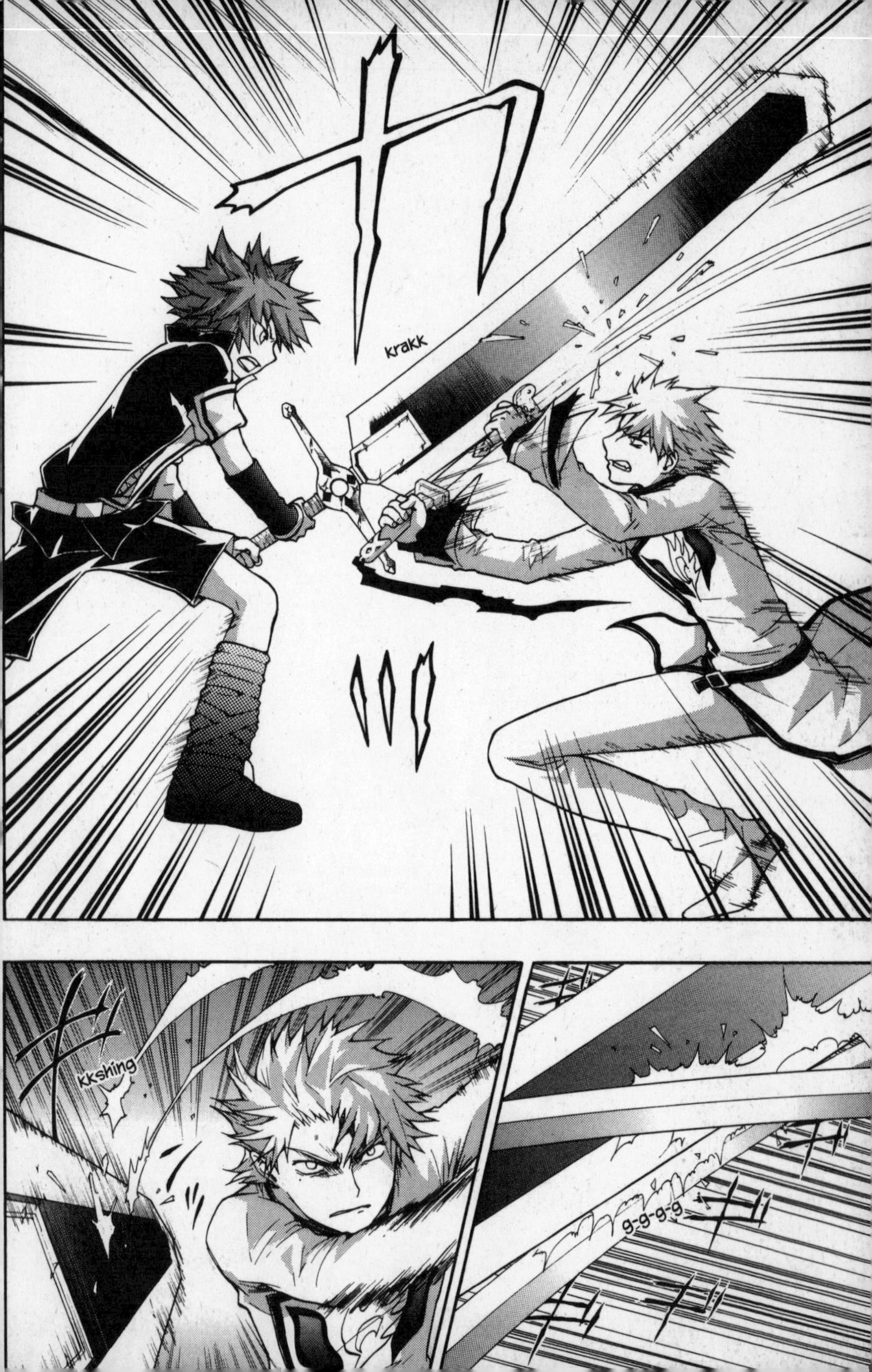
krakk
g-g-g-g
kkshing

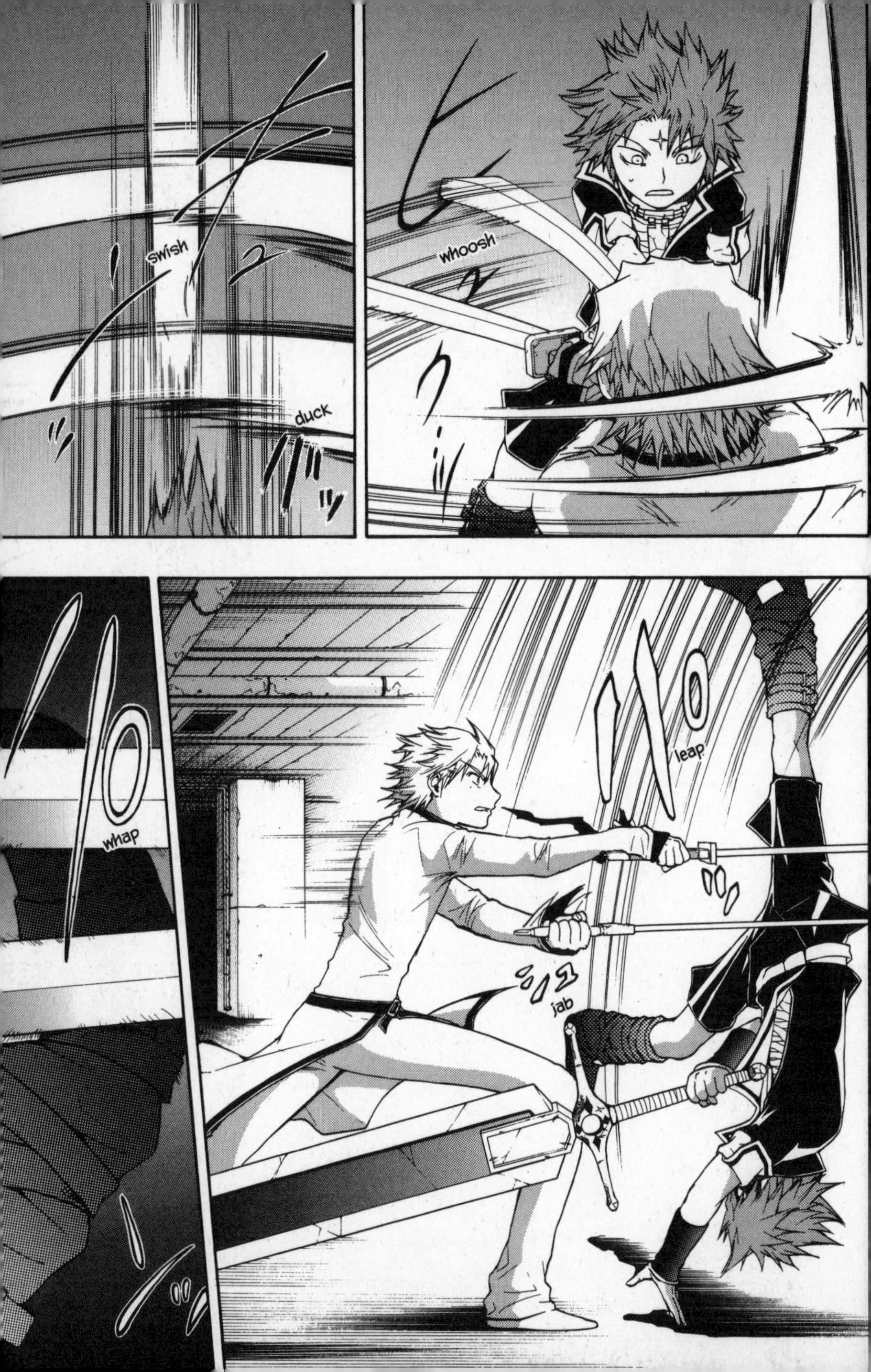
whoosh
swish
duck
leap
jab
whap

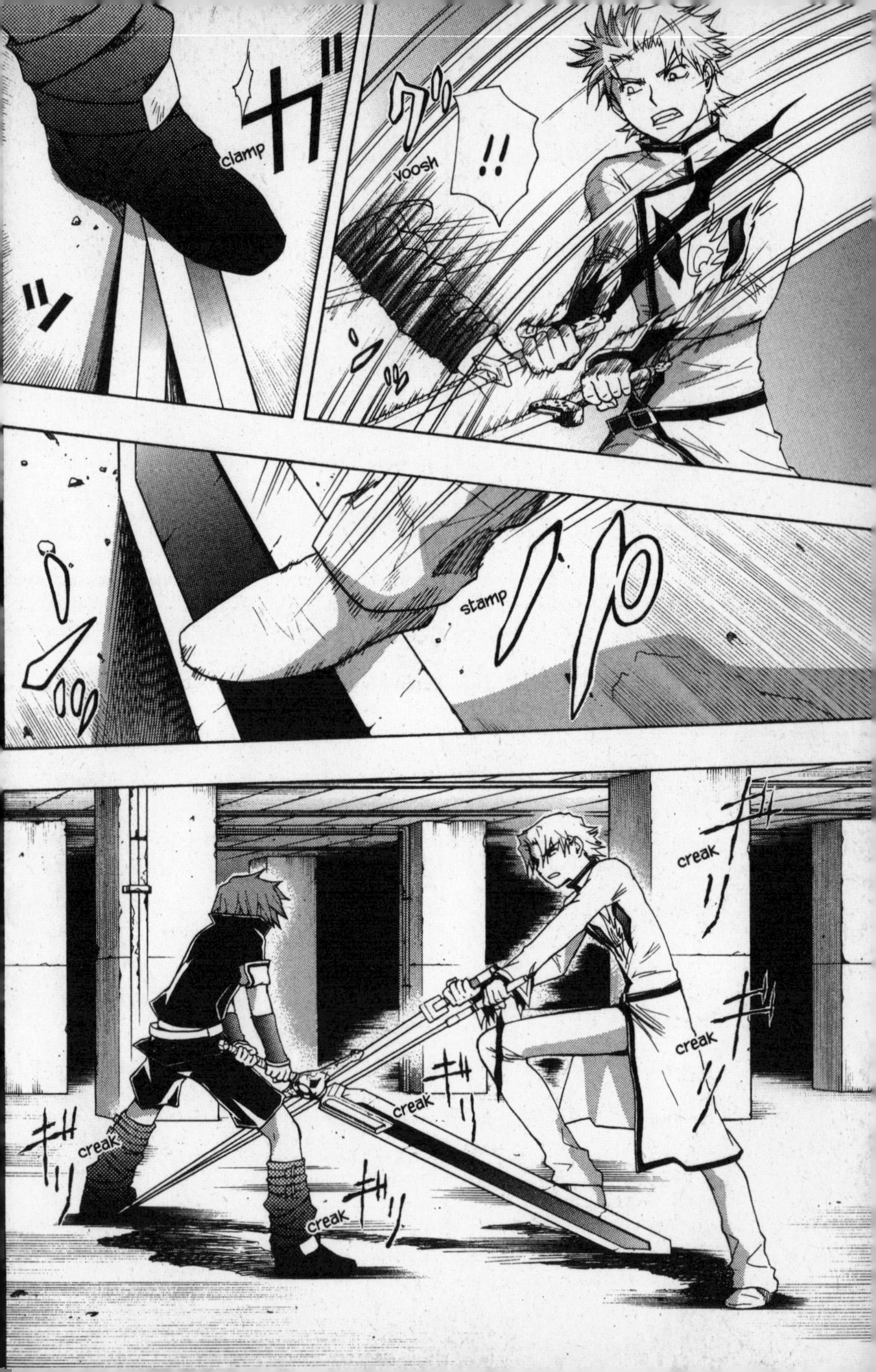

!!
voosh
clamp
stamp
creak
creak
creak
creak
creak

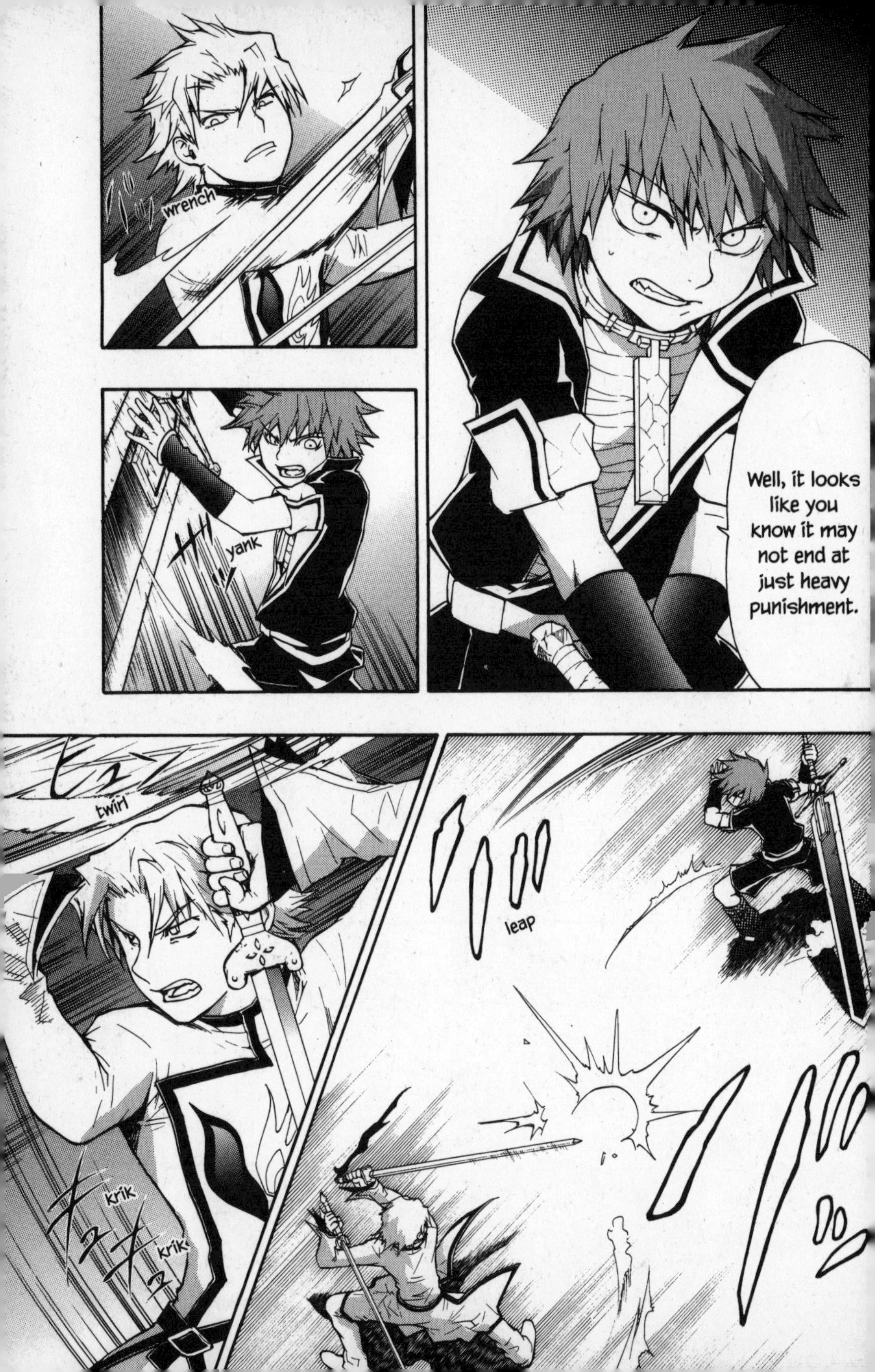
Well, it looks like you know it may not end at just heavy punishment.
wrench
yank
leap
twirl
krik
krik

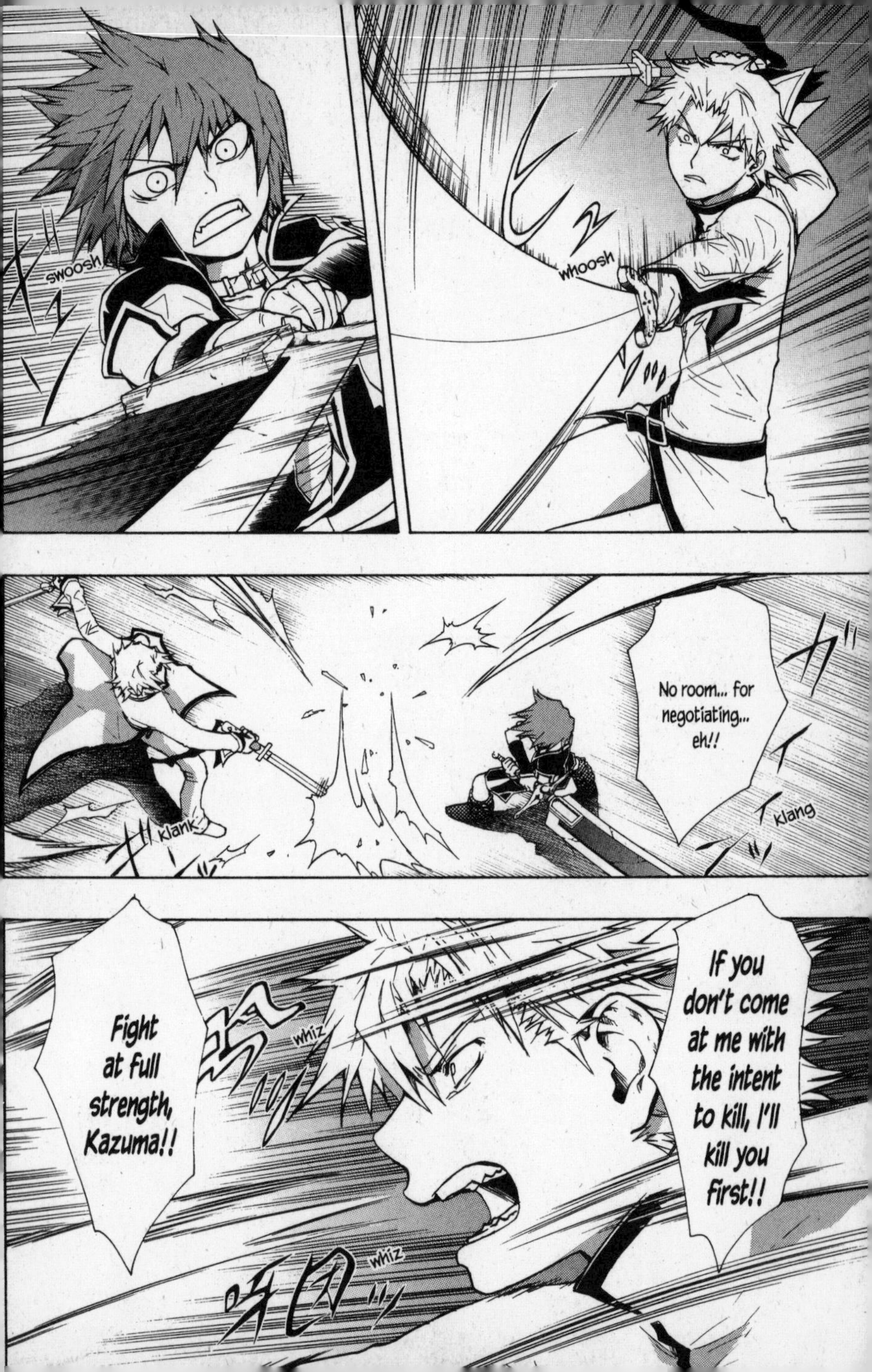
whoosh
swoosh
No room... for negotiating... eh!!
klang
klank
If you don't come at me with the intent to kill, I'll kill you first!!
whiz
Fight at full strength, Kazuma!!
whiz

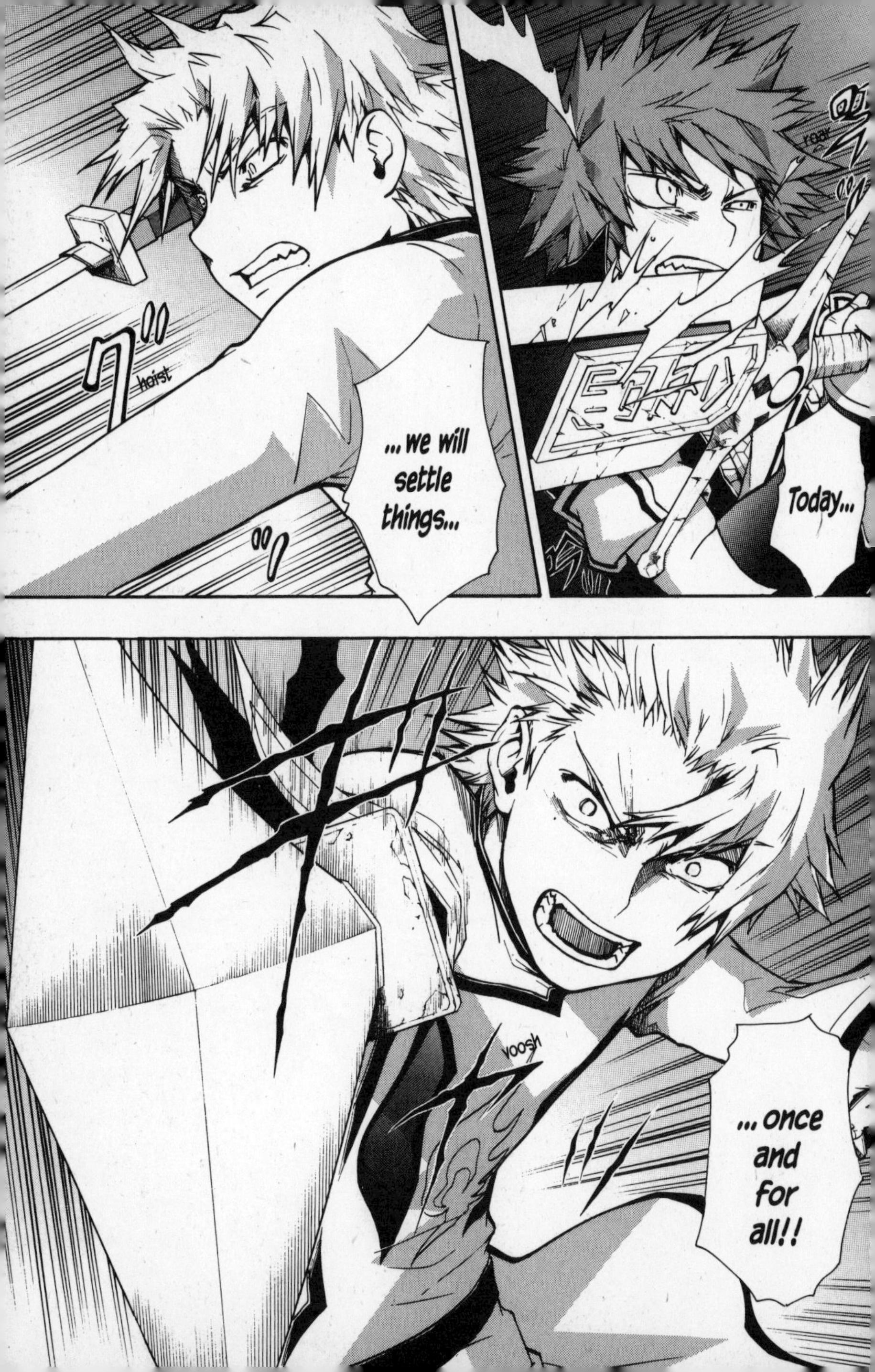
roar
Today...
hoist
...we will settle things...
voosh
...once and for all!!

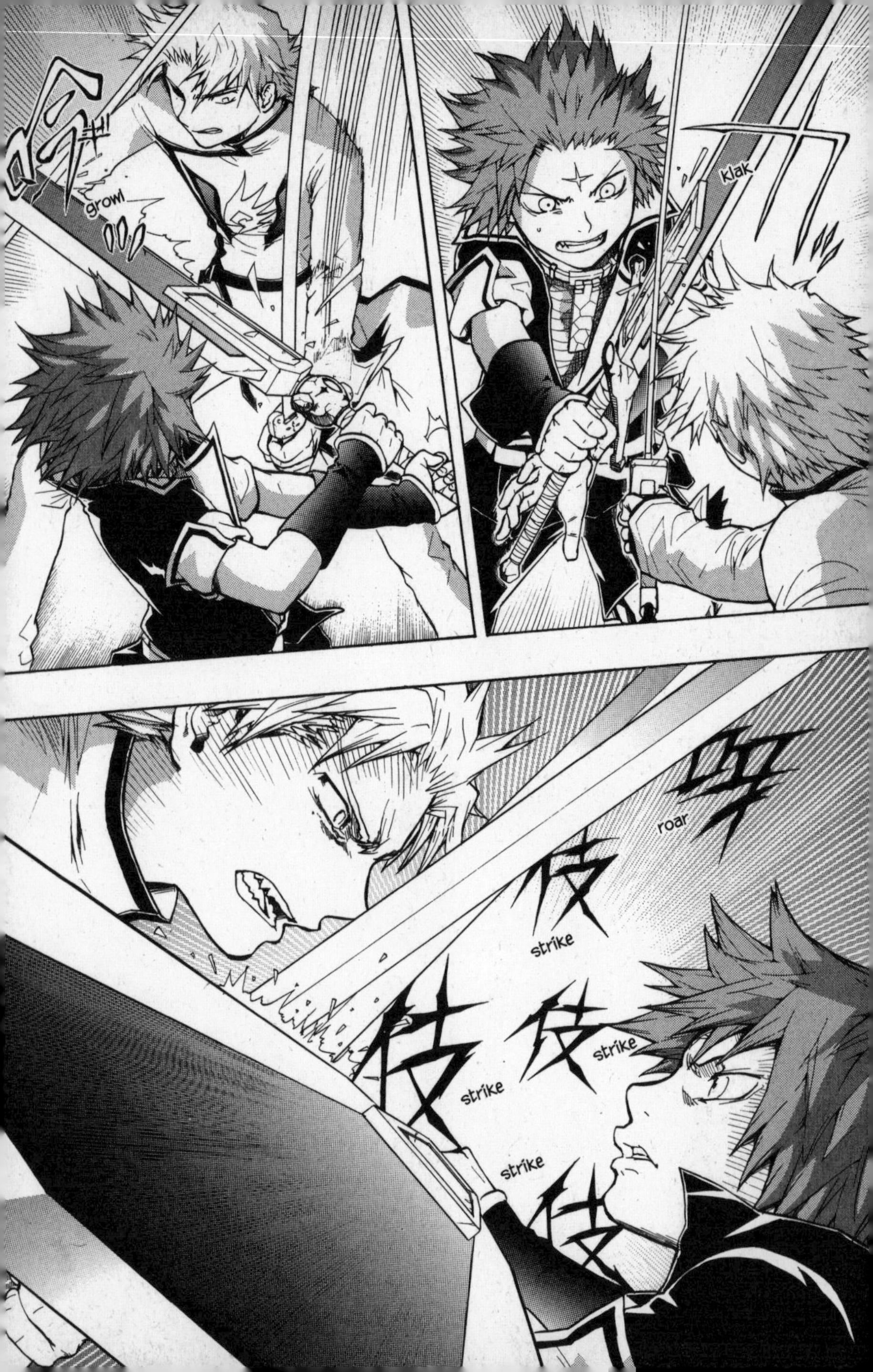
klak
growl
roar
strike
strike
strike
strike

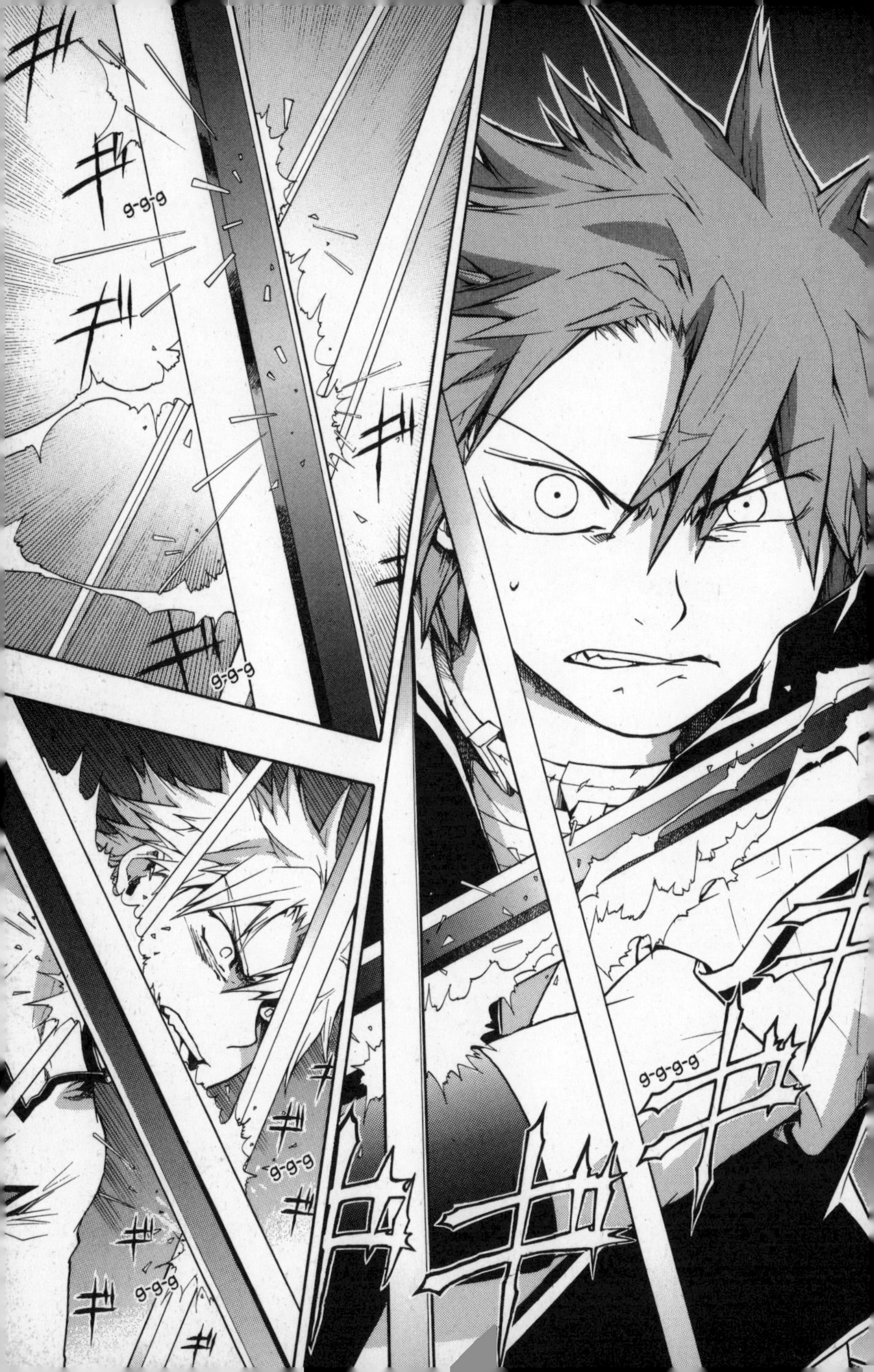
g-g-g-g
g-g-g
g-g-g
g-g-g
g-g-g

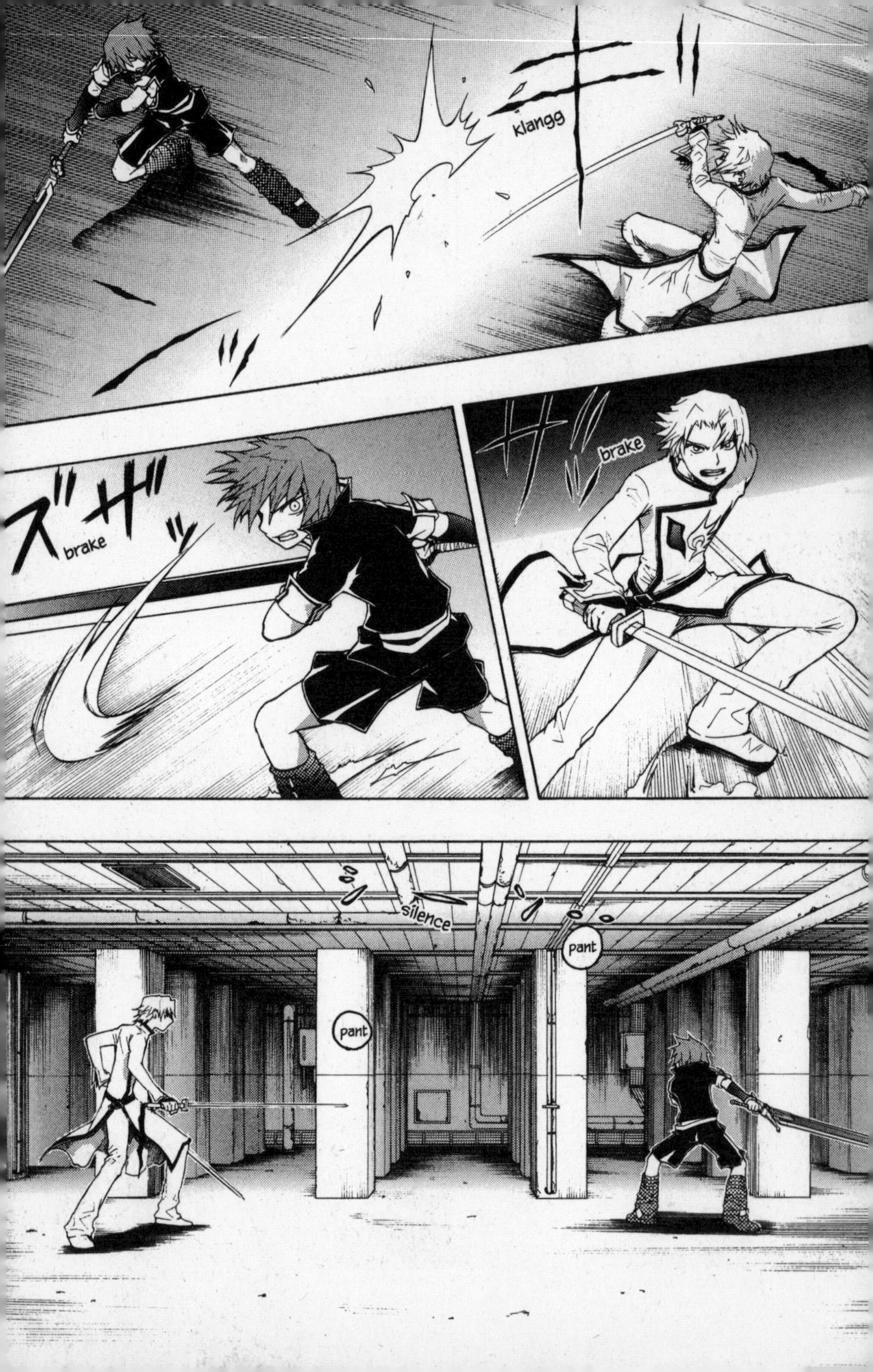
klangg
brake
ズザッ
brake
silence
pant
pant

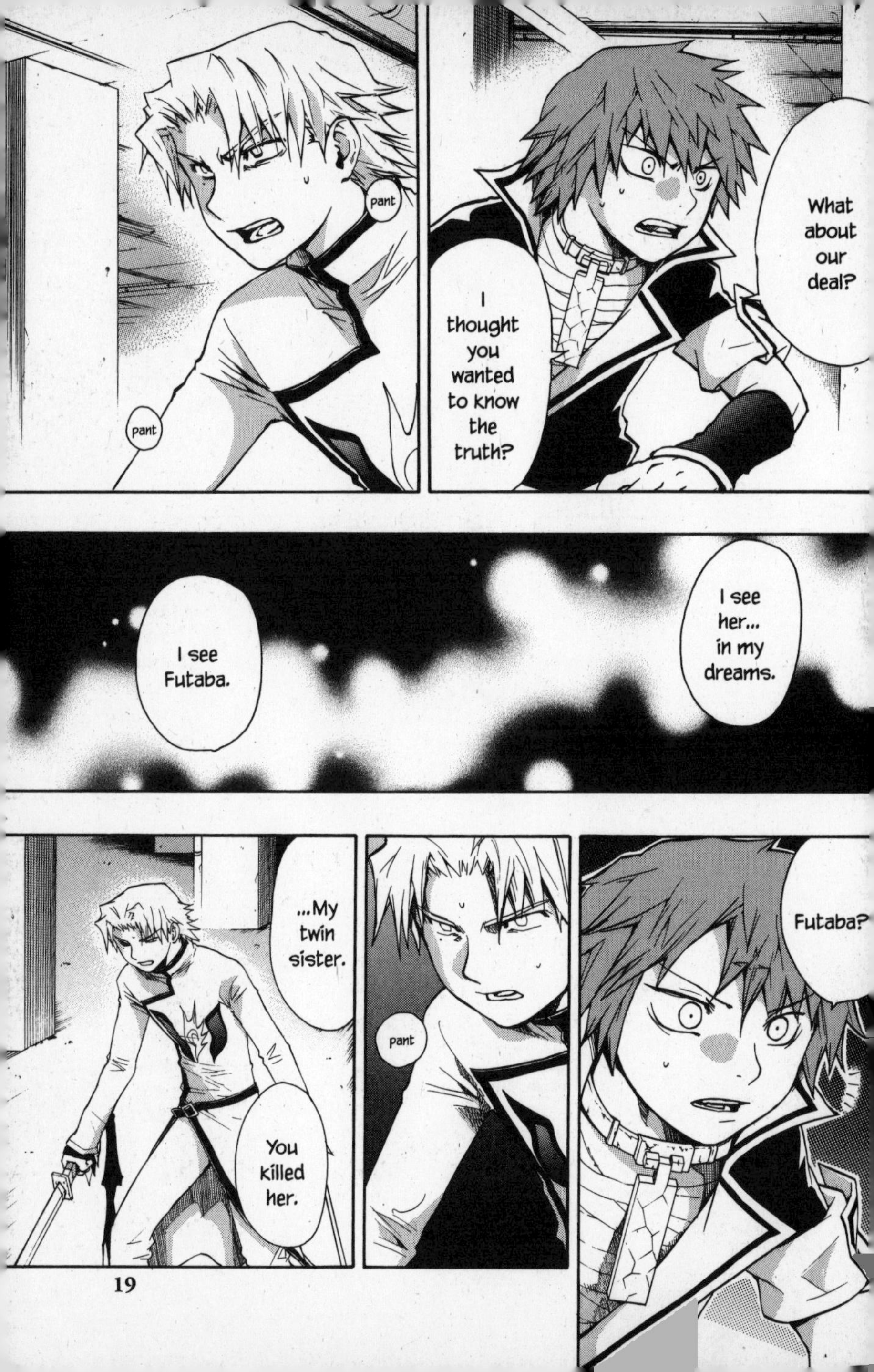
What about our deal?
I thought you wanted to know the truth?
pant
pant
I see her... in my dreams.
I see Futaba.
Futaba?
pant
...My twin sister.
You killed her.

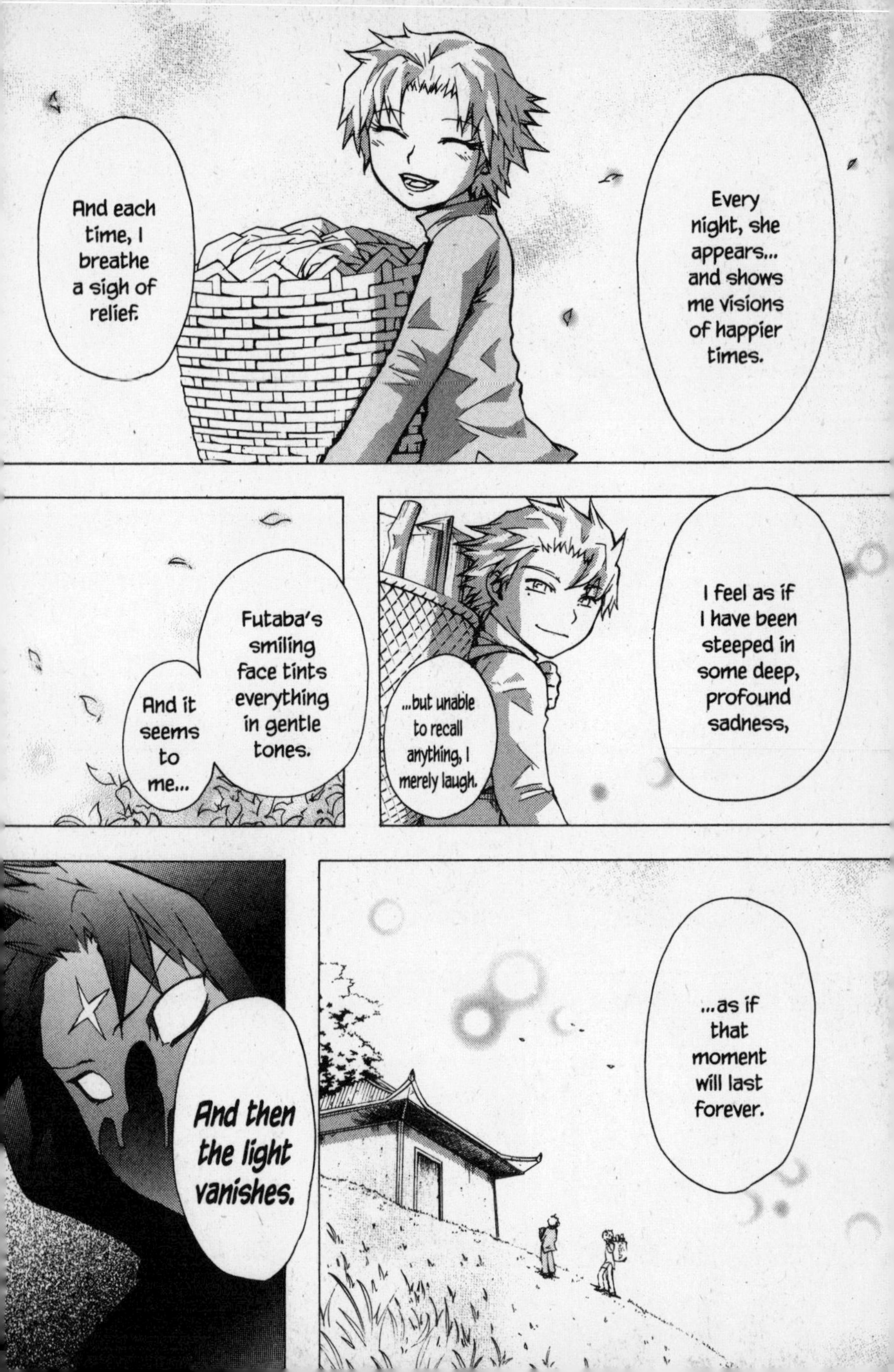
Every night, she appears... and shows me visions of happier times.
And each time, I breathe a sigh of relief.
I feel as if I have been steeped in some deep, profound sadness,
...but unable to recall anything, I merely laugh.
Futaba's smiling face tints everything in gentle tones.
And it seems to me...
...as if that moment will last forever.
And then the light vanishes.

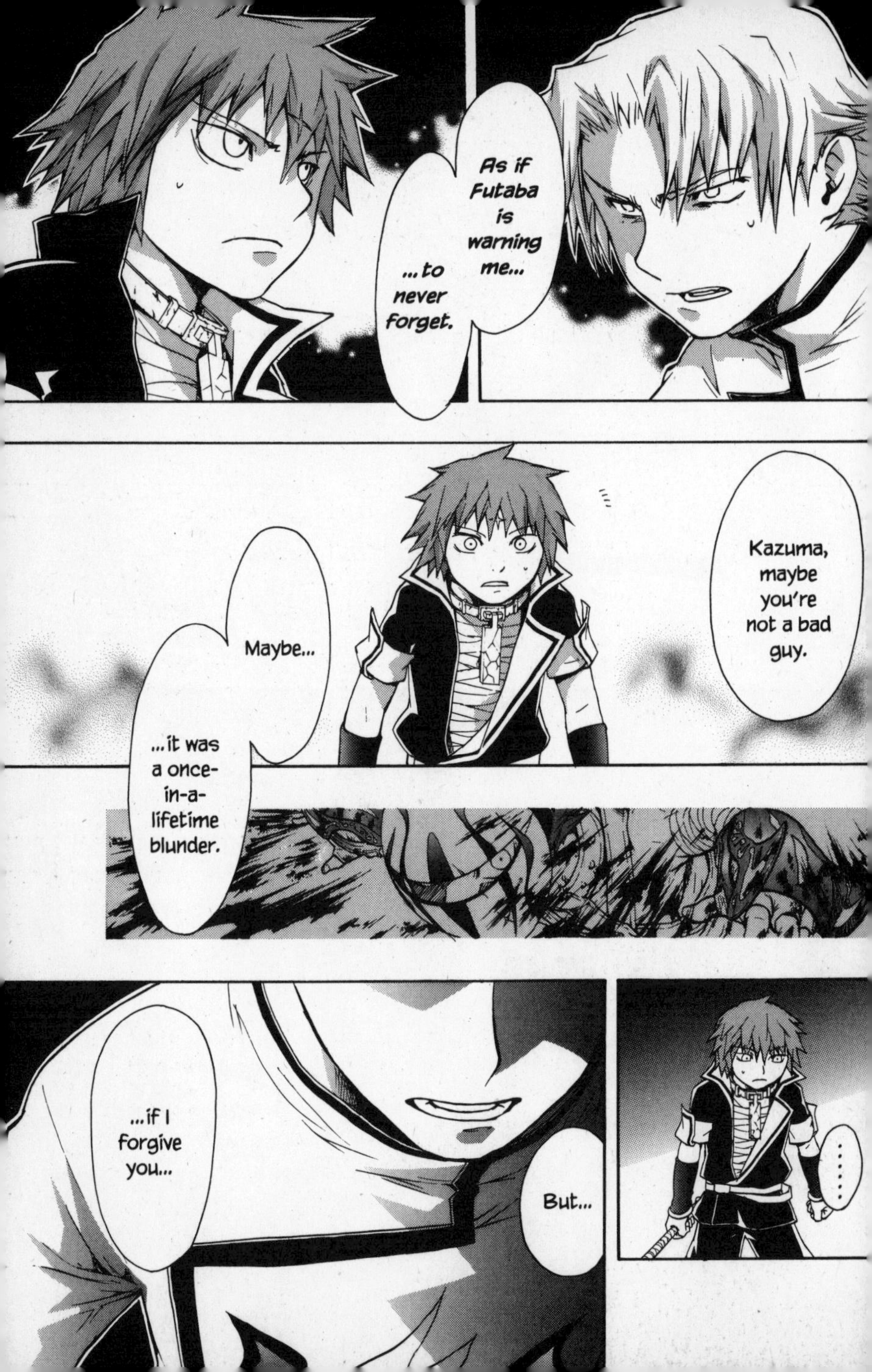
As if Futaba is warning me...
...to never forget.
Kazuma, maybe you're not a bad guy.
Maybe...
...it was a once-in-a-lifetime blunder.
......
But...
...if I forgive you...

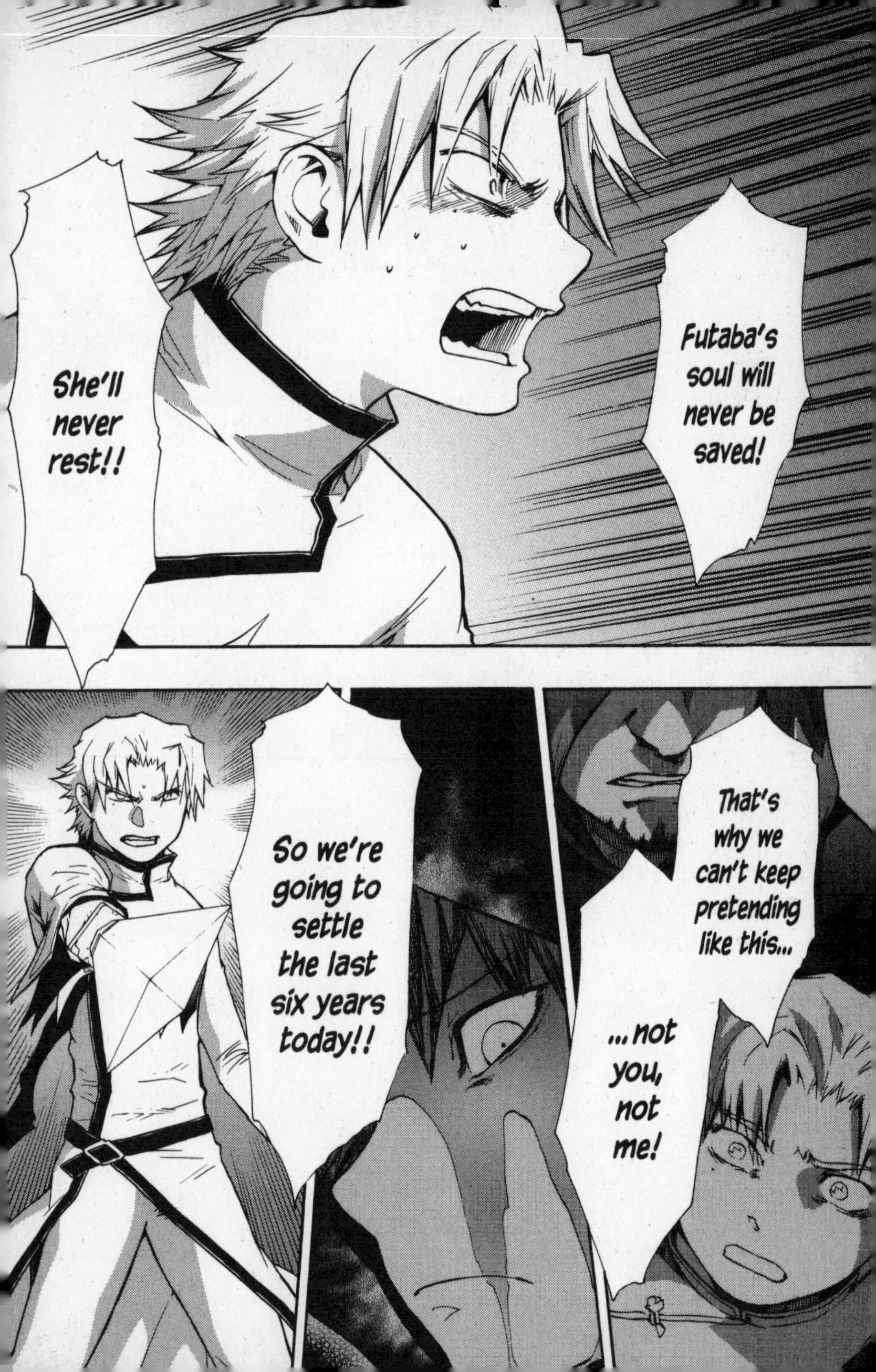
Futaba's soul will never be saved!
She'll never rest!!
That's why we can't keep pretending like this...
...not you, not me!
So we're going to settle the last six years today!!

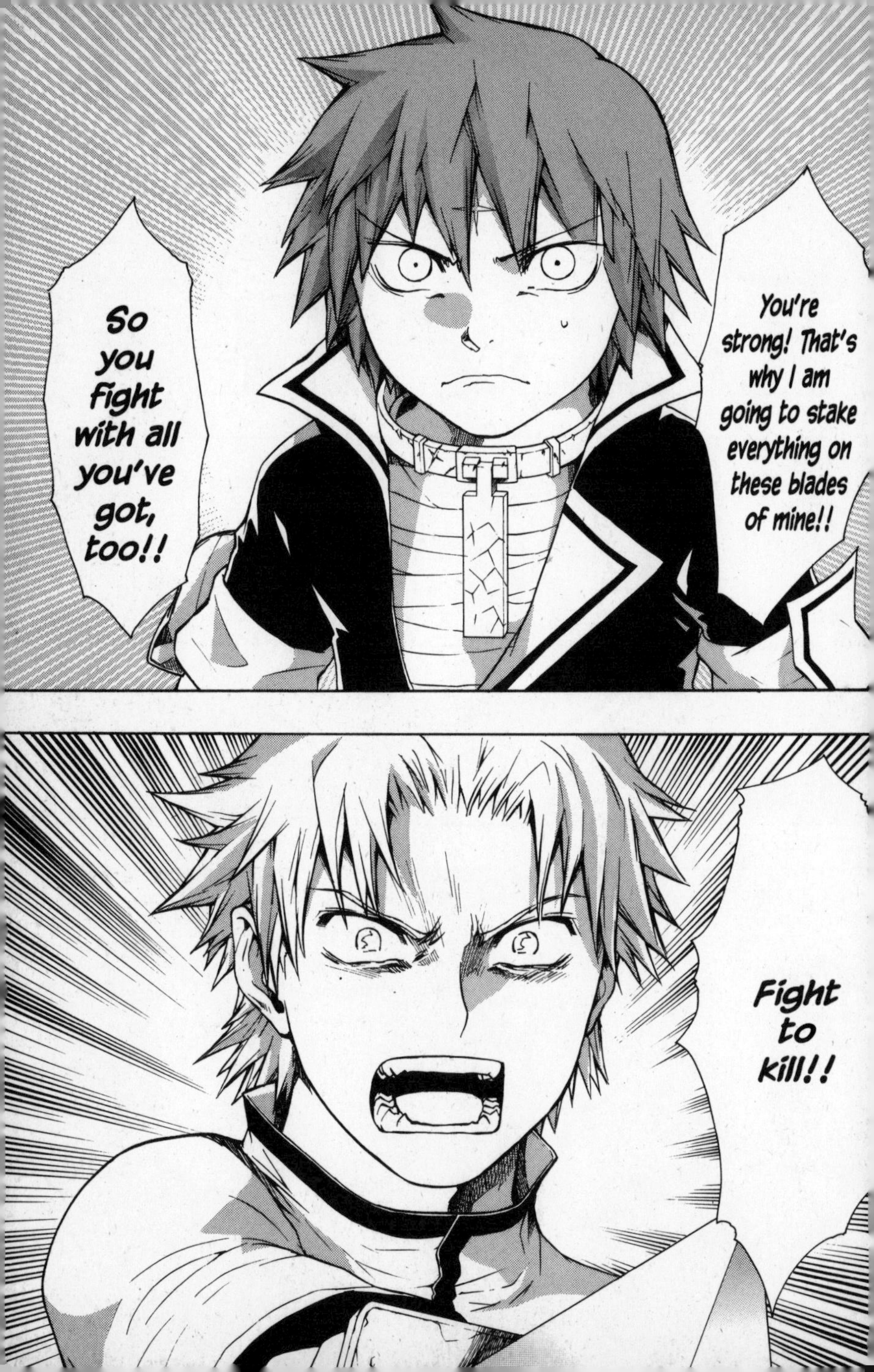
You're strong! That's why I am going to stake everything on these blades of mine!!
So you fight with all you've got, too!!
Fight to kill!!

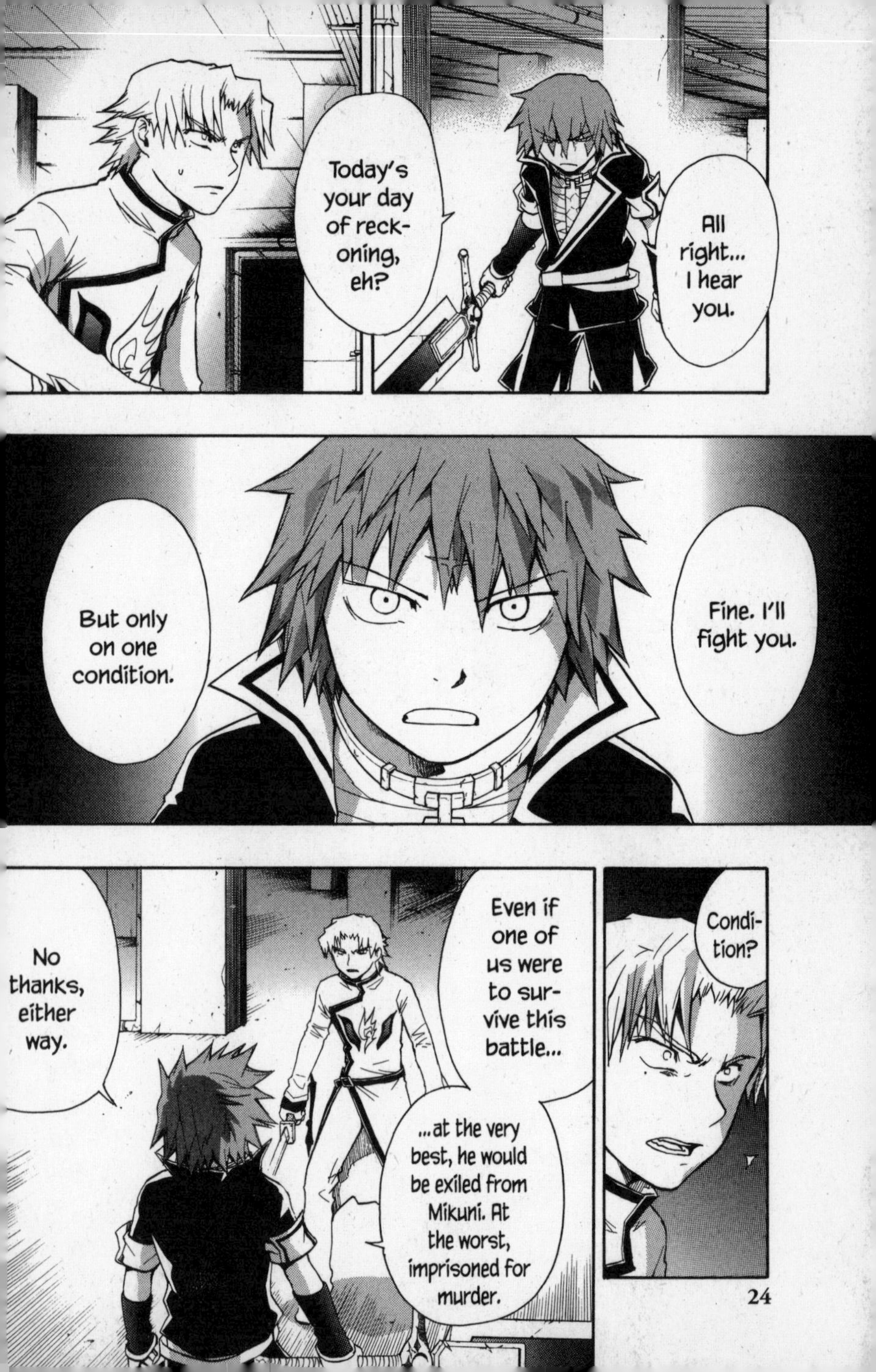
All right... I hear you.
Today's your day of reckoning, eh?
Fine. I'll fight you.
But only on one condition.
Condition?
Even if one of us were to survive this battle...
...at the very best, he would be exiled from Mikuni. At the worst, imprisoned for murder.
No thanks, either way.

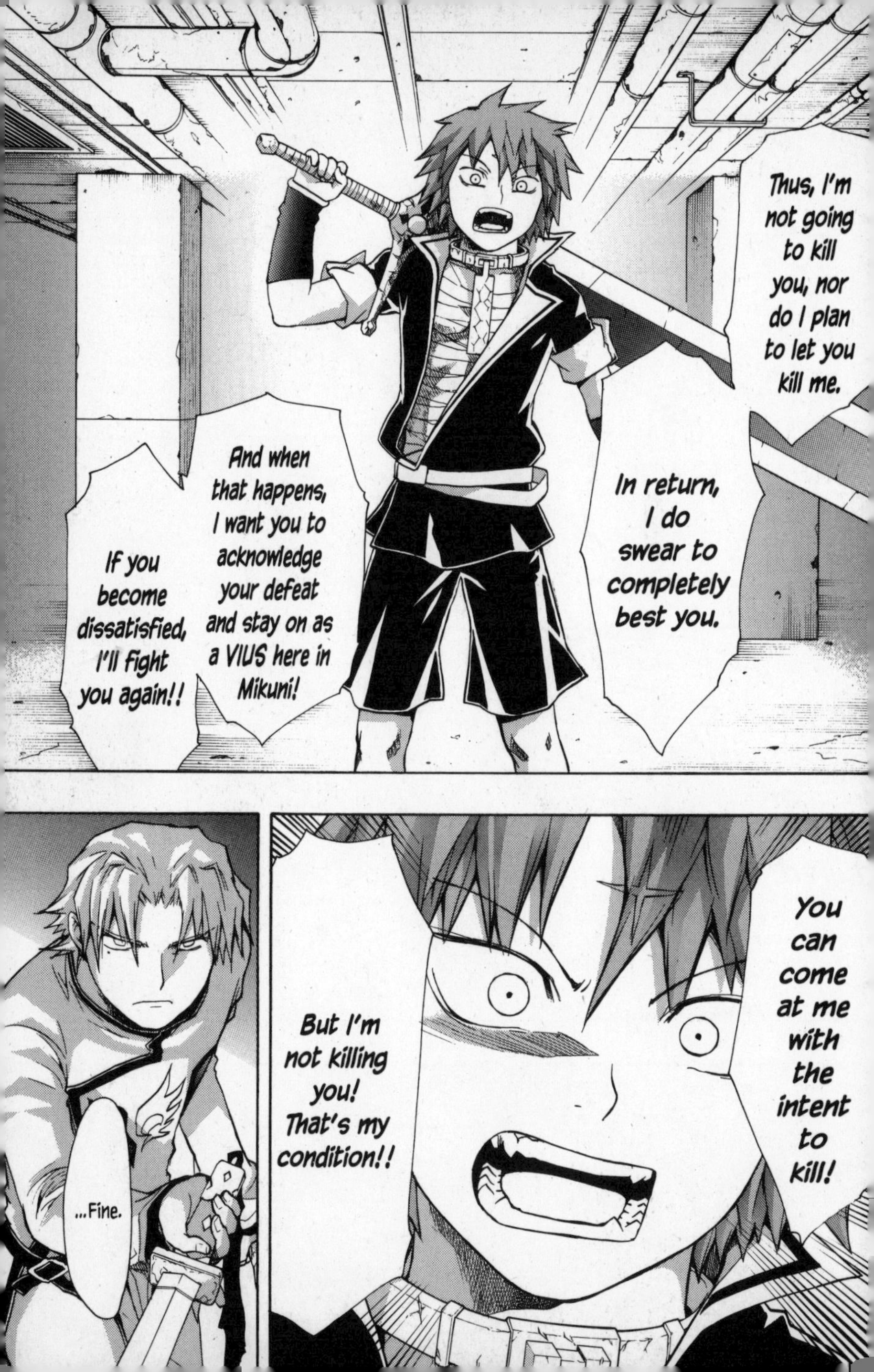
Thus, I'm not going to kill you, nor do I plan to let you kill me.
In return, I do swear to completely best you.
And when that happens, I want you to acknowledge your defeat and stay on as a VIUS here in Mikuni!
If you become dissatisfied, I'll fight you again!!
You can come at me with the intent to kill!
But I'm not killing you! That's my condition!!
...Fine.

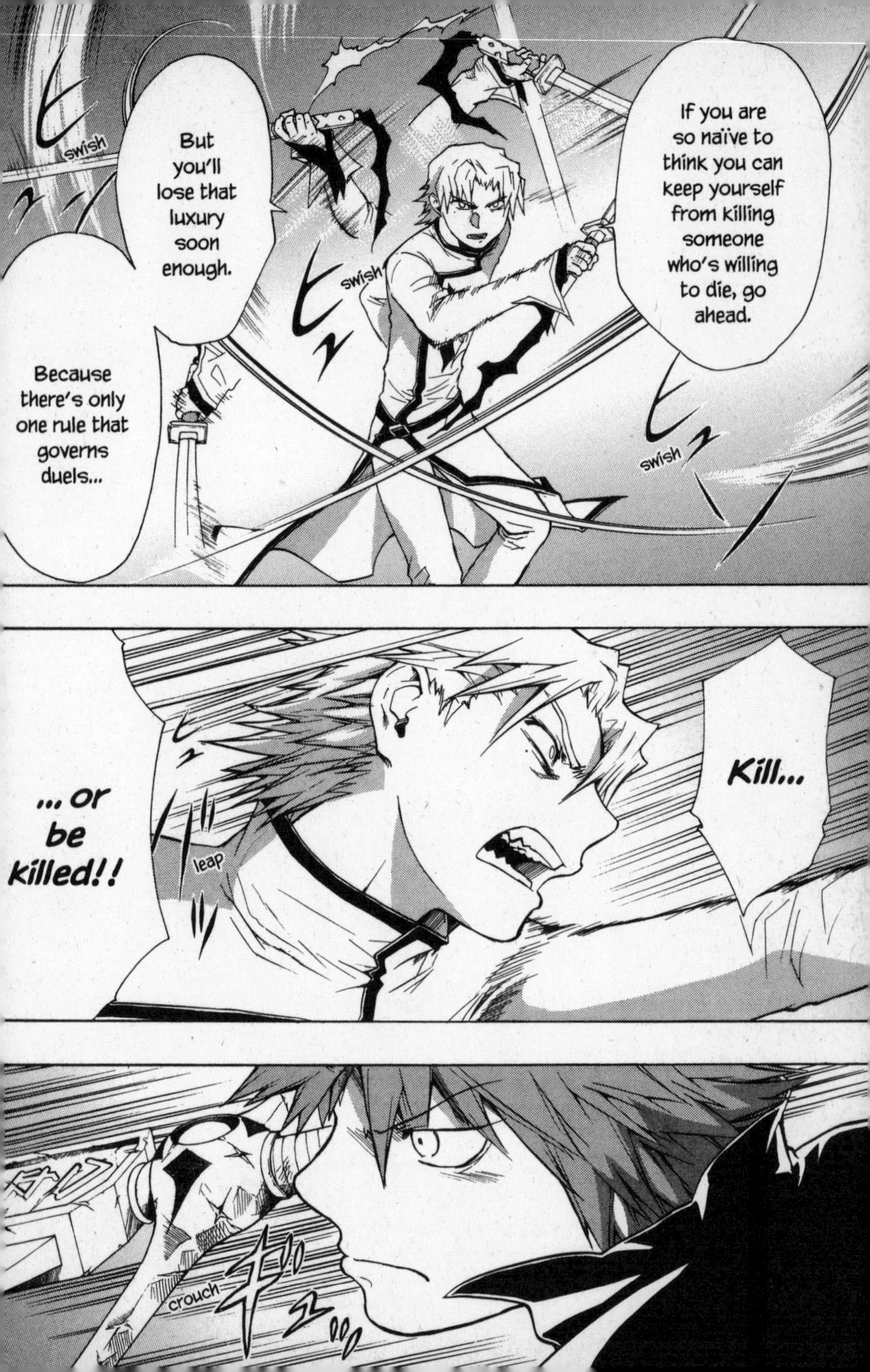
If you are so naïve to think you can keep yourself from killing someone who's willing to die, go ahead.
swish
swish
But you'll lose that luxury soon enough.
swish
Because there's only one rule that governs duels...
Kill...
... or be killed!!
leap
crouch

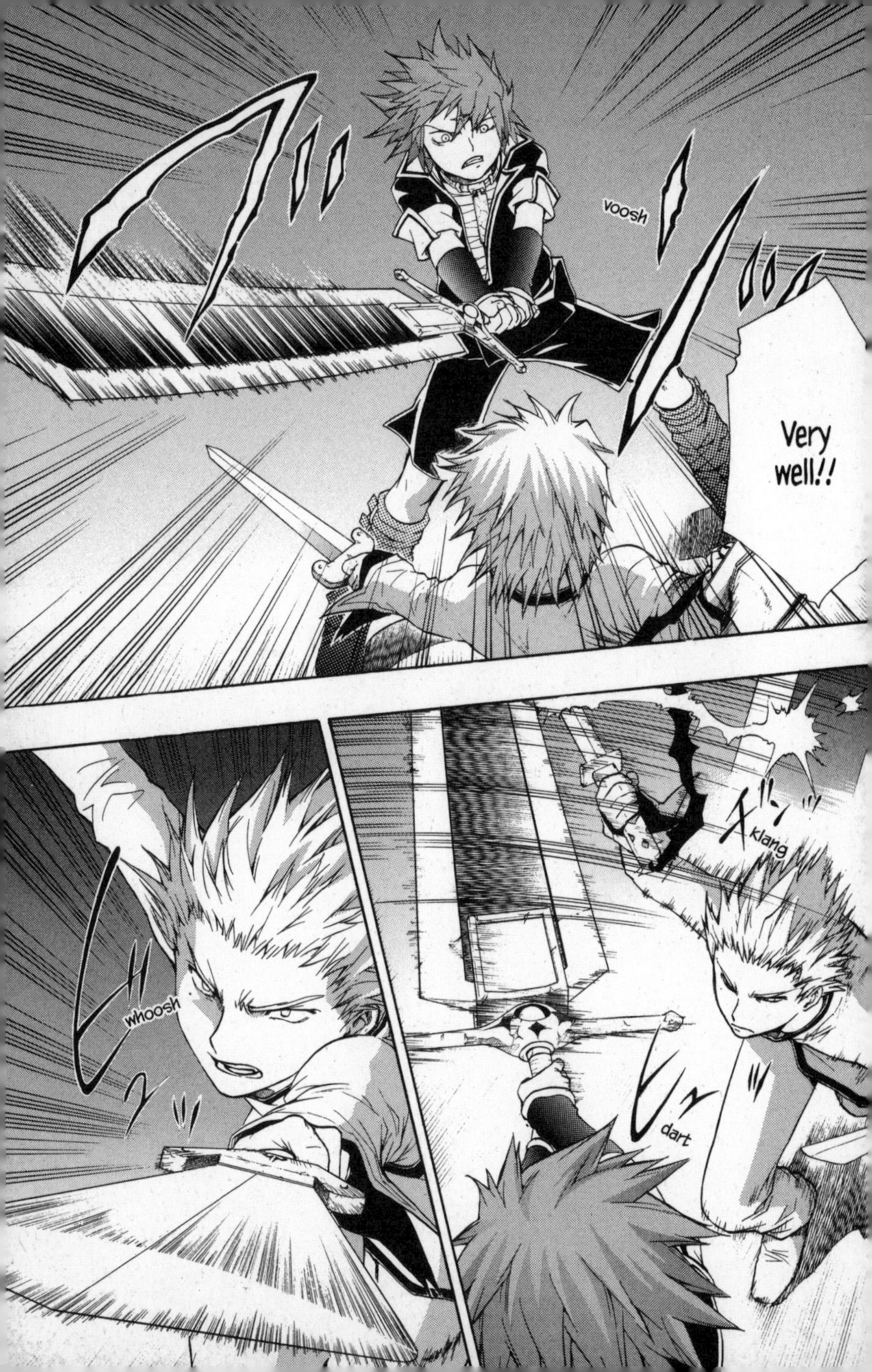
voosh
Very well!!
klang
dart
whoosh

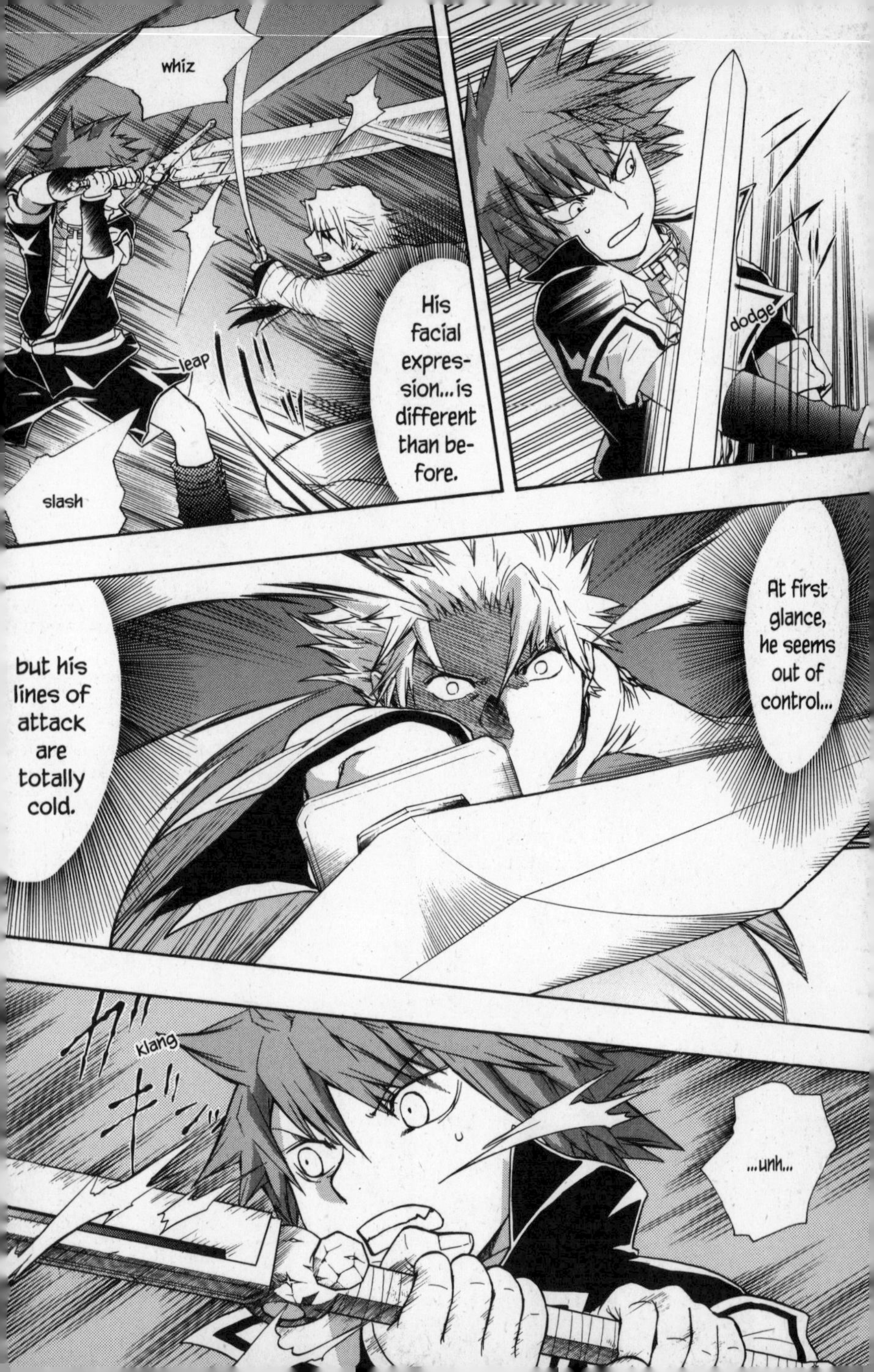
dodge
whiz
His facial expres-sion...is different than be-fore.
leap
slash
At first glance, he seems out of control...
but his lines of attack are totally cold.
...unh...
Klang

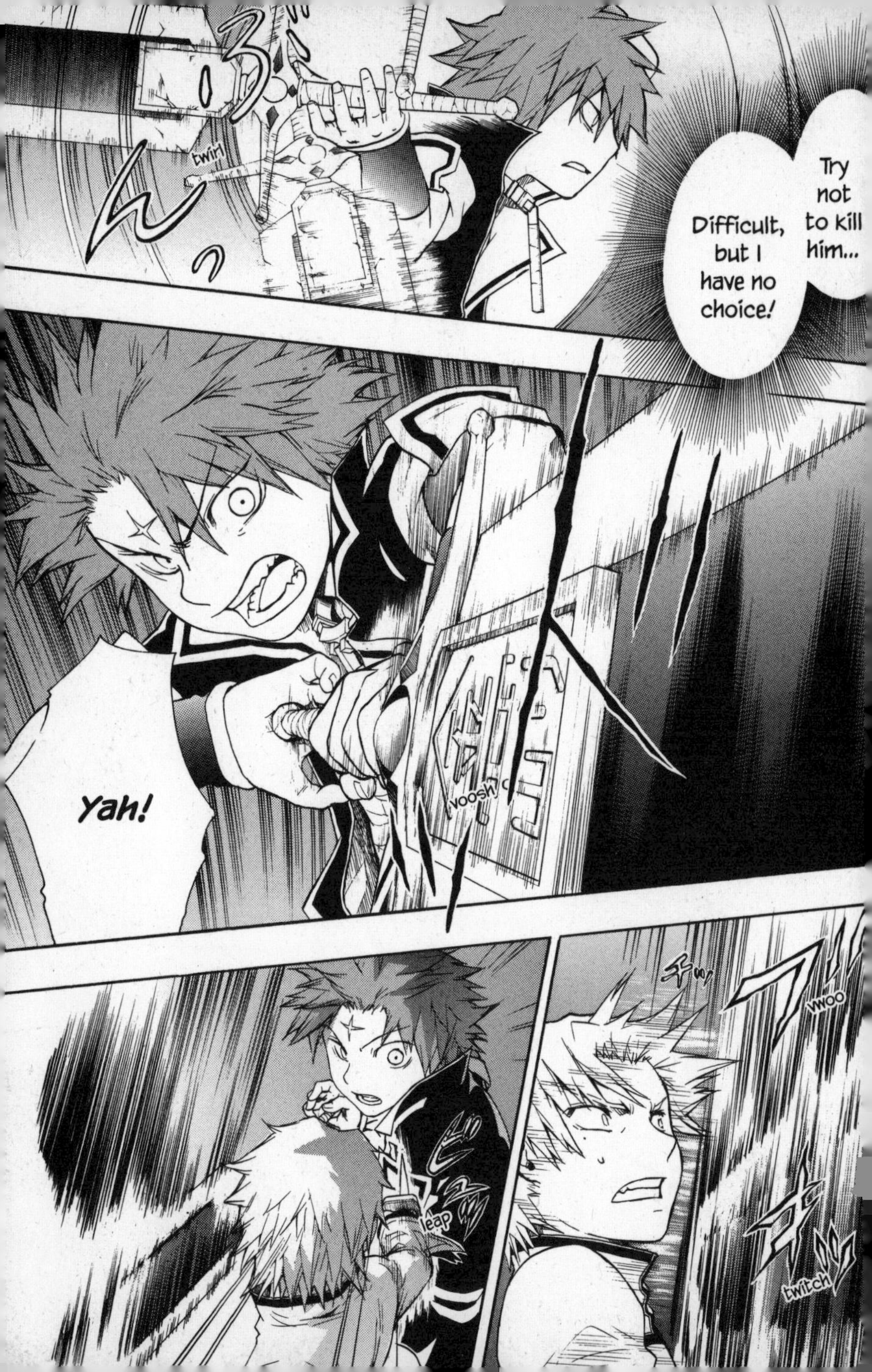
Try not to kill him...
Difficult, but I have no choice!
twirl
voosh
Yah!
vwoo
twitch
leap

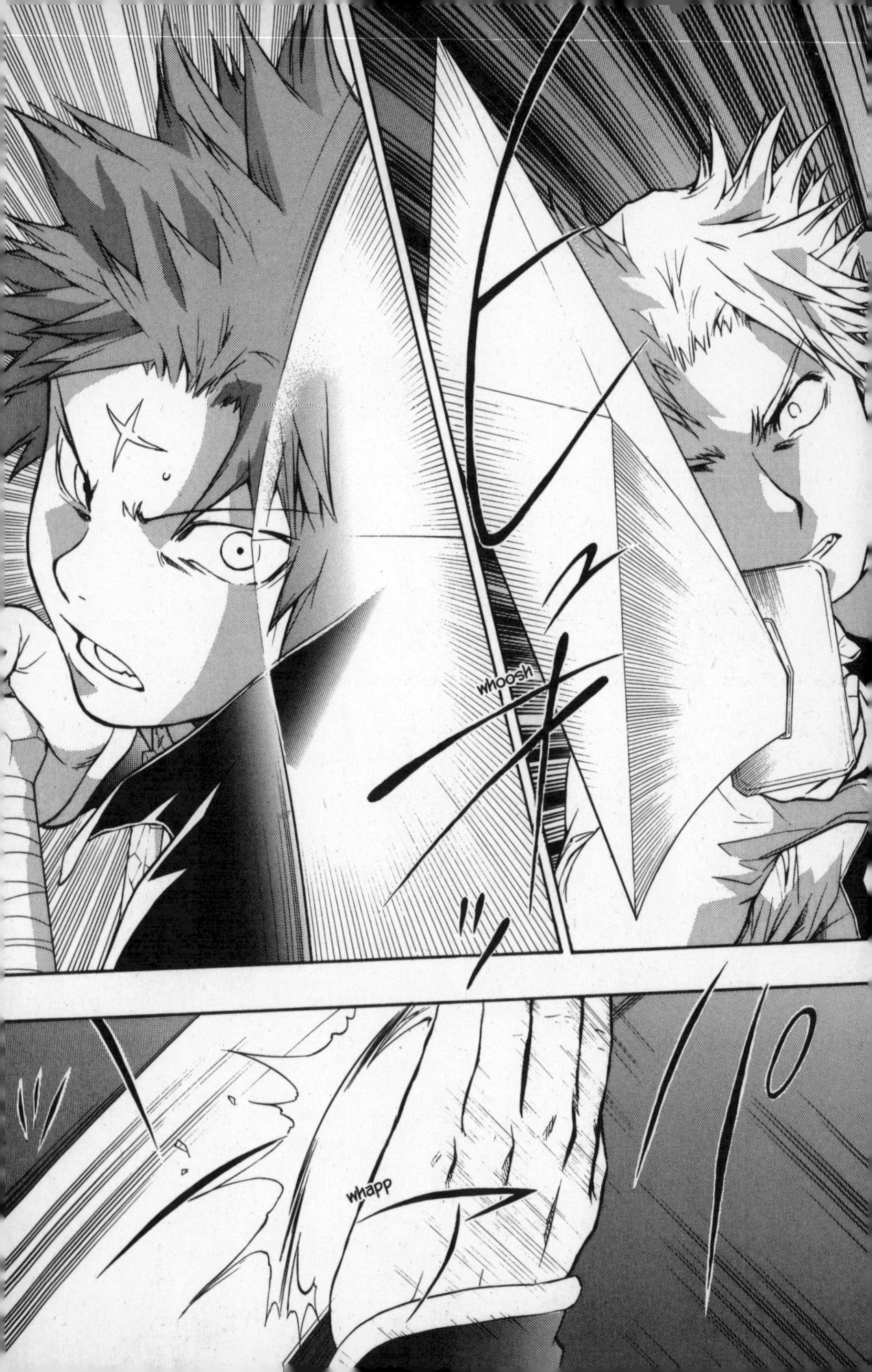
whoosh
whapp

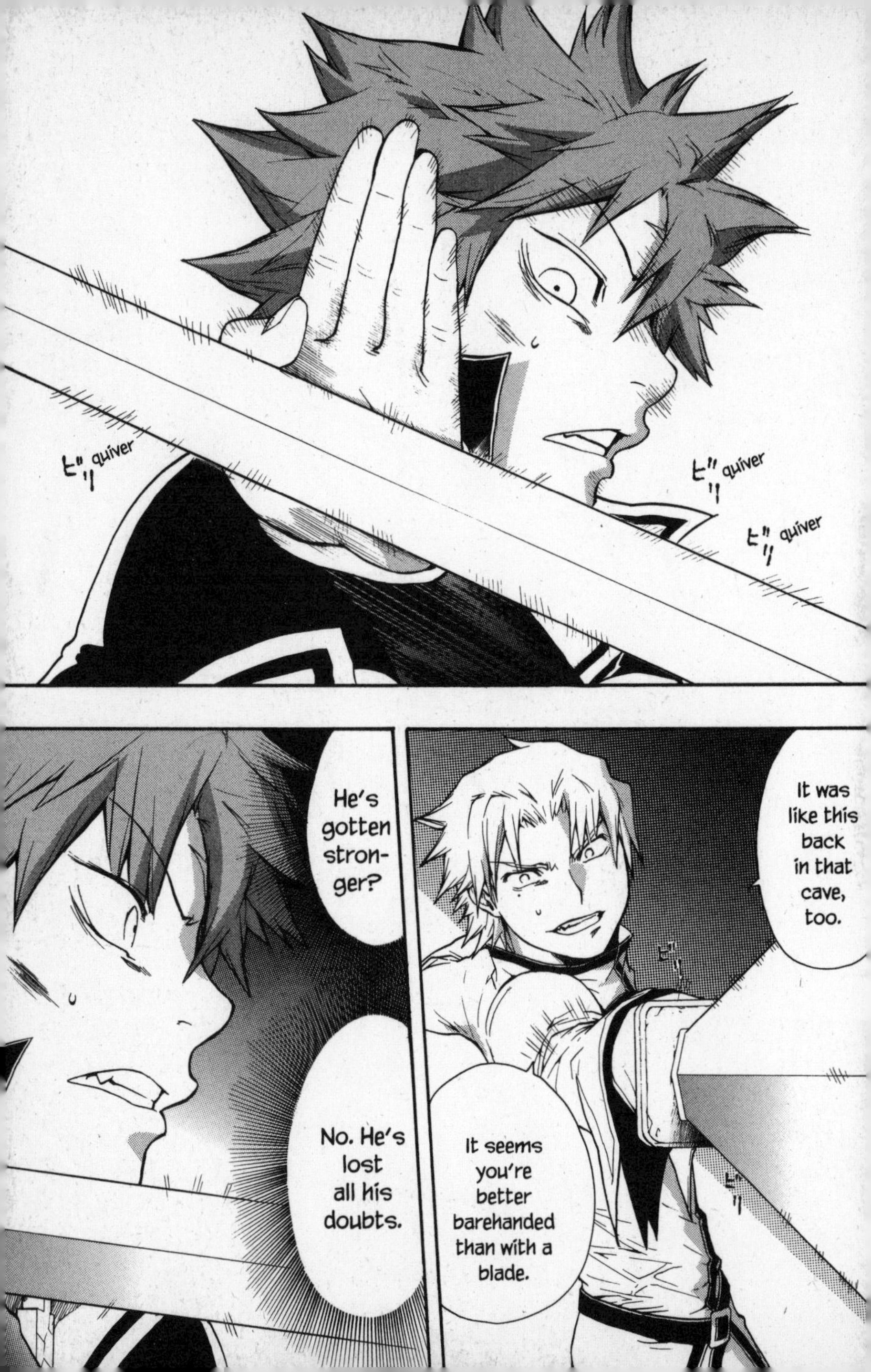
ビリ quiver
ビリ quiver
ビリ quiver
It was like this back in that cave, too.
ビリ
It seems you're better barehanded than with a blade.
ビリ
He's gotten stronger?
No. He's lost all his doubts.

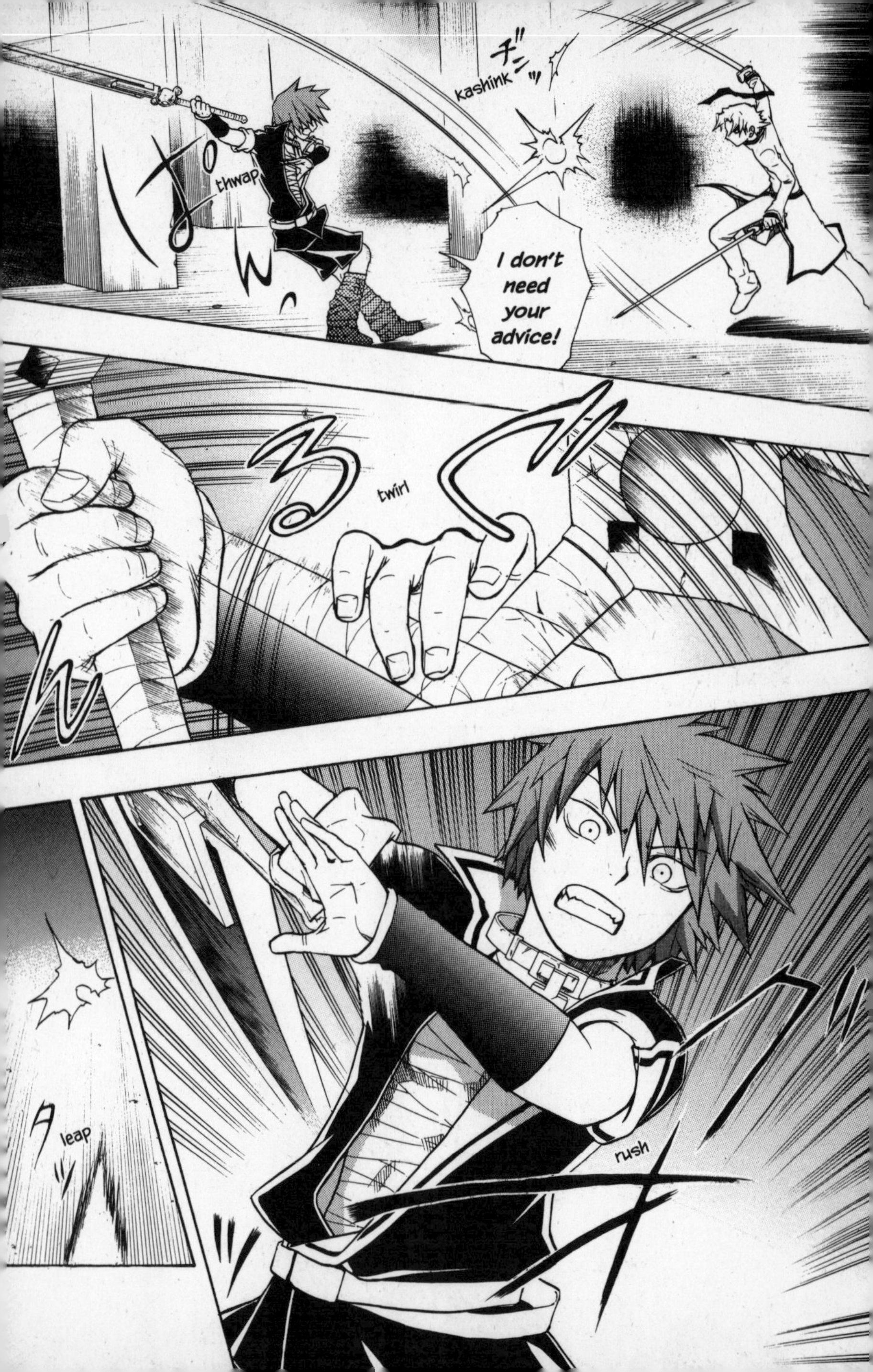
kashink
I don't need your advice!
thwap
twirl
rush
leap

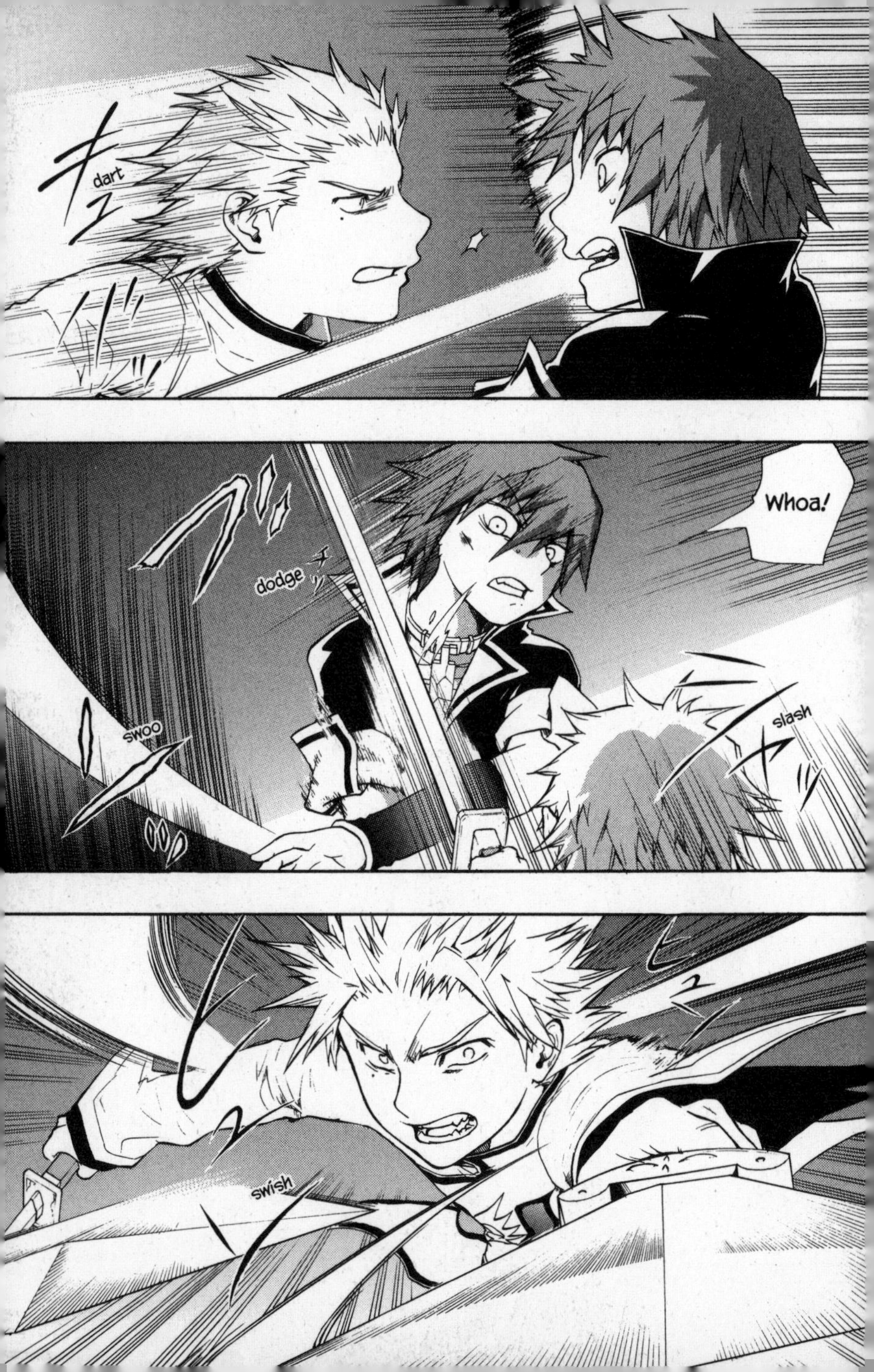
dart
Whoa!
dodge
slash
swoo
swish

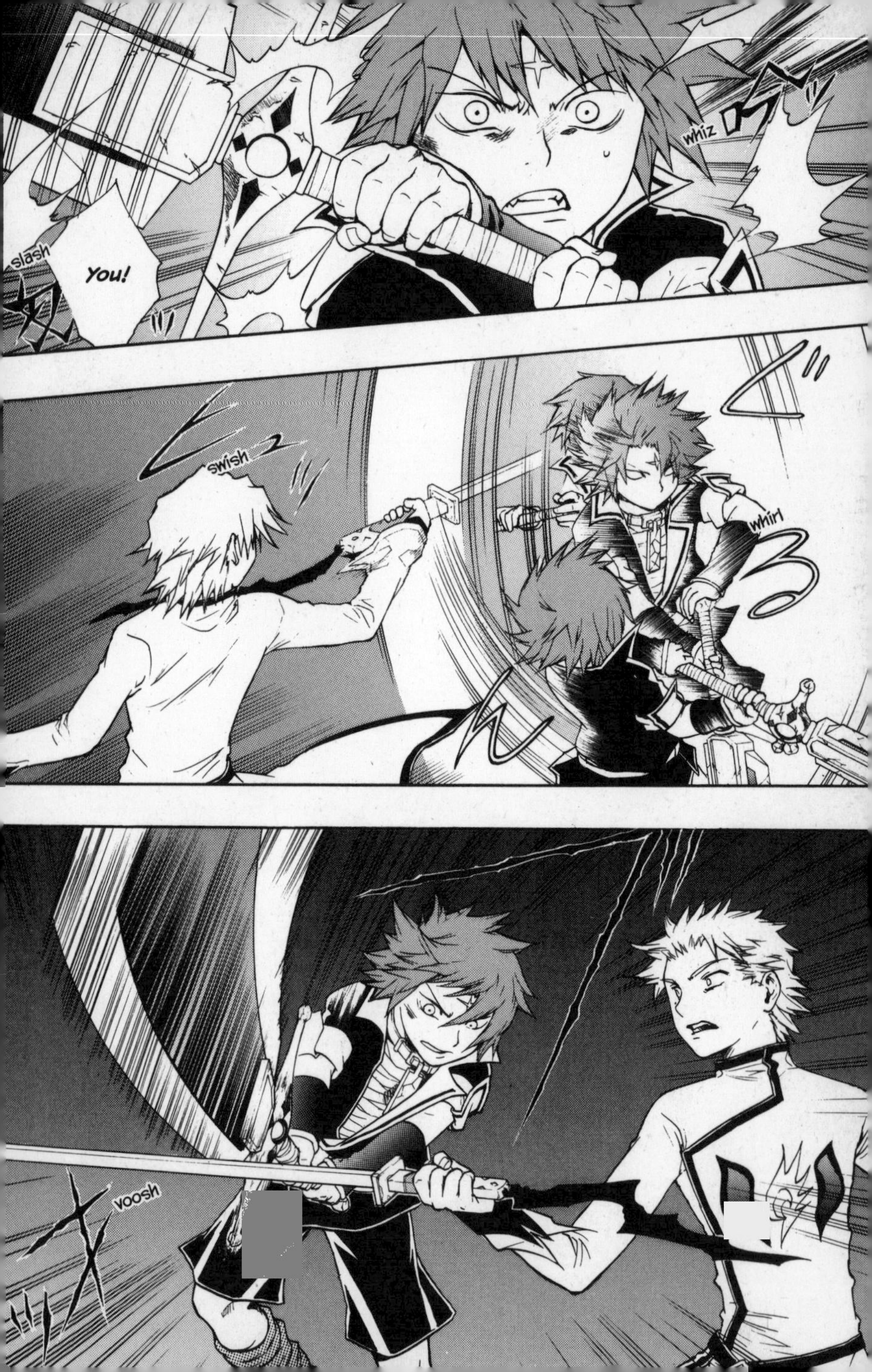
whiz
You!
slash
whirl
swish
voosh

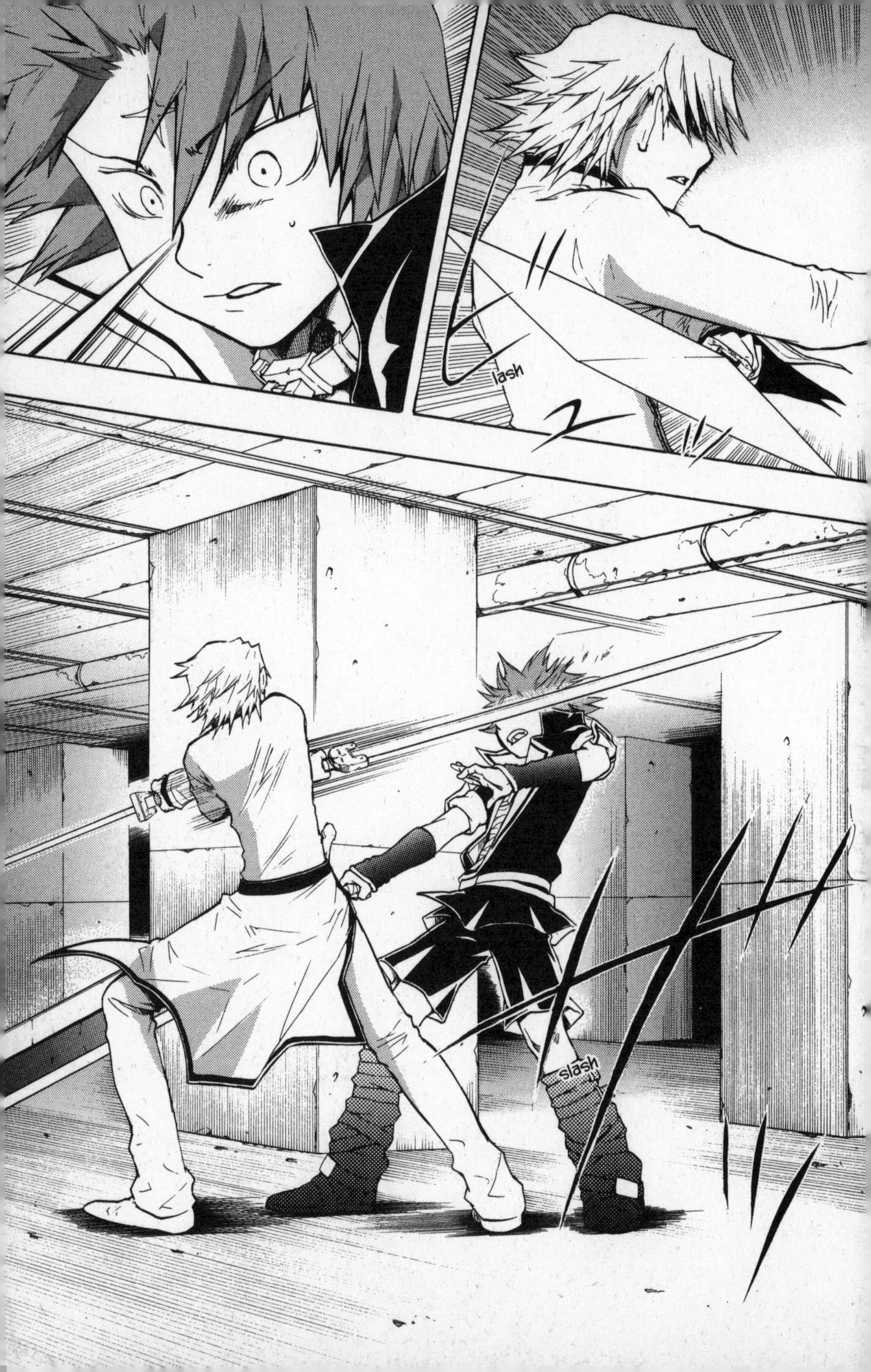
lash
slash

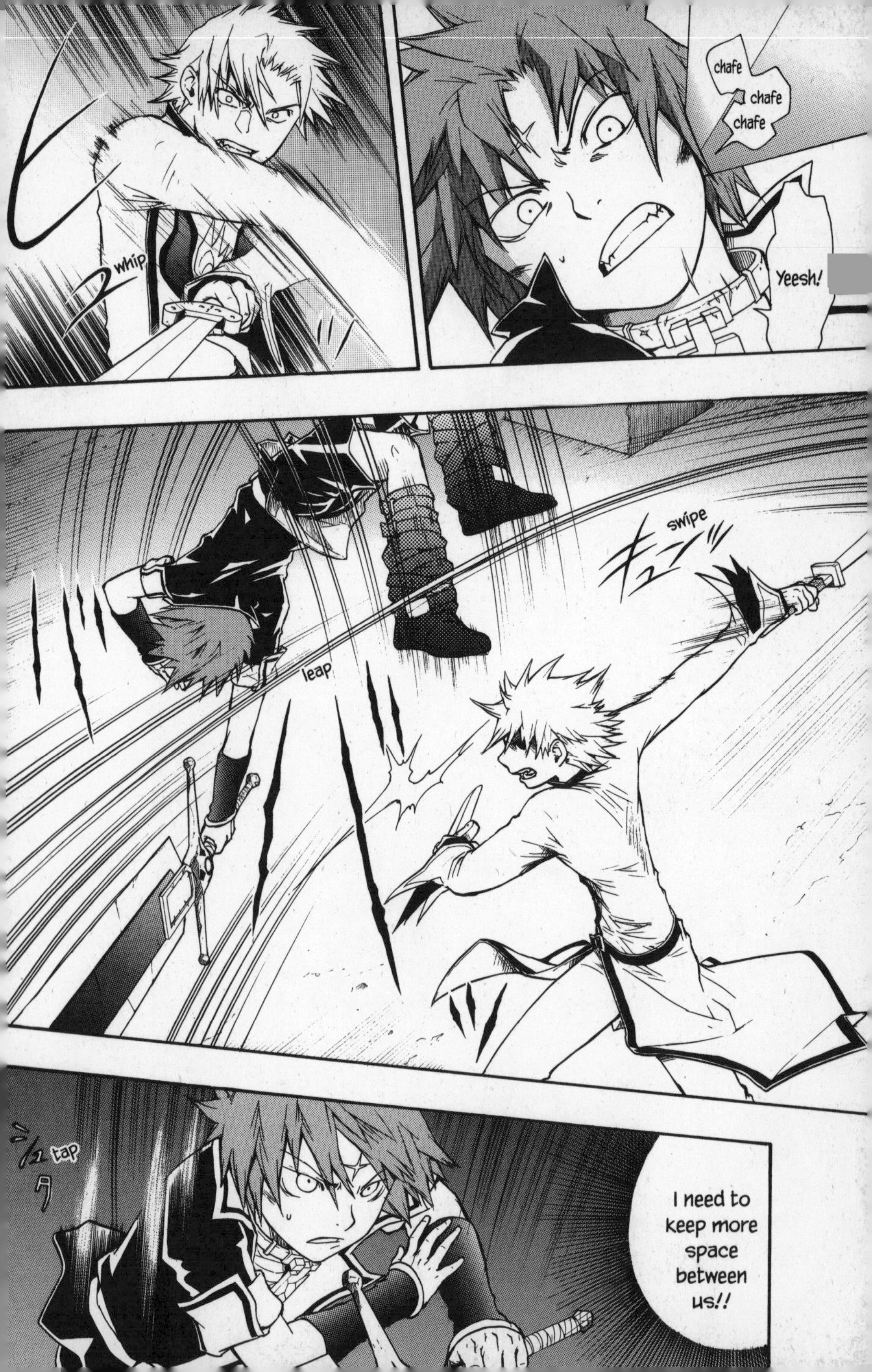
chafe
chafe
chafe
Yeesh!
whip
swipe
leap
I need to keep more space between us!!
tap

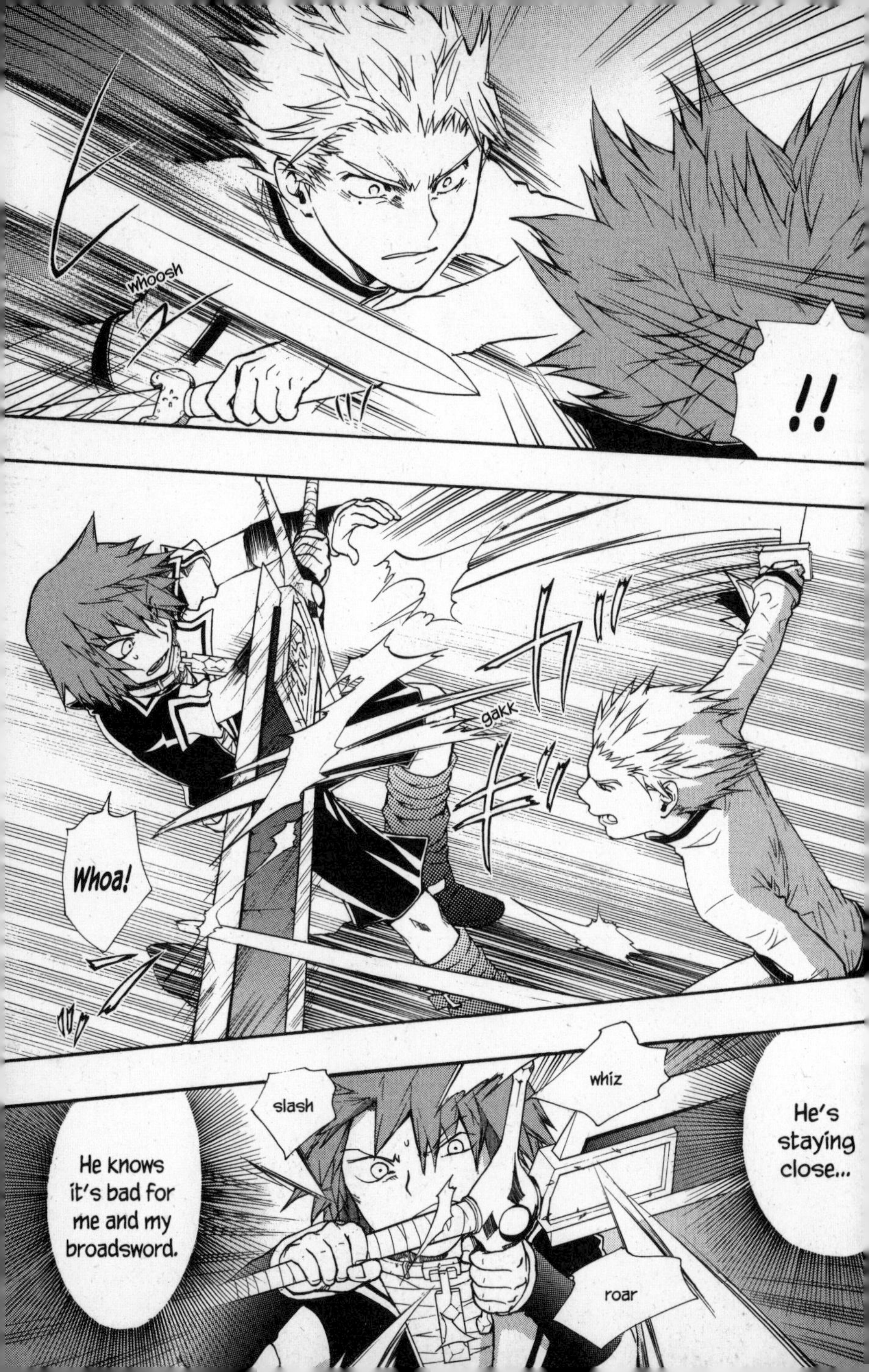
!!
whoosh
gakk
Whoa!
He's staying close...
whiz
slash
He knows it's bad for me and my broadsword.
roar

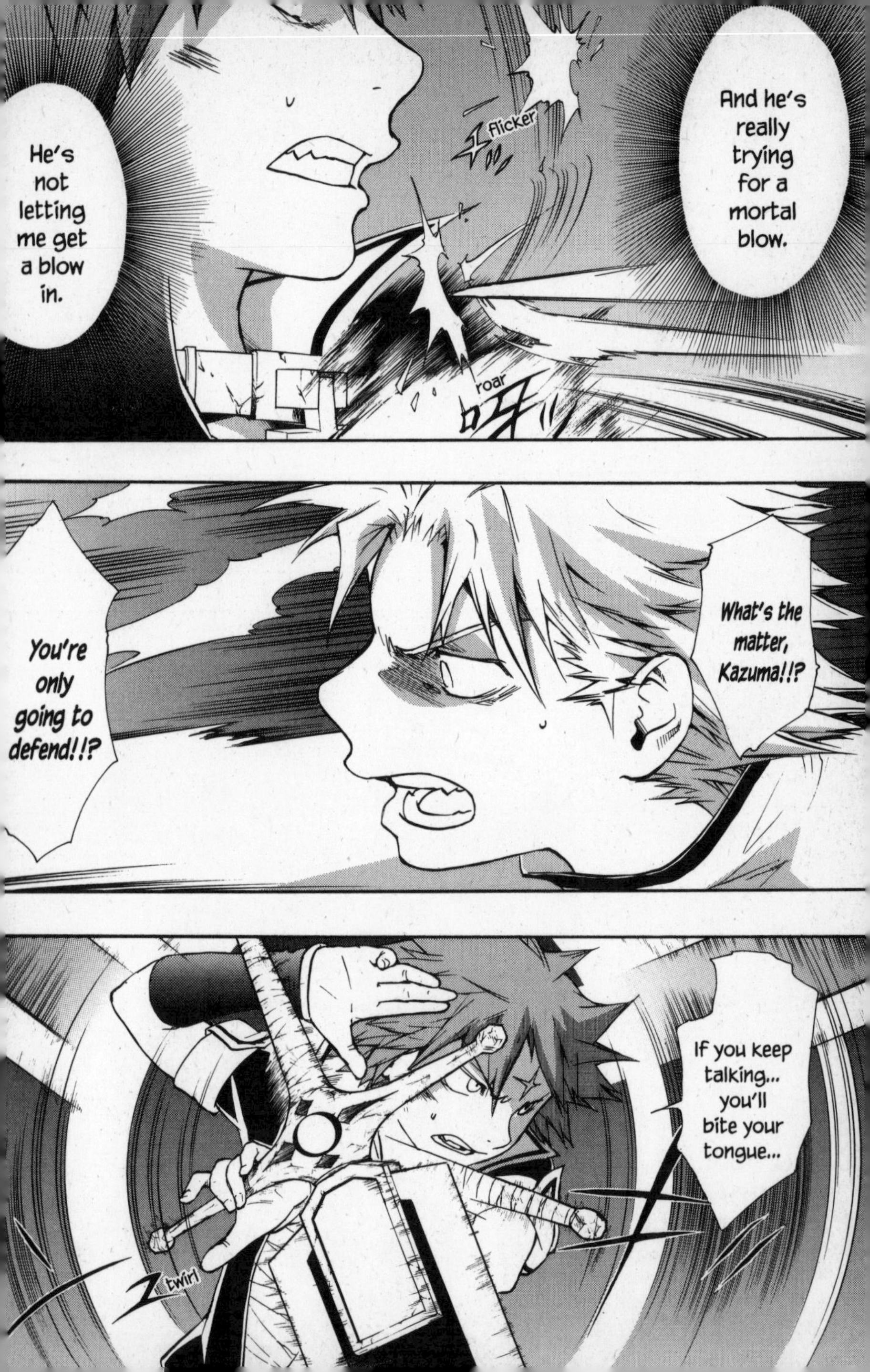
And he's really trying for a mortal blow.
flicker
He's not letting me get a blow in.
roar
What's the matter, Kazuma!!?
You're only going to defend!!?
If you keep talking... you'll bite your tongue...
twirl

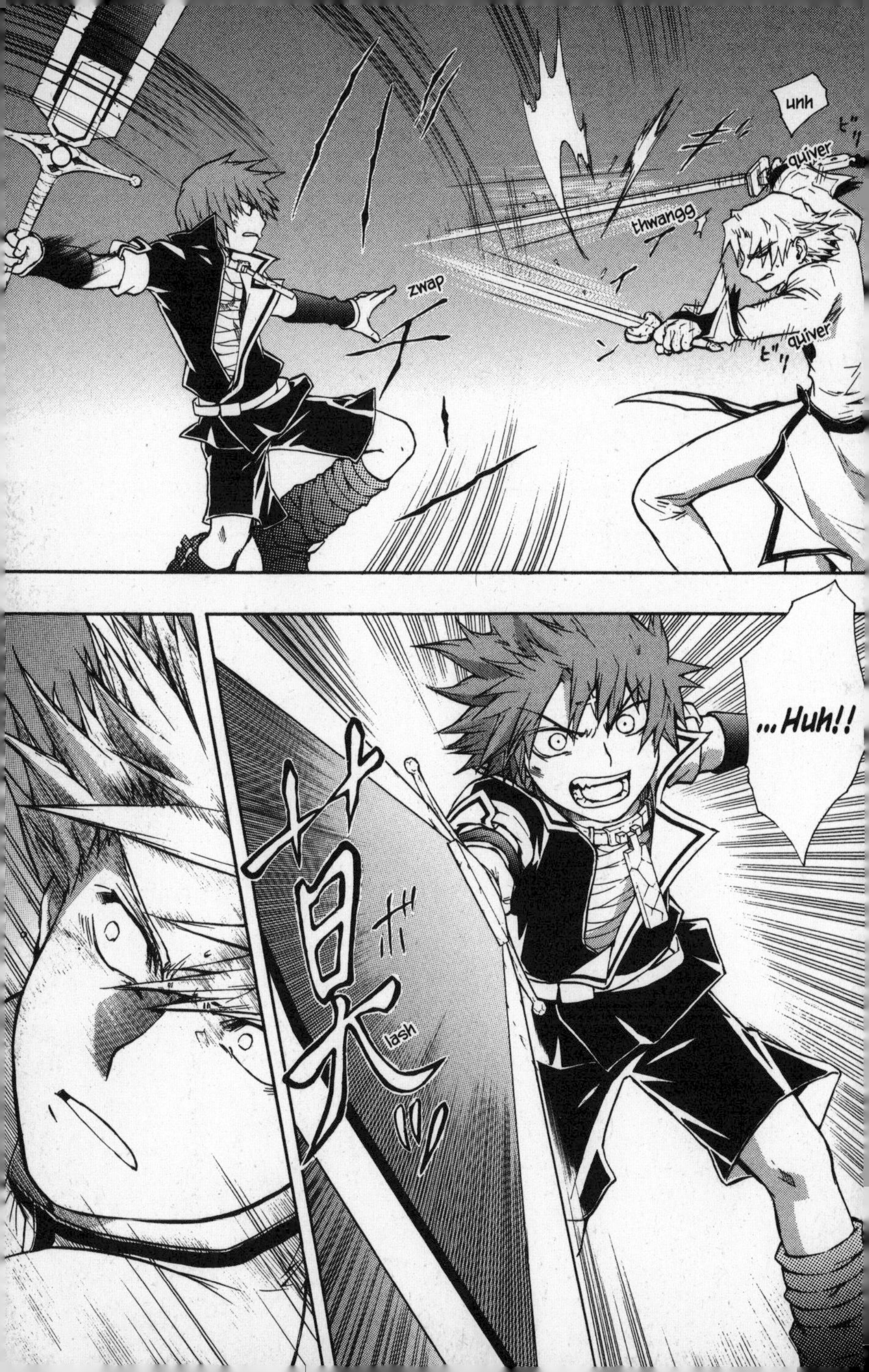
unh
quiver
thwangg
quiver
zwap
...Huh!!
lash

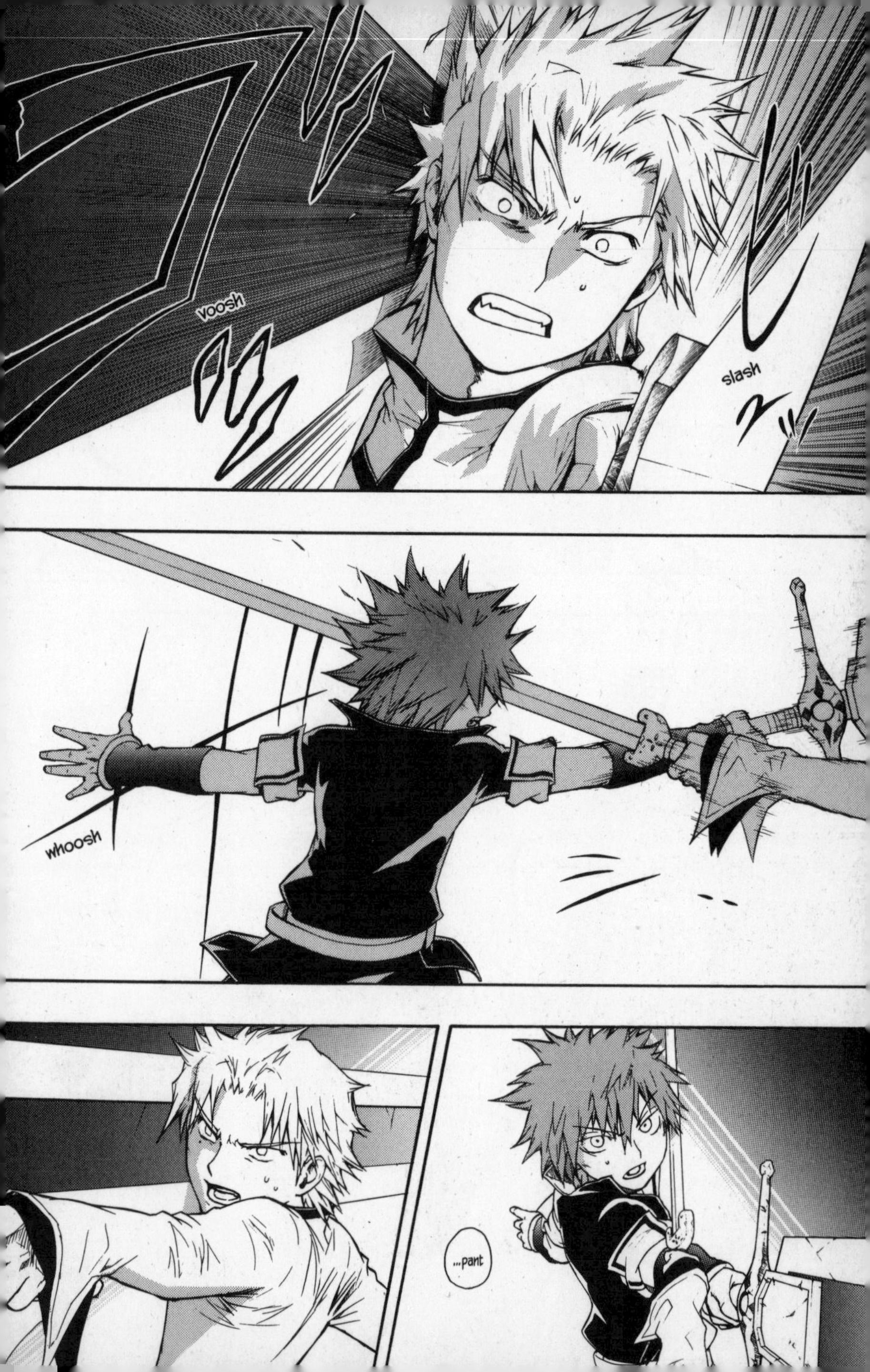
slash
voosh
whoosh
...pant

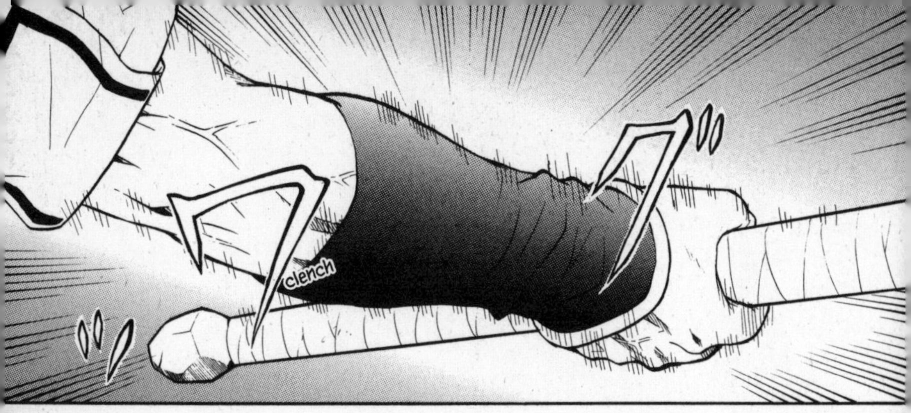
clench
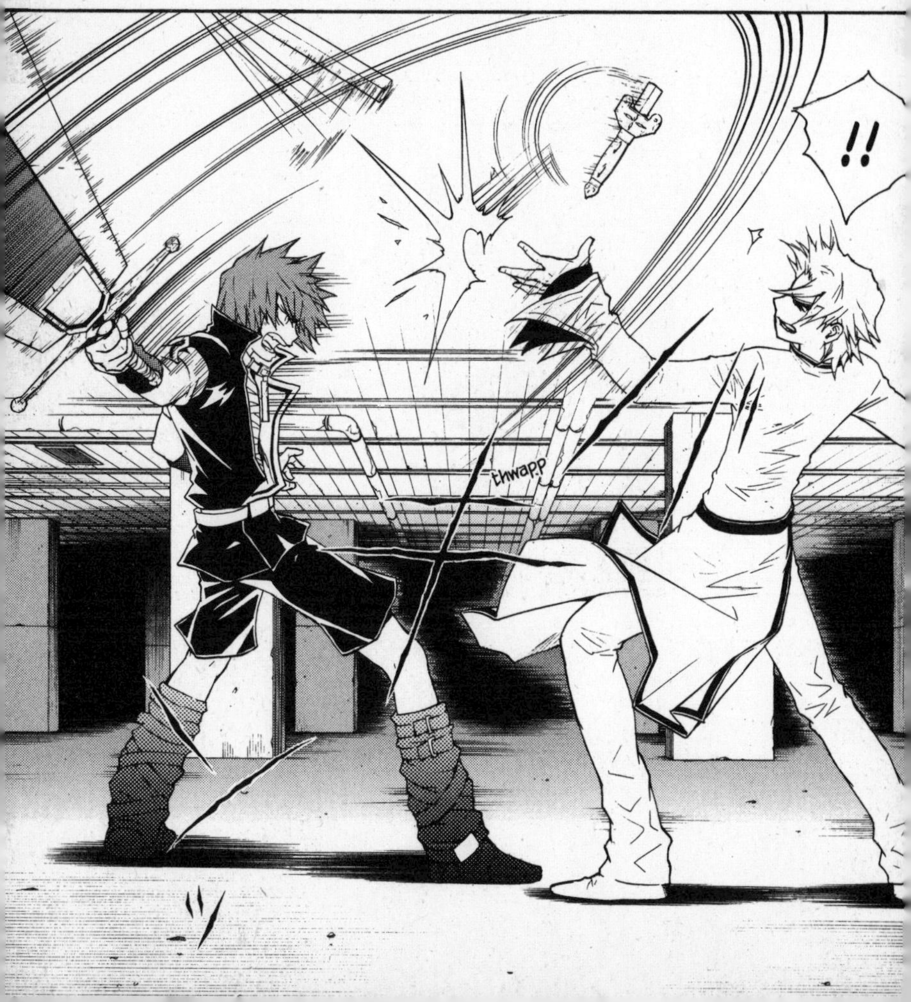
!!
thwapp

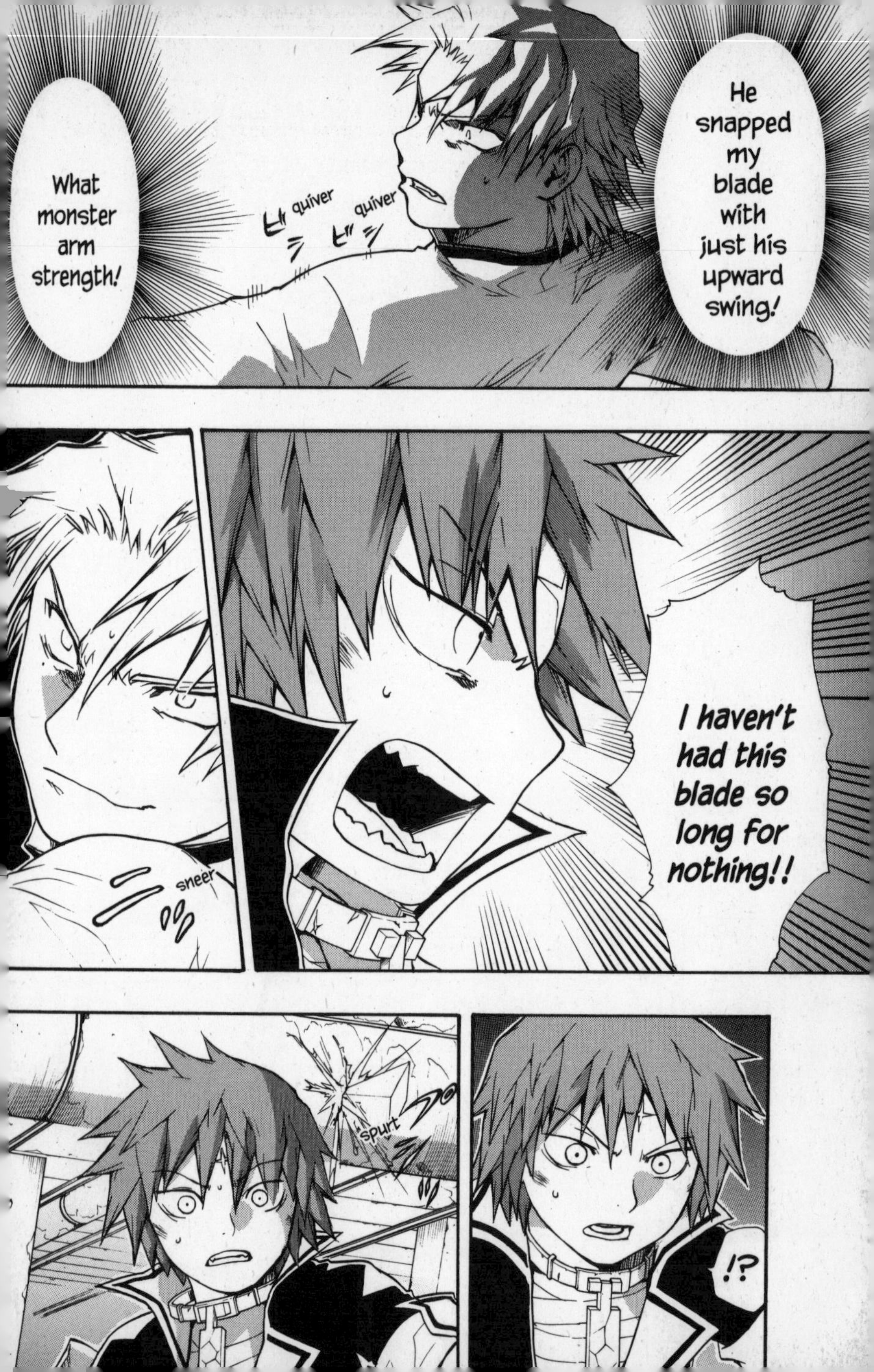
He snapped my blade with just his upward swing!
quiver
quiver
What monster arm strength!
I haven't had this blade so long for nothing!!
sneer
!?
spurt

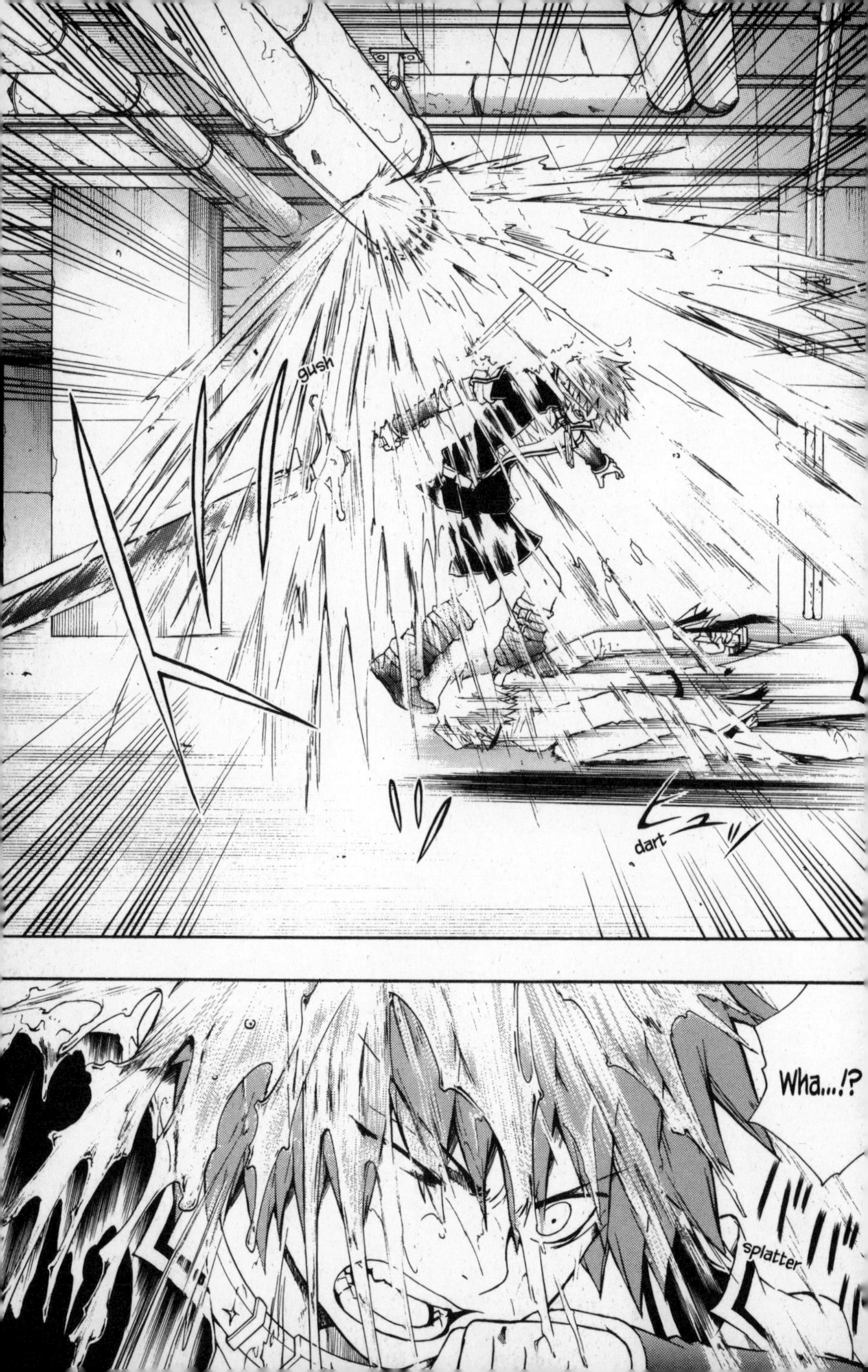
gush
dart
Wha...!?
splatter

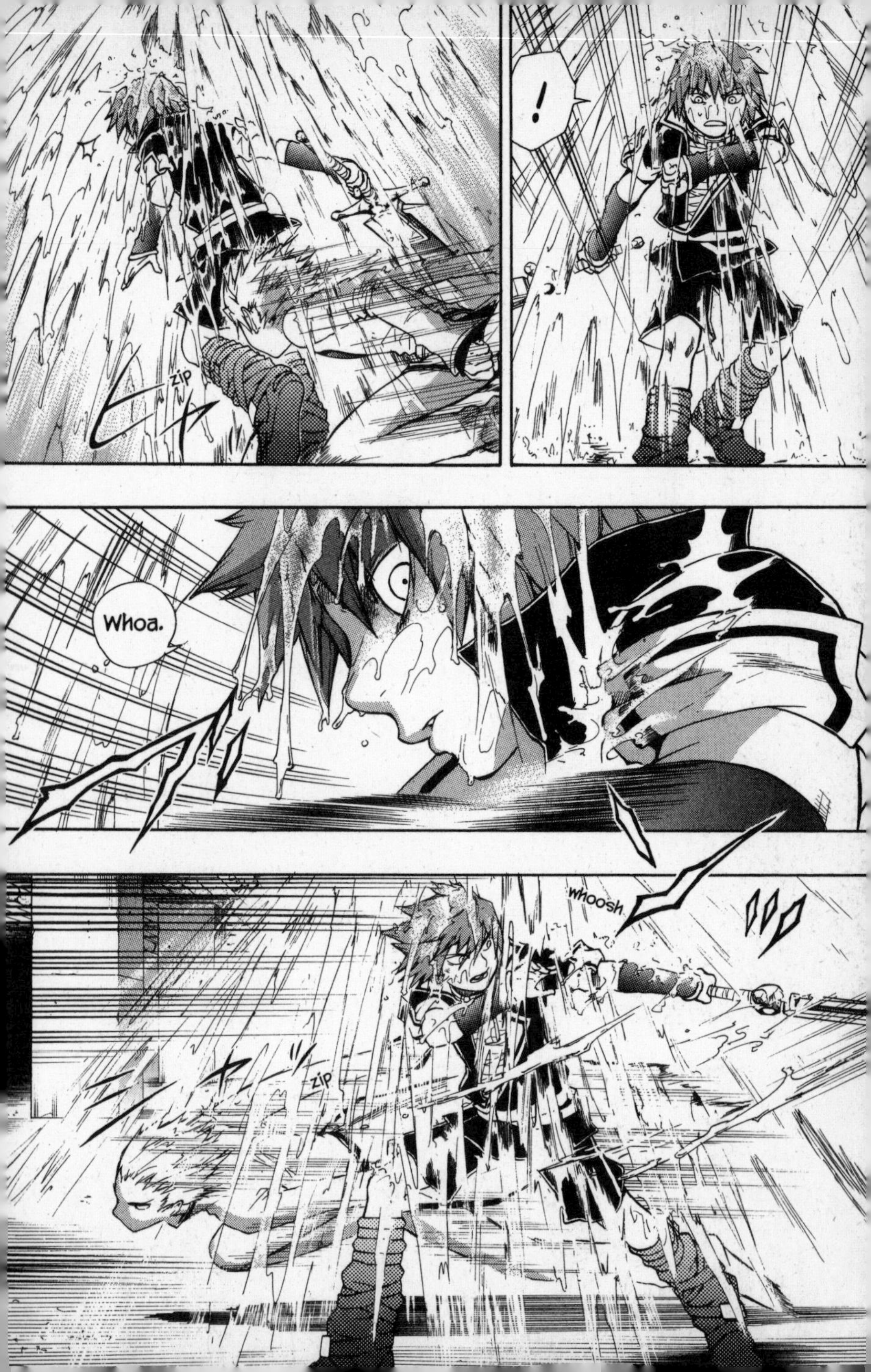
!
zip
Whoa.
whoosh
zip

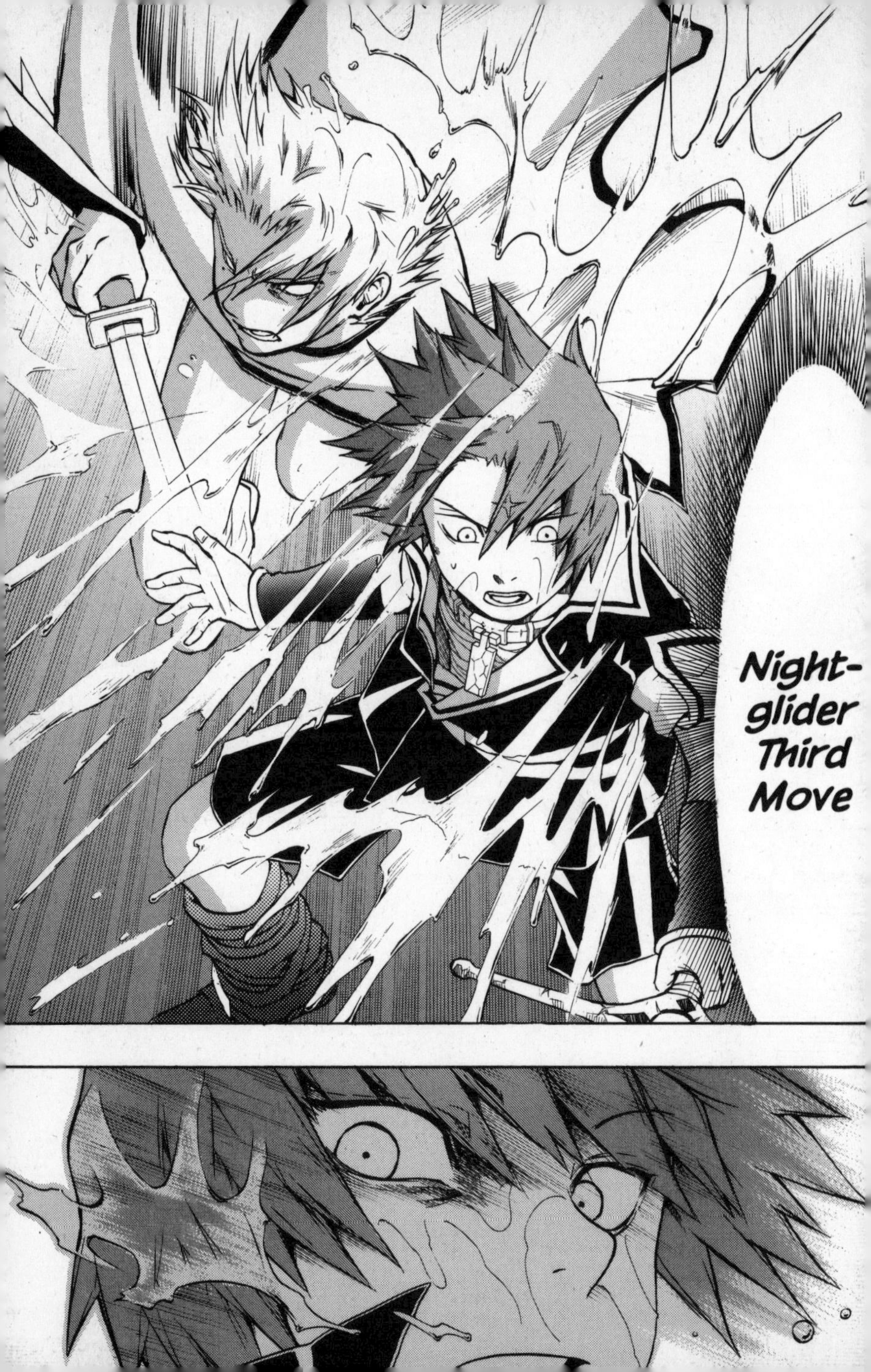
Night-
glider
Third
Move

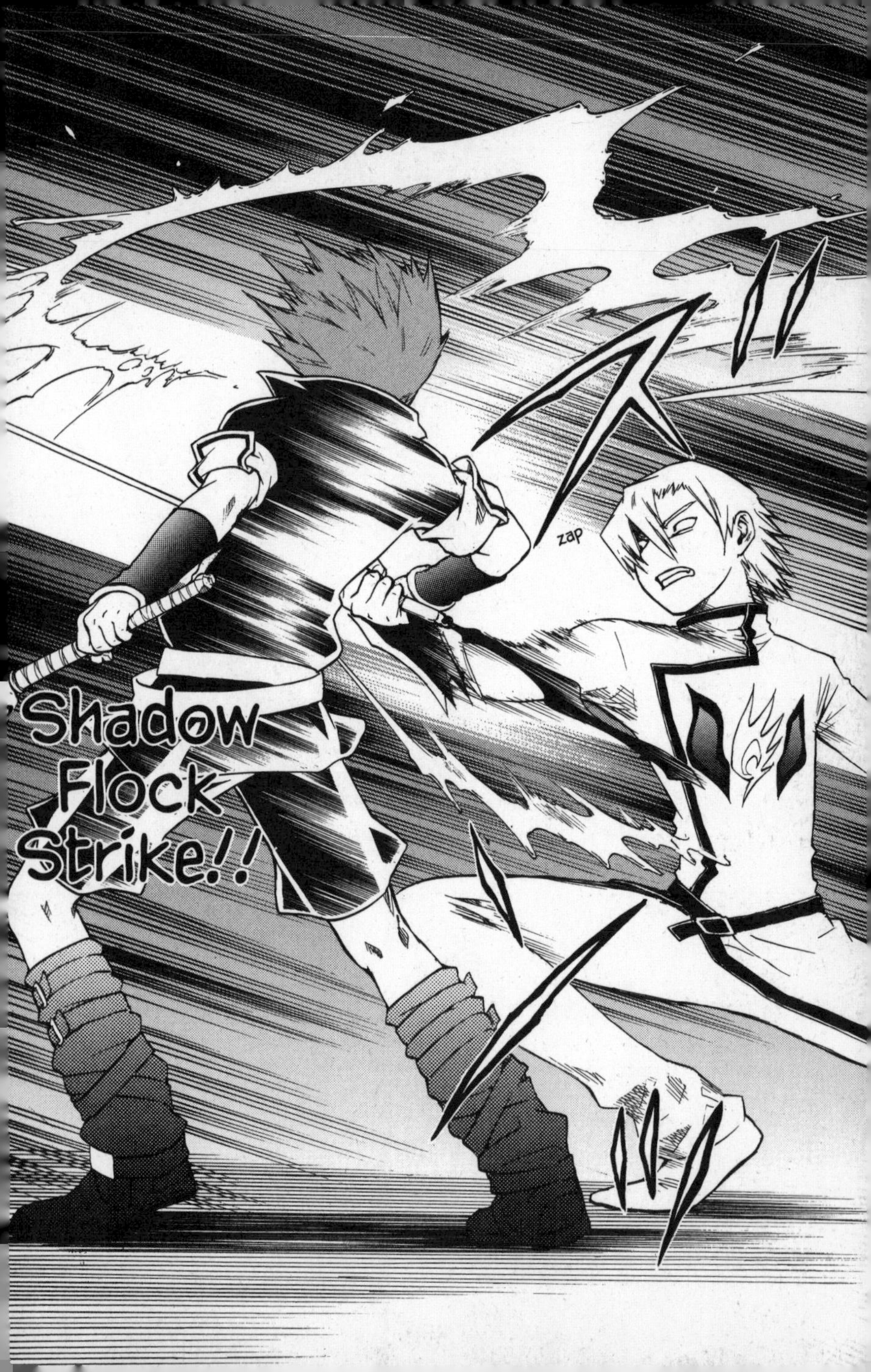
zap
Shadow Flock Strike!!

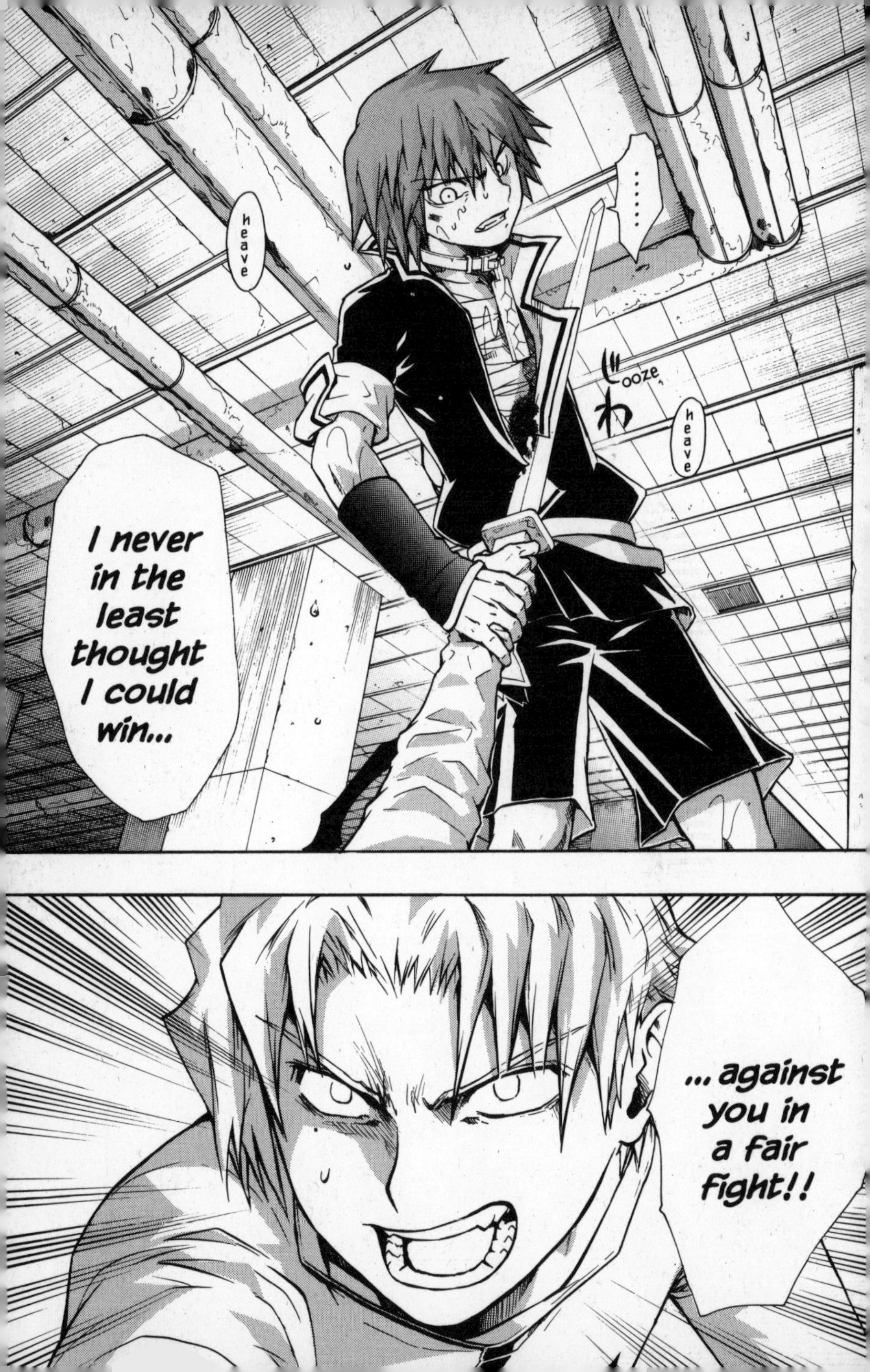
......
heave
じわ
ooze
heave
I never in the least thought I could win...
...against you in a fair fight!!

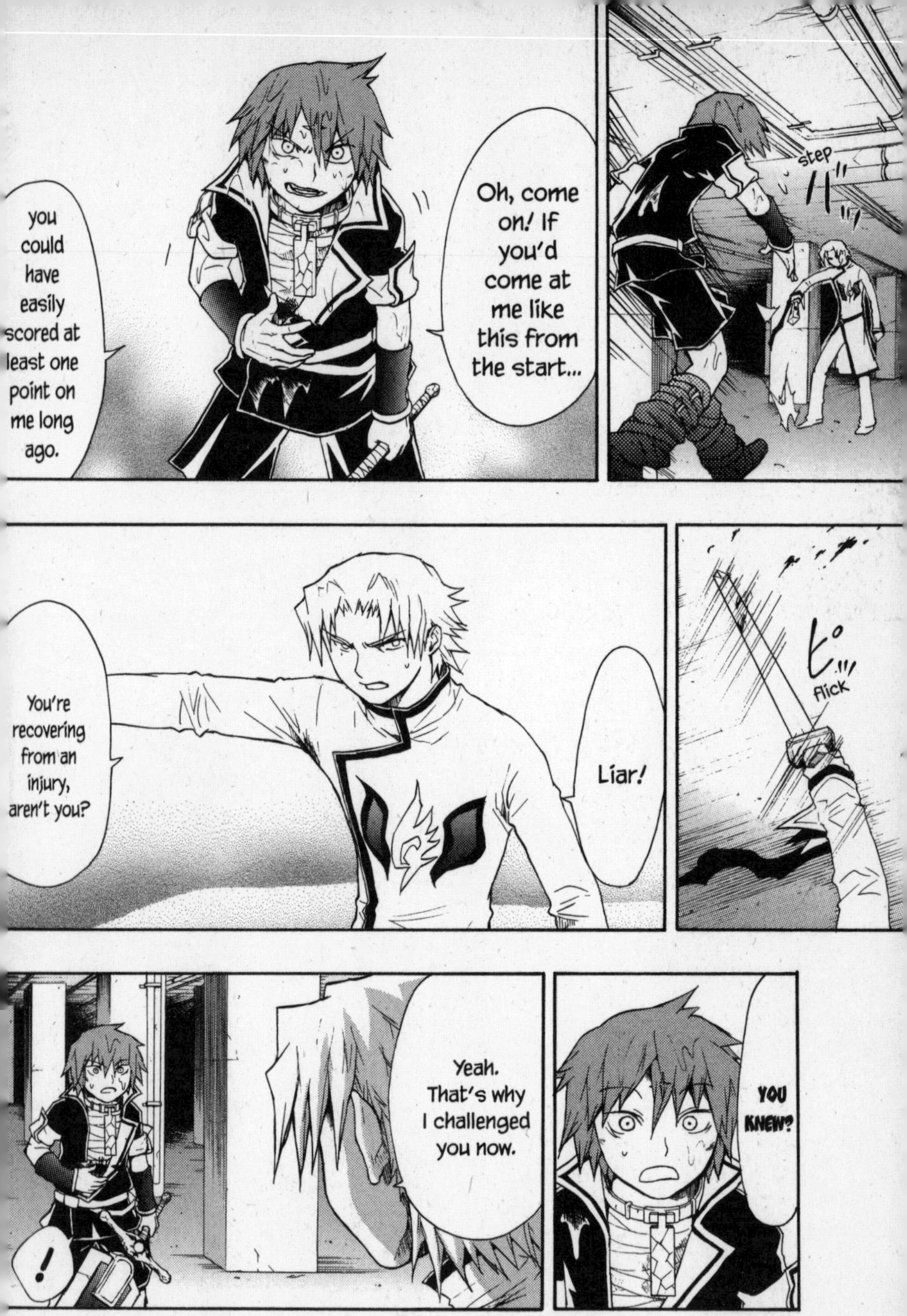
step
Oh, come on! If you'd come at me like this from the start...
you could have easily scored at least one point on me long ago.
ピ
flick
Liar!
You're recovering from an injury, aren't you?
YOU KNEW?
Yeah. That's why I challenged you now.
!

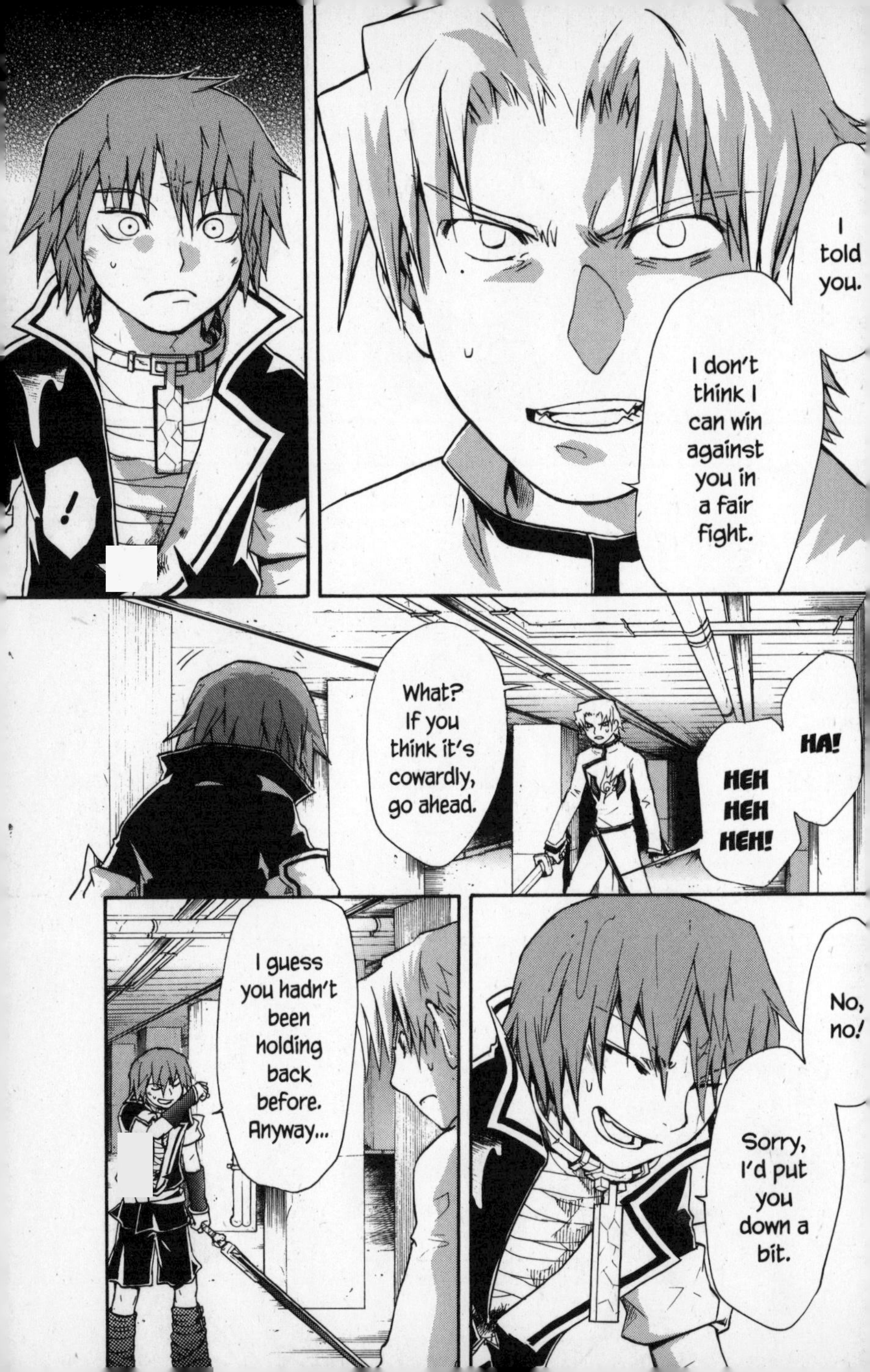
I told you.
I don't think I can win against you in a fair fight.
!
HA! HEH HEH HEH!
What? If you think it's cowardly, go ahead.
No, no!
Sorry, I'd put you down a bit.
I guess you hadn't been holding back before. Anyway...

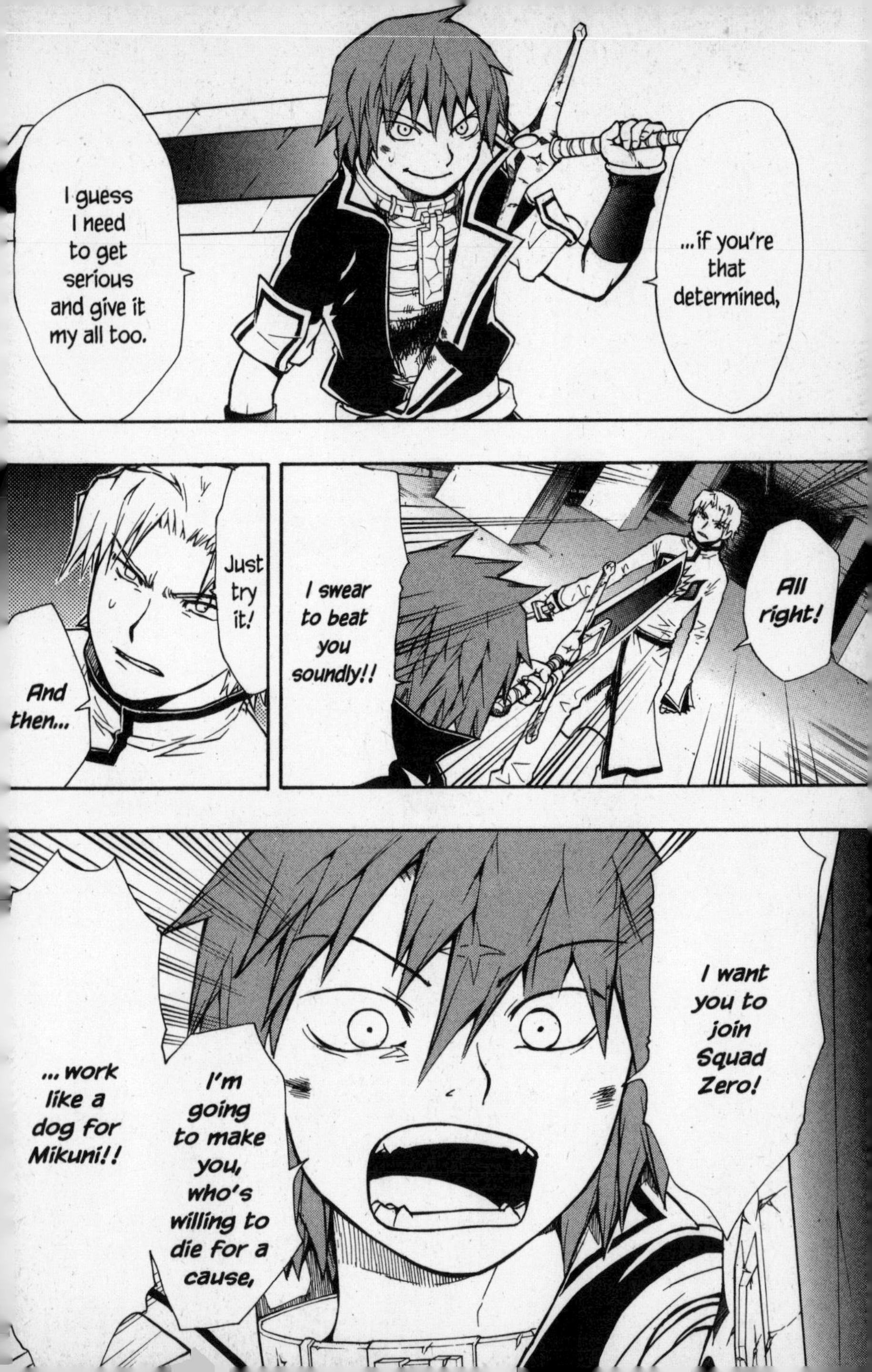
...if you're that determined,
I guess I need to get serious and give it my all too.
All right!
I swear to beat you soundly!!
Just try it!
And then...
I want you to join Squad Zero!
I'm going to make you, who's willing to die for a cause,
...work like a dog for Mikuni!!

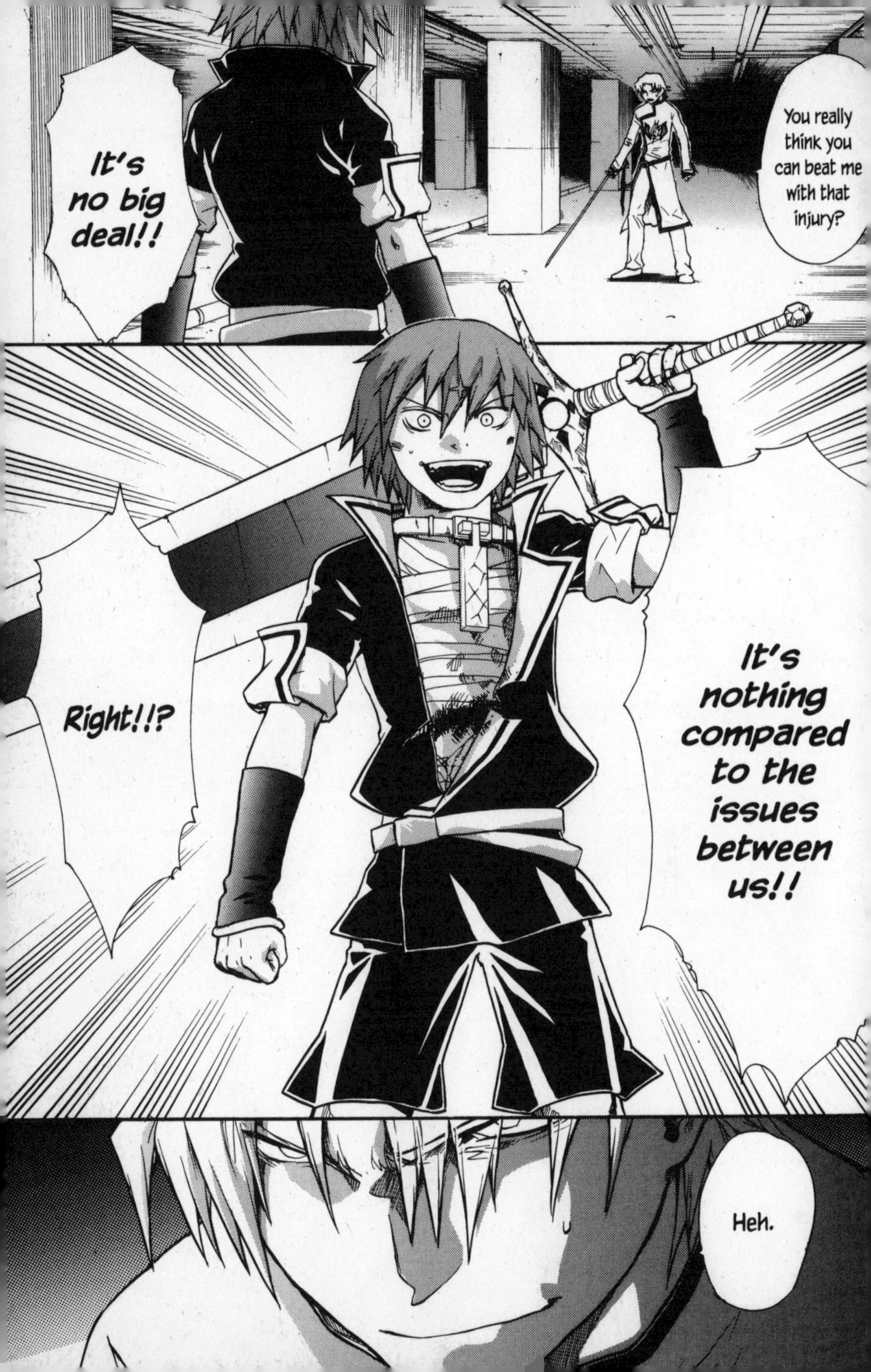
You really think you can beat me with that injury?
It's no big deal!!
It's nothing compared to the issues between us!!
Right!!?
Heh.

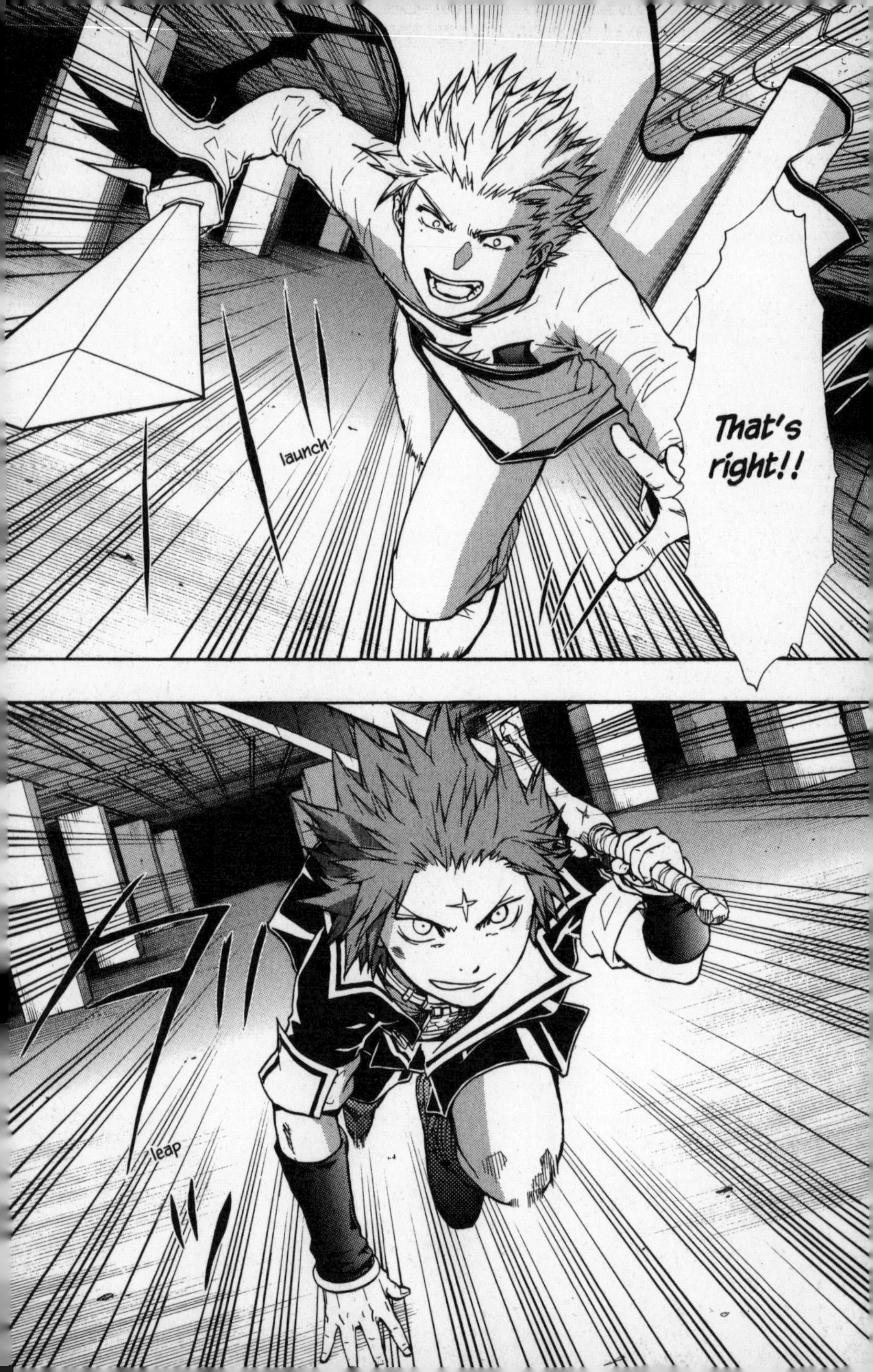
That's right!!
launch
leap

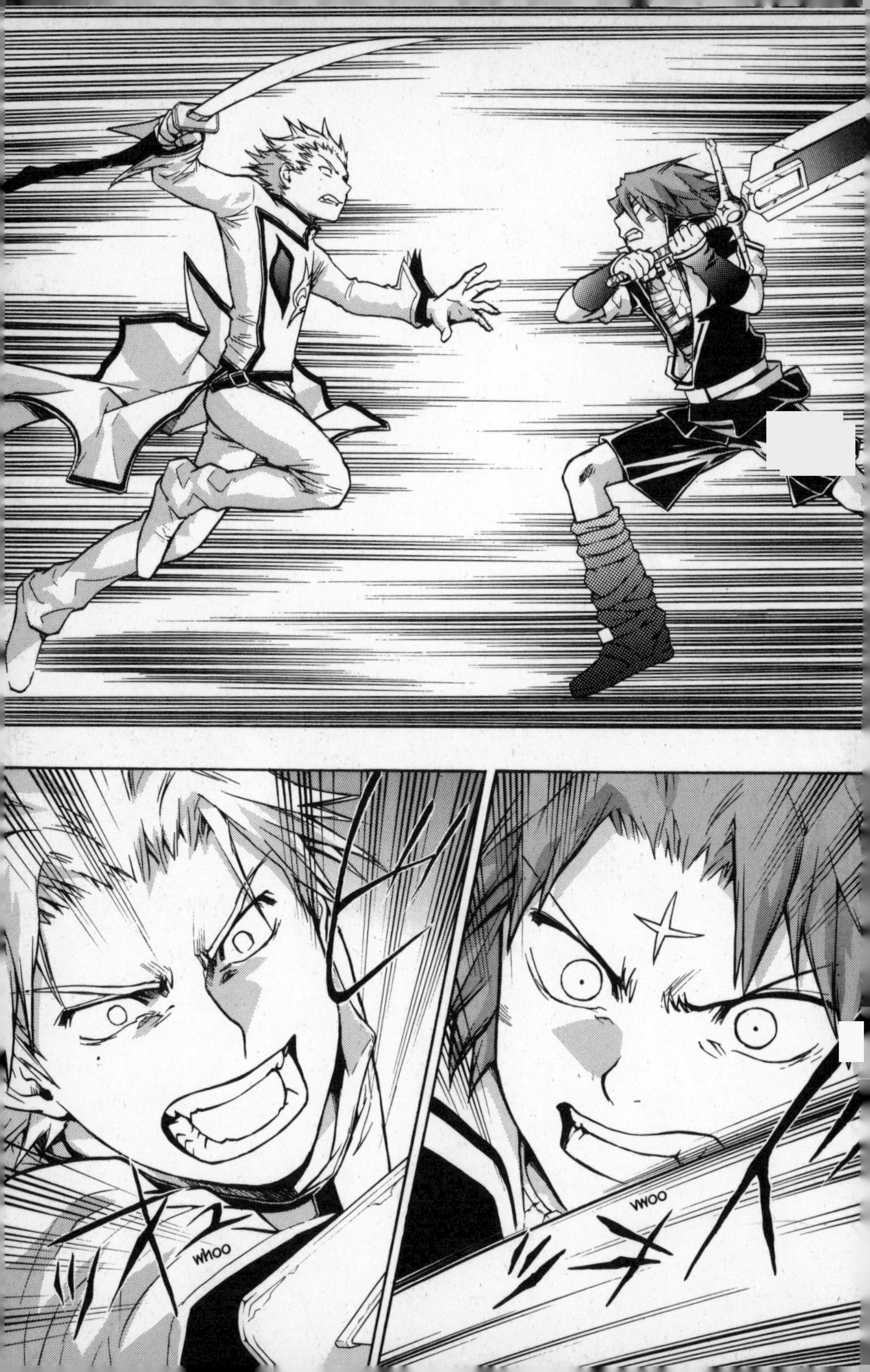
VWOO
whoo

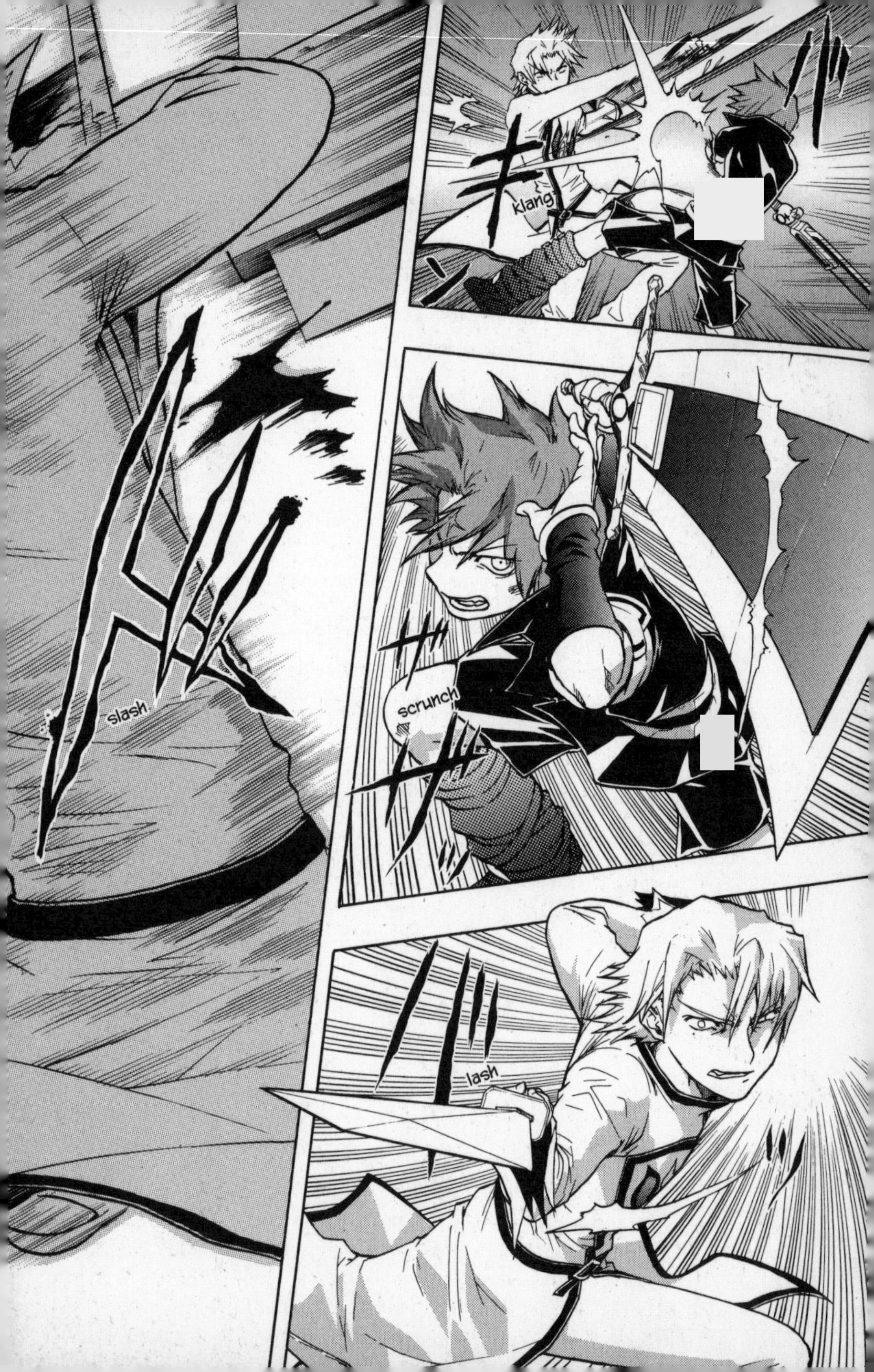
klang
scrunch
lash
slash

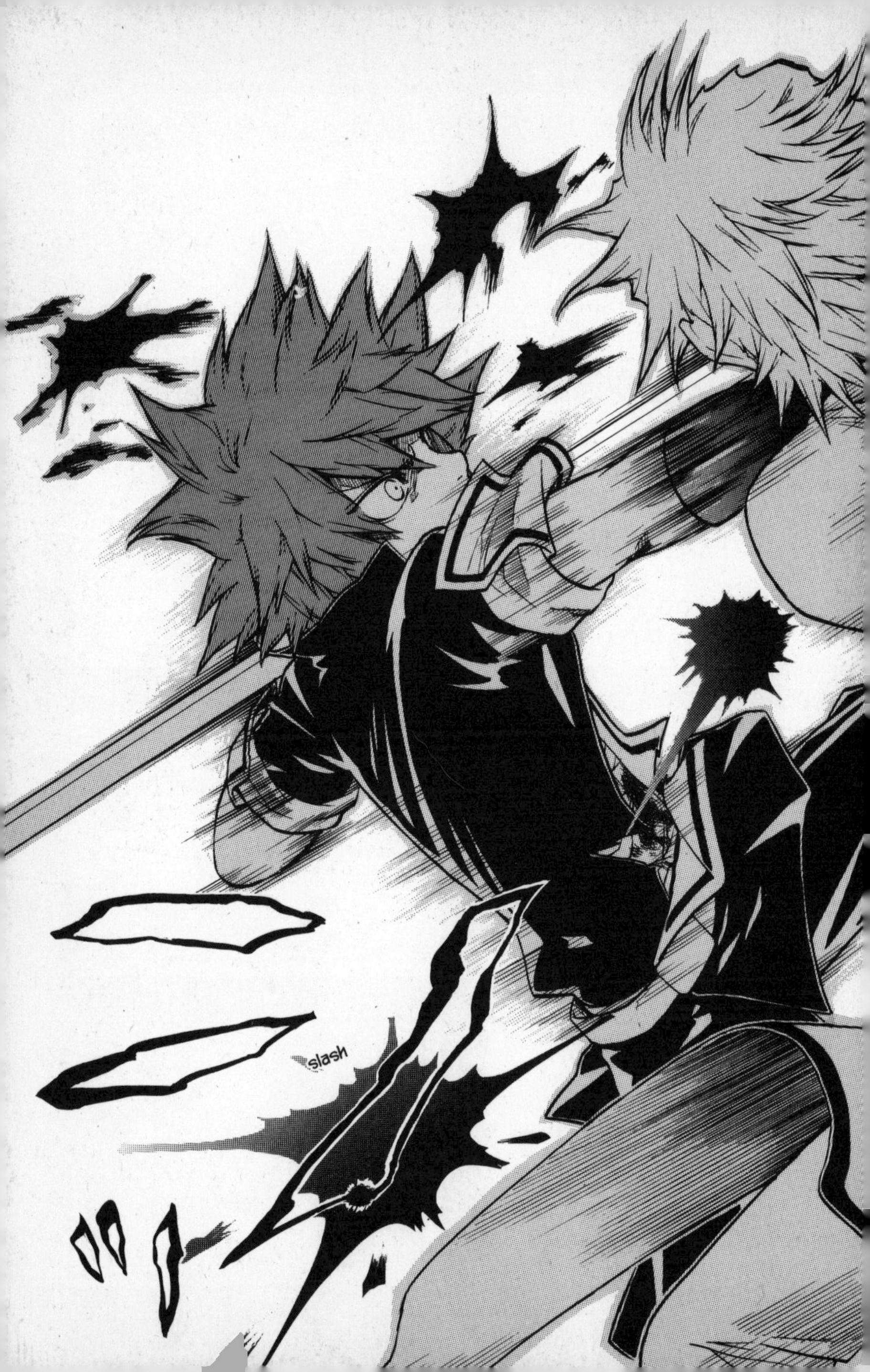
slash

What Happened One Day 1

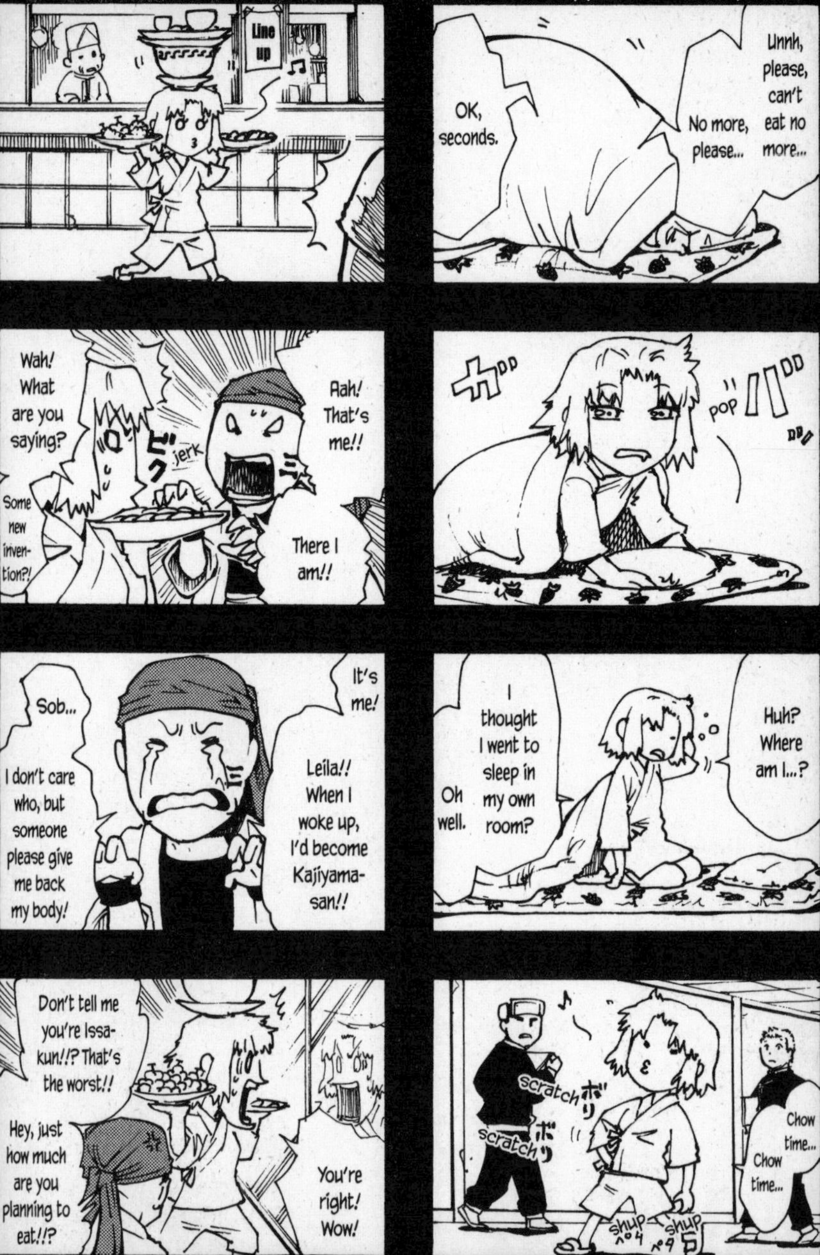
Unnh, please, can't eat no more...
No more, please...
OK, seconds.
POP
Huh? Where am I...?
I thought I went to sleep in my own room?
Oh well.
Chow time... Chow time...
scratch ボリ
scratch ボリ
shup
shup
Line up
Aah! That's me!!
There I am!!
jerk
Wah! What are you saying?
Some new invention?!
It's me!
Leila!! When I woke up, I'd become Kajiyama-san!!
Sob...
I don't care who, but someone please give me back my body!
Don't tell me you're Issa-kun!!? That's the worst!!
You're right! Wow!
Hey, just how much are you planning to eat!!?

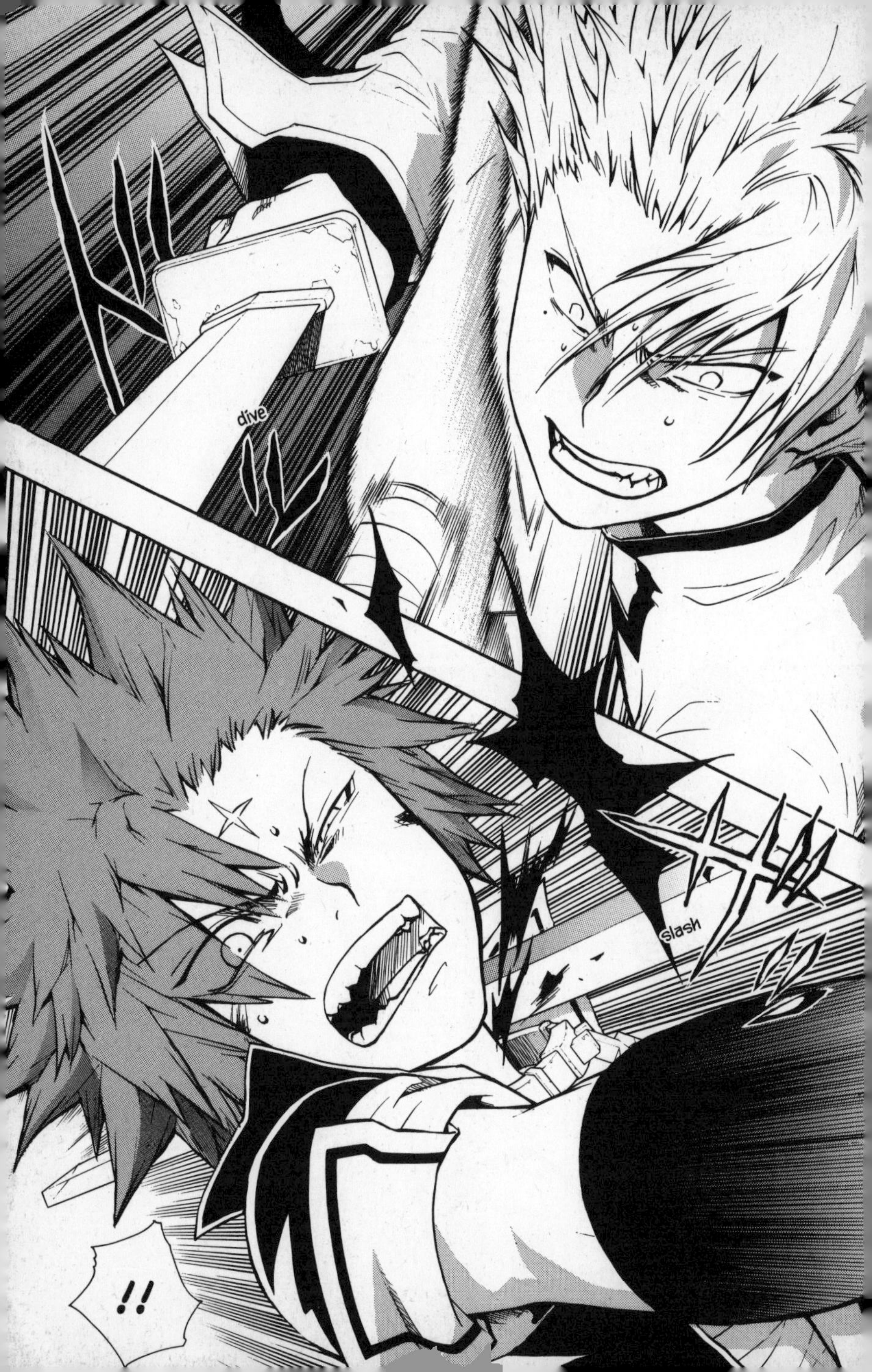
dive
slash
!!

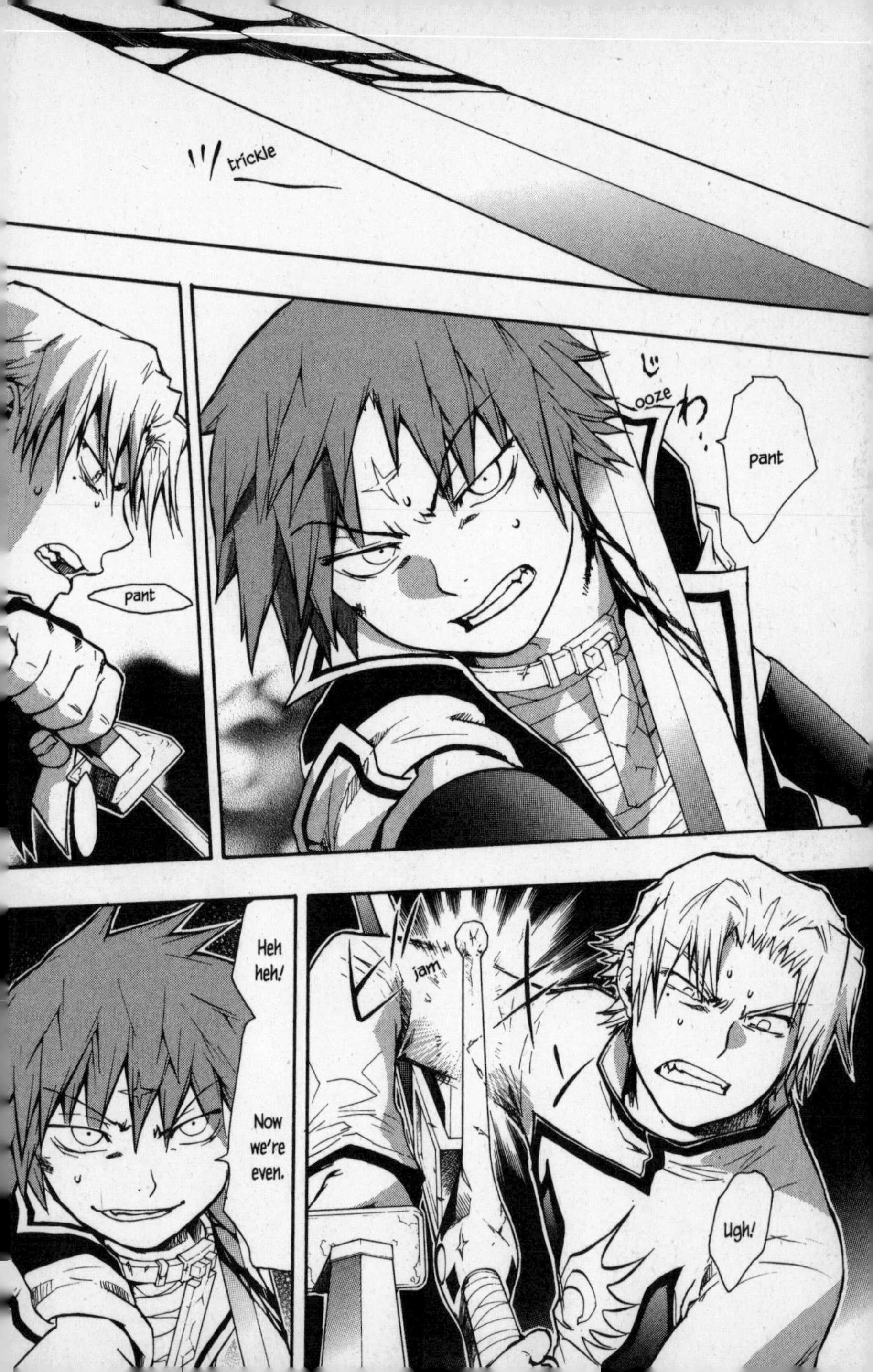

trickle
じわ
ooze
pant
pant
jam
Ugh!
Heh heh!
Now we're even.

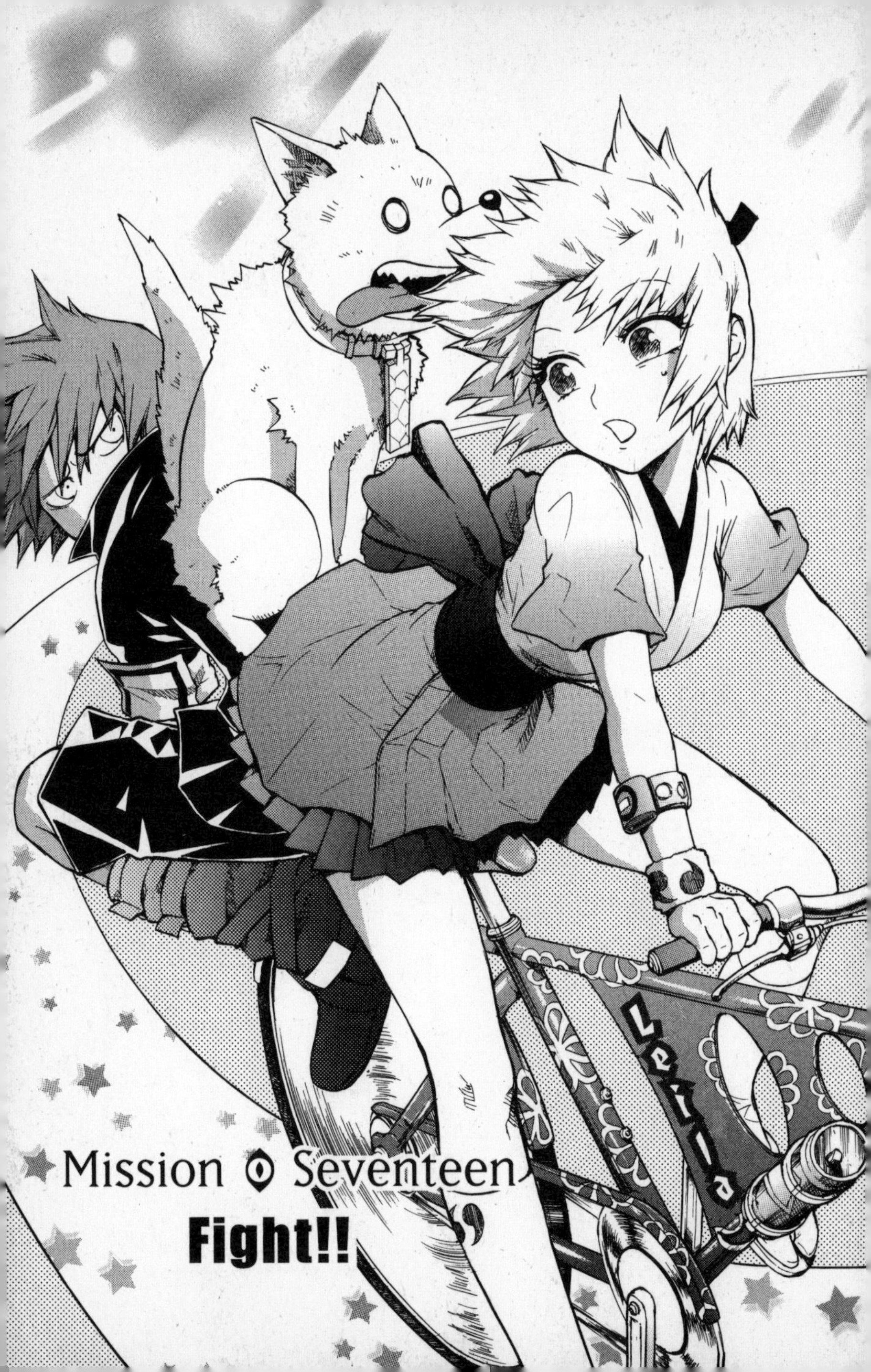
Mission Seventeen
Fight!!

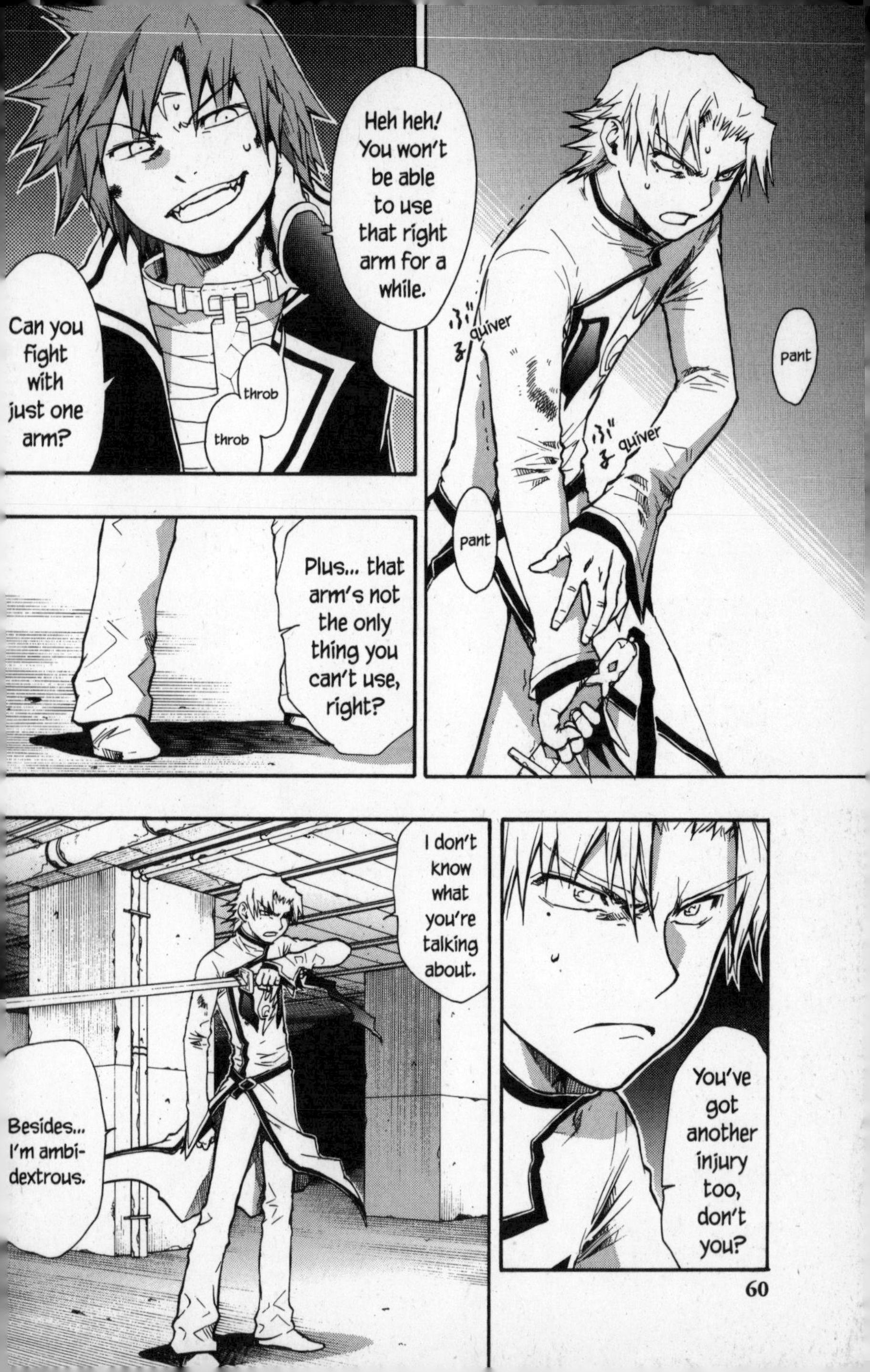
quiver
pant
quiver
pant
Heh heh! You won't be able to use that right arm for a while.
Can you fight with just one arm?
throb
throb
Plus... that arm's not the only thing you can't use, right?
You've got another injury too, don't you?
I don't know what you're talking about.
Besides... I'm ambi-dextrous.

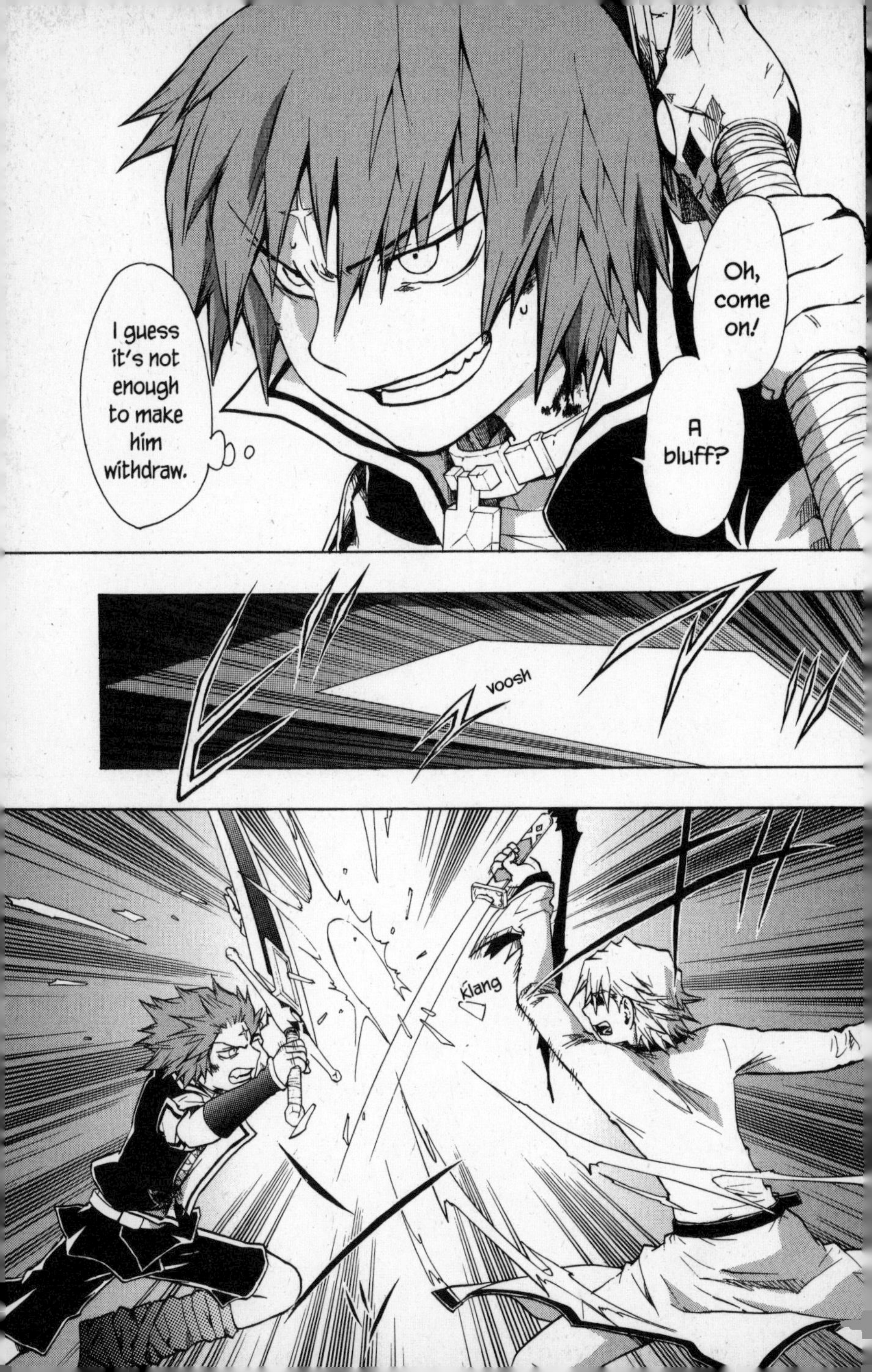
Oh, come on!
A bluff?
I guess it's not enough to make him withdraw.
voosh
klang

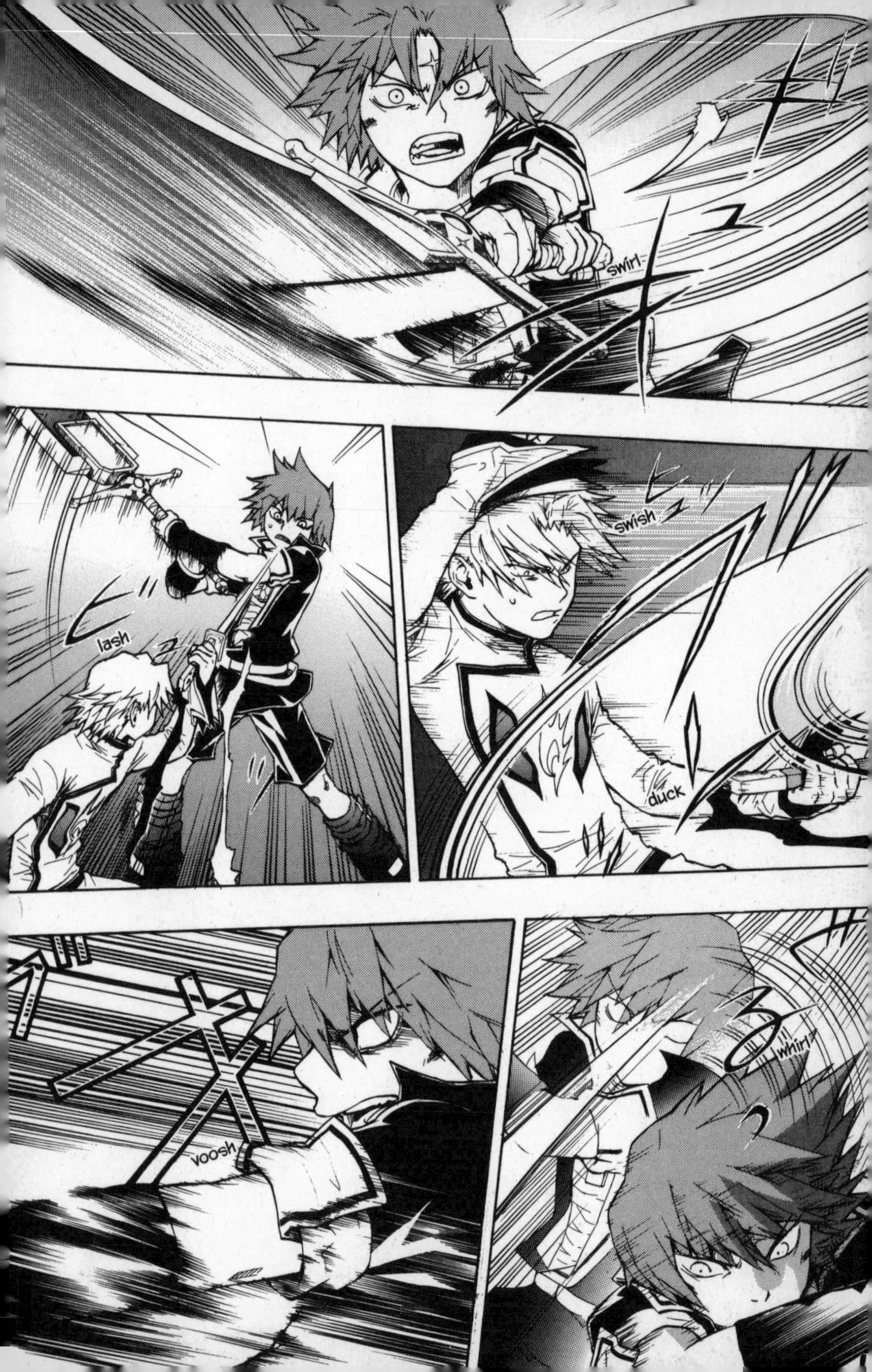
swirl
swish
duck
lash
whirl
voosh

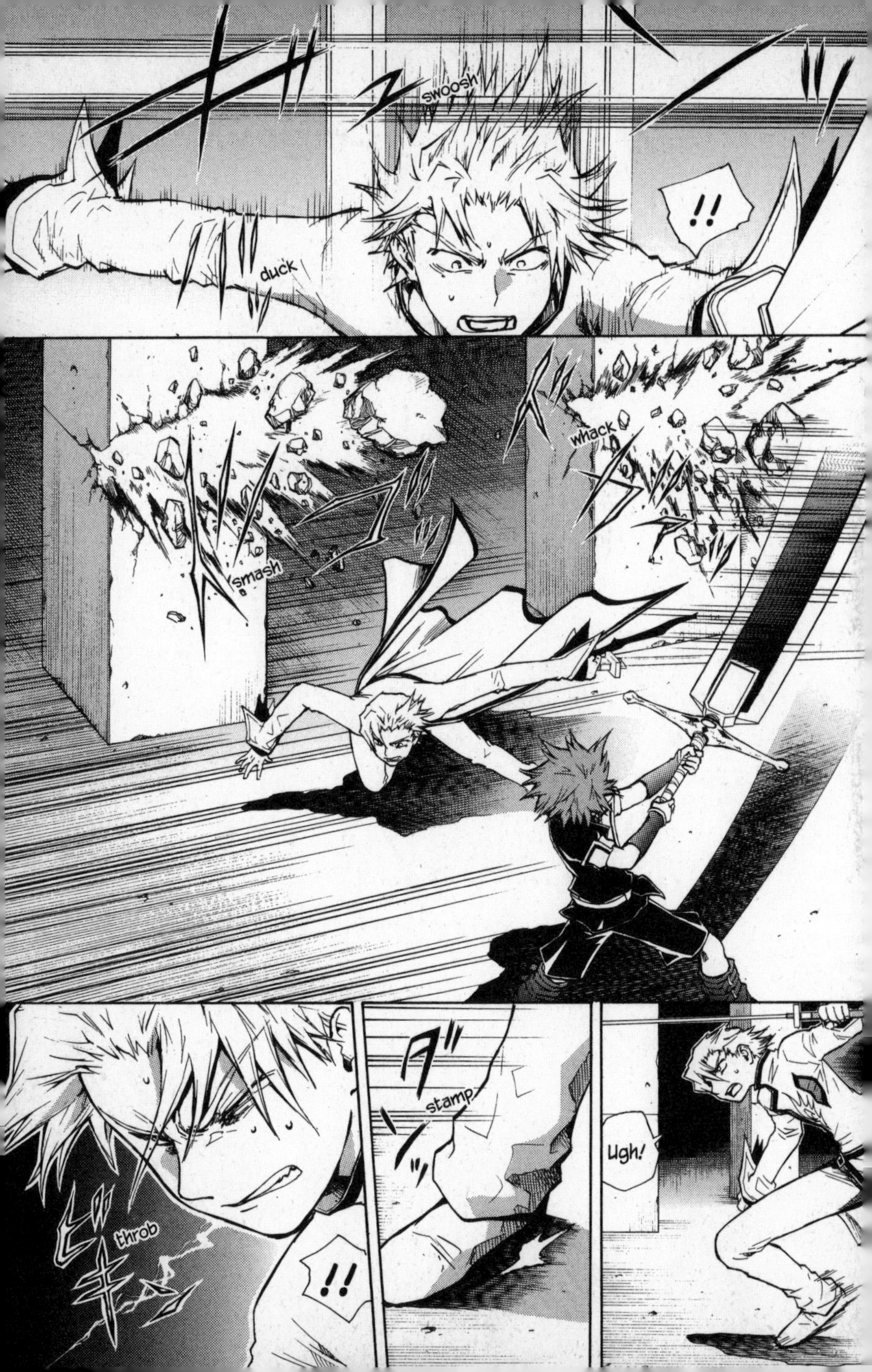
swoosh
!!
duck
whack
smash
Ugh!
stamp
!!
throb

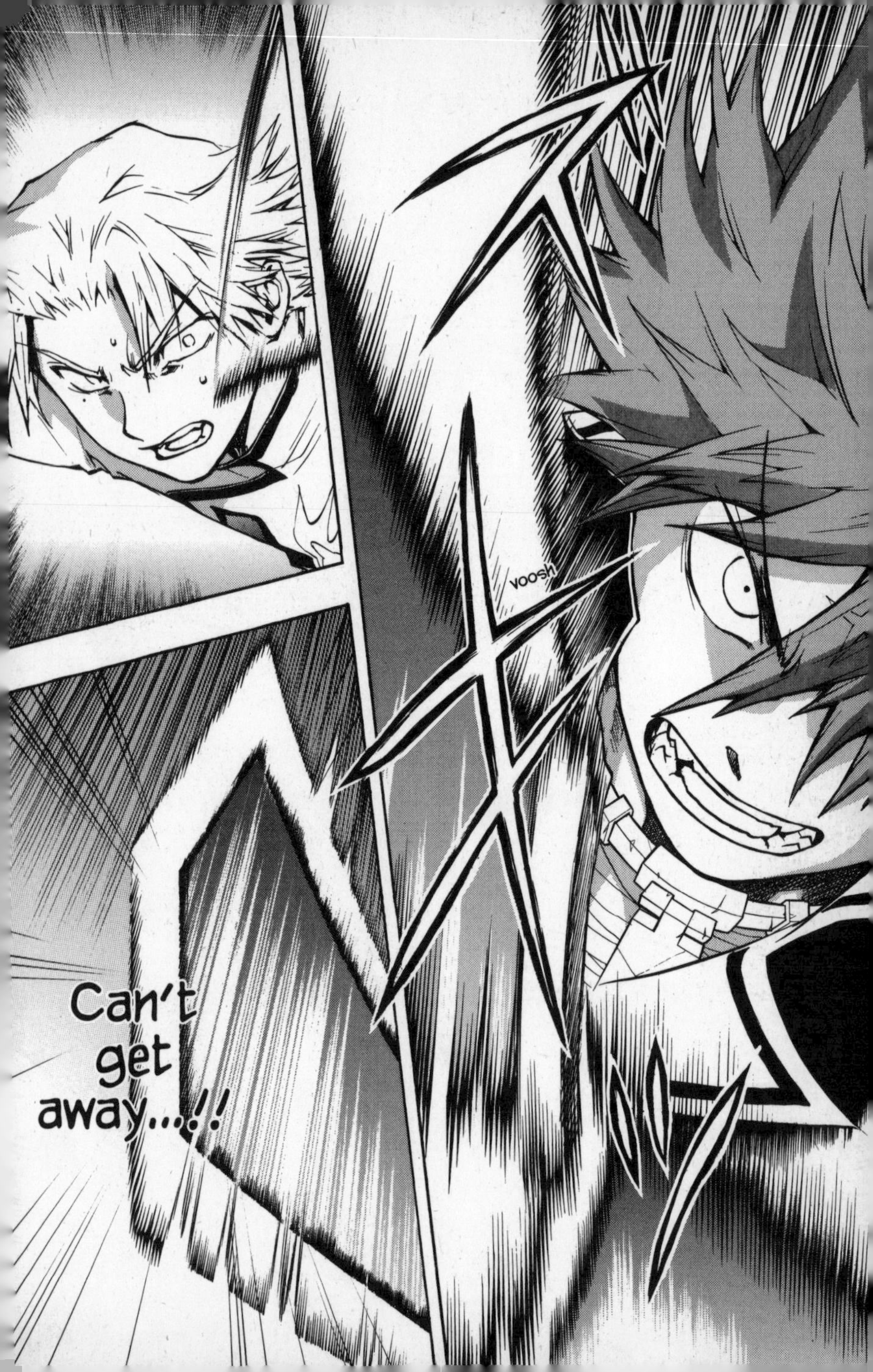
voosh
Can't get away...!!

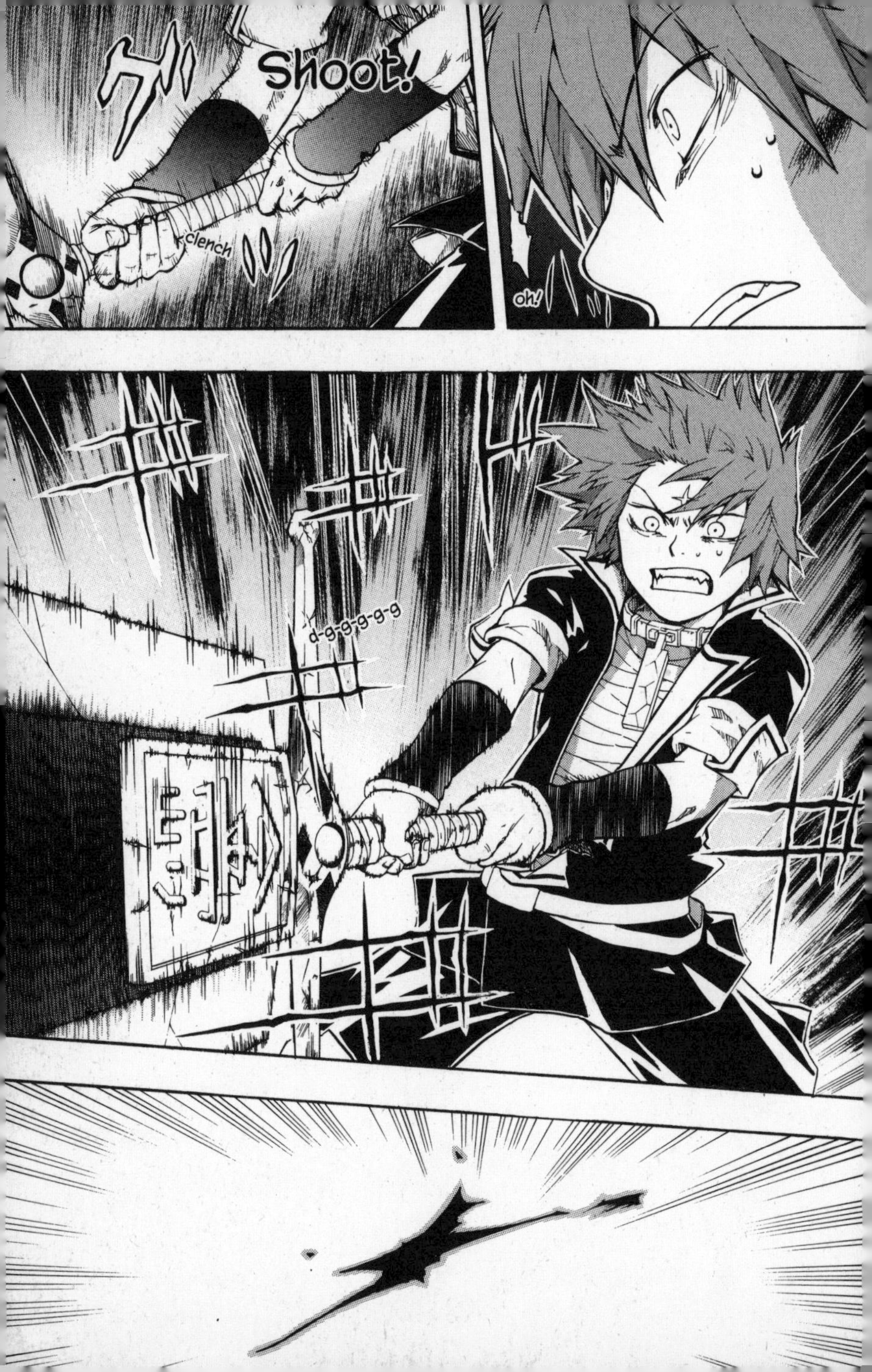
oh!
Shoot!
clench
d-g-g-g-g-g

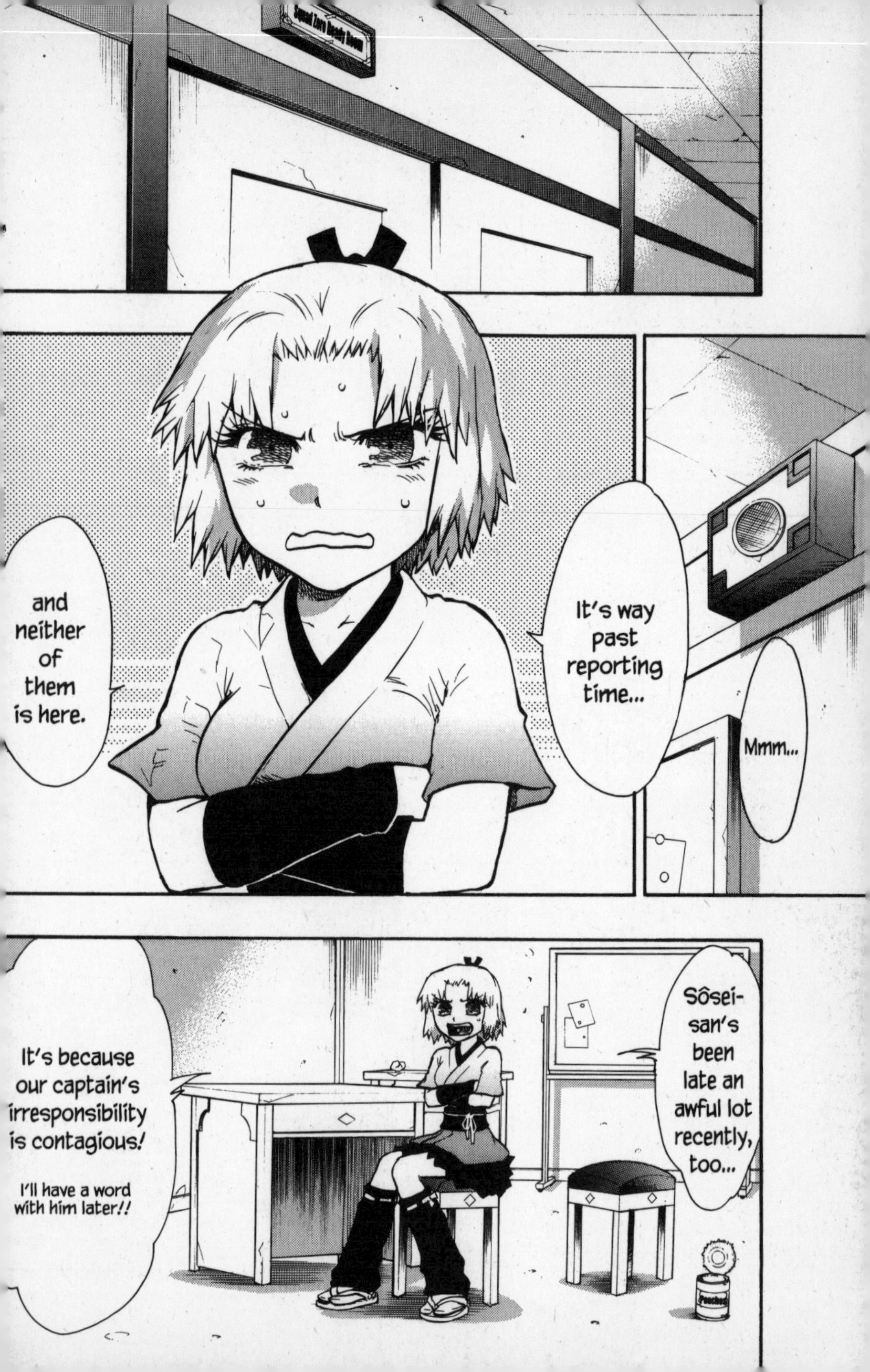
Squad Zero Ready Room
Mmm...
It's way past reporting time...
and neither of them is here.
Sôsei-san's been late an awful lot recently, too...
It's because our captain's irresponsibility is contagious!
I'll have a word with him later!!
Peaches

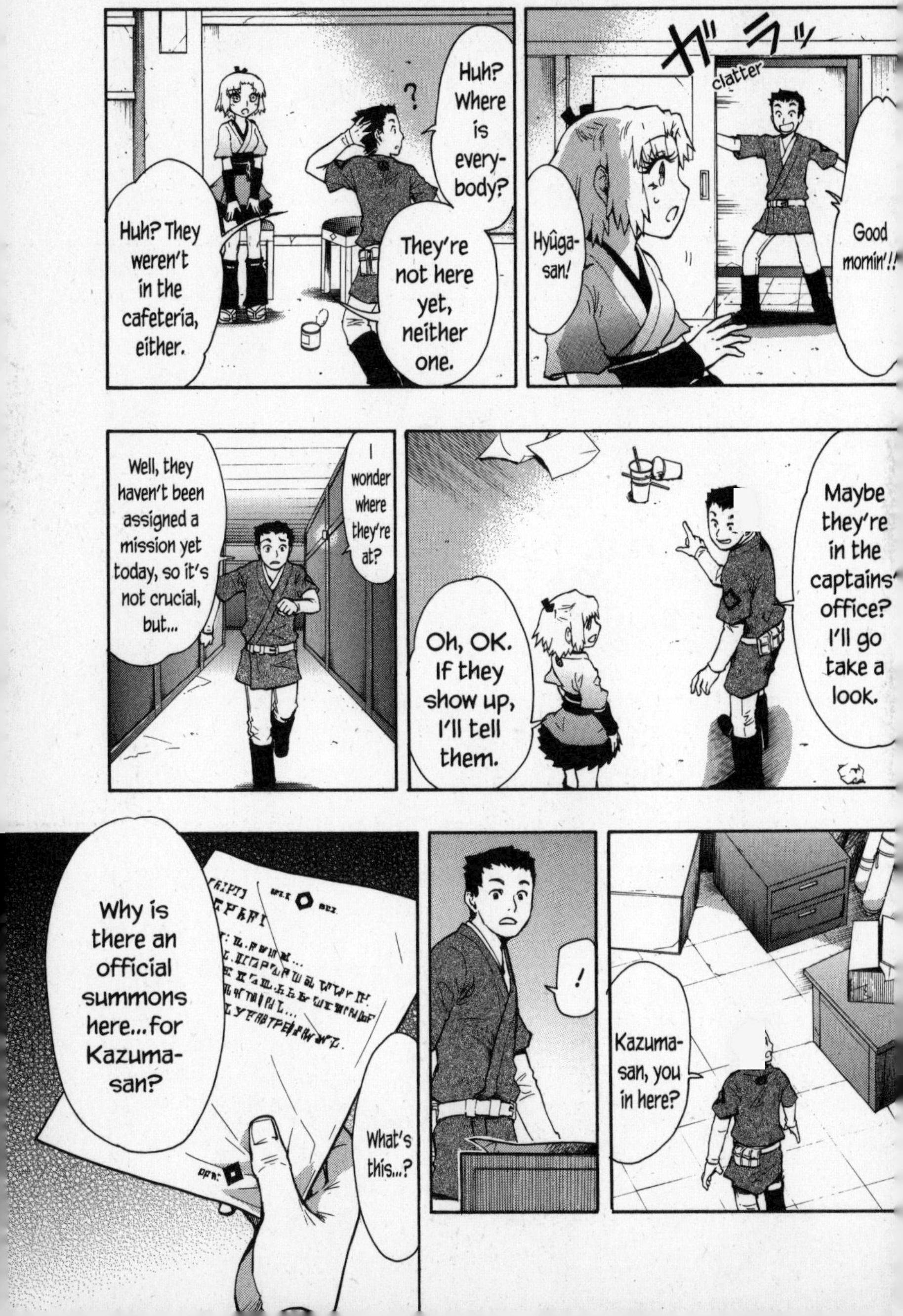
ガラッ
clatter
Good mornin'!!
Hyûga-san!
Huh? Where is every-body?
?
They're not here yet, neither one.
Huh? They weren't in the cafeteria, either.
Maybe they're in the captains' office? I'll go take a look.
Oh, OK. If they show up, I'll tell them.
I wonder where they're at?
Well, they haven't been assigned a mission yet today, so it's not crucial, but...
Kazuma-san, you in here?
!
What's this...?
Why is there an official summons here...for Kazuma-san?

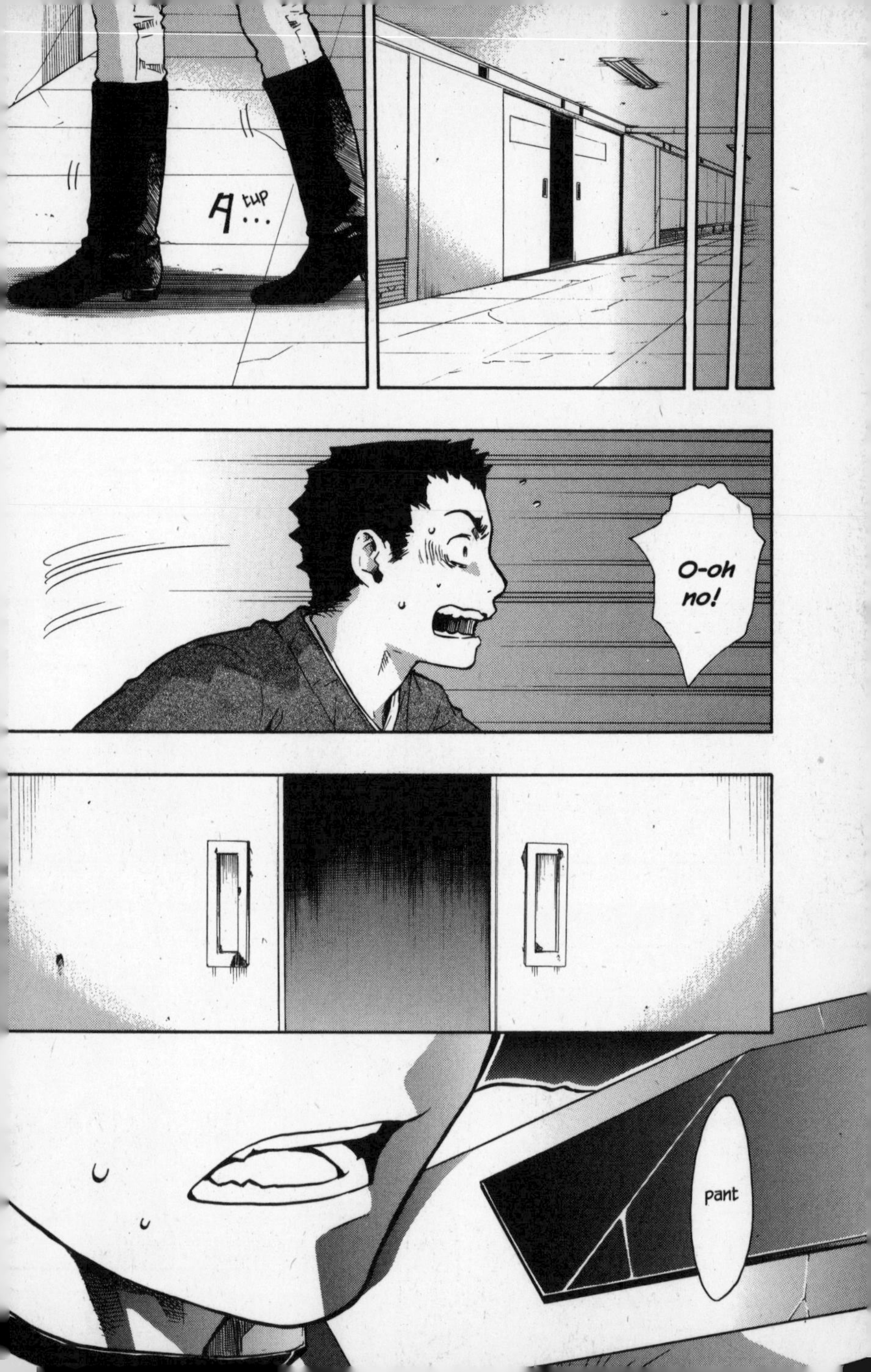
tup...
O-oh no!
pant

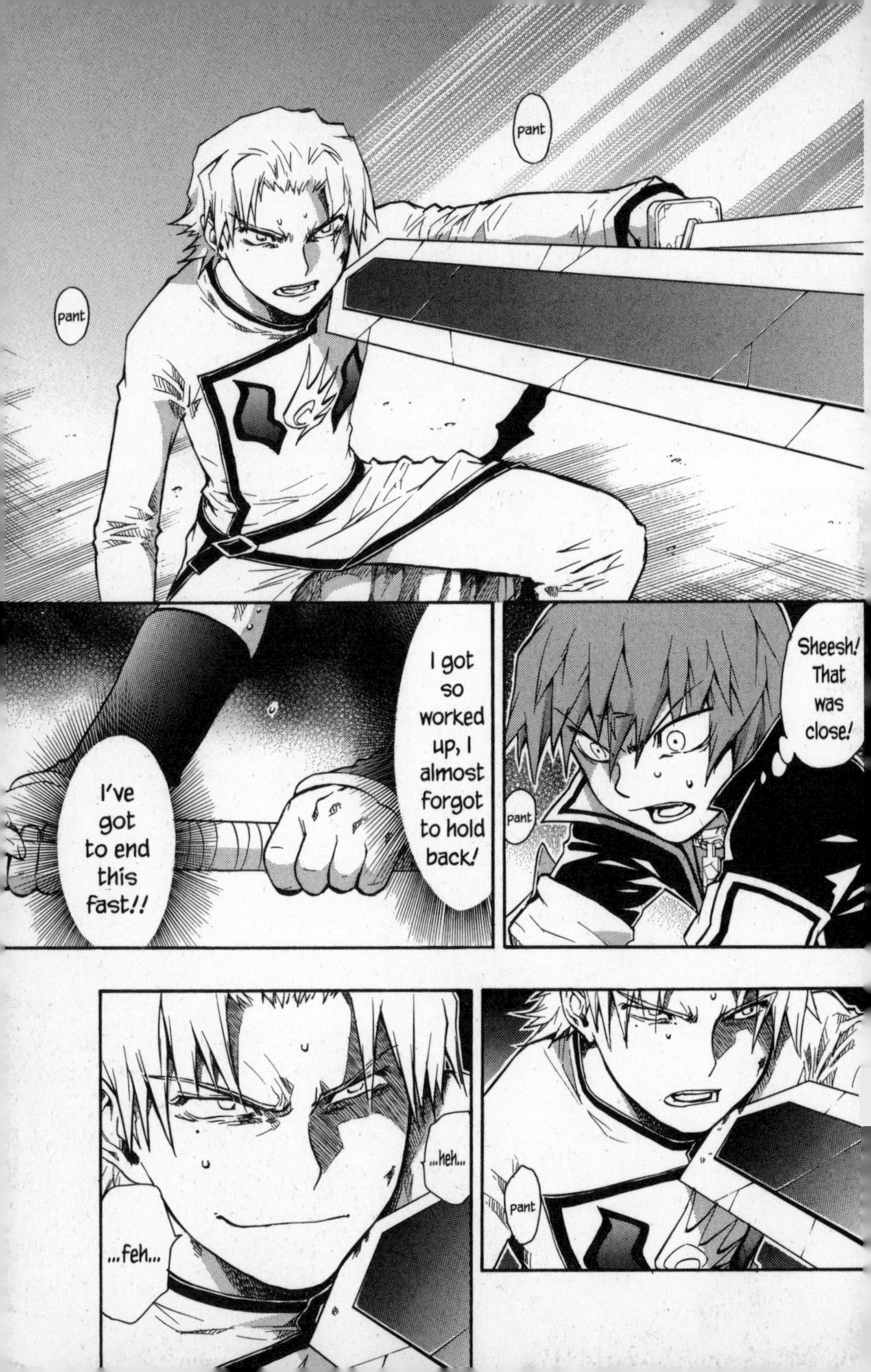
pant
pant
Sheesh! That was close!
pant
I got so worked up, I almost forgot to hold back!
I've got to end this fast!!
pant
...heh...
...feh...

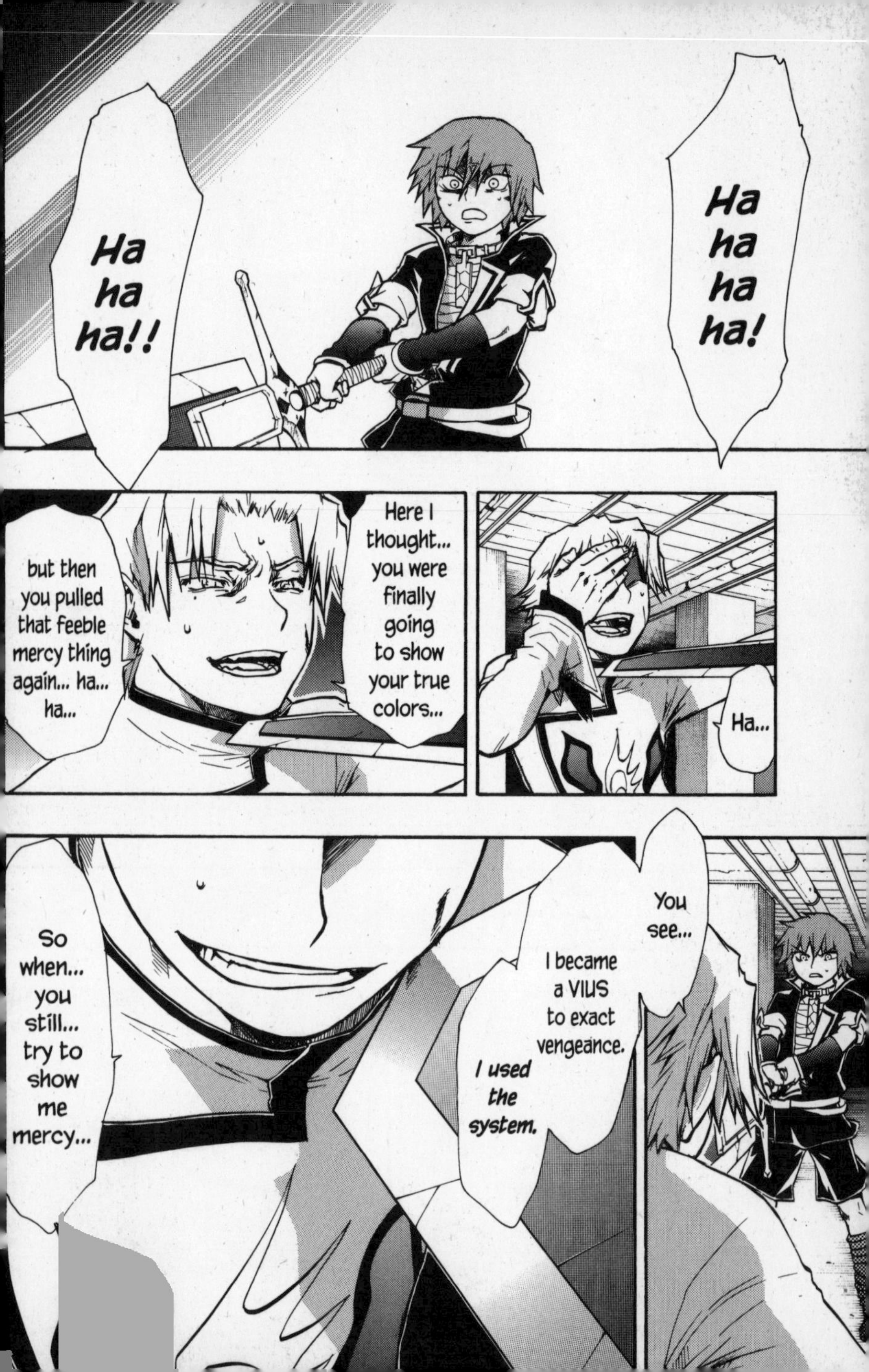
Ha ha ha ha!
Ha ha ha!!
Ha...
Here I thought... you were finally going to show your true colors...
but then you pulled that feeble mercy thing again... ha... ha...
You see...
I became a VIUS to exact vengeance.
I used the system.
So when... you still... try to show me mercy...

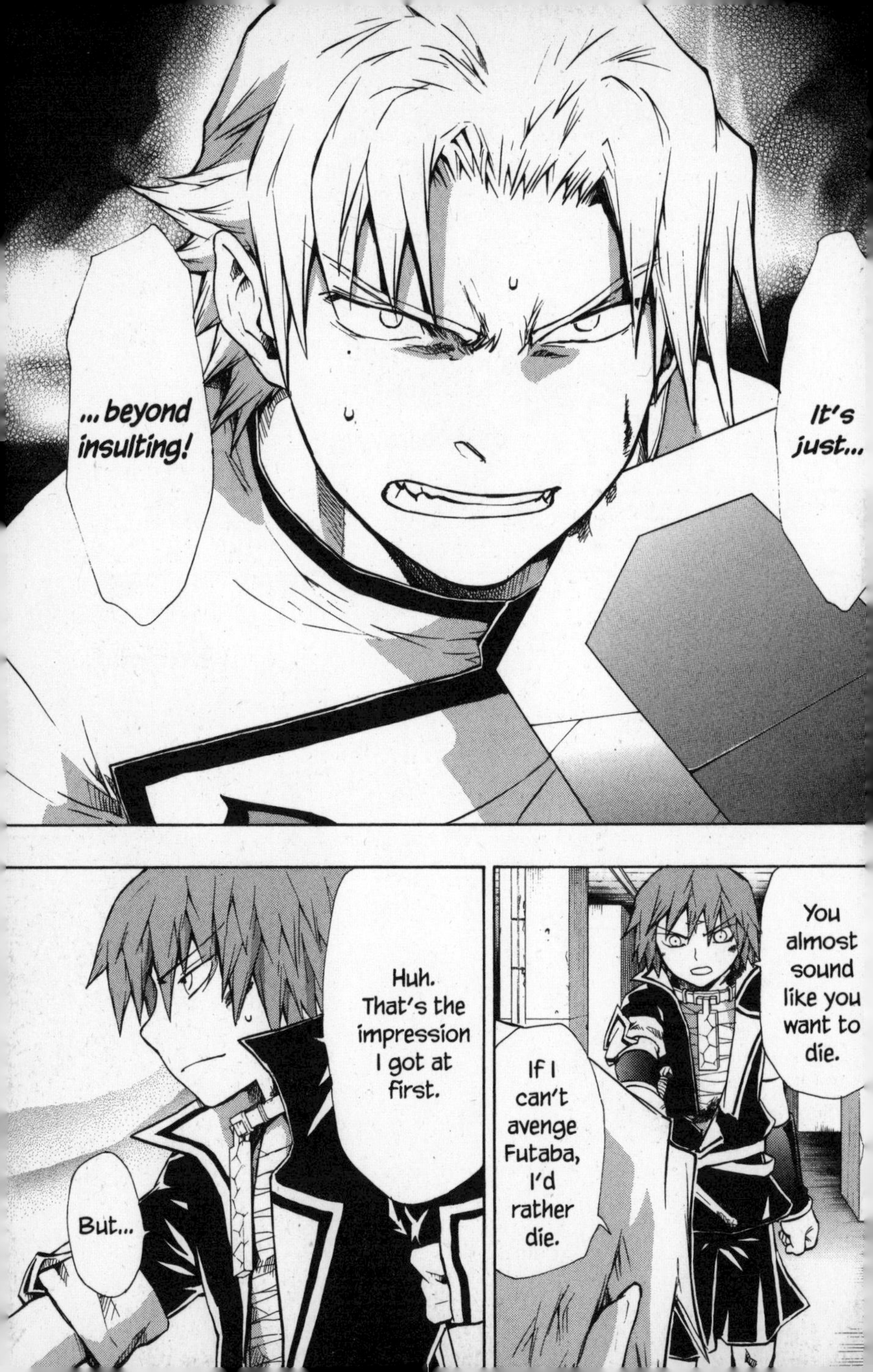
It's just...
...beyond insulting!
You almost sound like you want to die.
If I can't avenge Futaba, I'd rather die.
Huh. That's the impression I got at first.
But...

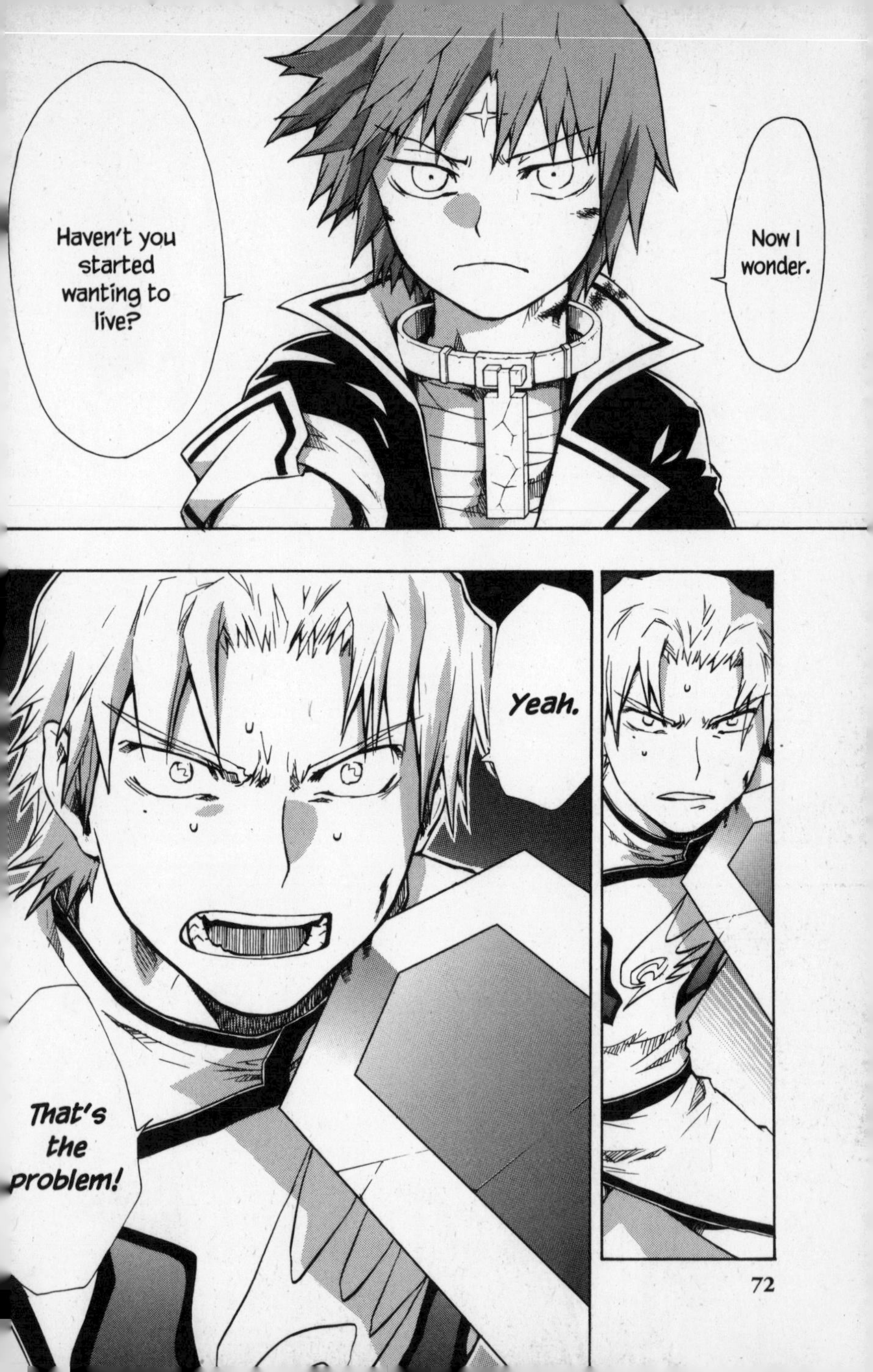
Now I wonder.
Haven't you started wanting to live?
Yeah.
That's the problem!

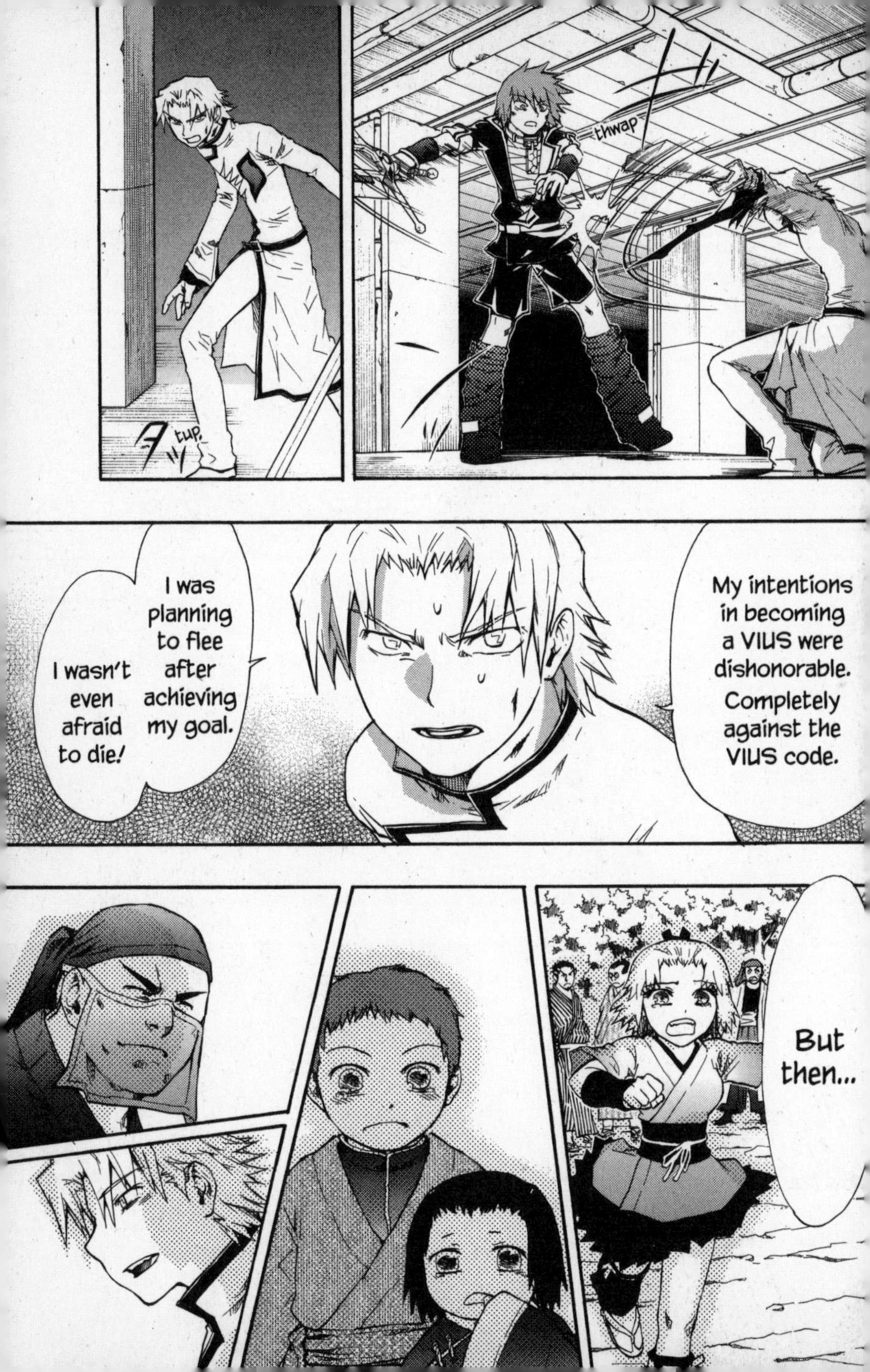
thwap
tup.
My intentions in becoming a VIUS were dishonorable. Completely against the VIUS code.
I was planning to flee after achieving my goal.
I wasn't even afraid to die!
But then...

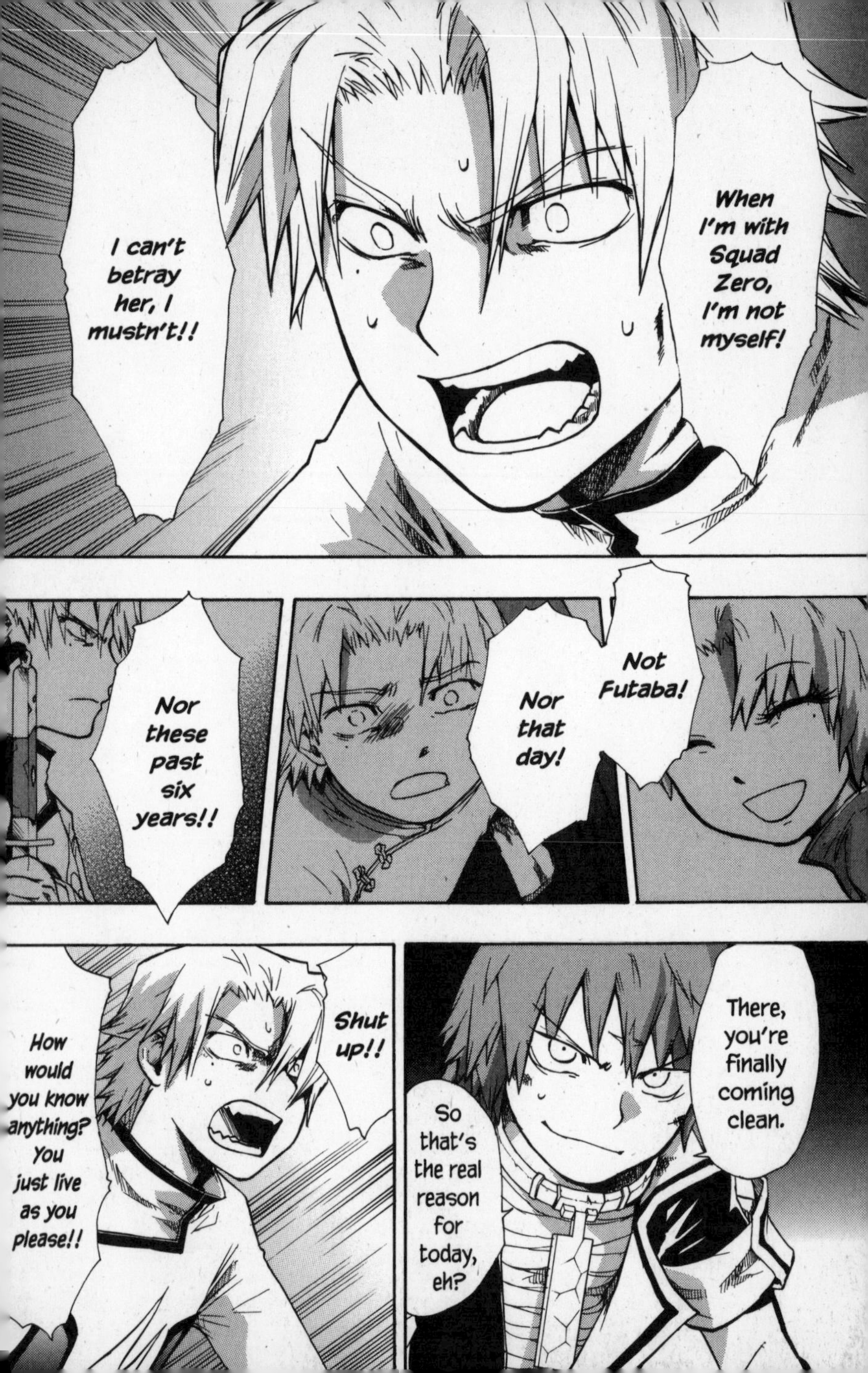
When I'm with Squad Zero, I'm not myself!
I can't betray her, I mustn't!!
Not Futaba!
Nor that day!
Nor these past six years!!
There, you're finally coming clean.
So that's the real reason for today, eh?
Shut up!!
How would you know anything? You just live as you please!!

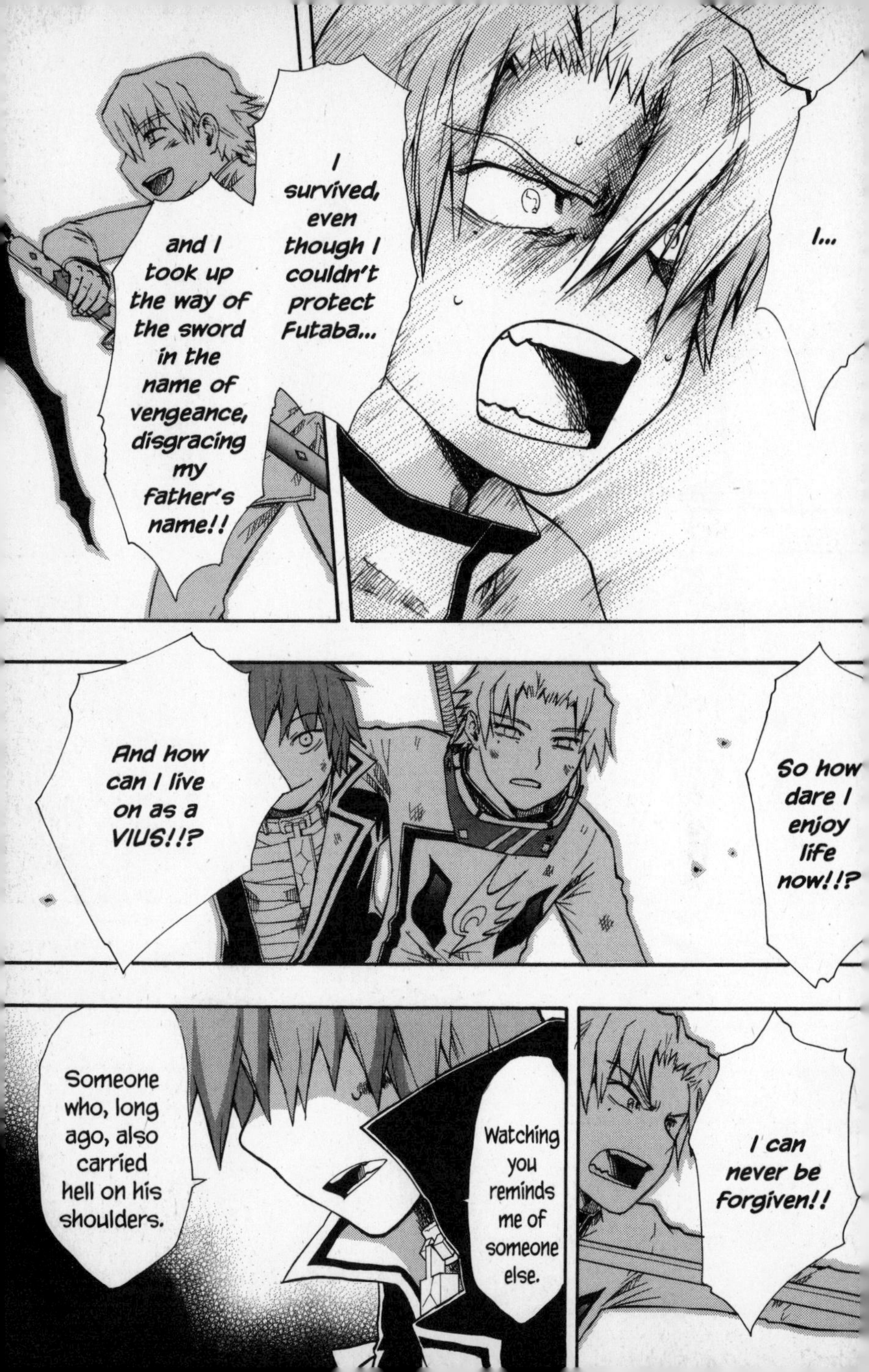
I...
I survived, even though I couldn't protect Futaba...
and I took up the way of the sword in the name of vengeance, disgracing my father's name!!
So how dare I enjoy life now!!?
And how can I live on as a VIUS!!?
I can never be forgiven!!
Watching you reminds me of someone else.
Someone who, long ago, also carried hell on his shoulders.

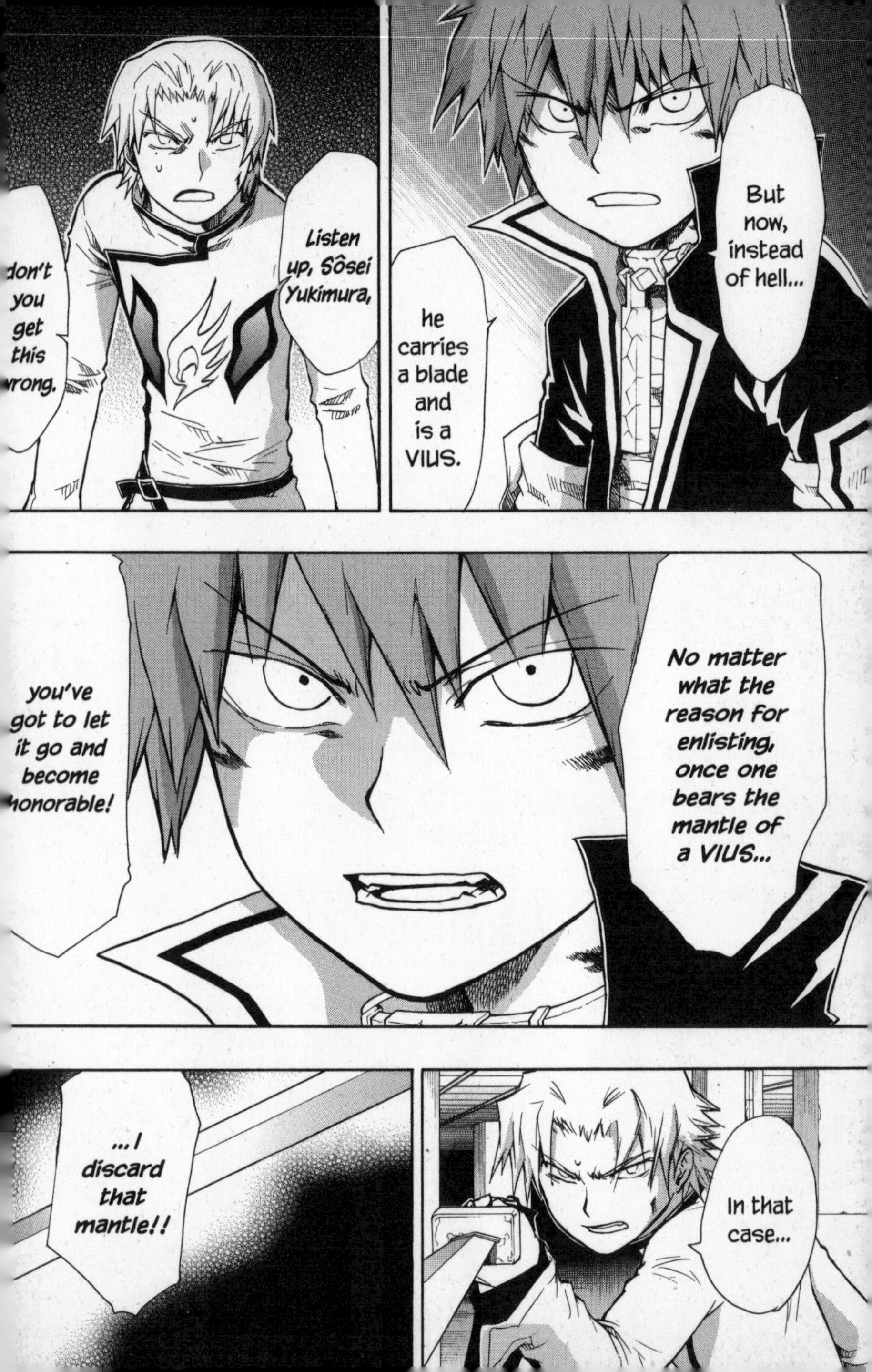
But now, instead of hell...
he carries a blade and is a VIUS.
Listen up, Sôsei Yukimura,
don't you get this wrong.
No matter what the reason for enlisting, once one bears the mantle of a VIUS...
you've got to let it go and become honorable!
In that case...
...I discard that mantle!!

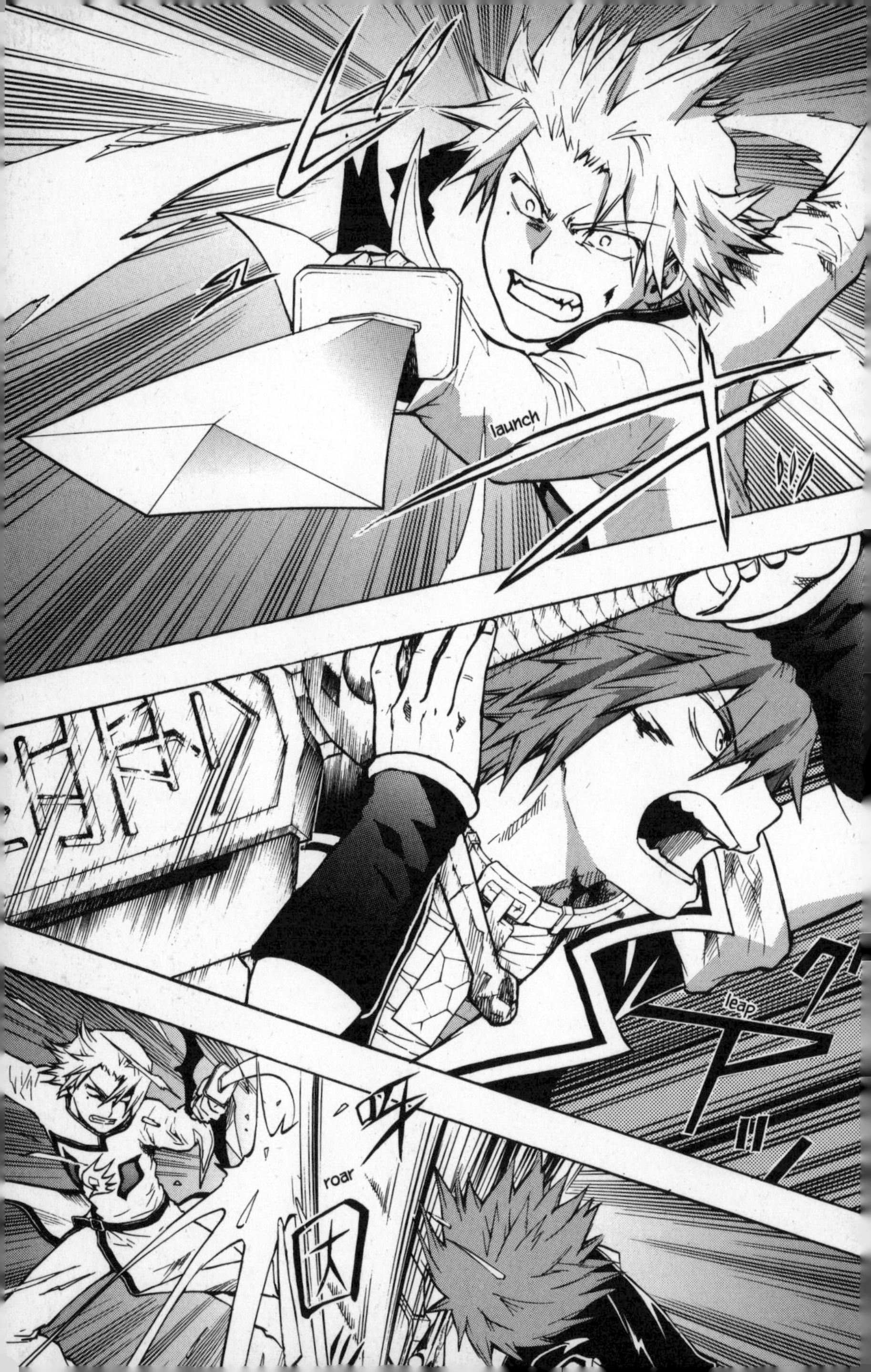
launch
leap
roar

swish
swoosh
I can't lose!
If I lose here, it'll even make a lie out of my vengeful soul!!

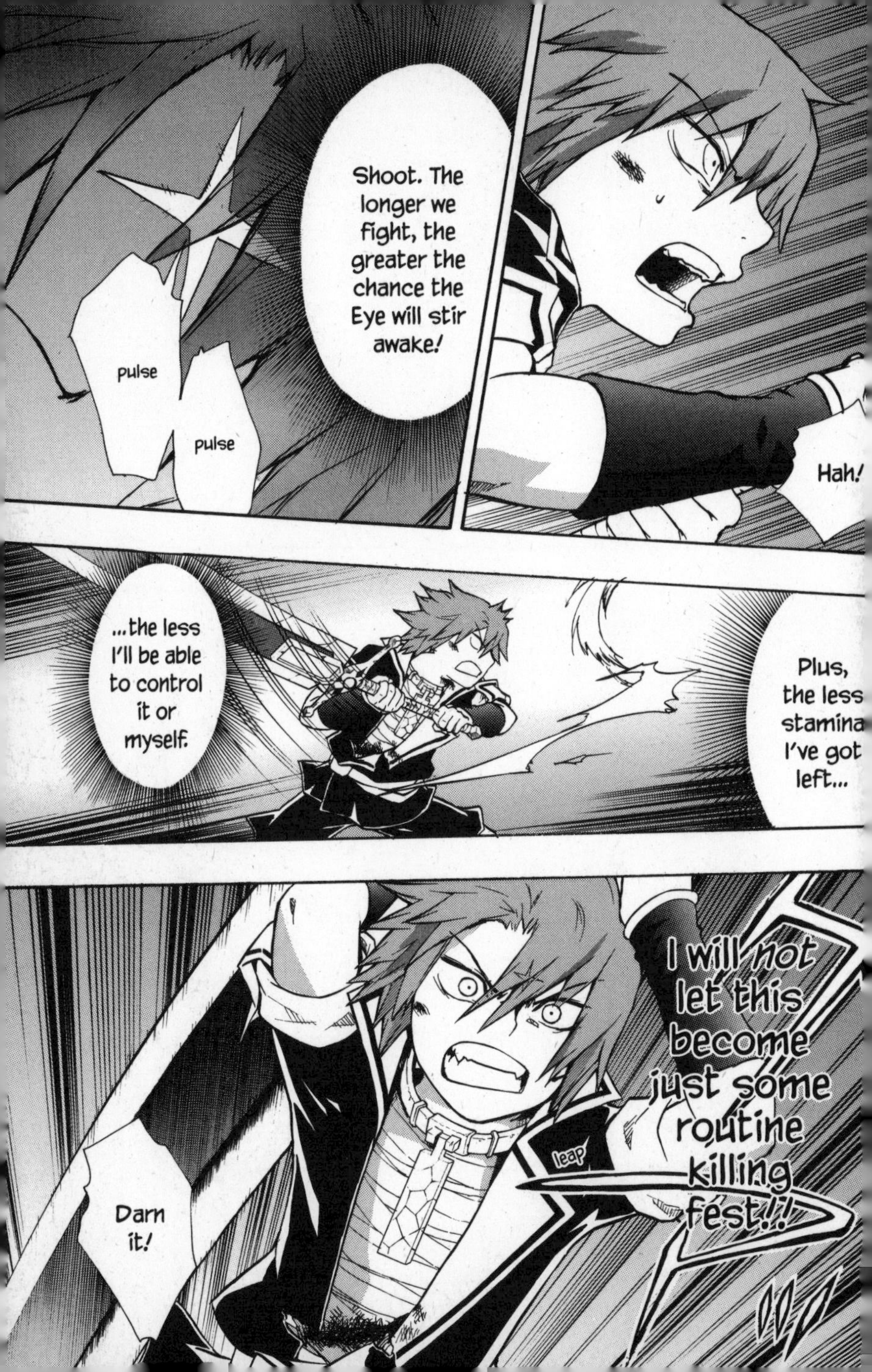
Hah!
Shoot. The longer we fight, the greater the chance the Eye will stir awake!
pulse
pulse
Plus, the less stamina I've got left...
...the less I'll be able to control it or myself.
I will *not* let this become just some routine killing fest!!
leap
Darn it!

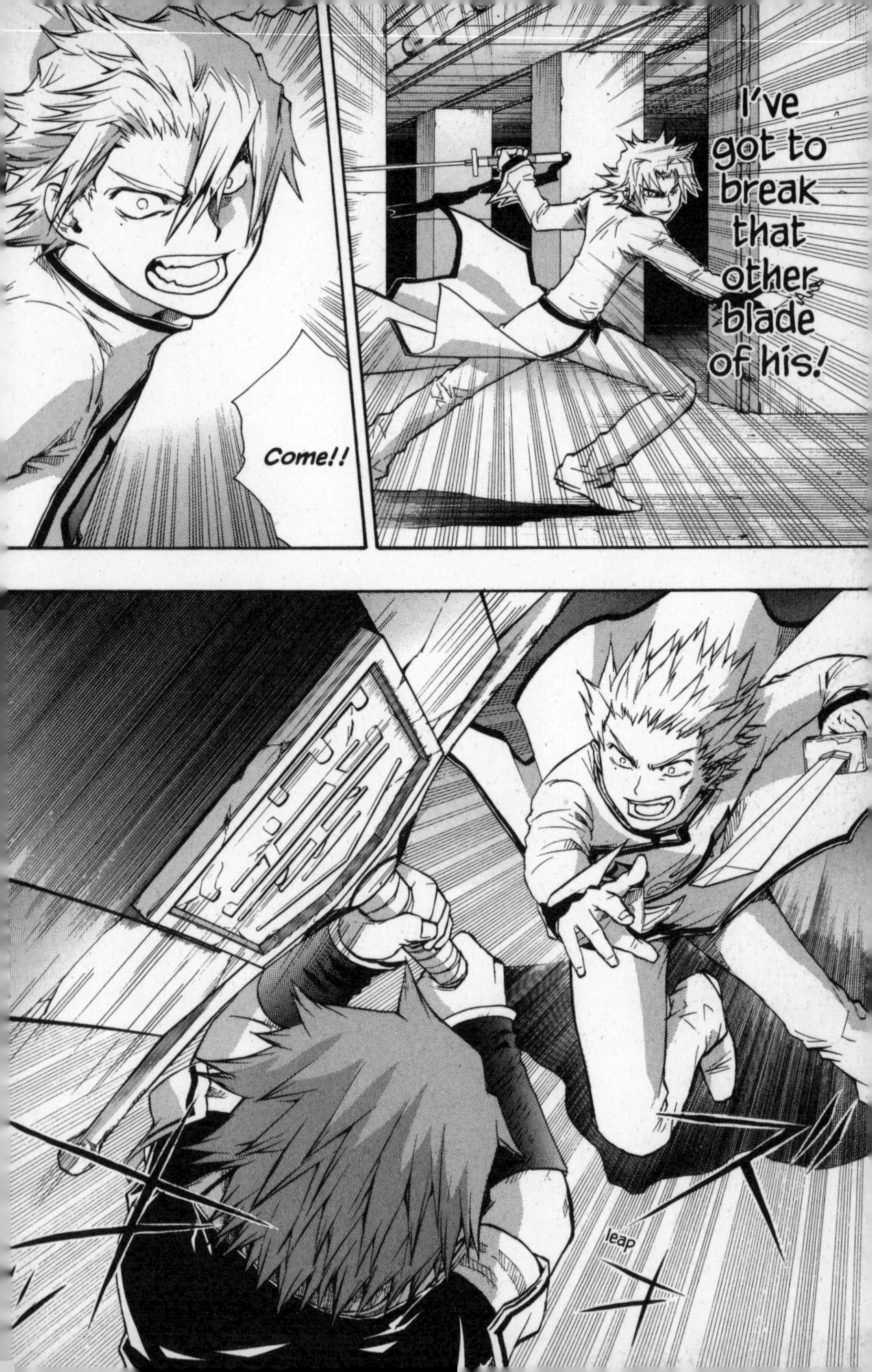
I've got to break that other blade of his!
Come!!
leap

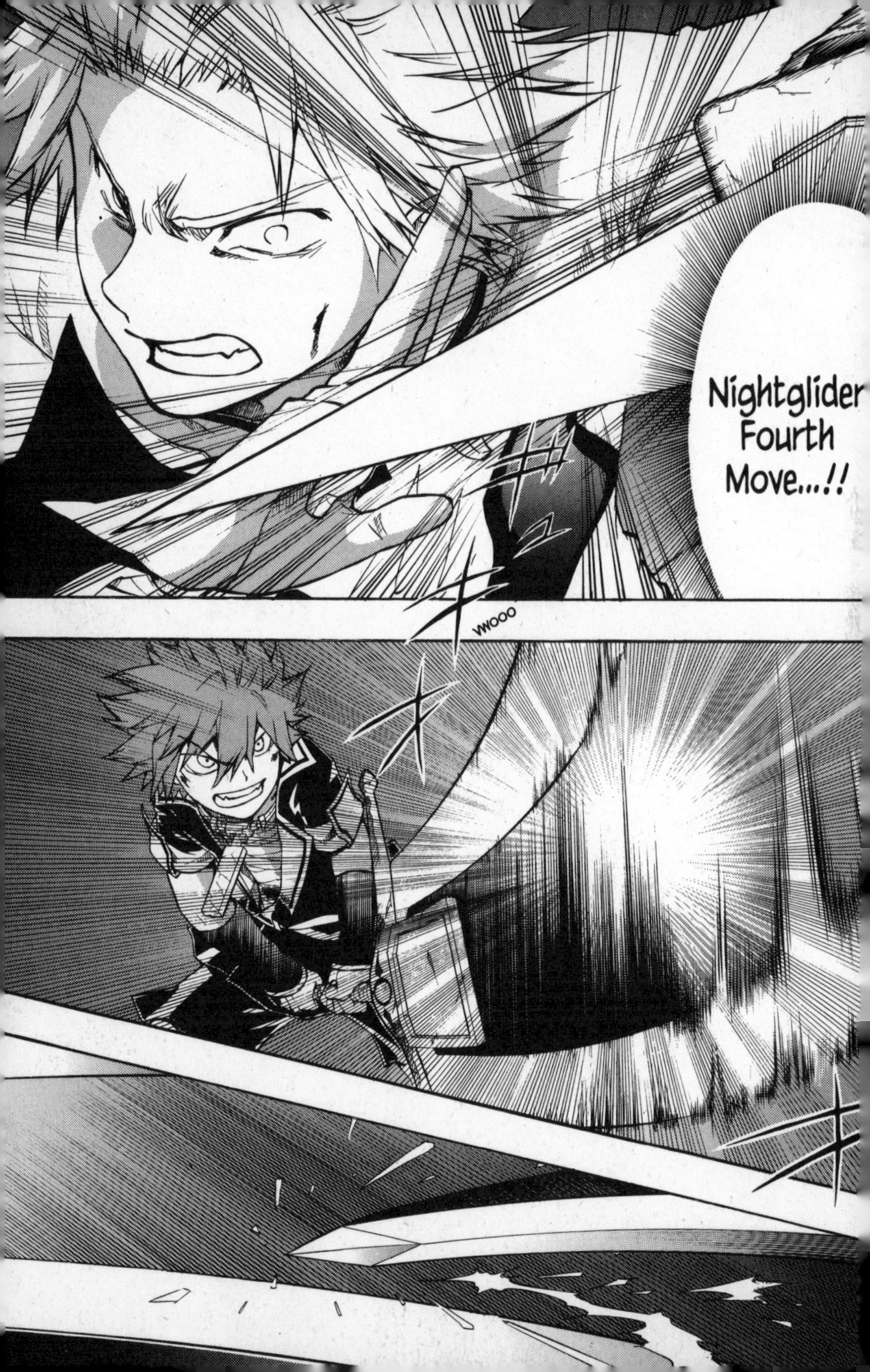
Nightglider Fourth Move...!!
VWOOO

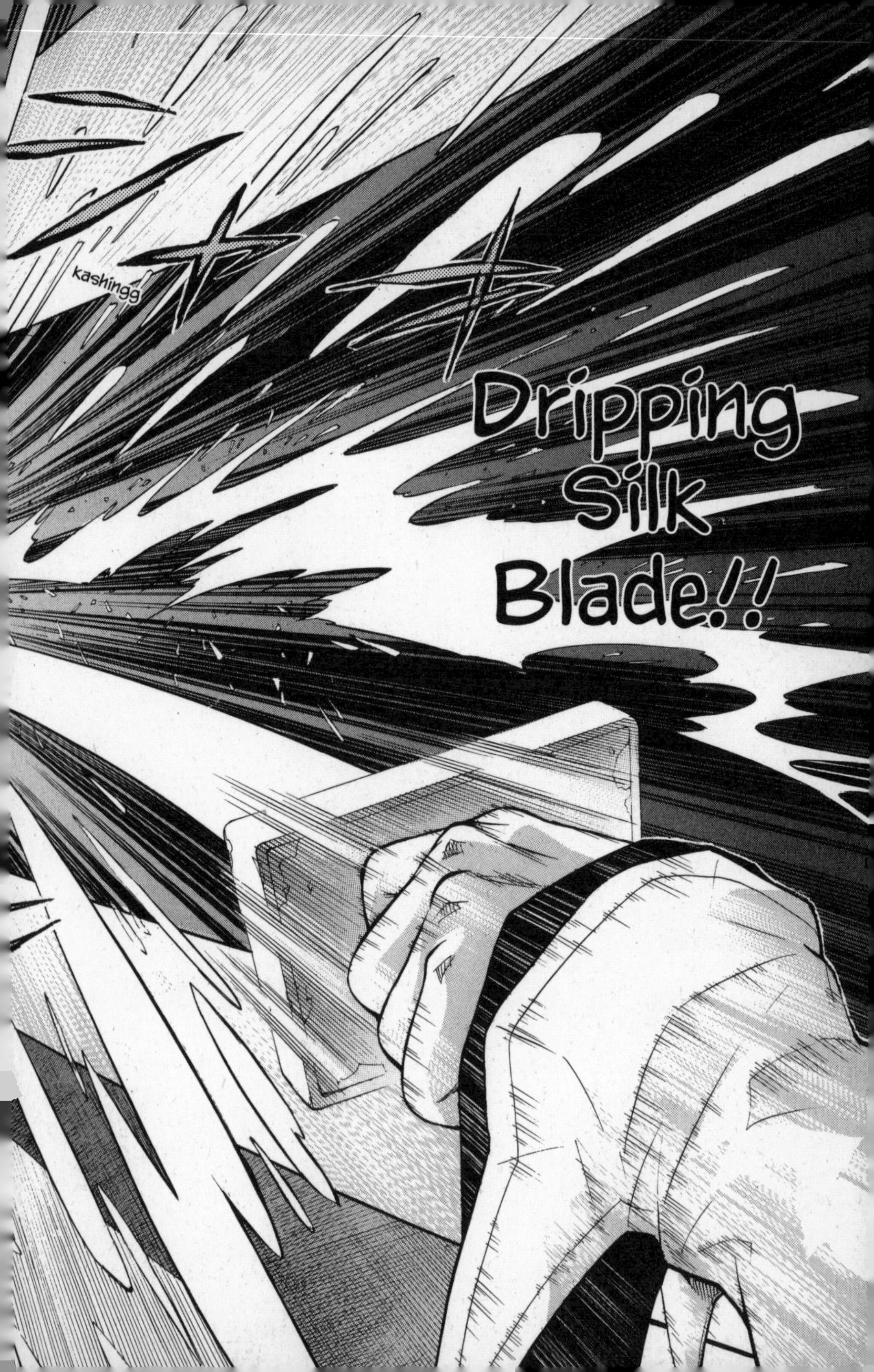
kashingg
Dripping Silk Blade!!

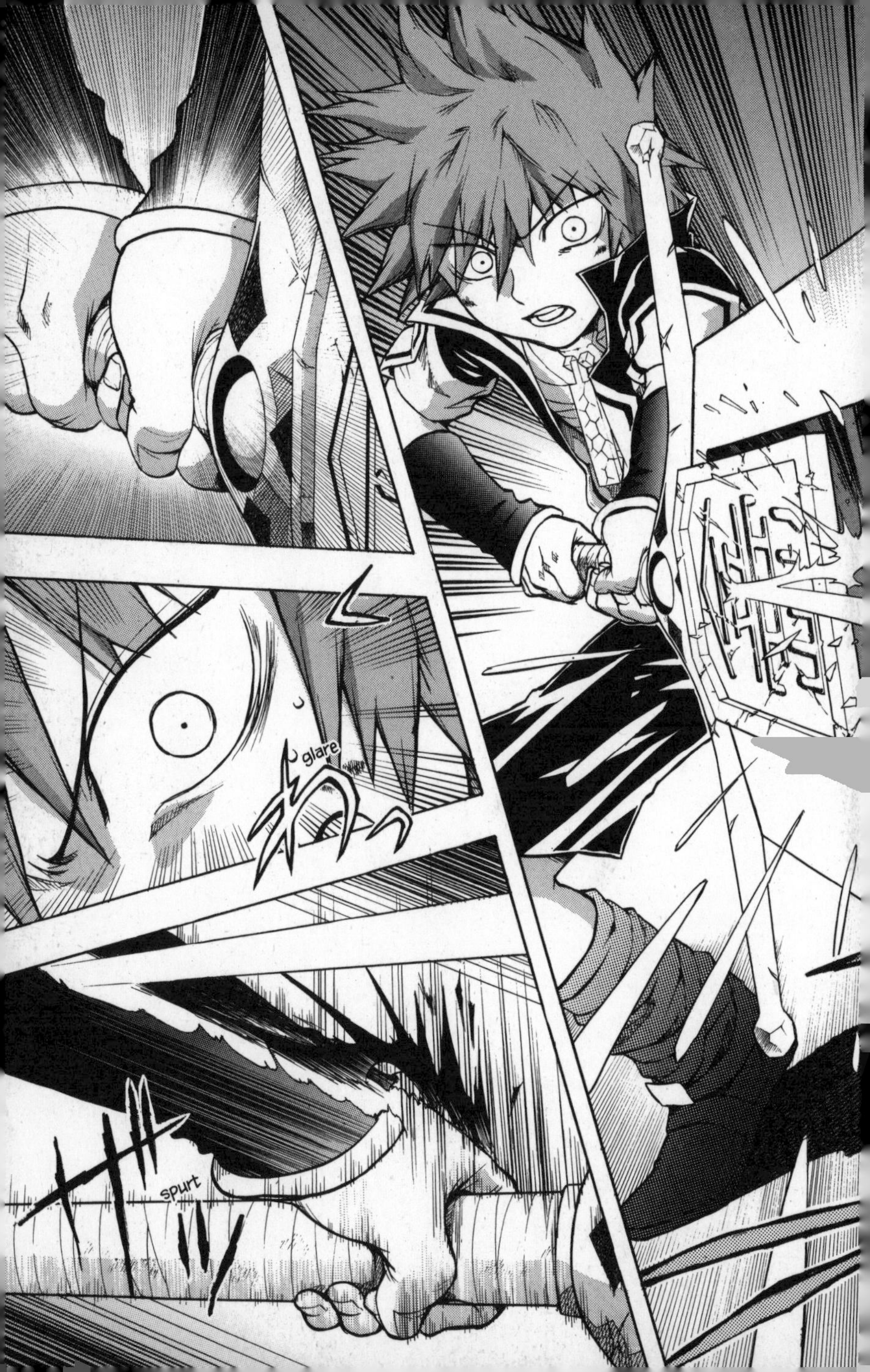
glare
spurt

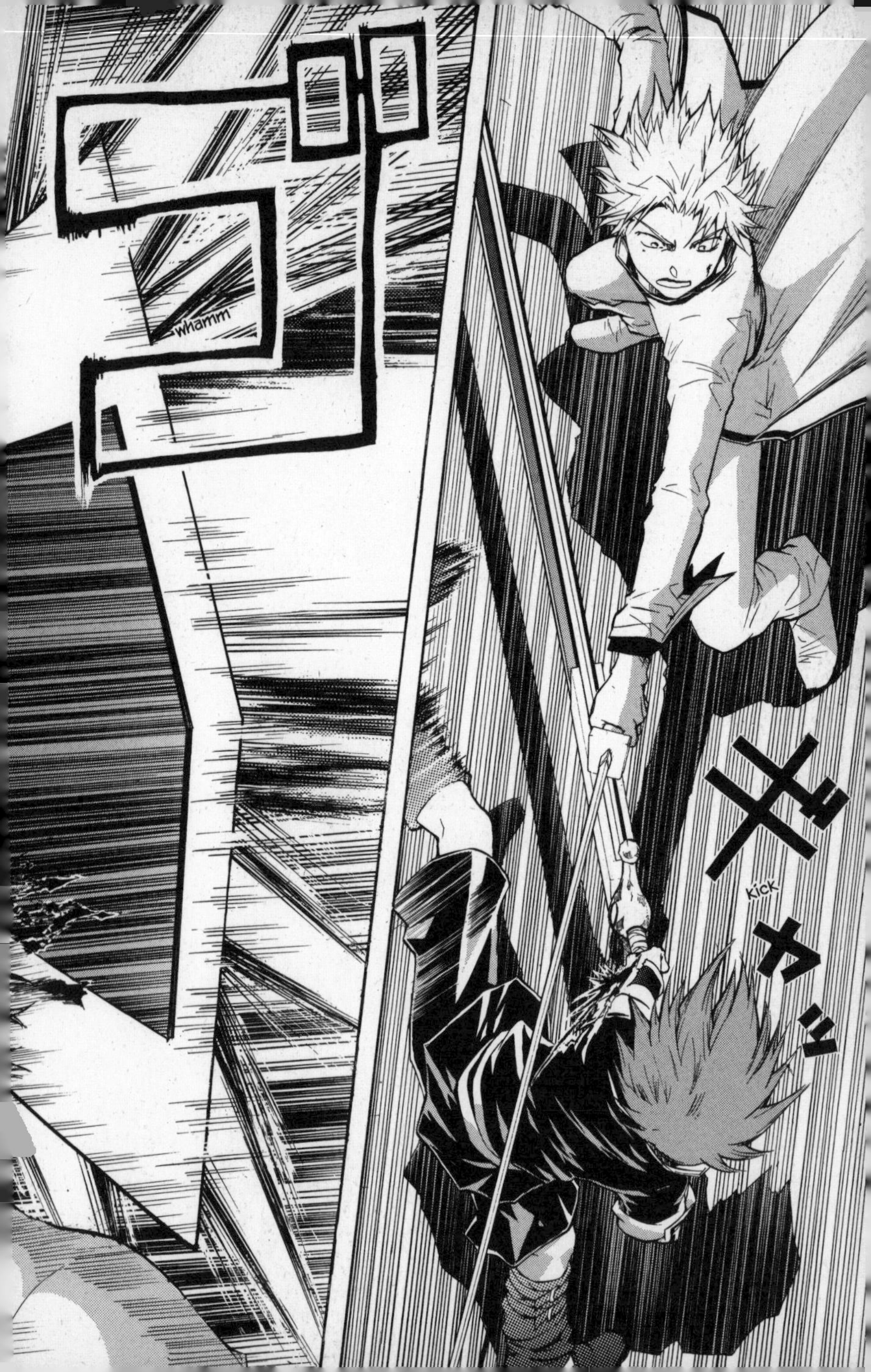
kick
whamm

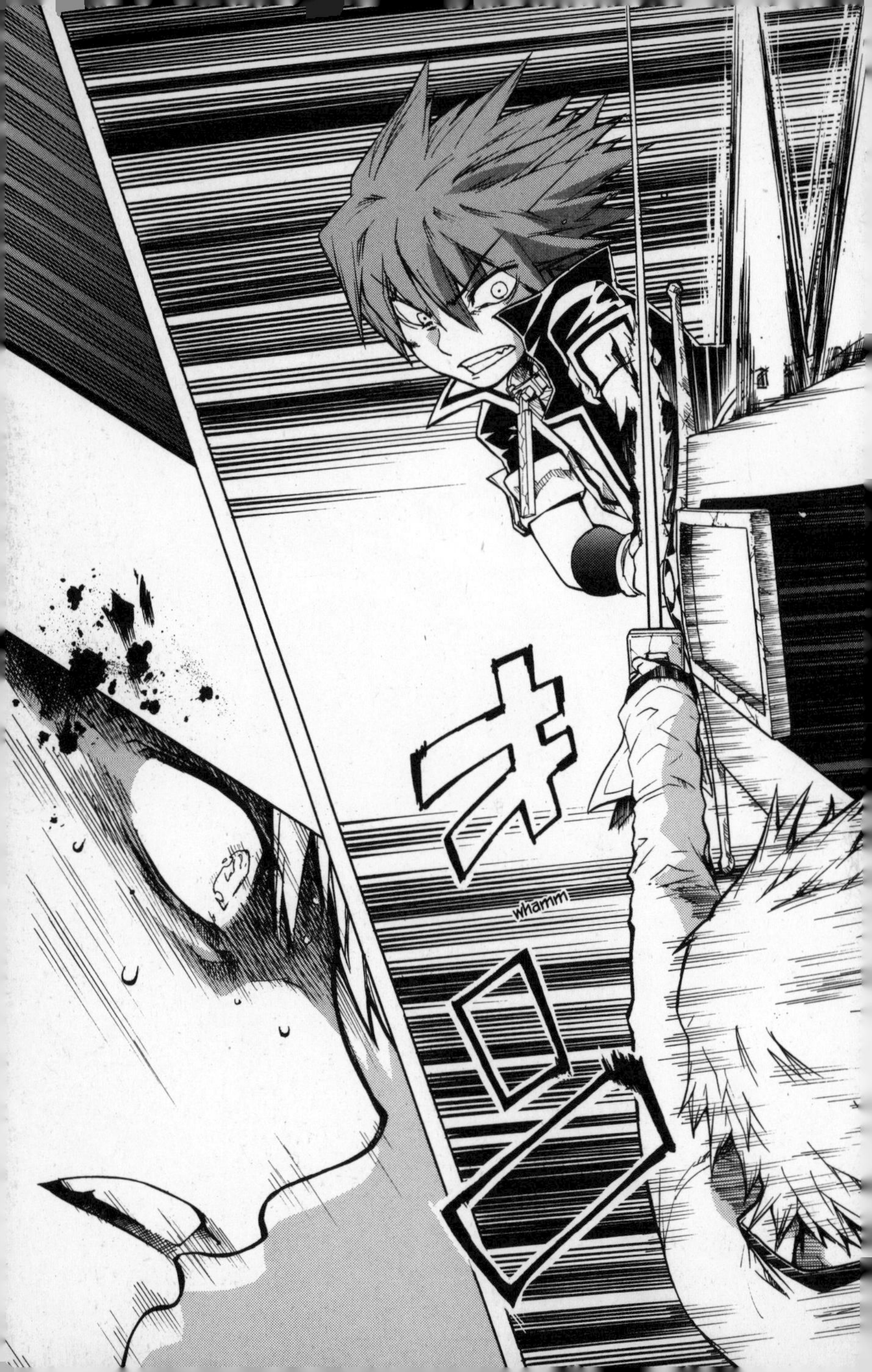
whamm

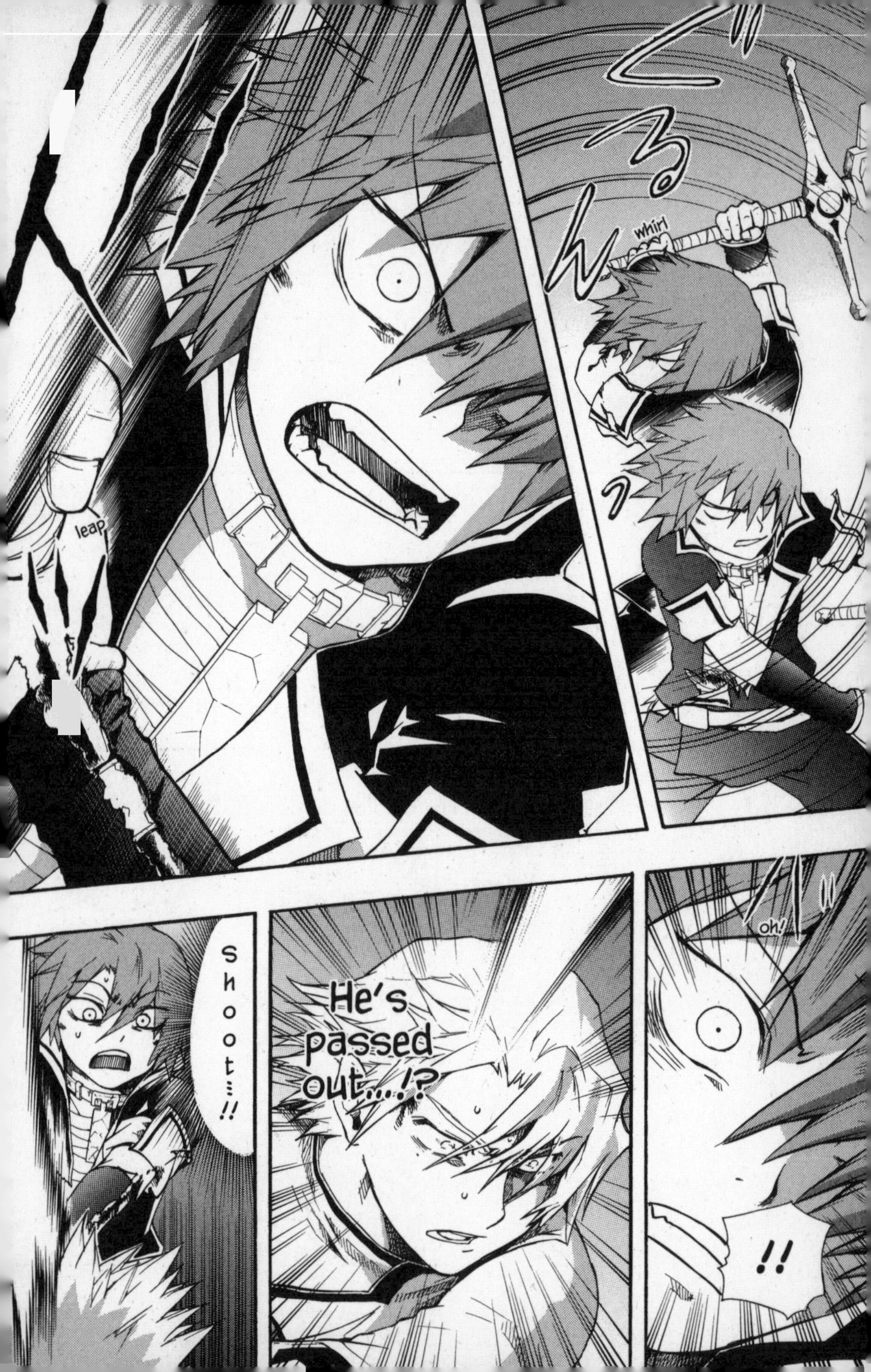
whirl
leap
oh!
!!
He's passed out...!?
Shoot...!!

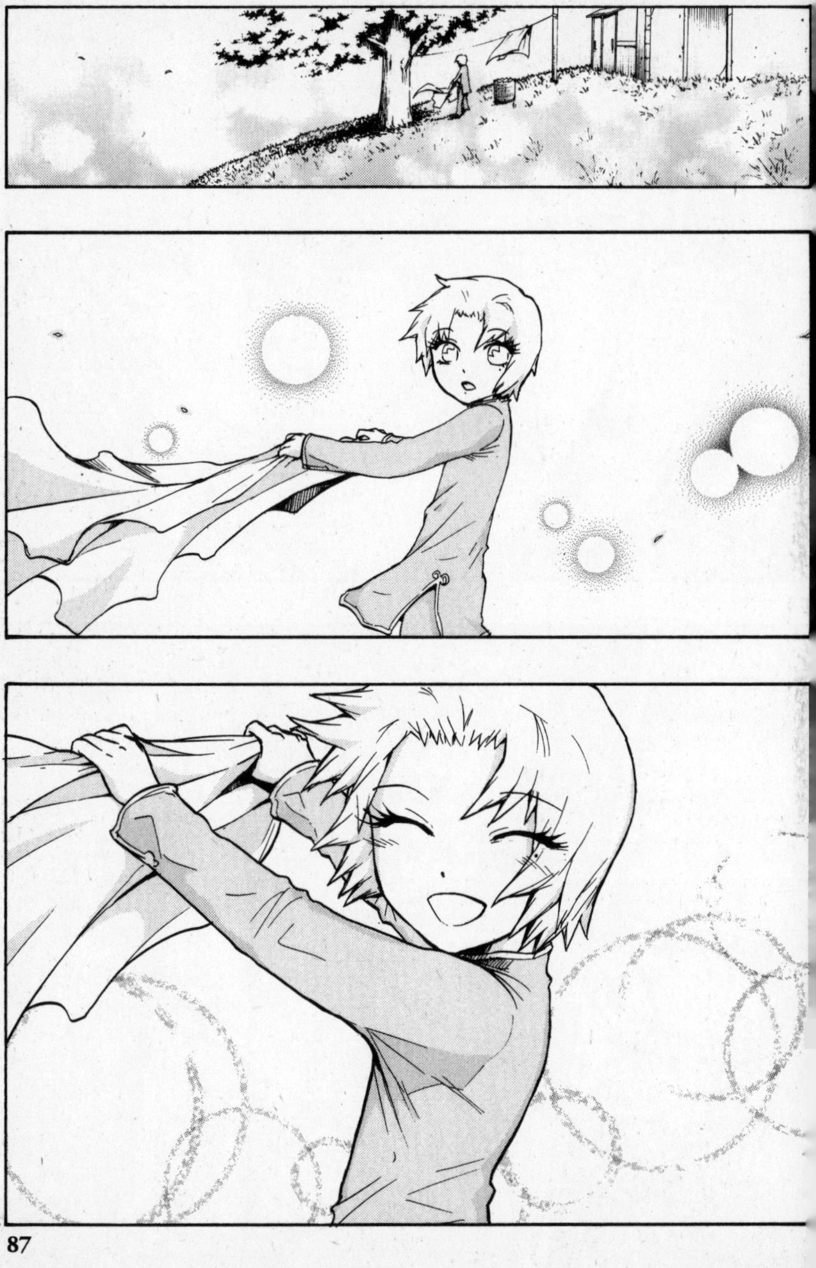

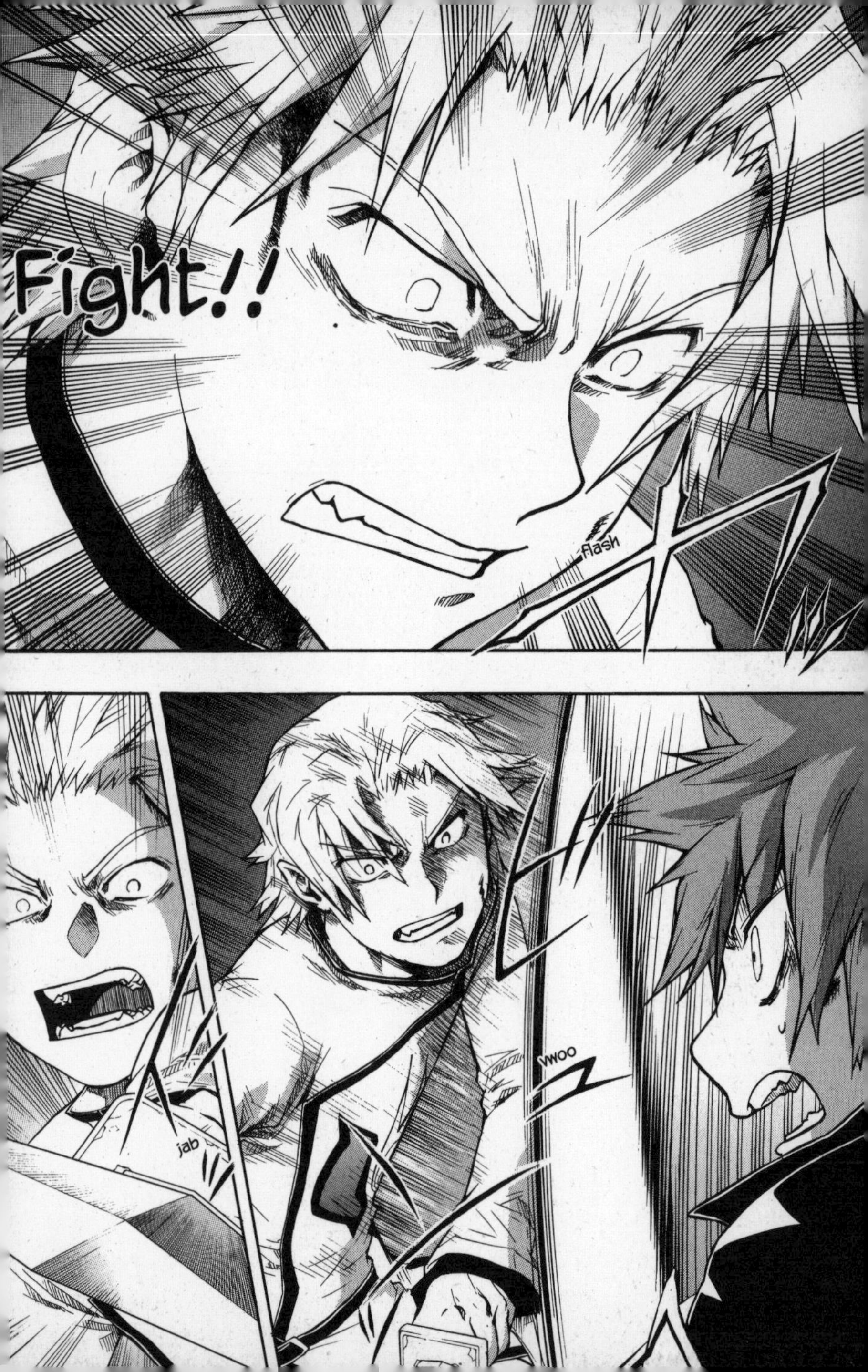
Fight!!
flash
VWOO
jab

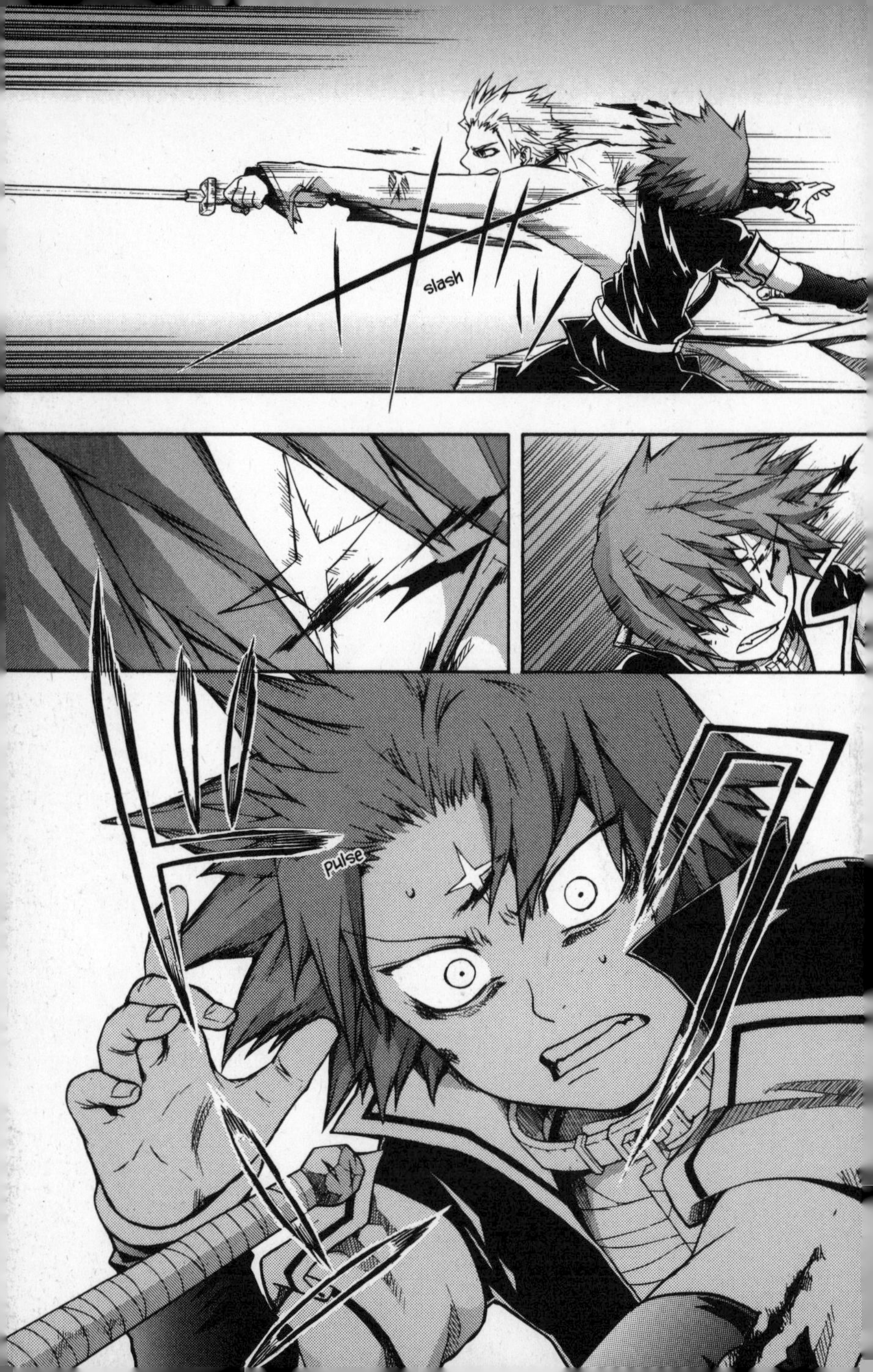
slash
pulse

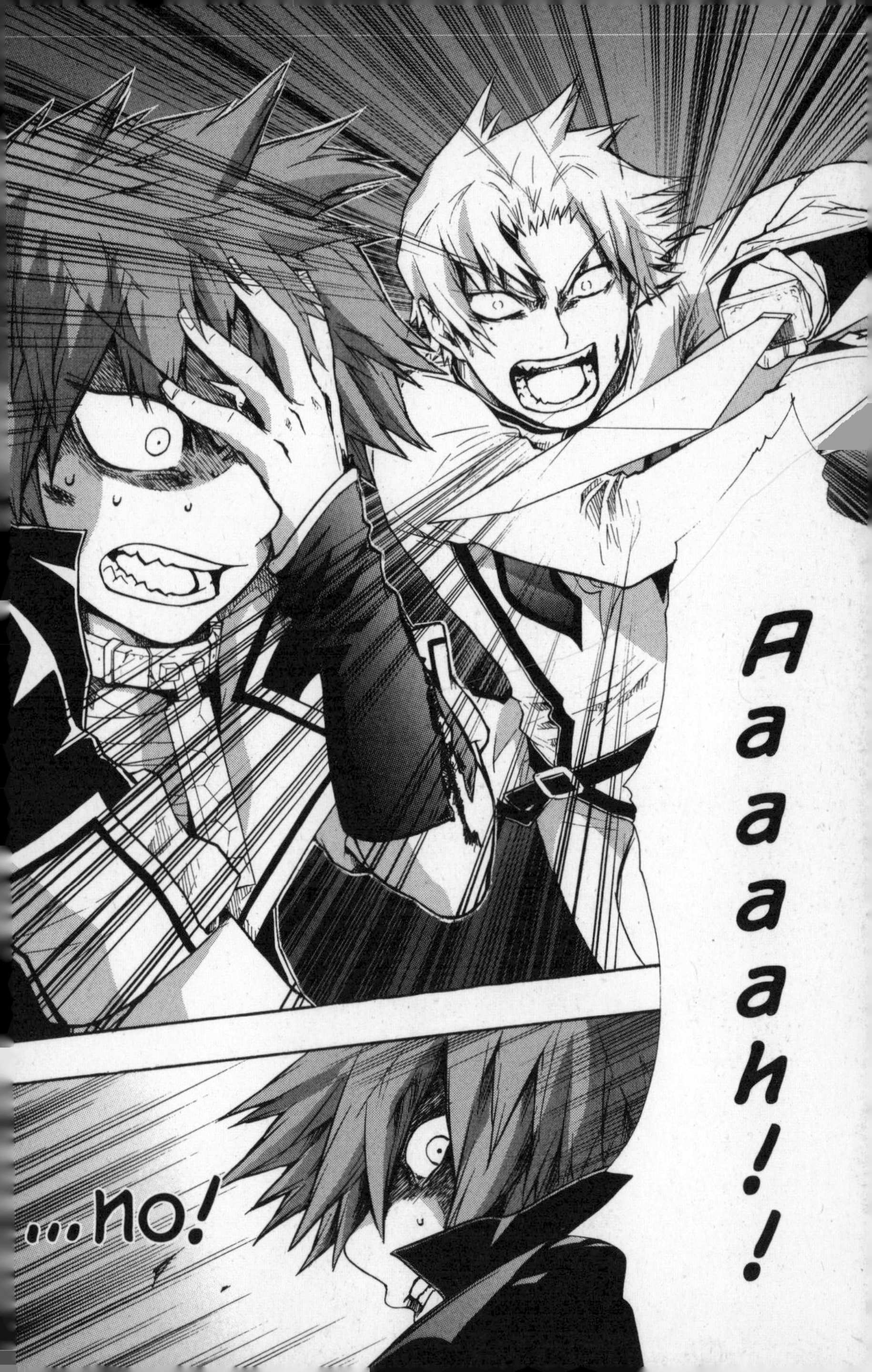
Aaaaah!!
...no!

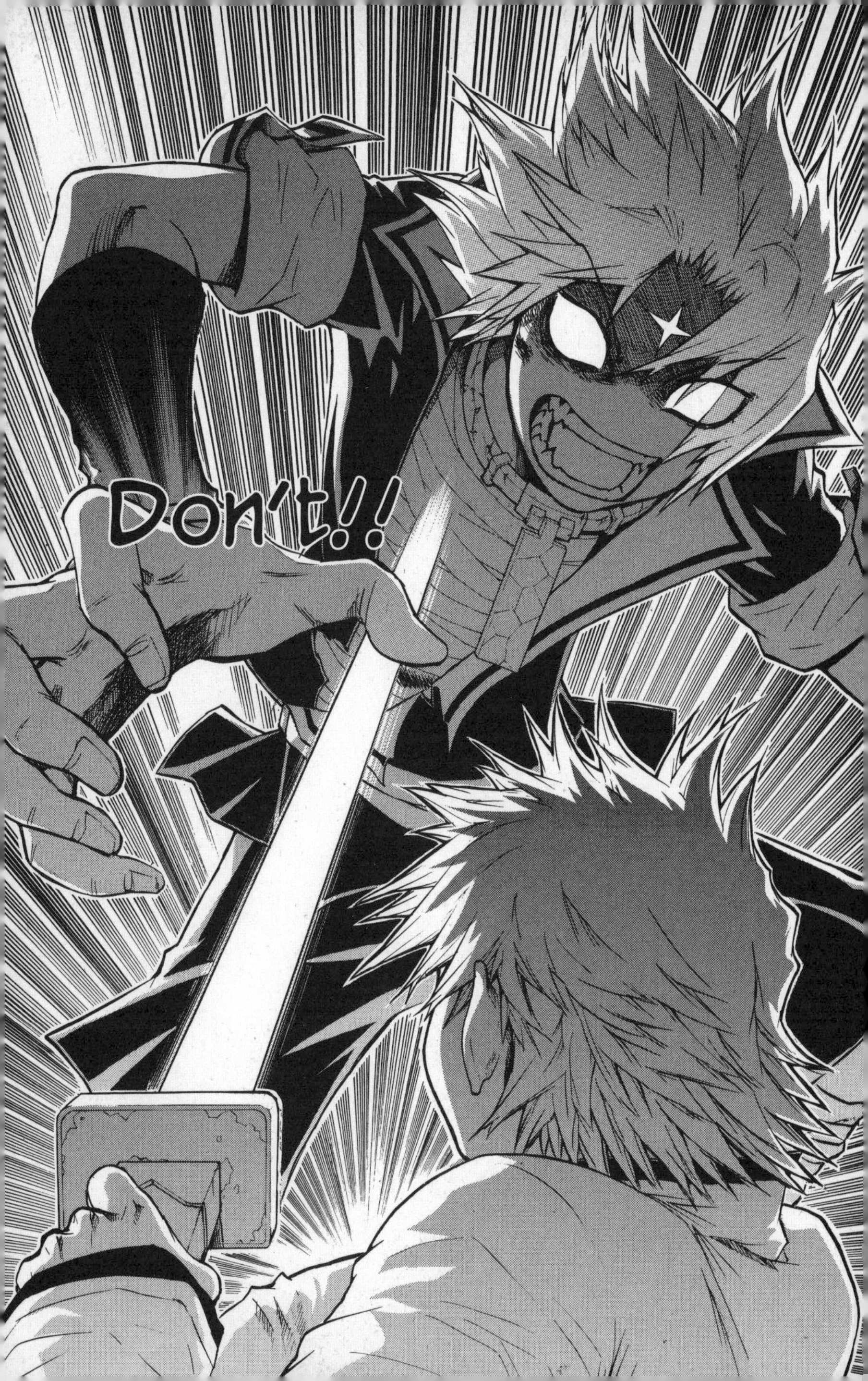
Don't!!

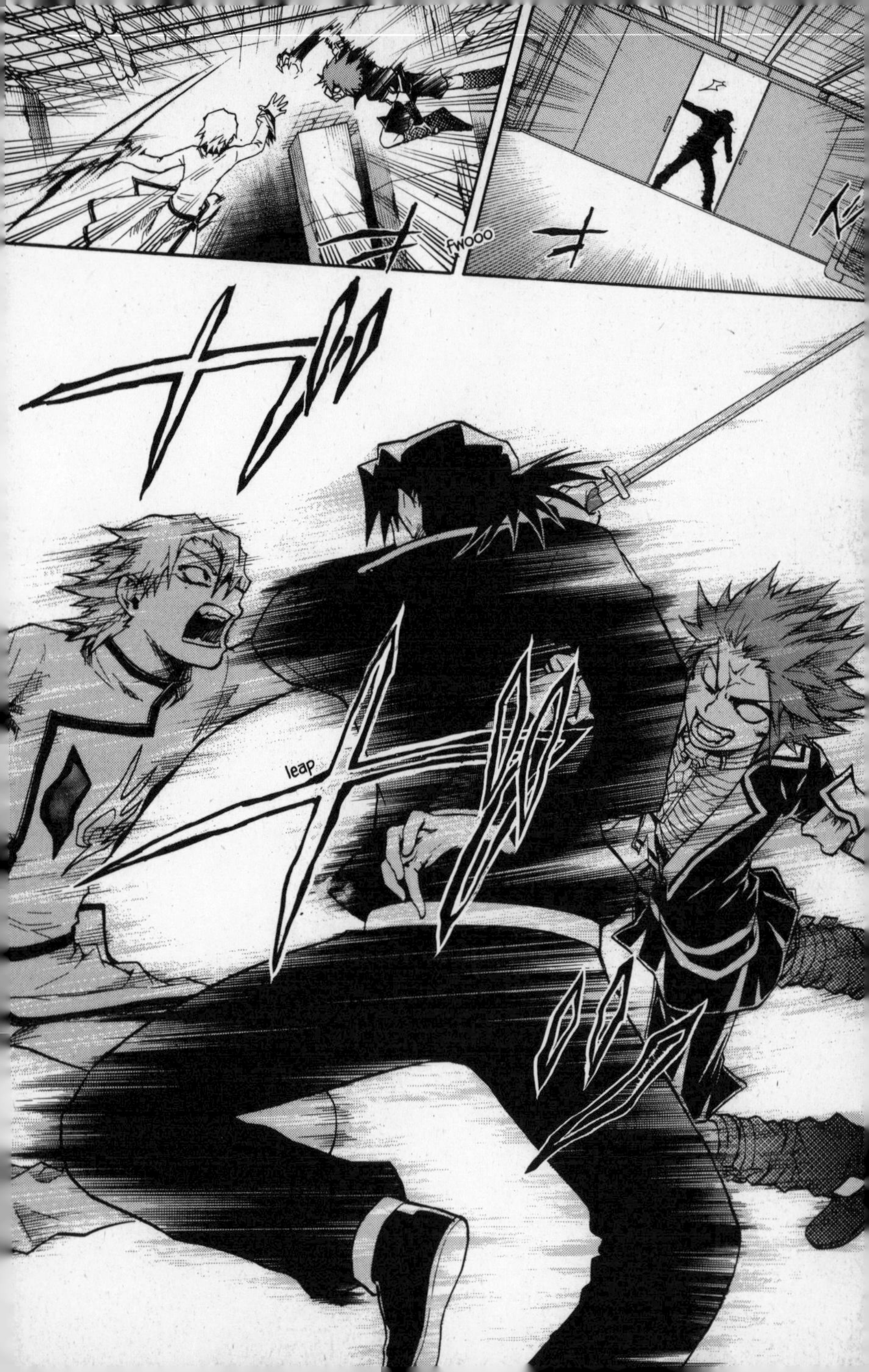
fwooo
leap

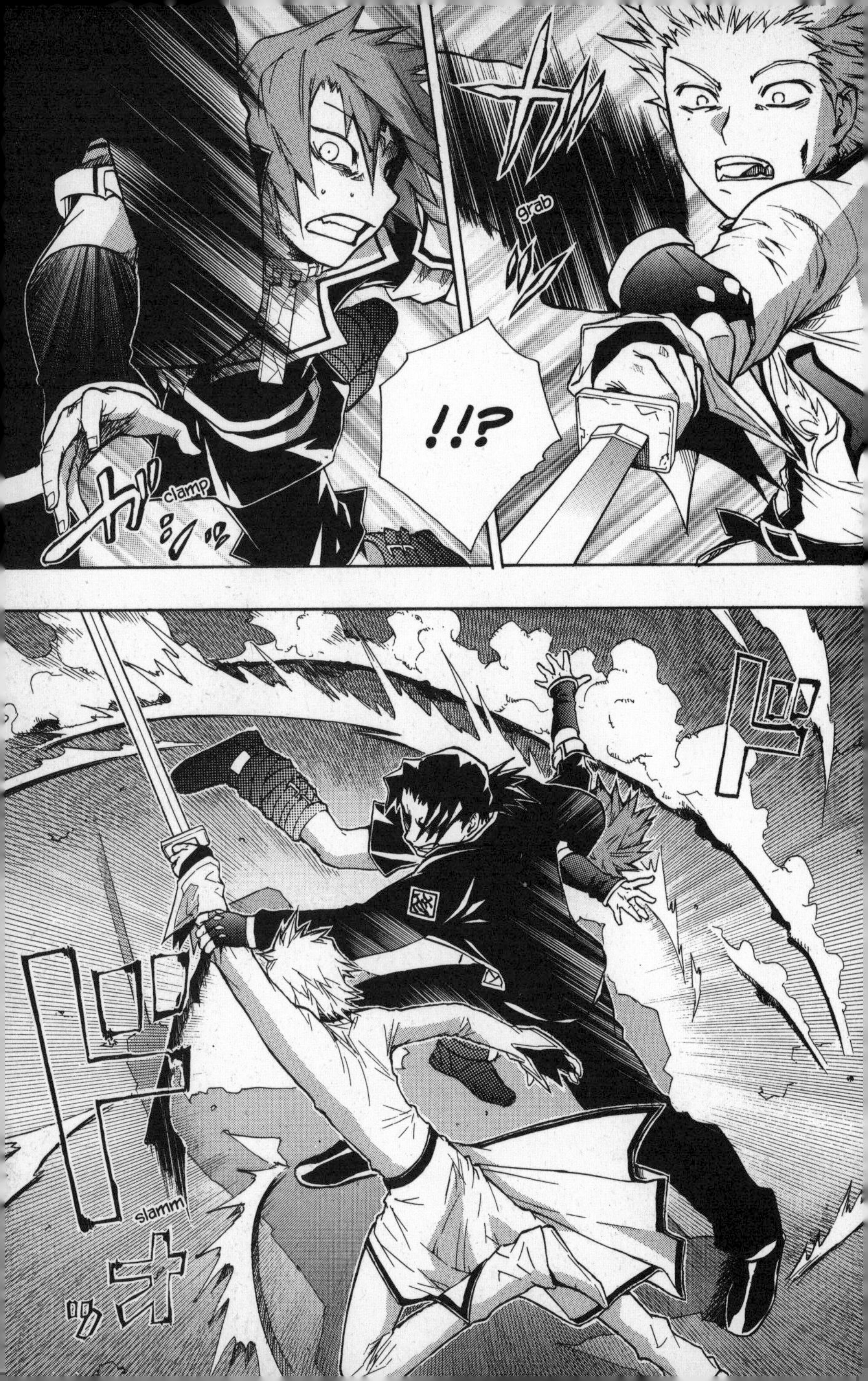
grab
!!?
clamp
slamm

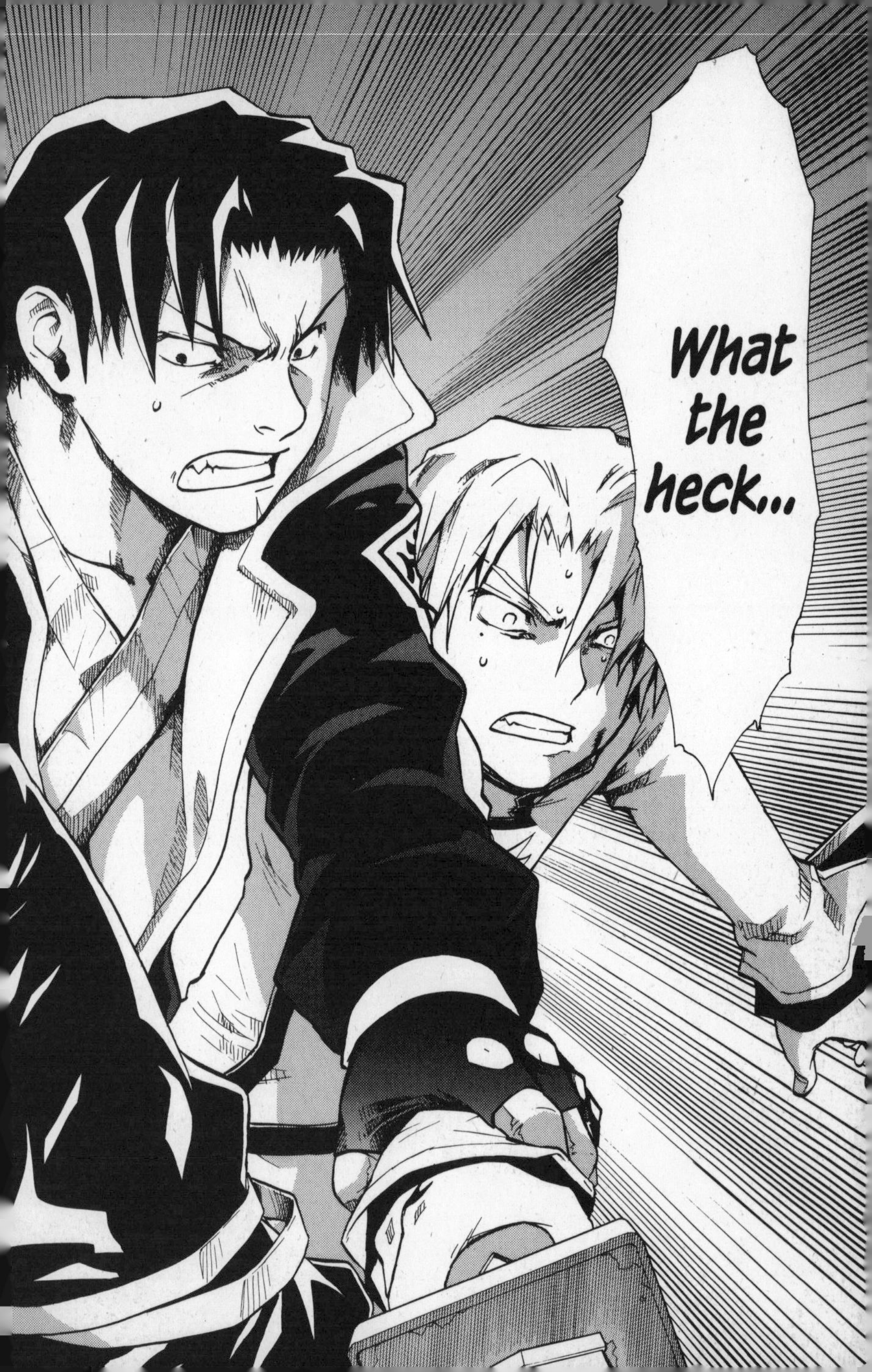
What the heck...

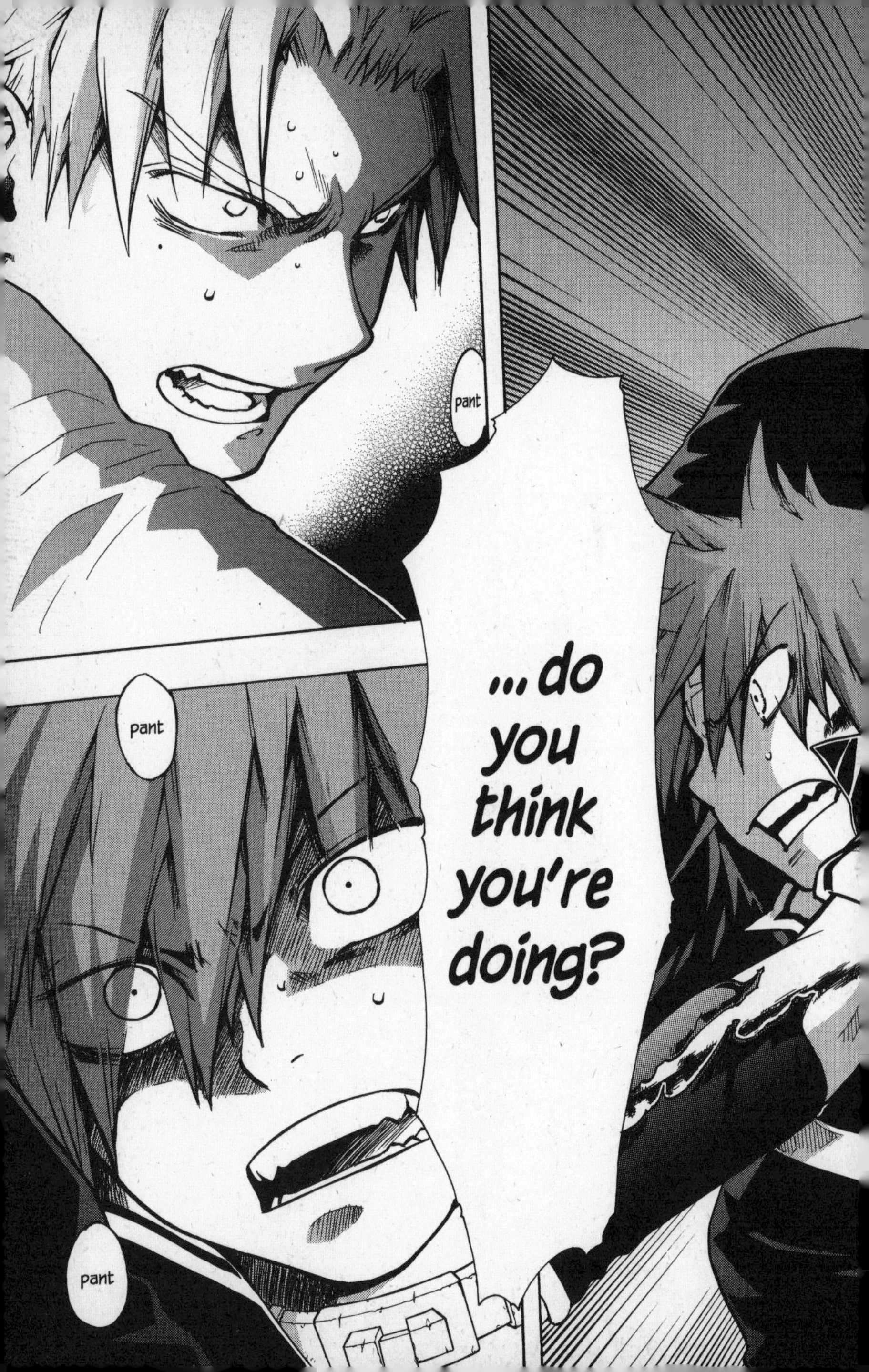
...do you think you're doing?
pant
pant
pant

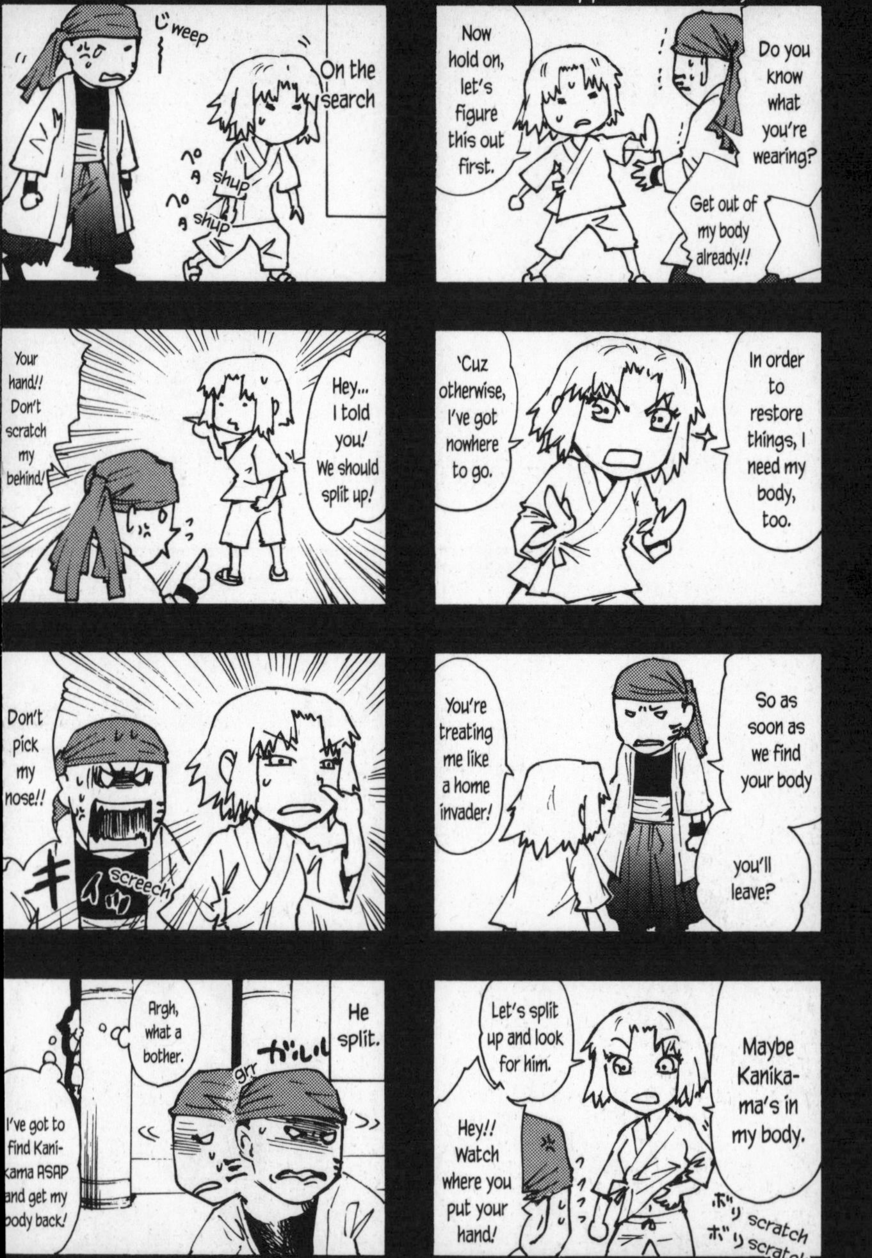
Do you know what you're wearing?
Now hold on, let's figure this out first.
Get out of my body already!!
On the search
じ weep
へ shup
へ shup
In order to restore things, I need my body, too.
'Cuz otherwise, I've got nowhere to go.
Hey... I told you! We should split up!
Your hand!! Don't scratch my behind!
So as soon as we find your body
you'll leave?
You're treating me like a home invader!
Don't pick my nose!!
screech
Maybe Kanika-ma's in my body.
Let's split up and look for him.
Hey!! Watch where you put your hand!
ボリ scratch
ボリ scratch
He split.
ガルル grr
Argh, what a bother.
I've got to find Kani-kama ASAP and get my body back!

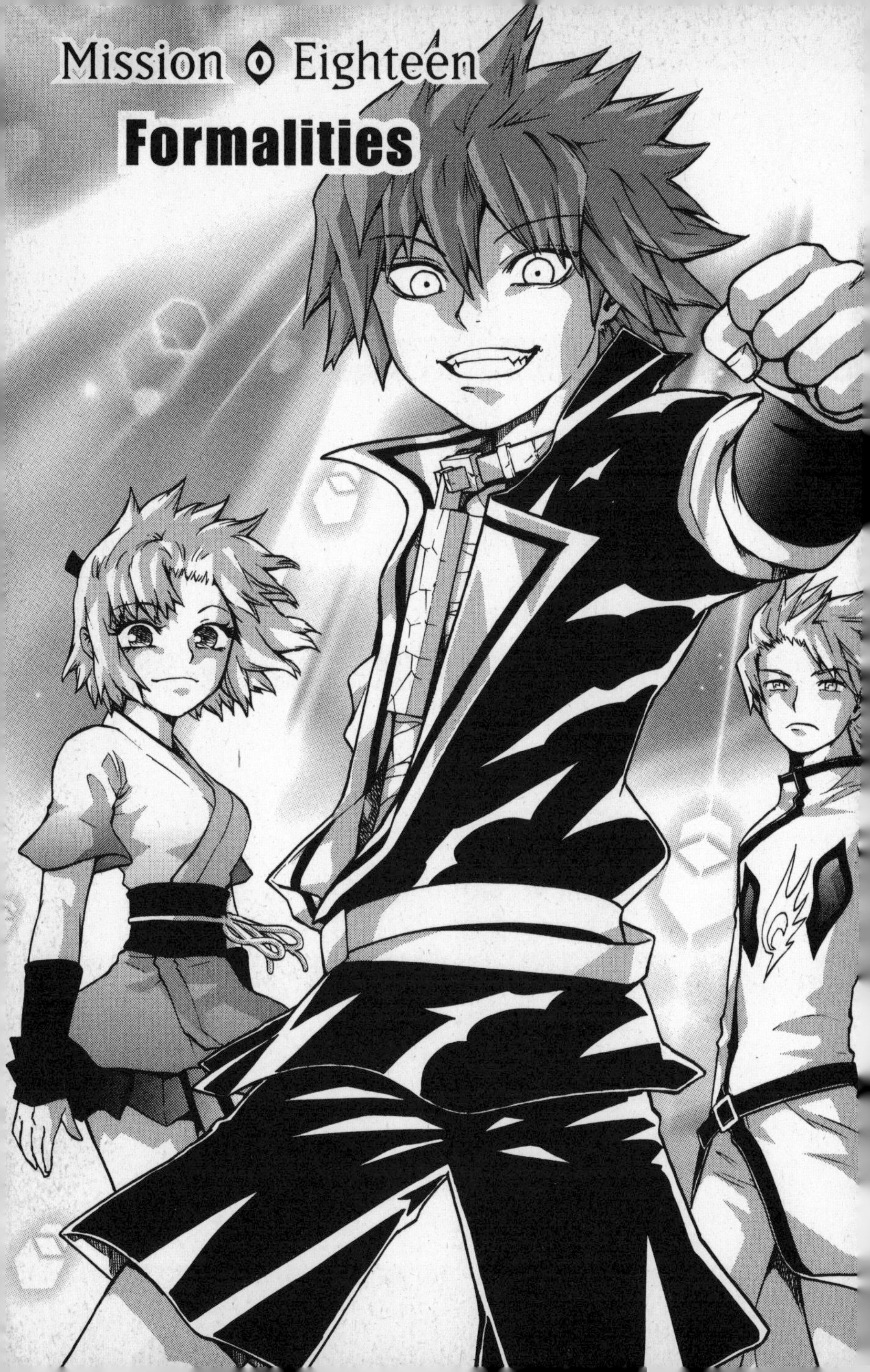
Mission Eighteen
Formalities

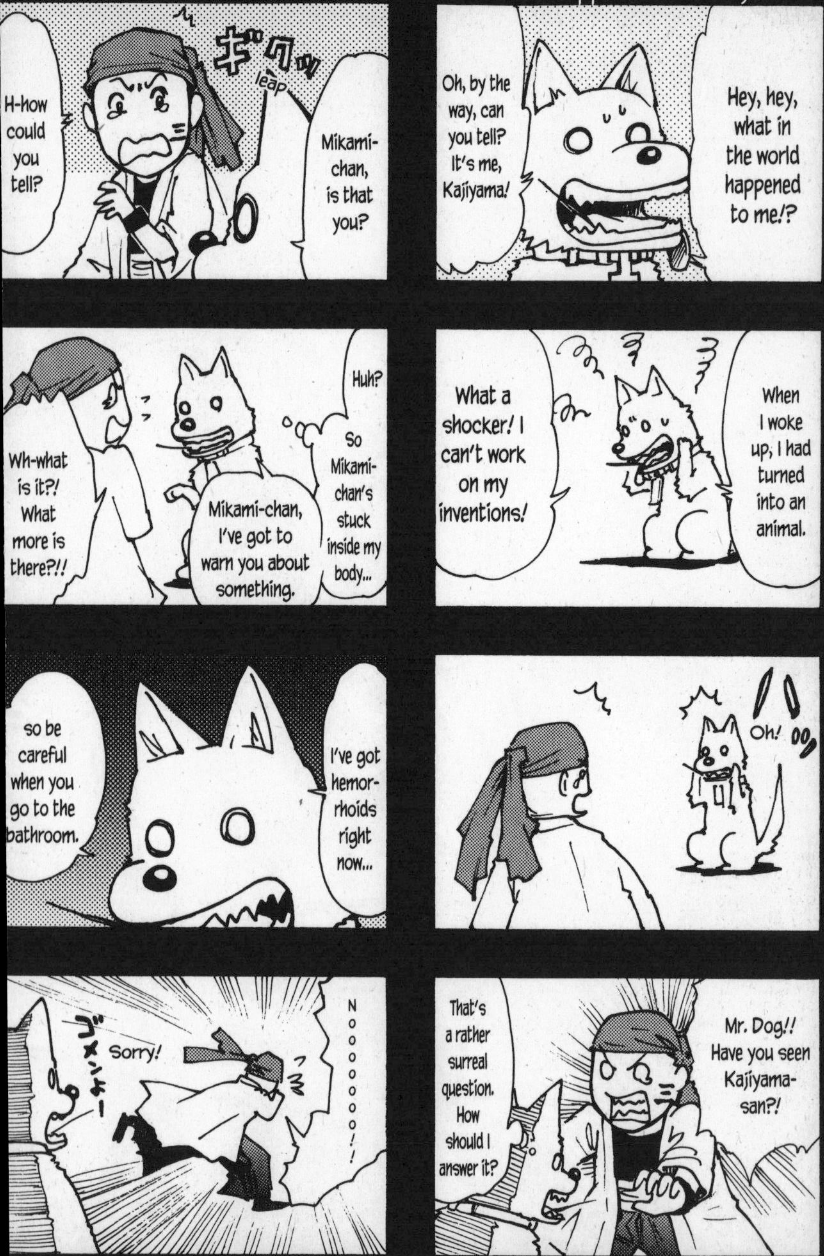
Hey, hey, what in the world happened to me!?
Oh, by the way, can you tell? It's me, Kajiyama!
When I woke up, I had turned into an animal.
What a shocker! I can't work on my inventions!
Oh!
Mr. Dog!! Have you seen Kajiyama-san?!
That's a rather surreal question. How should I answer it?
Mikami-chan, is that you?
leap
H-how could you tell?
Huh?
So Mikami-chan's stuck inside my body...
Mikami-chan, I've got to warn you about something.
Wh-what is it?! What more is there?!!
I've got hemorrhoids right now...
so be careful when you go to the bathroom.
Noooooooooo!
Sorry!
ゴメンよー

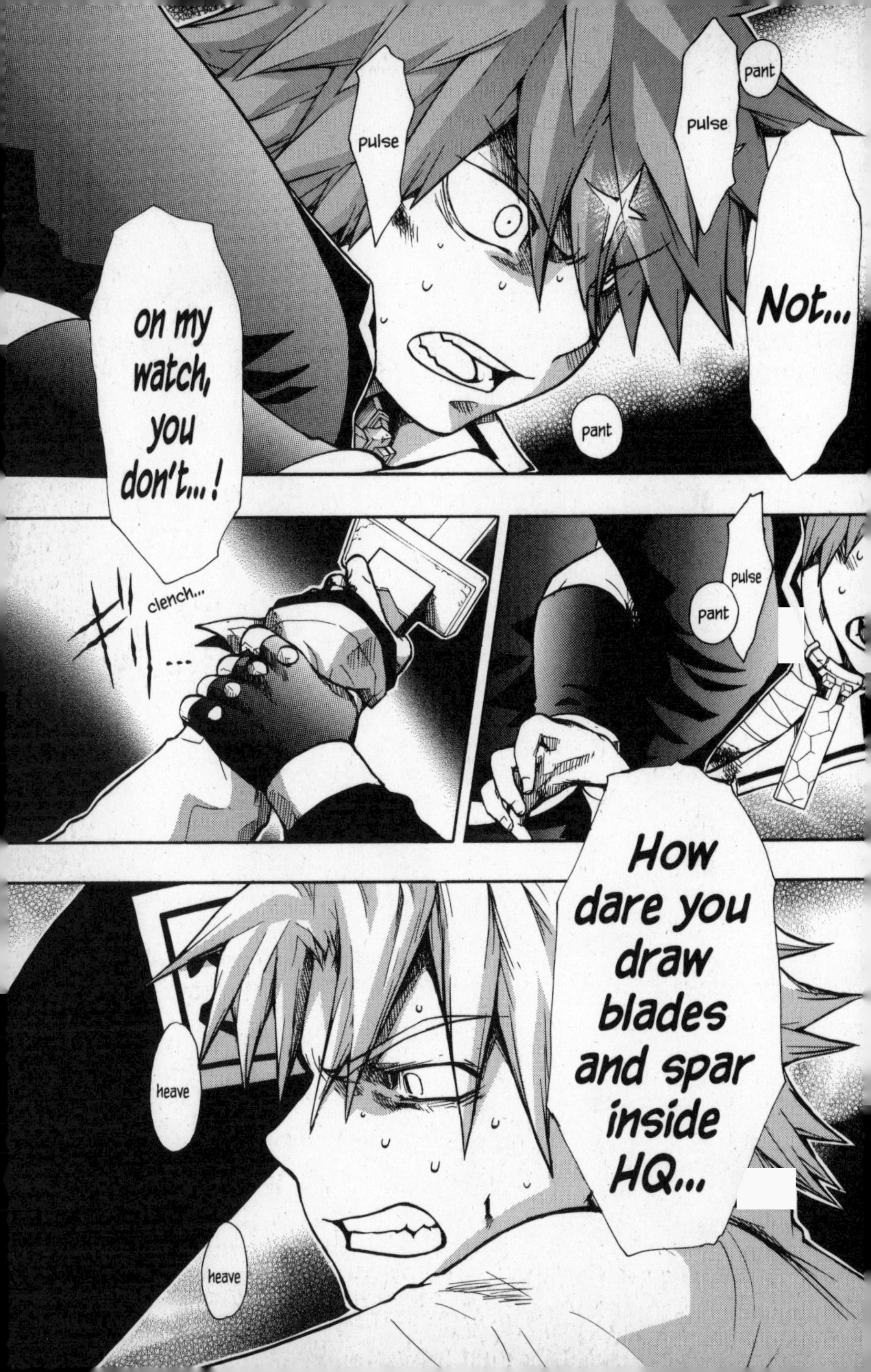

pant
pulse
Not...
pulse
pant
on my watch, you don't...!
pulse
pant
clench...
ギリ...
How dare you draw blades and spar inside HQ...
heave
heave

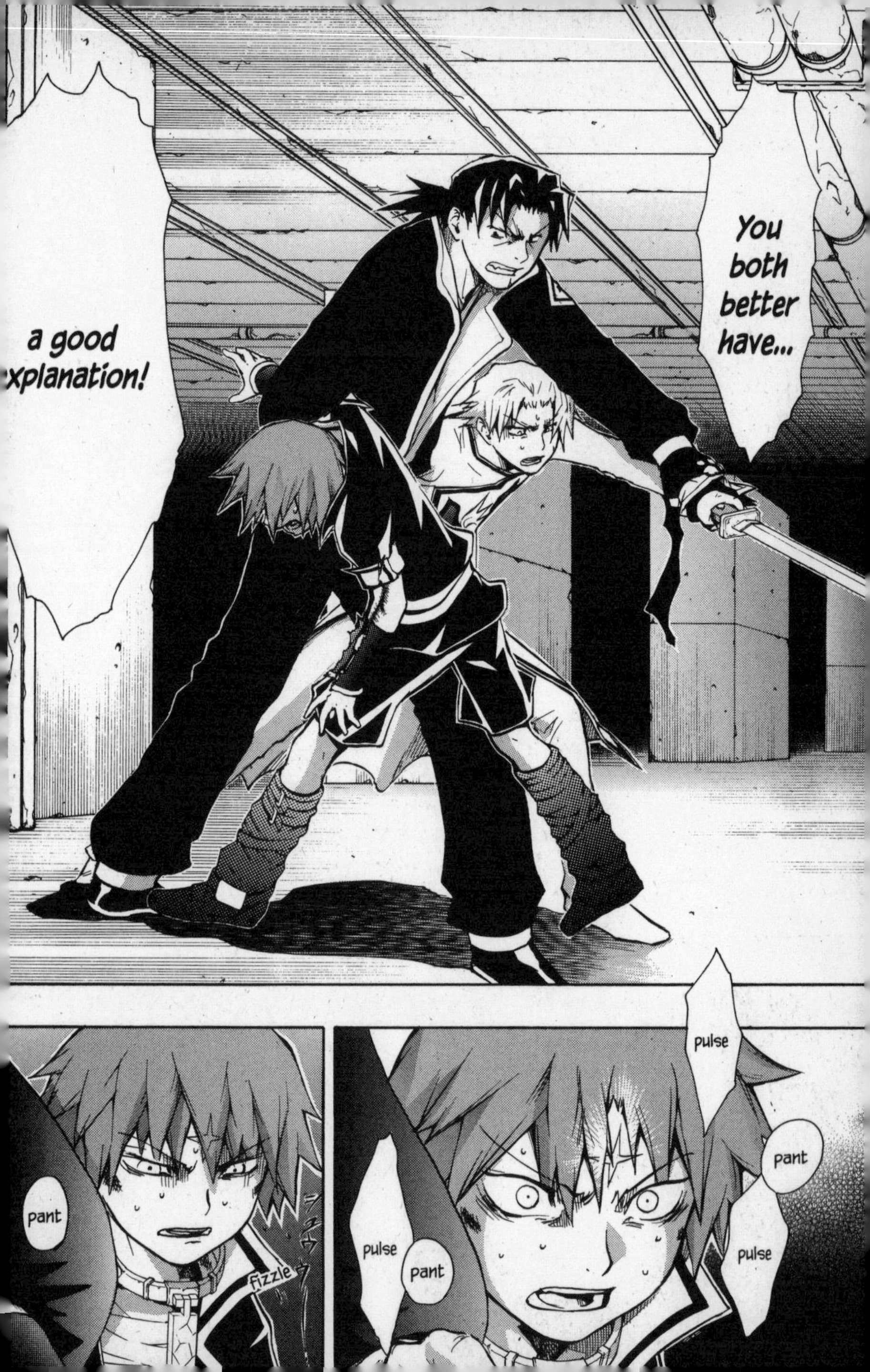
You both better have...
a good xplanation!
pulse
pant
pulse
pant
pulse
fizzle
pant

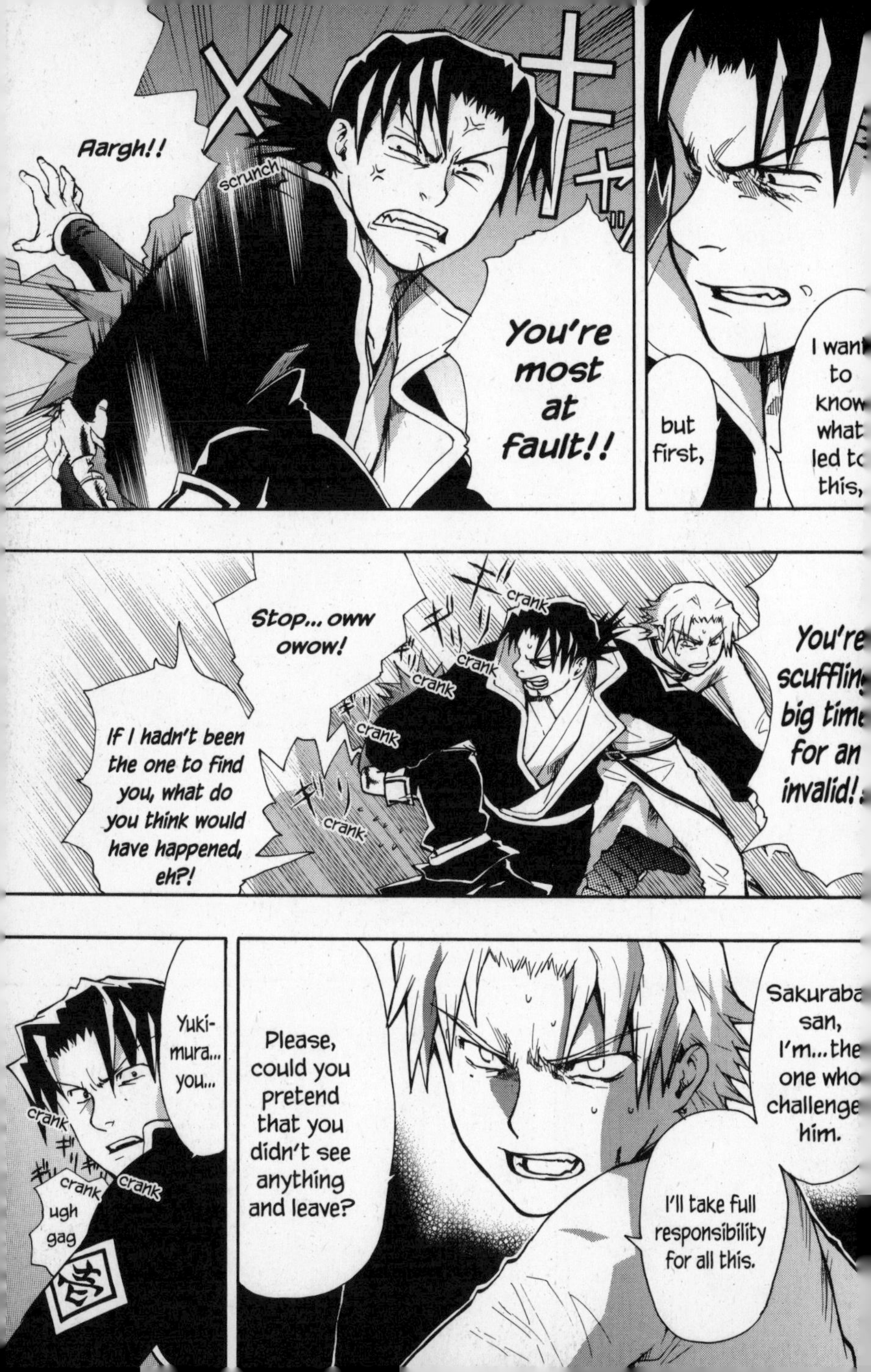
I want to know what led to this,
but first,
You're most at fault!!
scrunch
Aargh!!
You're scufflin big tim for an invalid!
crank
crank
crank
crank
crank
Stop... oww owow!
If I hadn't been the one to find you, what do you think would have happened, eh?!
Sakuraba san, I'm...the one who challenge him.
I'll take full responsibility for all this.
Please, could you pretend that you didn't see anything and leave?
Yuki-mura... you...
crank
crank
crank
ugh gag

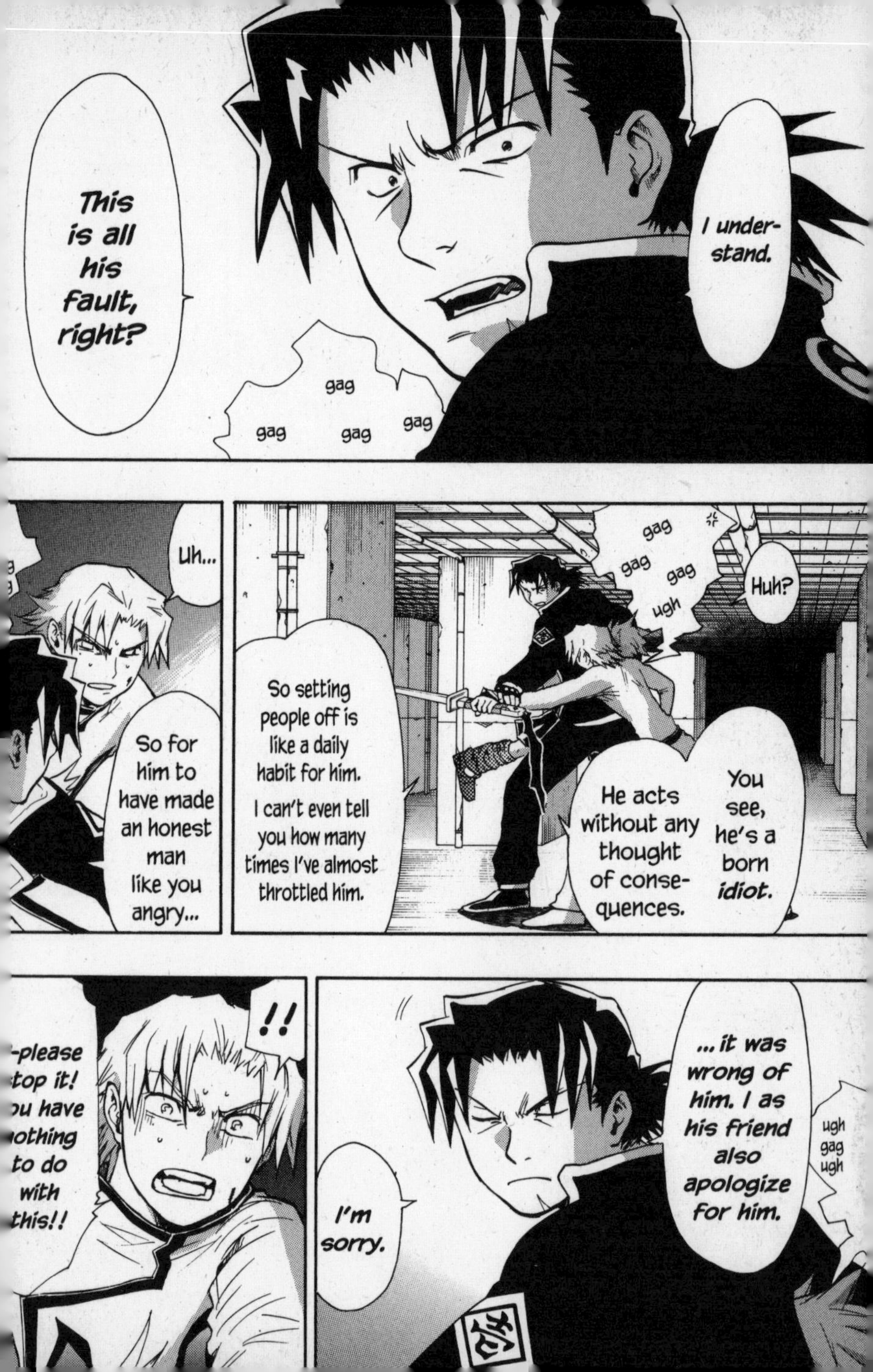
I under-stand.
This is all his fault, right?
gag gag gag gag
Huh?
gag gag gag ugh
You see, he's a born idiot.
He acts without any thought of conse-quences.
So setting people off is like a daily habit for him.
I can't even tell you how many times I've almost throttled him.
Uh...
So for him to have made an honest man like you angry...
...it was wrong of him. I as his friend also apologize for him.
I'm sorry.
ugh gag ugh
!!
-please top it! ou have othing to do with this!!

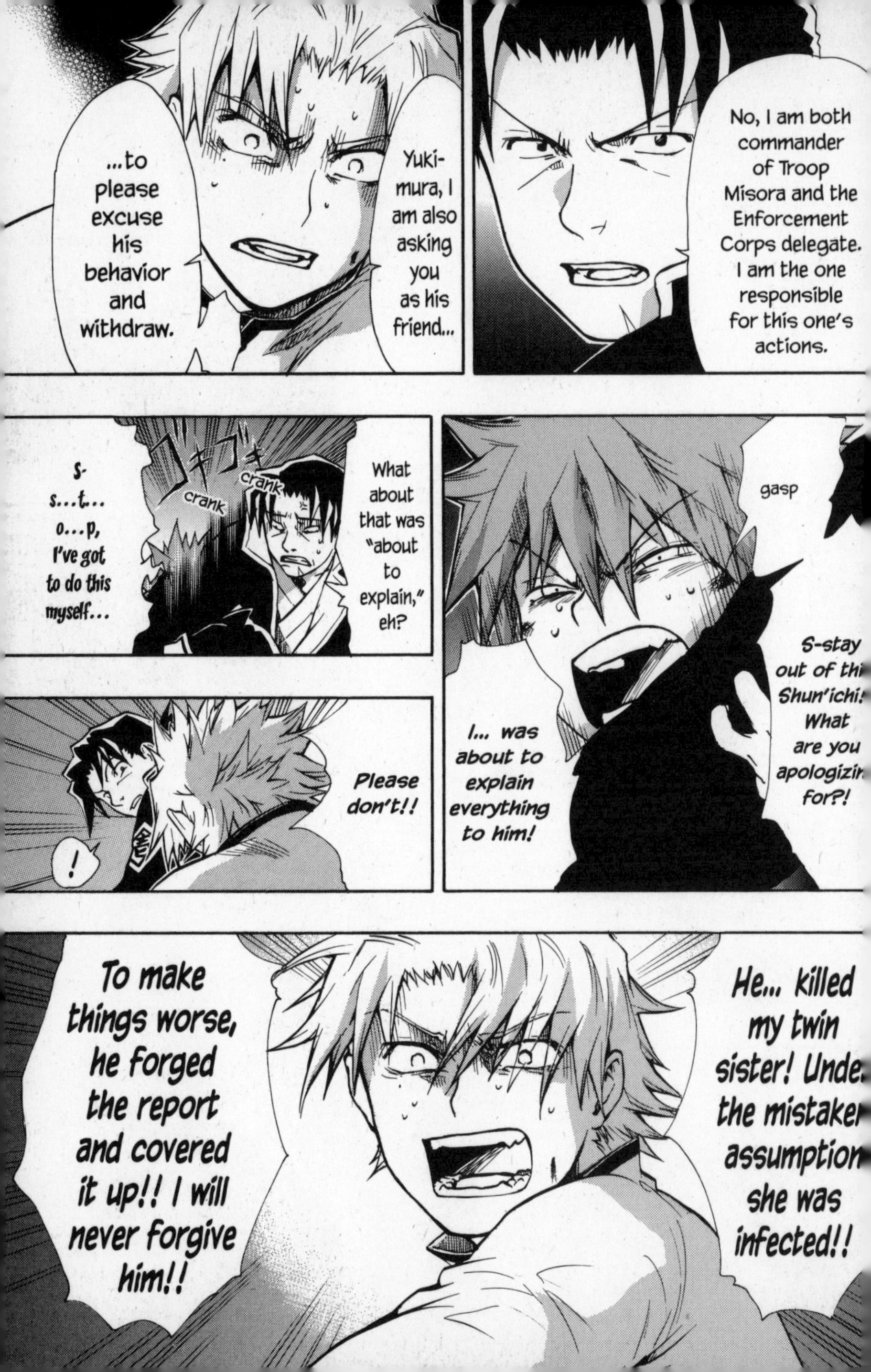
No, I am both commander of Troop Misora and the Enforcement Corps delegate. I am the one responsible for this one's actions.
Yuki-mura, I am also asking you as his friend...
...to please excuse his behavior and withdraw.
gasp
S-stay out of thi Shun'ichi! What are you apologizi for?!
I... was about to explain everything to him!
What about that was "about to explain," eh?
crank
crank
s- s...t... o...p, I've got to do this myself...
Please don't!!
!
He... killed my twin sister! Unde the mistake assumption she was infected!!
To make things worse, he forged the report and covered it up!! I will never forgive him!!

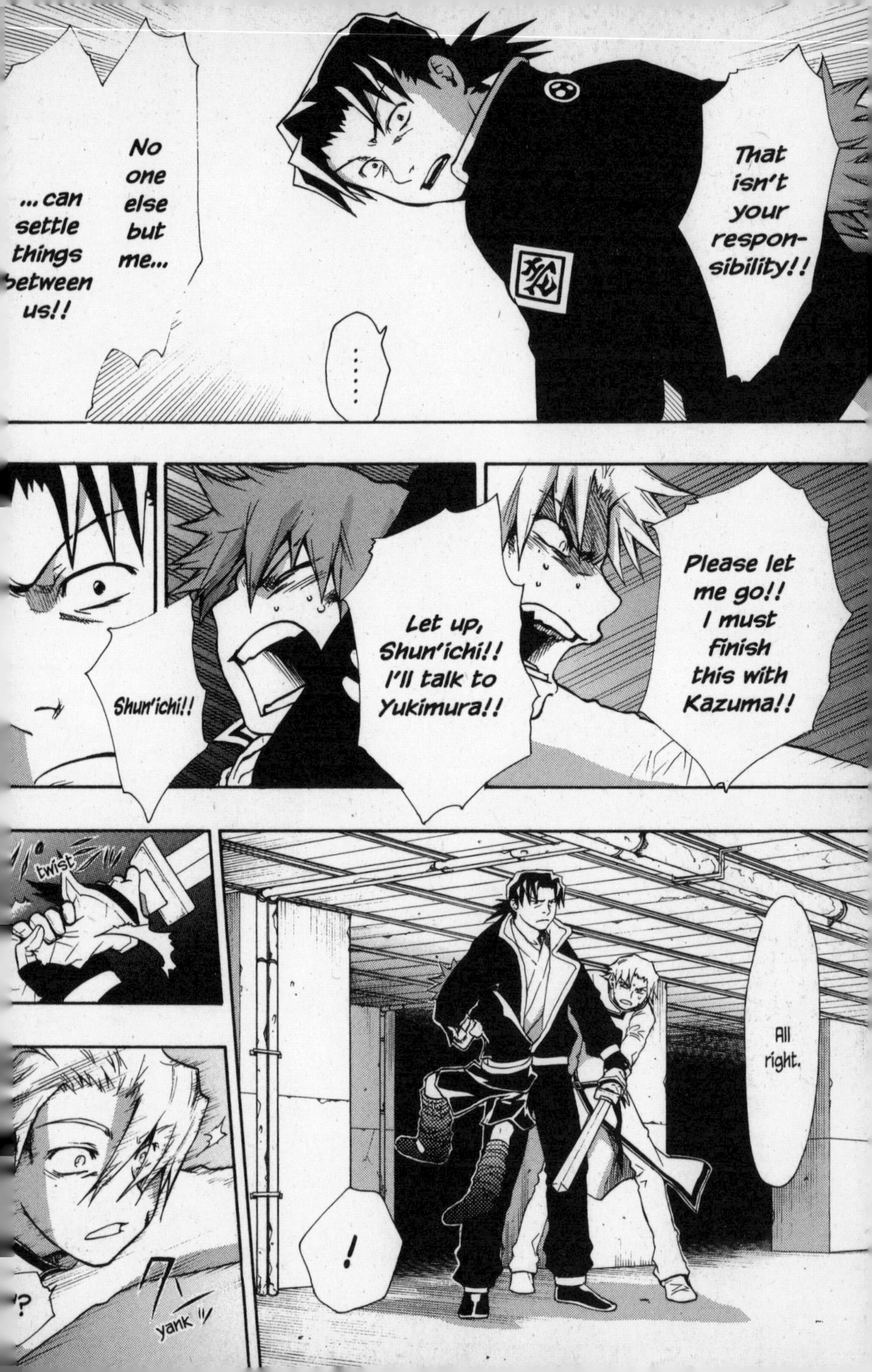

That isn't your respon-sibility!!
No one else but me...
...can settle things between us!!
......
Please let me go!! I must finish this with Kazuma!!
Let up, Shun'ichi!! I'll talk to Yukimura!!
Shun'ichi!!
All right.
!
twist
?
yank

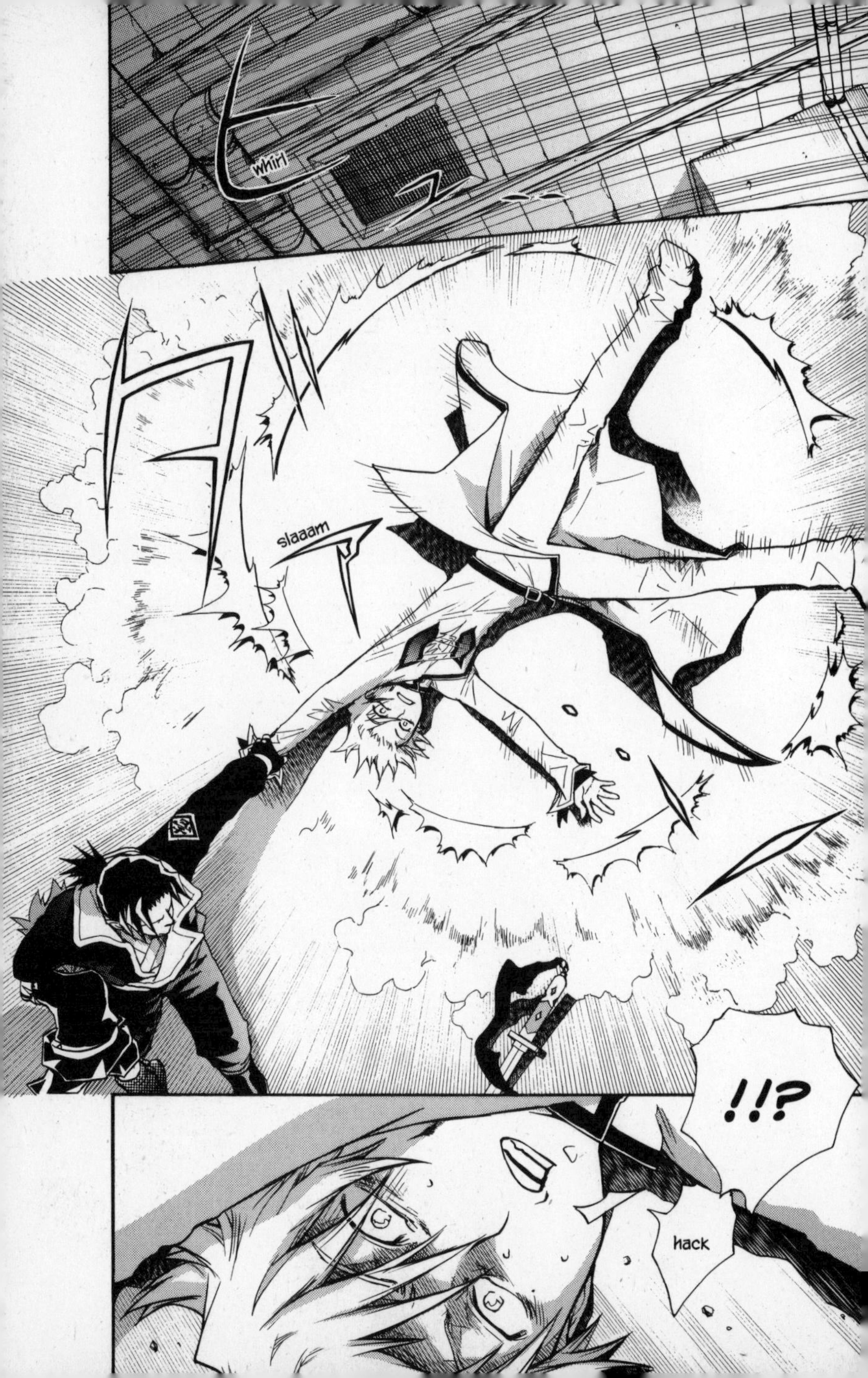
whirl
slaaam
!!?
hack

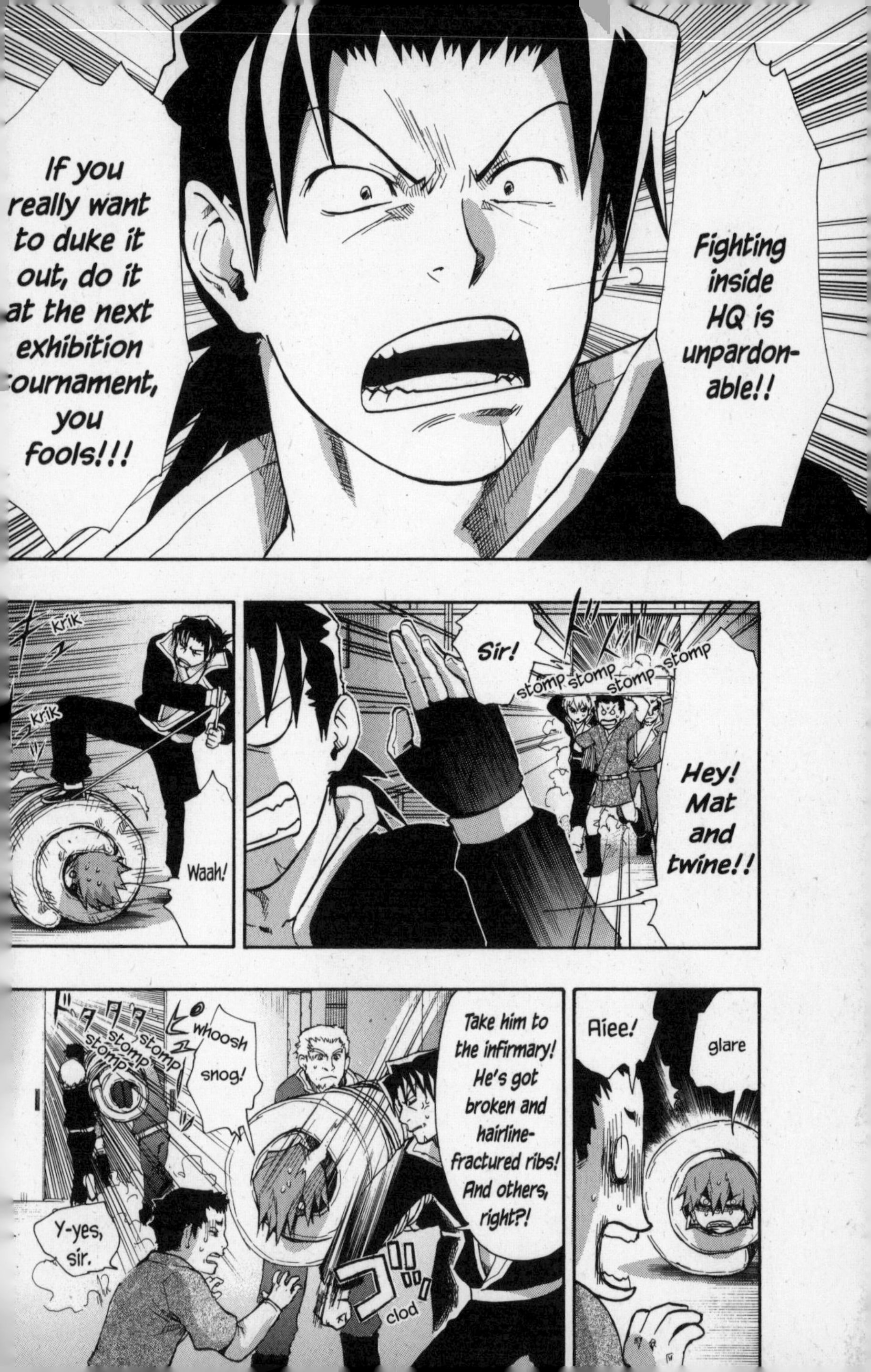
Fighting inside HQ is unpardonable!!
If you really want to duke it out, do it at the next exhibition tournament, you fools!!!
Sir!
stomp stomp stomp stomp
Hey! Mat and twine!!
krik
krik
Waah!
Aiee!
glare
Take him to the infirmary! He's got broken and hairline-fractured ribs! And others, right?!
whoosh
snog!
stomp stomp stomp
Y-yes, sir.
clod

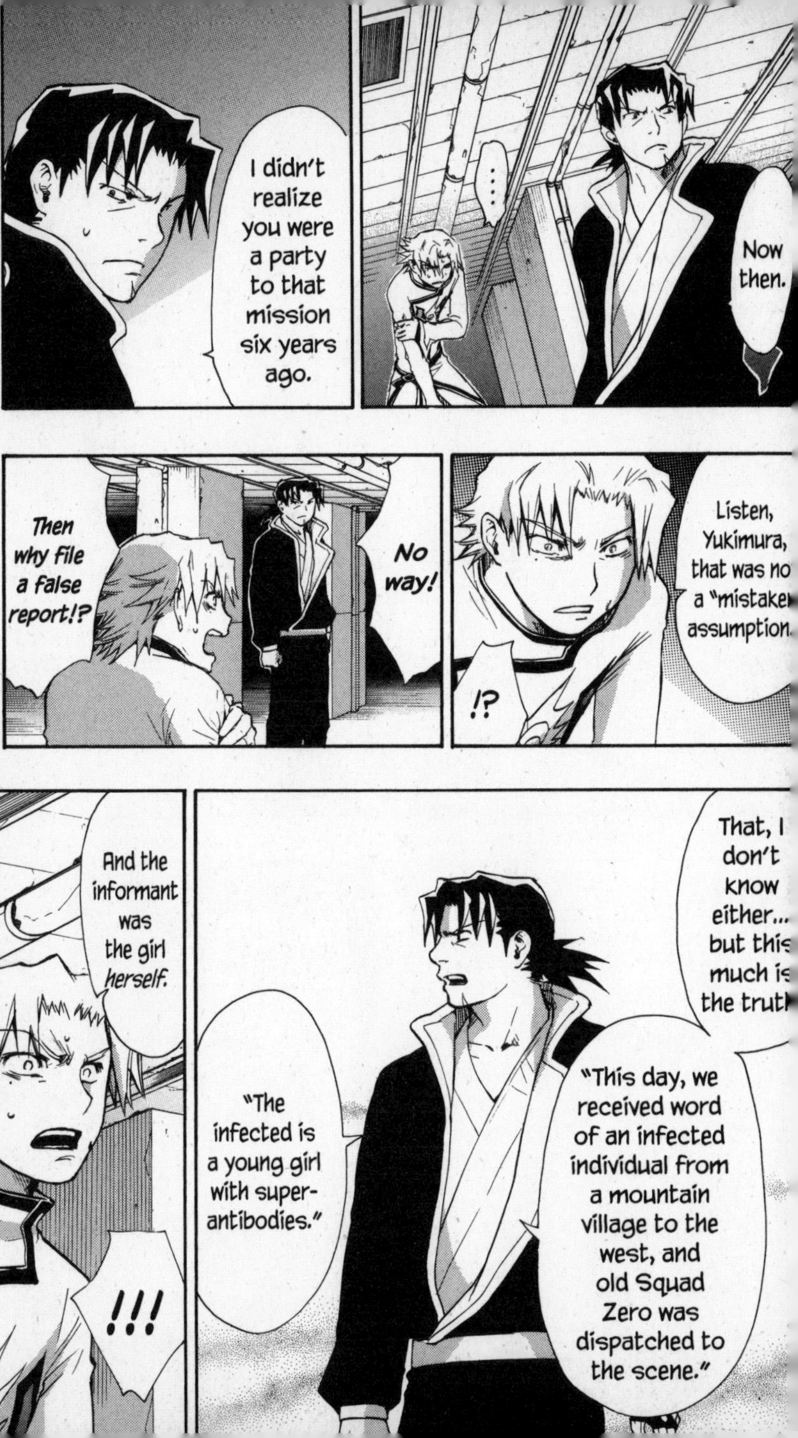

Now then.
....
I didn't realize you were a party to that mission six years ago.
Listen, Yukimura, that was no a "mistake assumption.
!?
No way!
Then why file a false report!?
That, I don't know either... but this much is the trut
"This day, we received word of an infected individual from a mountain village to the west, and old Squad Zero was dispatched to the scene."
"The infected is a young girl with super-antibodies."
And the informant was the girl herself.
!!!

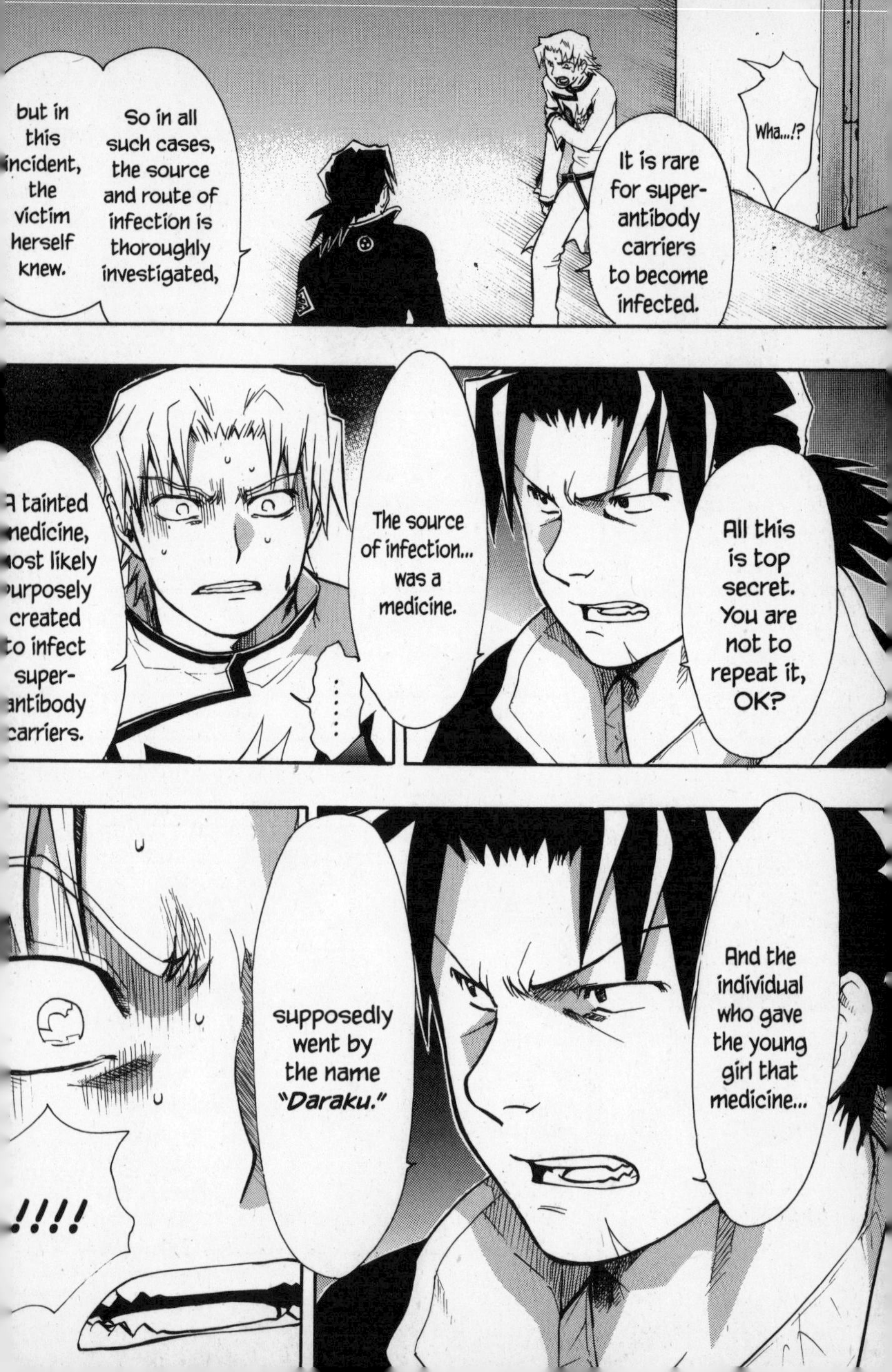

Wha...!?
It is rare for super-antibody carriers to become infected.
So in all such cases, the source and route of infection is thoroughly investigated,
but in this incident, the victim herself knew.
All this is top secret. You are not to repeat it, OK?
The source of infection... was a medicine.
......
A tainted medicine, most likely purposely created to infect super-antibody carriers.
And the individual who gave the young girl that medicine...
supposedly went by the name *"Daraku."*
!!!!

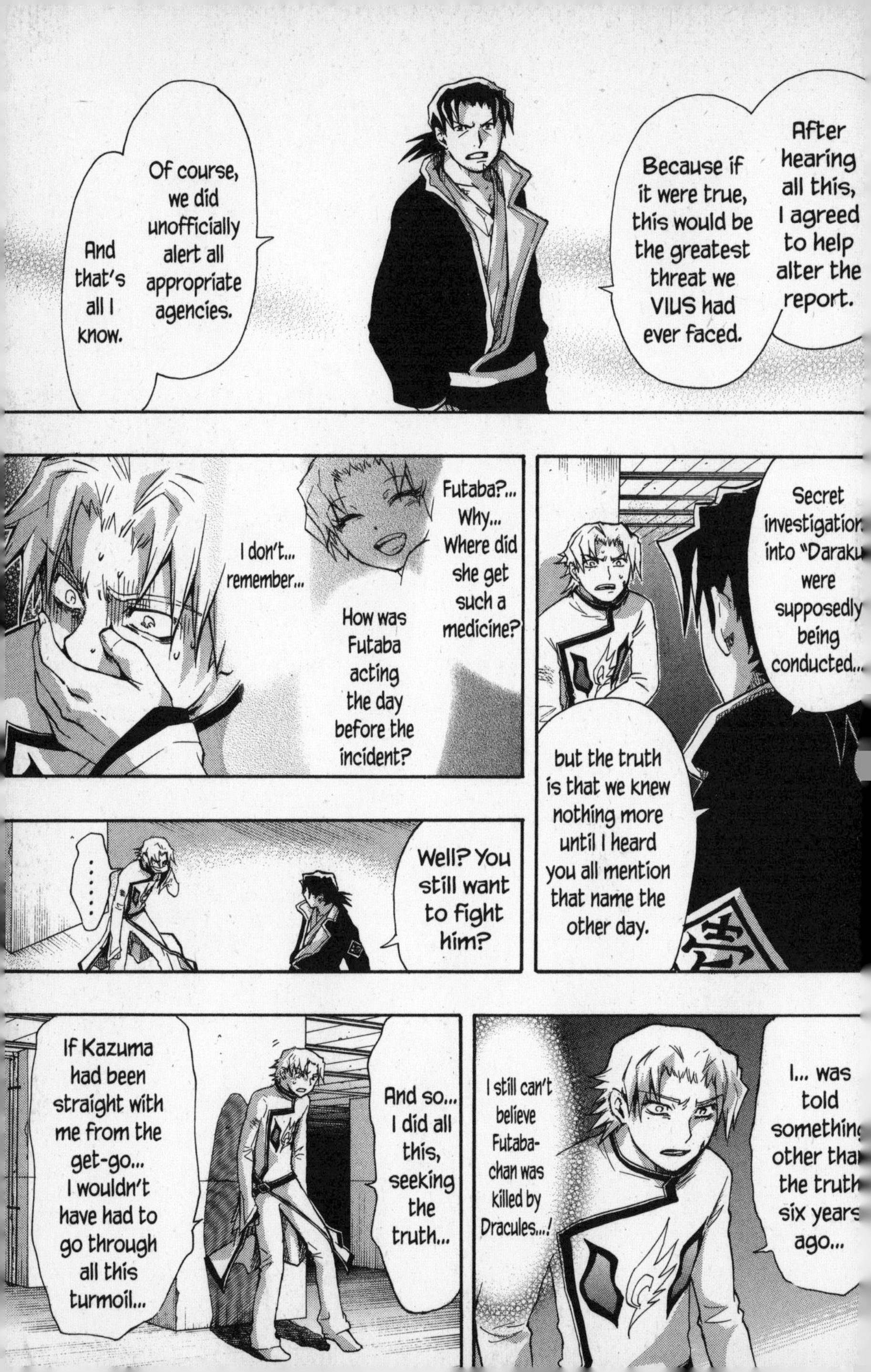
After hearing all this, I agreed to help alter the report.
Because if it were true, this would be the greatest threat we VIUS had ever faced.
Of course, we did unofficially alert all appropriate agencies.
And that's all I know.
Secret investigatio into "Daraku were supposedly being conducted...
but the truth is that we knew nothing more until I heard you all mention that name the other day.
Futaba?... Why... Where did she get such a medicine?
How was Futaba acting the day before the incident?
I don't... remember...
Well? You still want to fight him?
......
I... was told somethin other tha the truth six years ago...
I still can't believe Futaba-chan was killed by Dracules...!
And so... I did all this, seeking the truth...
If Kazuma had been straight with me from the get-go... I wouldn't have had to go through all this turmoil...

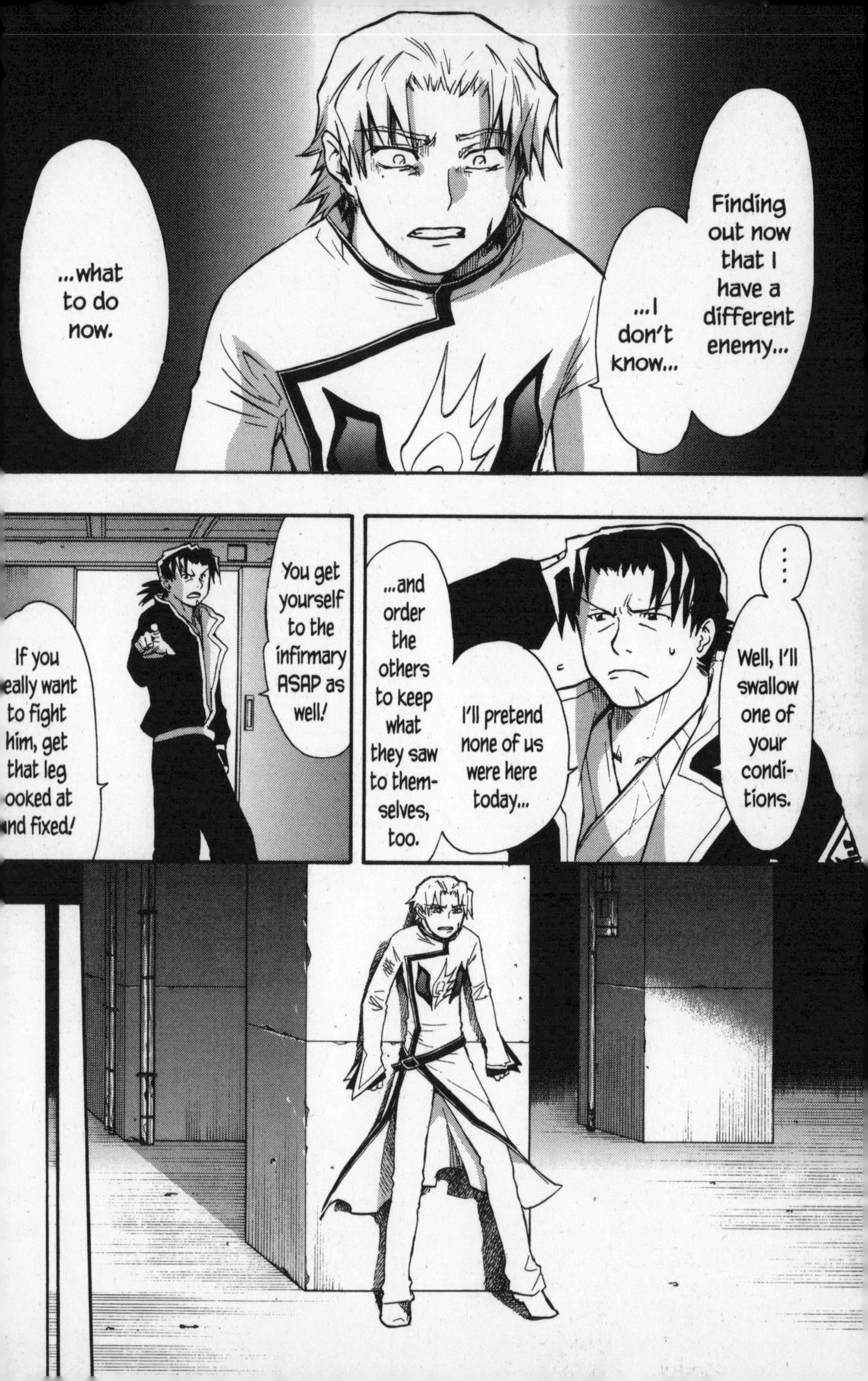
Finding out now that I have a different enemy...
...I don't know...
...what to do now.
....
Well, I'll swallow one of your conditions.
I'll pretend none of us were here today...
...and order the others to keep what they saw to themselves, too.
You get yourself to the infirmary ASAP as well!
If you eally want to fight him, get that leg ooked at nd fixed!

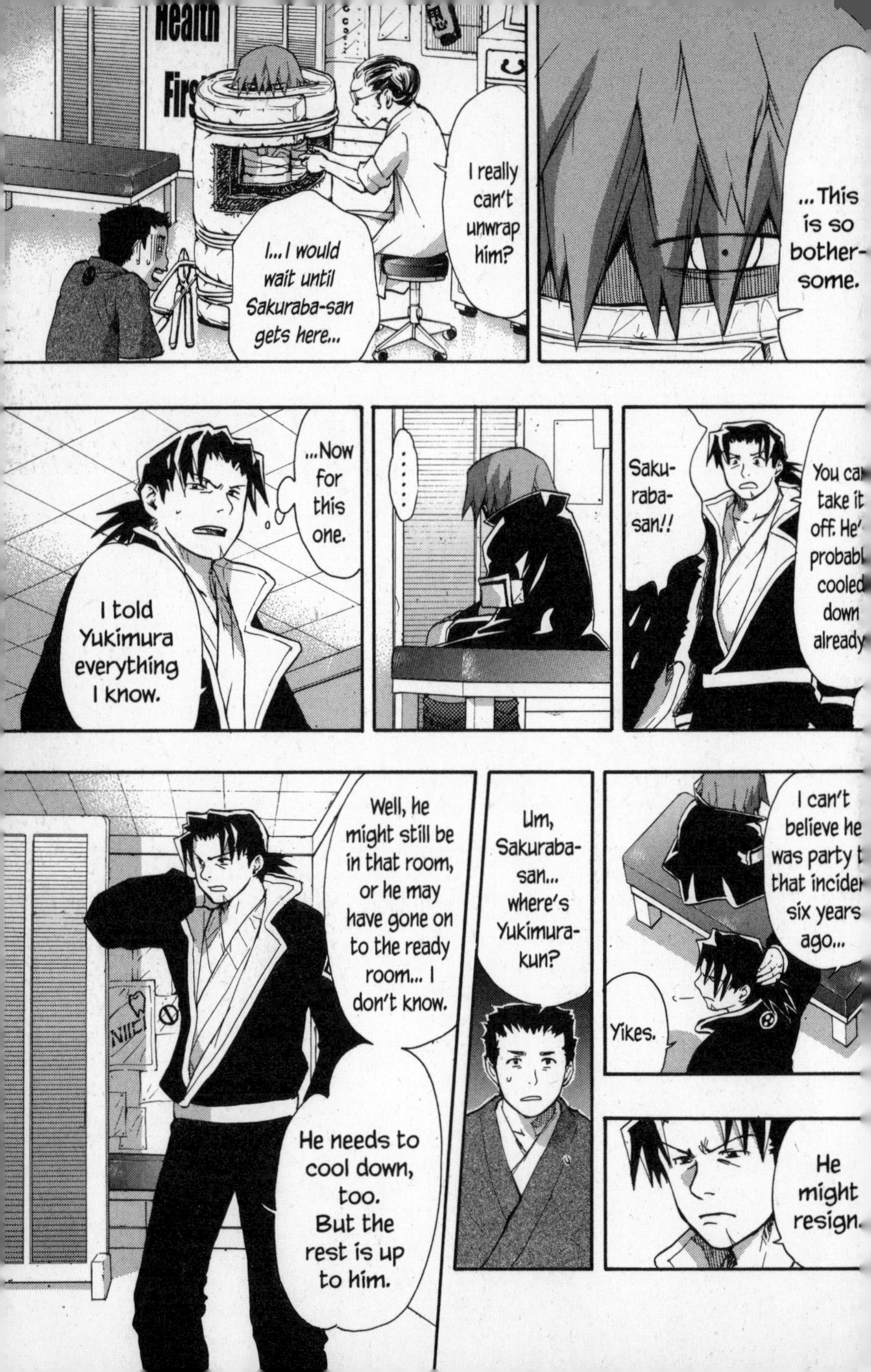
...This is so bother-some.
I really can't unwrap him?
I...I would wait until Sakuraba-san gets here...
Health
You ca take it off. He' probabl cooled down already
Saku-raba-san!!
......
...Now for this one.
I told Yukimura everything I know.
I can't believe he was party t that incide six years ago...
Yikes.
He might resign.
Um, Sakuraba-san... where's Yukimura-kun?
Well, he might still be in that room, or he may have gone on to the ready room... I don't know.
He needs to cool down, too. But the rest is up to him.

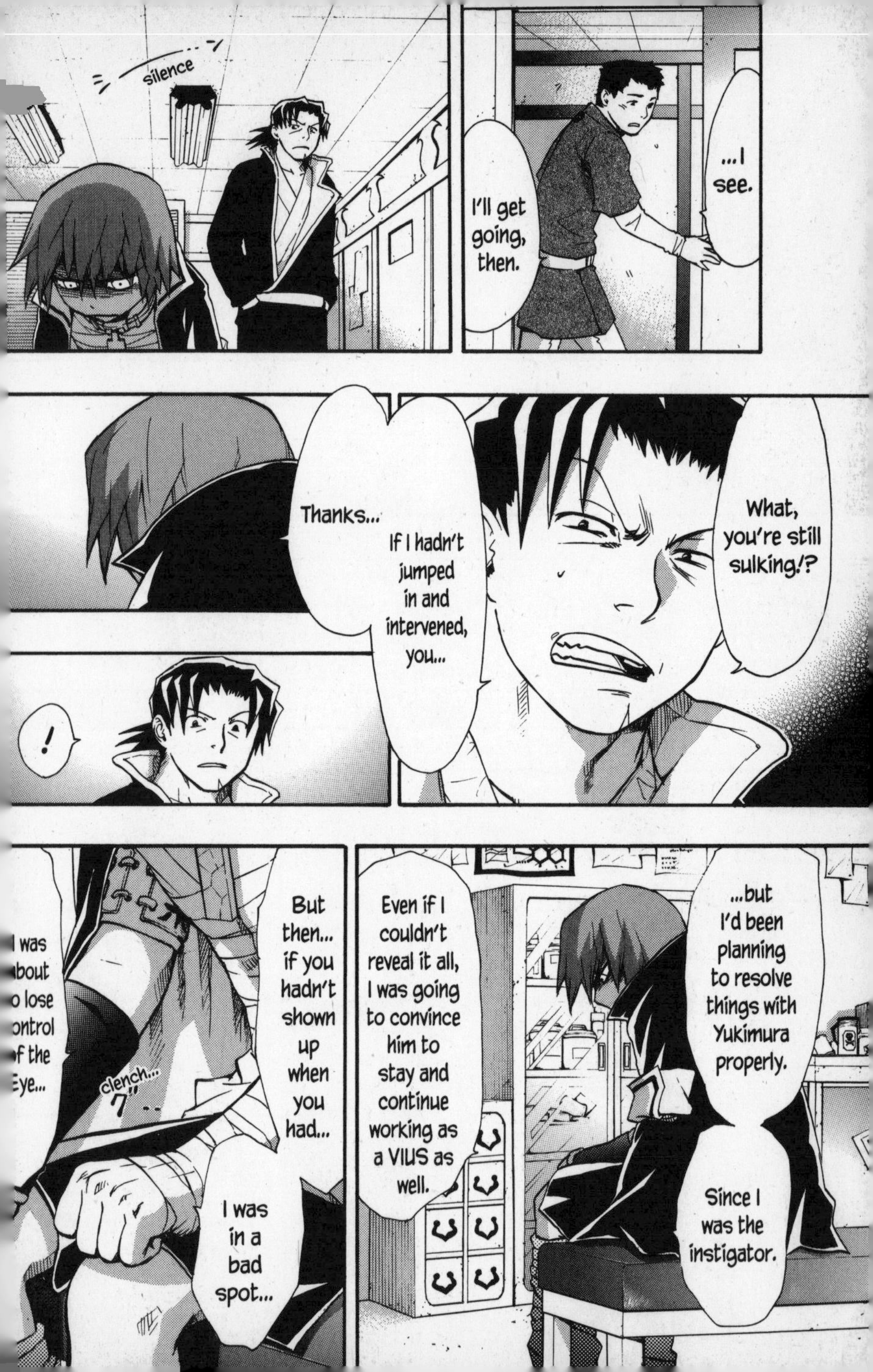

...I see.
I'll get going, then.
silence
What, you're still sulking!?
Thanks... If I hadn't jumped in and intervened, you...
!
...but I'd been planning to resolve things with Yukimura properly.
Since I was the instigator.
Even if I couldn't reveal it all, I was going to convince him to stay and continue working as a VIUS as well.
But then... if you hadn't shown up when you had...
I was in a bad spot...
clench...
I was bout o lose ontrol f the Eye...

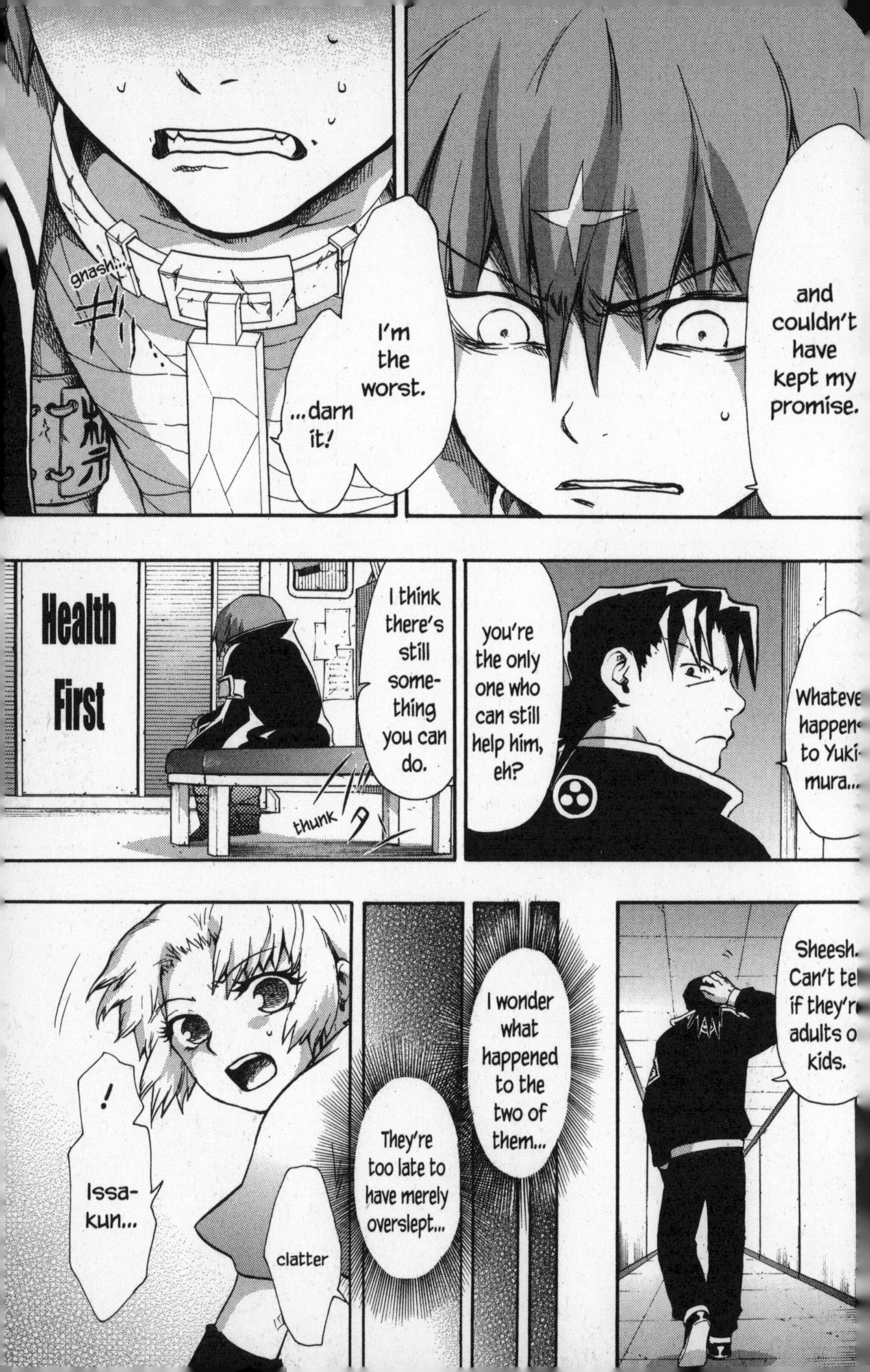
and couldn't have kept my promise.
I'm the worst.
...darn it!
gnash...
Whateve happen to Yuki-mura...
you're the only one who can still help him, eh?
I think there's still some-thing you can do.
thunk
Health First
Sheesh. Can't te if they'r adults o kids.
I wonder what happened to the two of them...
They're too late to have merely overslept...
clatter
!
Issa-kun...

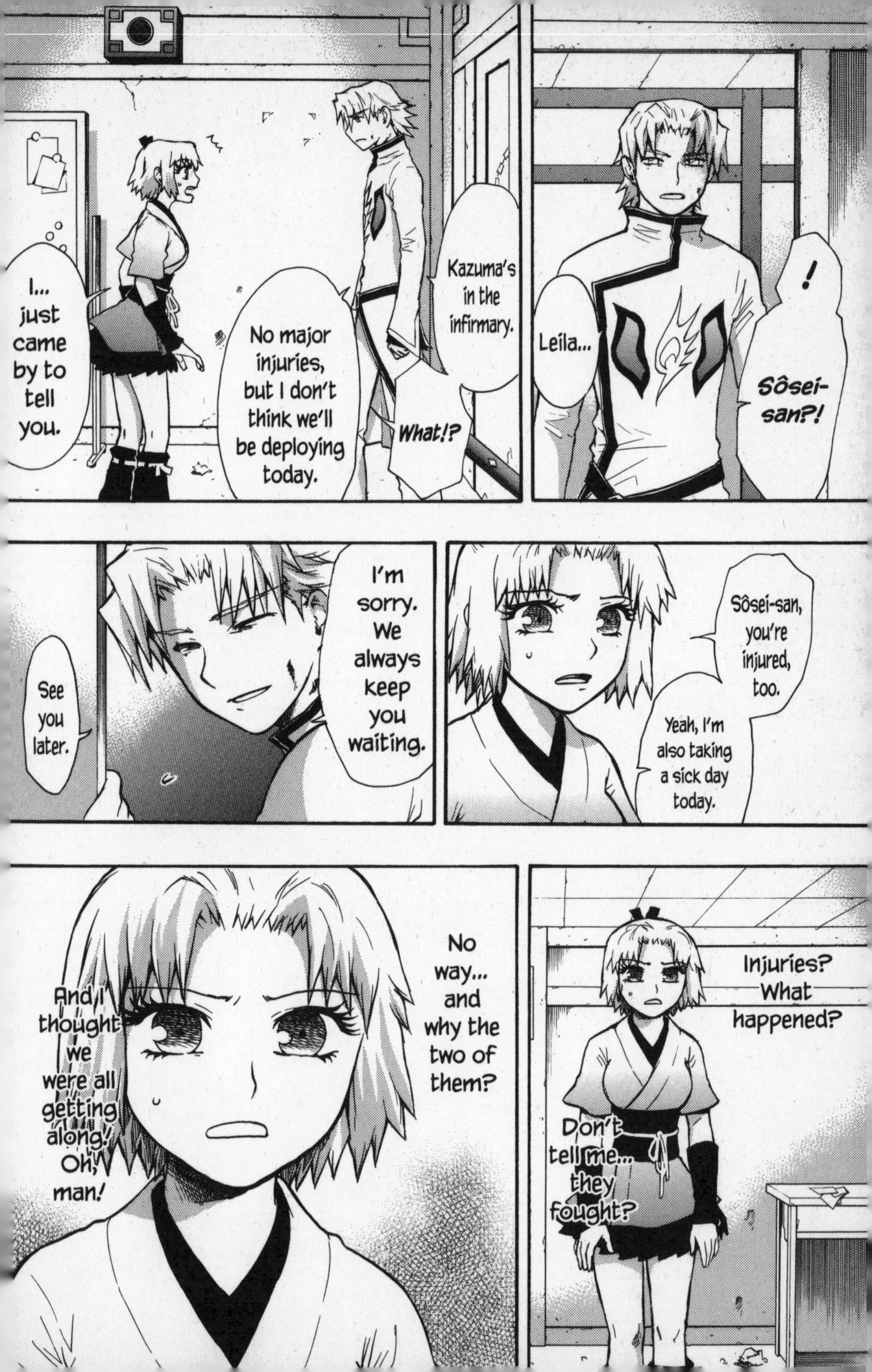
!
Sôsei-san?!
Leila...
Kazuma's in the infirmary.
What!?
No major injuries, but I don't think we'll be deploying today.
I... just came by to tell you.
Sôsei-san, you're injured, too.
Yeah, I'm also taking a sick day today.
I'm sorry. We always keep you waiting.
See you later.
Injuries? What happened?
Don't tell me... they fought?
No way... and why the two of them?
And I thought we were all getting along! Oh, man!

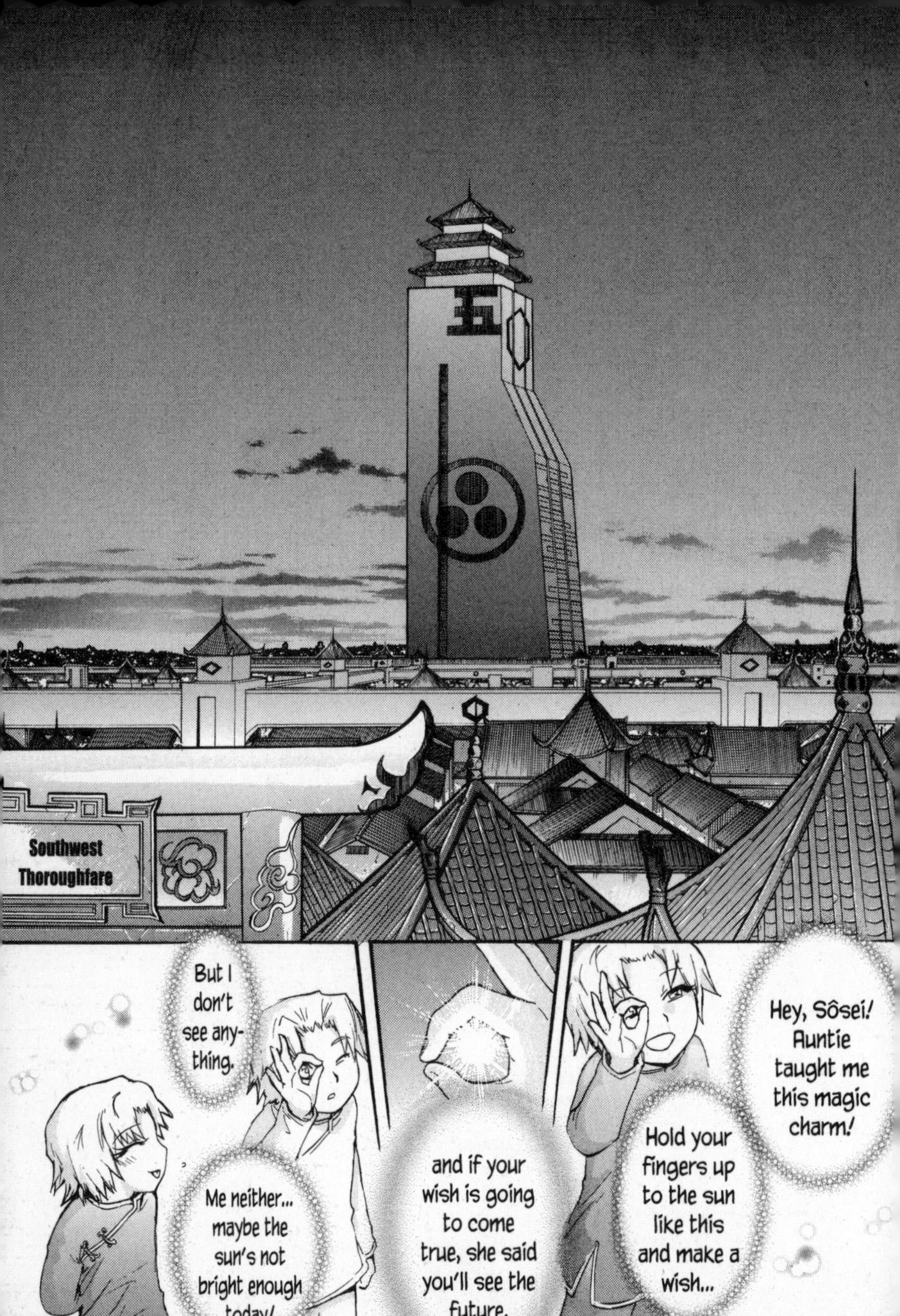
Southwest Thoroughfare
Hey, Sôsei! Auntie taught me this magic charm!
Hold your fingers up to the sun like this and make a wish...
and if your wish is going to come true, she said you'll see the future.
But I don't see anything.
Me neither... maybe the sun's not bright enough today!

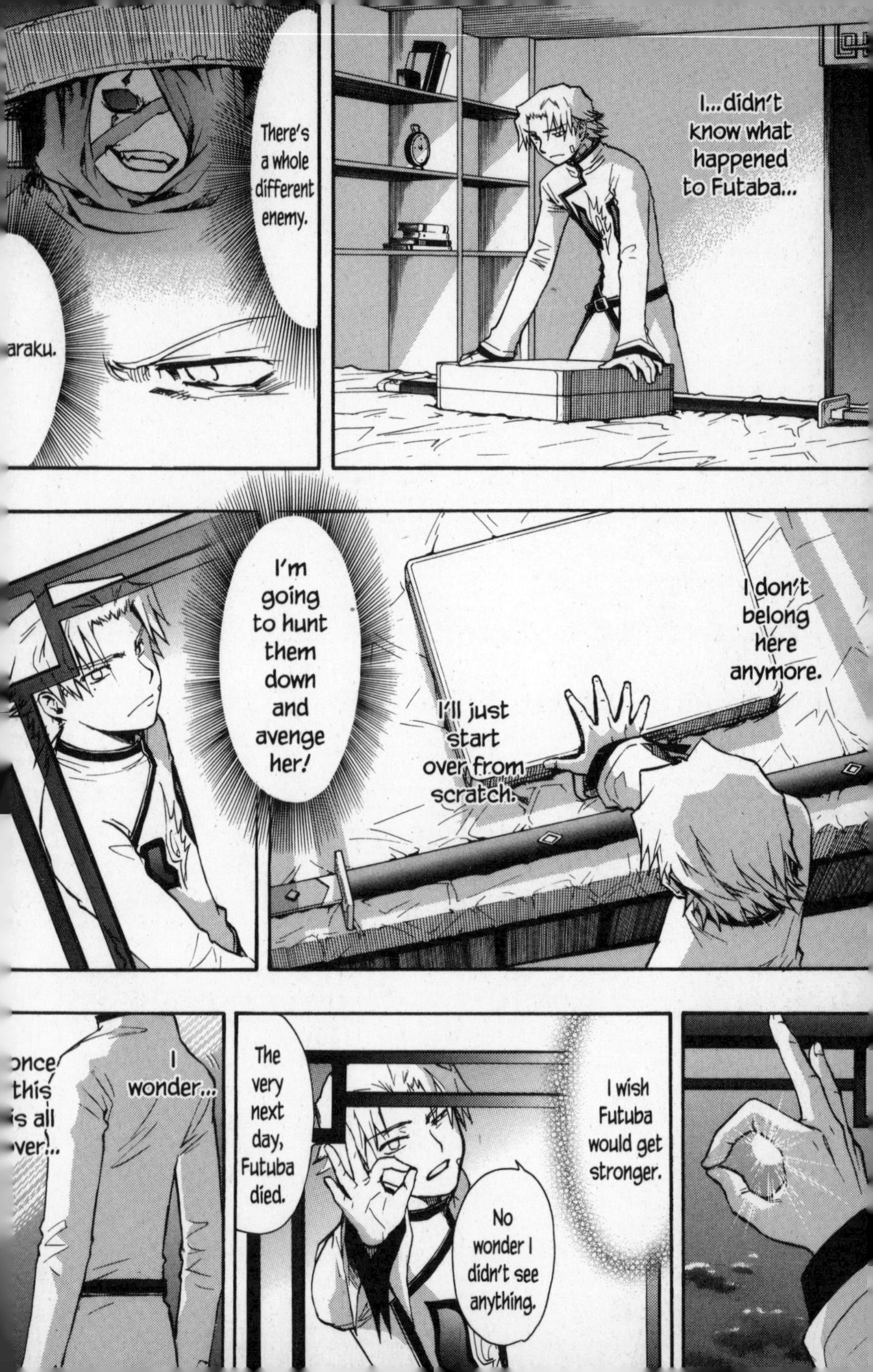
I...didn't know what happened to Futaba...
There's a whole different enemy.
araku.
I don't belong here anymore.
I'll just start over from scratch.
I'm going to hunt them down and avenge her!
I wish Futuba would get stronger.
The very next day, Futuba died.
No wonder I didn't see anything.
I wonder...
once this is all over...

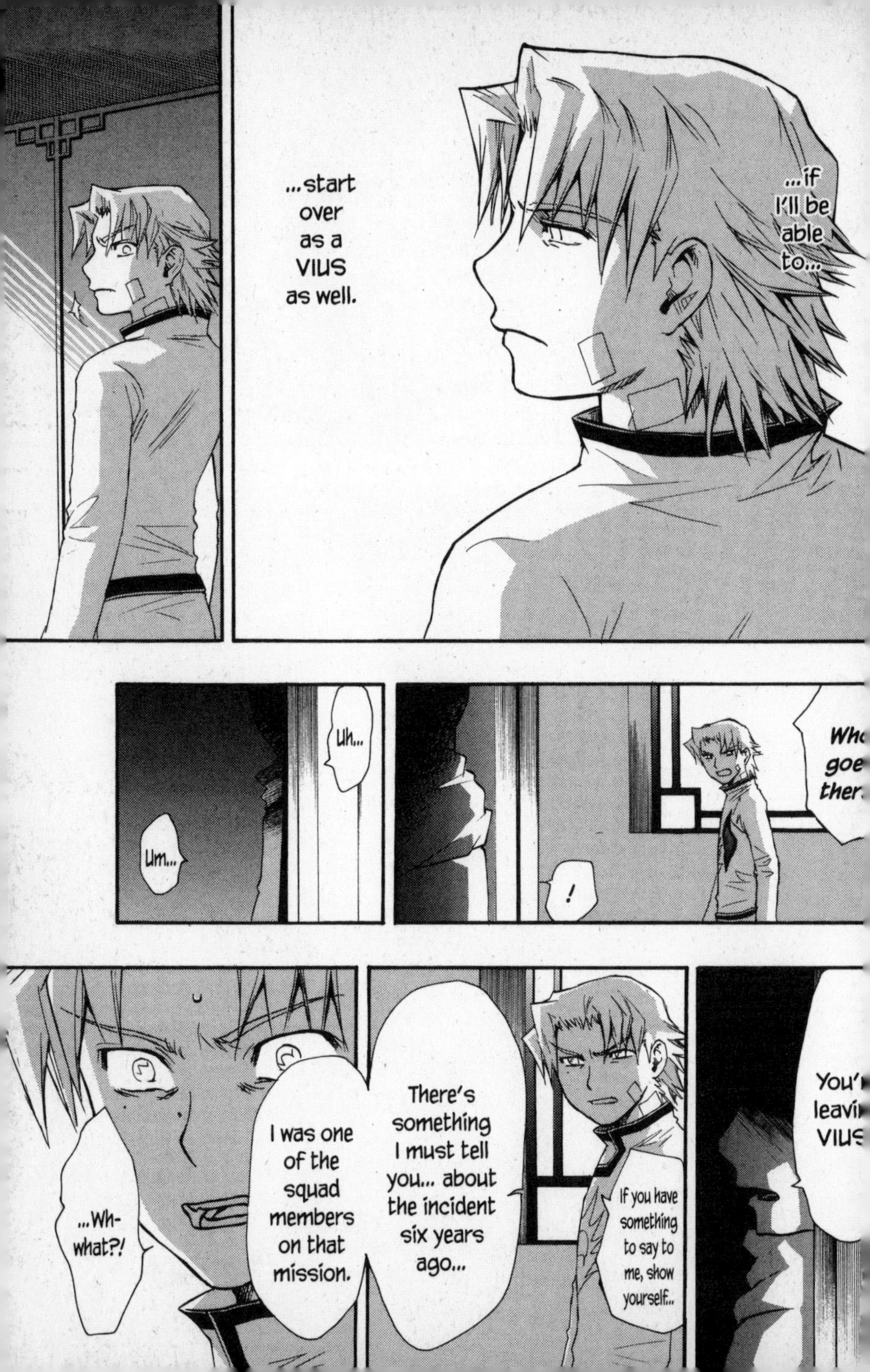
...if I'll be able to...
...start over as a VIUS as well.
Wh goe ther
!
Uh...
Um...
You' leavi VIUS
If you have something to say to me, show yourself...
There's something I must tell you... about the incident six years ago...
I was one of the squad members on that mission.
...Wh-what?!

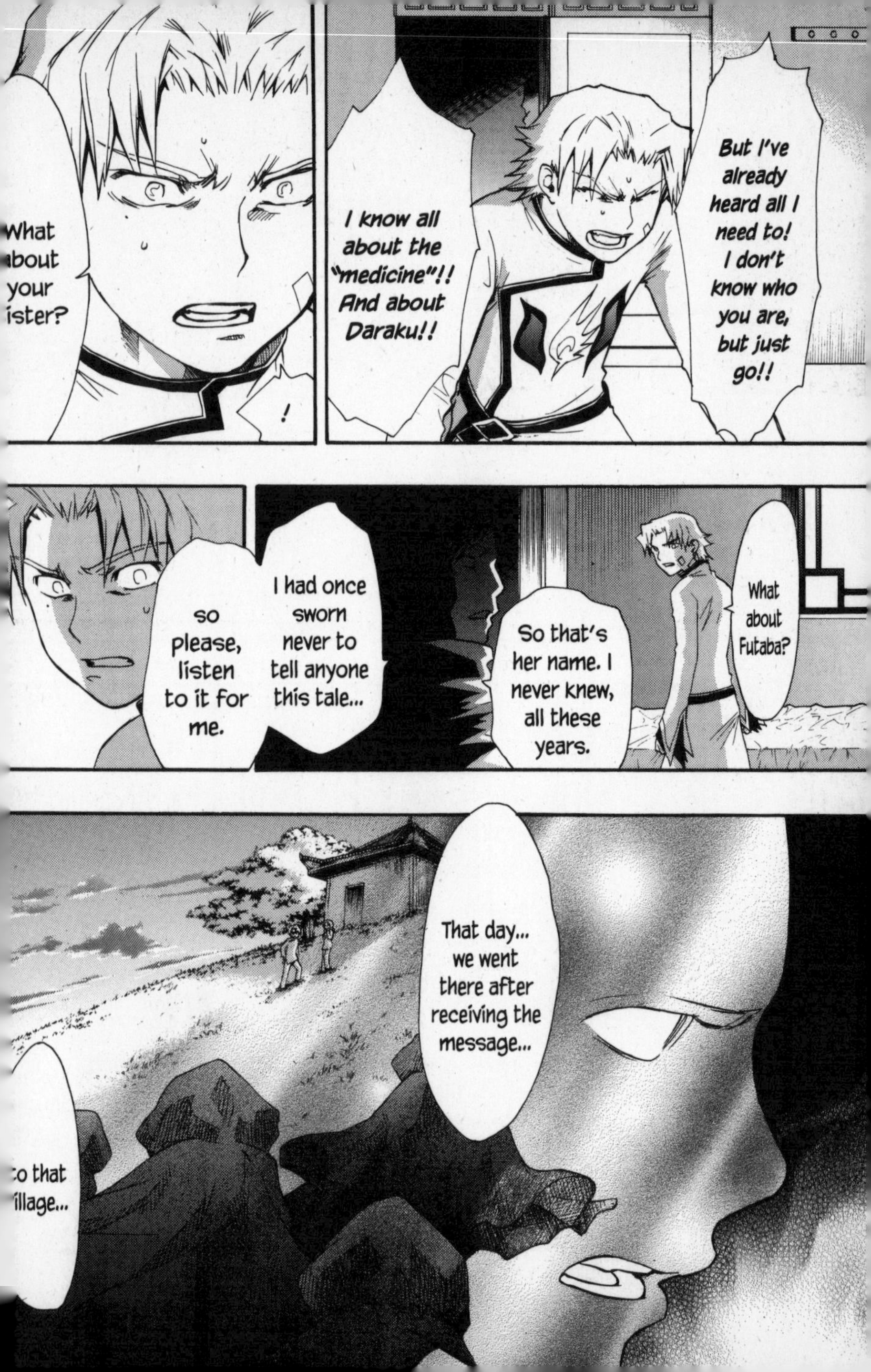
But I've already heard all I need to! I don't know who you are, but just go!!
I know all about the "medicine"!! And about Daraku!!
!
What about your ister?
What about Futaba?
So that's her name. I never knew, all these years.
I had once sworn never to tell anyone this tale...
so please, listen to it for me.
That day... we went there after receiving the message...
o that illage...

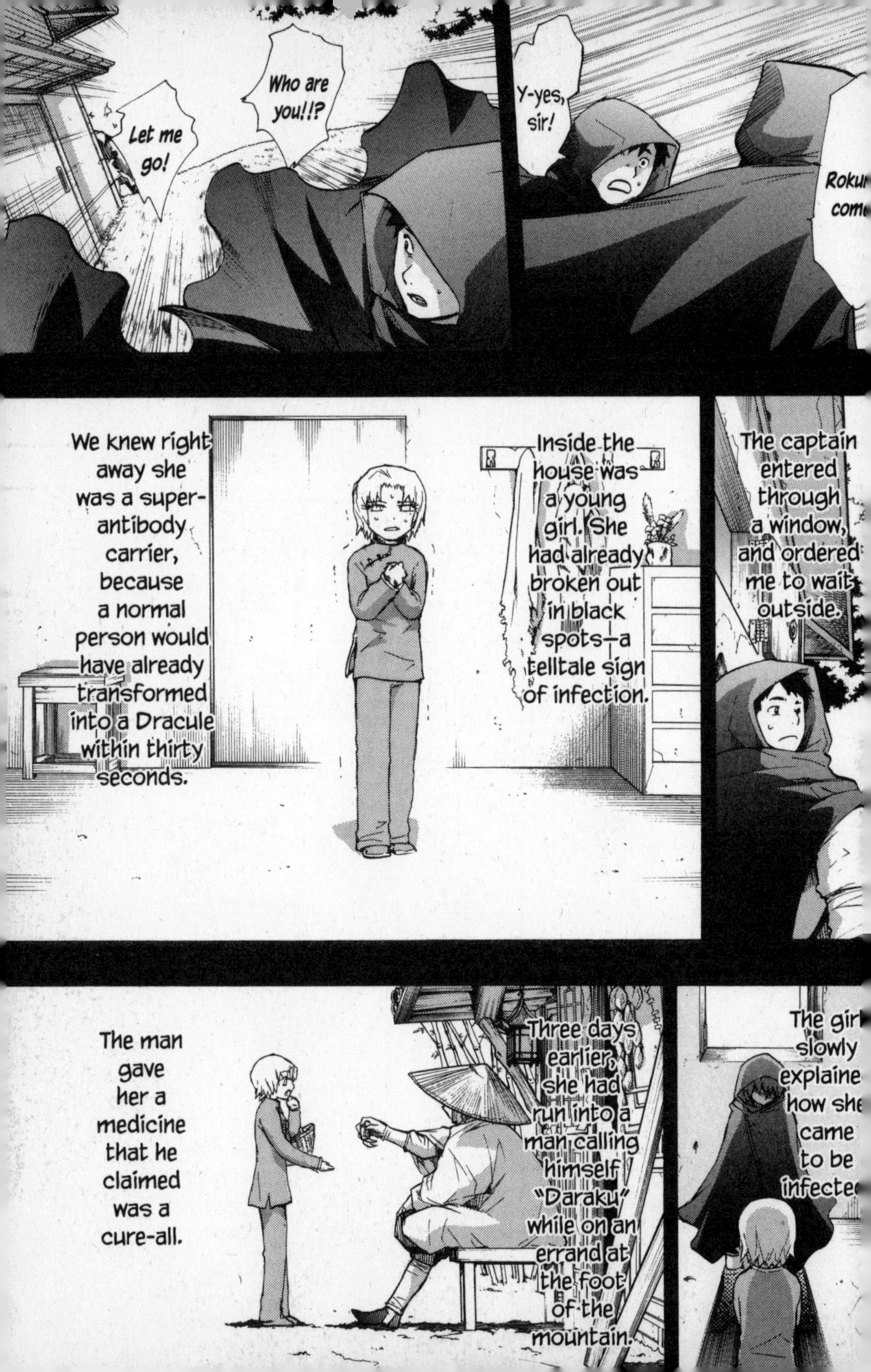
Roku com
Y-yes, sir!
Who are you!!?
Let me go!
The captain entered through a window, and ordered me to wait outside.
Inside the house was a young girl. She had already broken out in black spots—a telltale sign of infection.
We knew right away she was a super-antibody carrier, because a normal person would have already transformed into a Dracule within thirty seconds.
The gir slowly explaine how she came to be infecte
Three days earlier, she had run into a man calling himself "Daraku" while on an errand at the foot of the mountain.
The man gave her a medicine that he claimed was a cure-all.

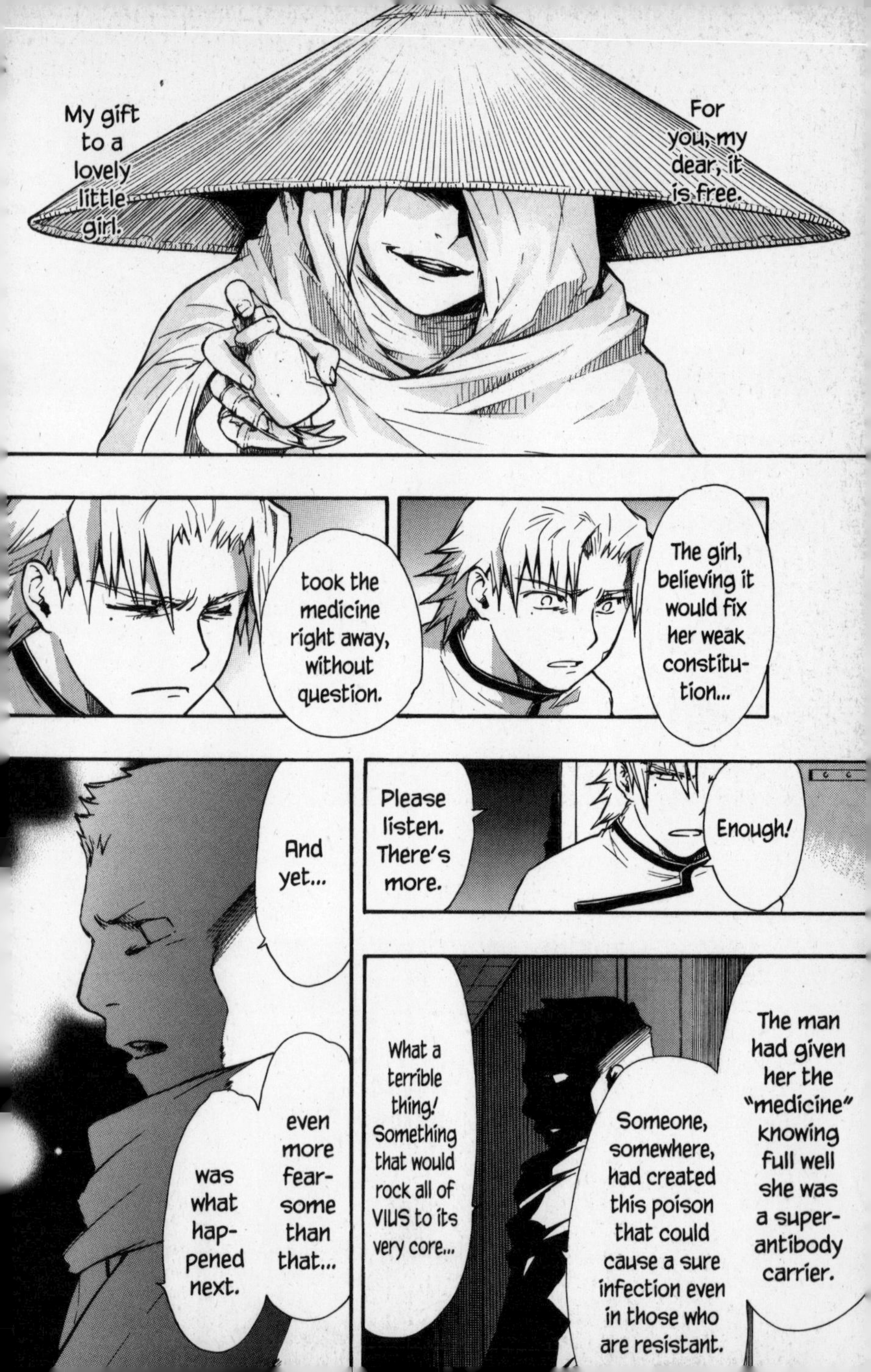
For you, my dear, it is free.
My gift to a lovely little girl.
The girl, believing it would fix her weak constitution...
took the medicine right away, without question.
Enough!
Please listen. There's more.
The man had given her the "medicine" knowing full well she was a super-antibody carrier.
Someone, somewhere, had created this poison that could cause a sure infection even in those who are resistant.
What a terrible thing! Something that would rock all of VIUS to its very core...
And yet...
even more fearsome than that...
was what happened next.

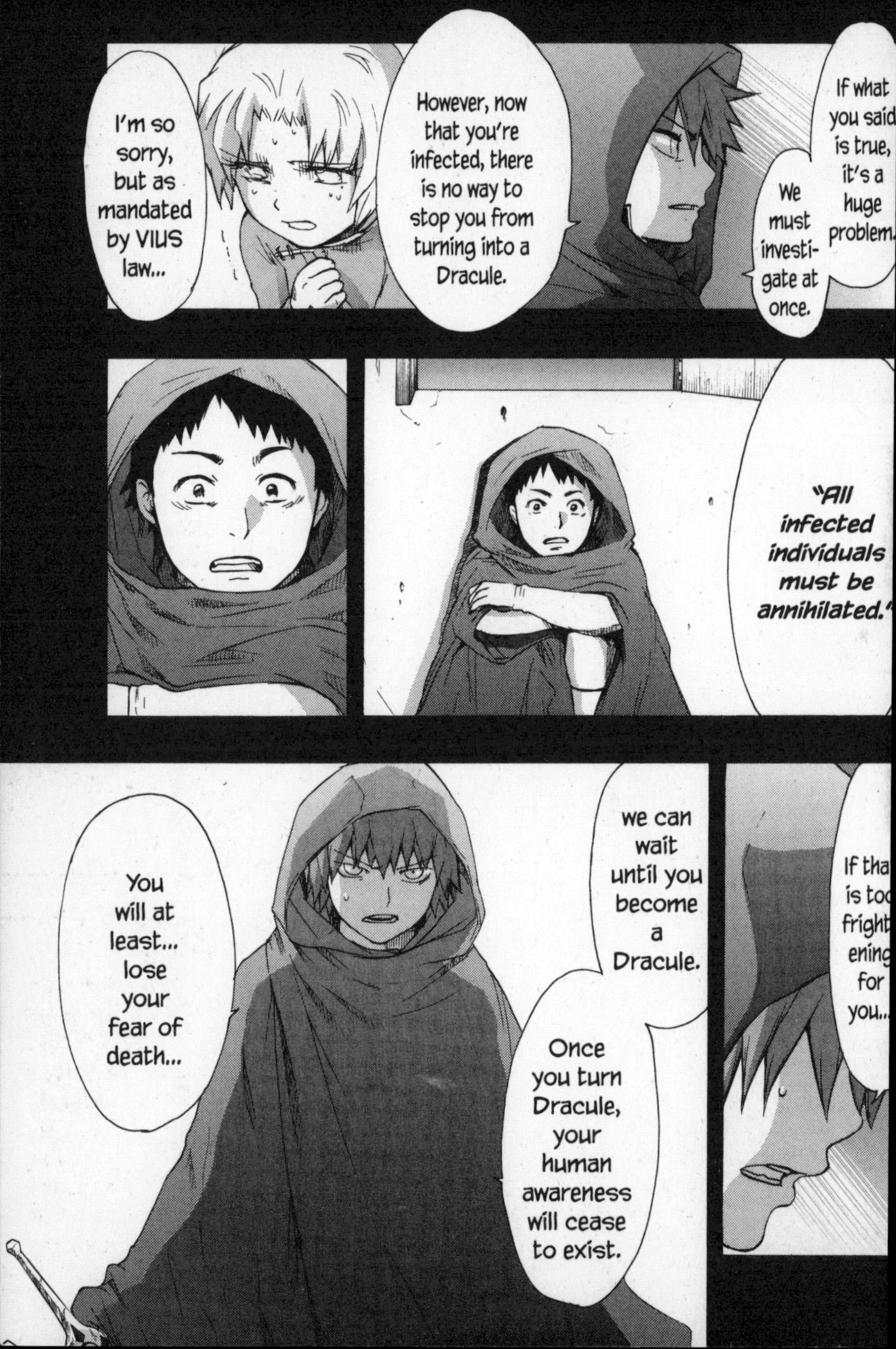

If what you said is true, it's a huge problem.
We must investigate at once.
However, now that you're infected, there is no way to stop you from turning into a Dracule.
I'm so sorry, but as mandated by VIUS law...
"All infected individuals must be annihilated."
If tha is to fright ening for you...
we can wait until you become a Dracule.
Once you turn Dracule, your human awareness will cease to exist.
You will at least... lose your fear of death...

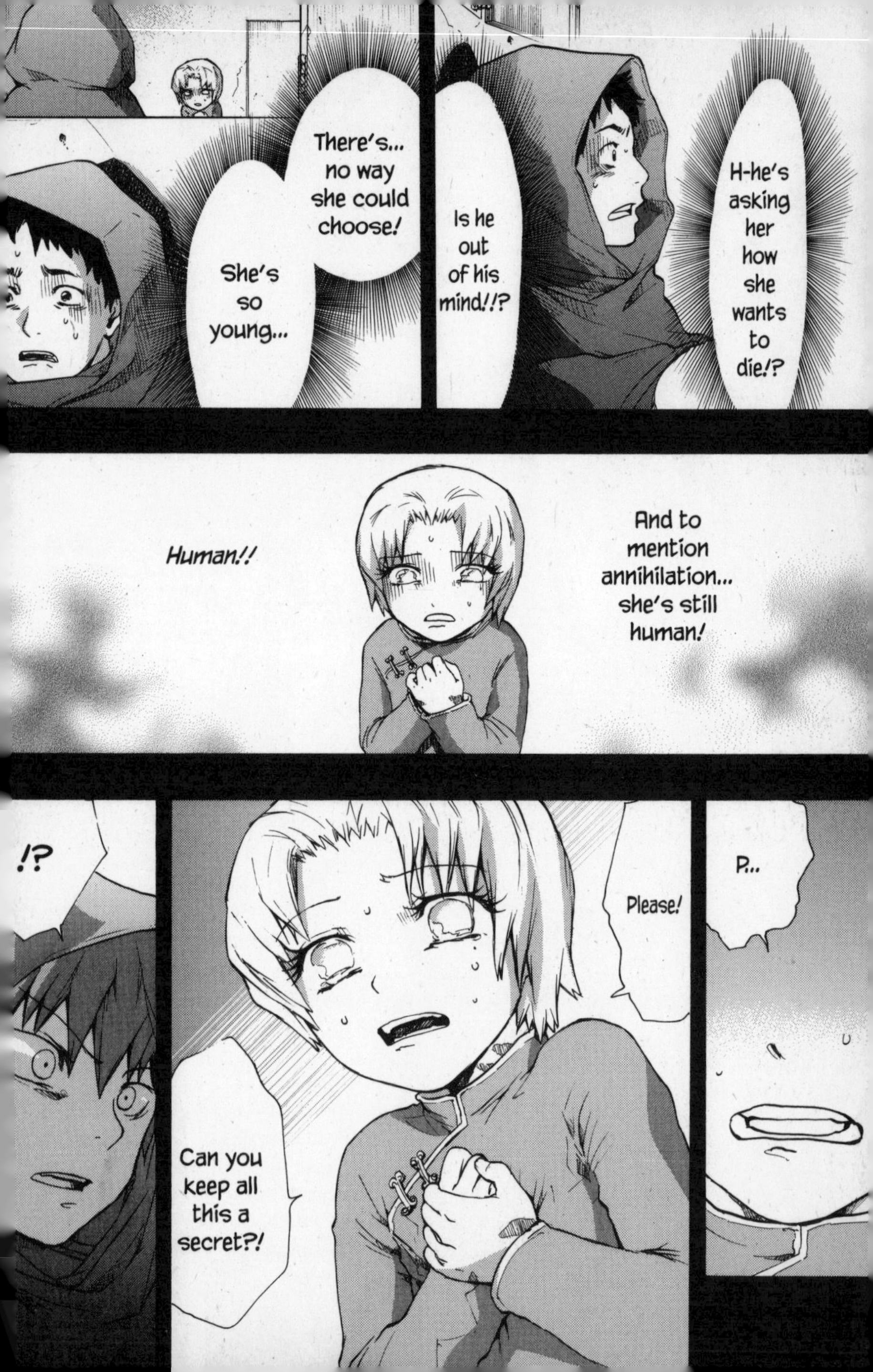
H-he's asking her how she wants to die!?
Is he out of his mind!!?
There's... no way she could choose!
She's so young...
And to mention annihilation... she's still human!
Human!!
P...
Please!
Can you keep all this a secret?!
!?

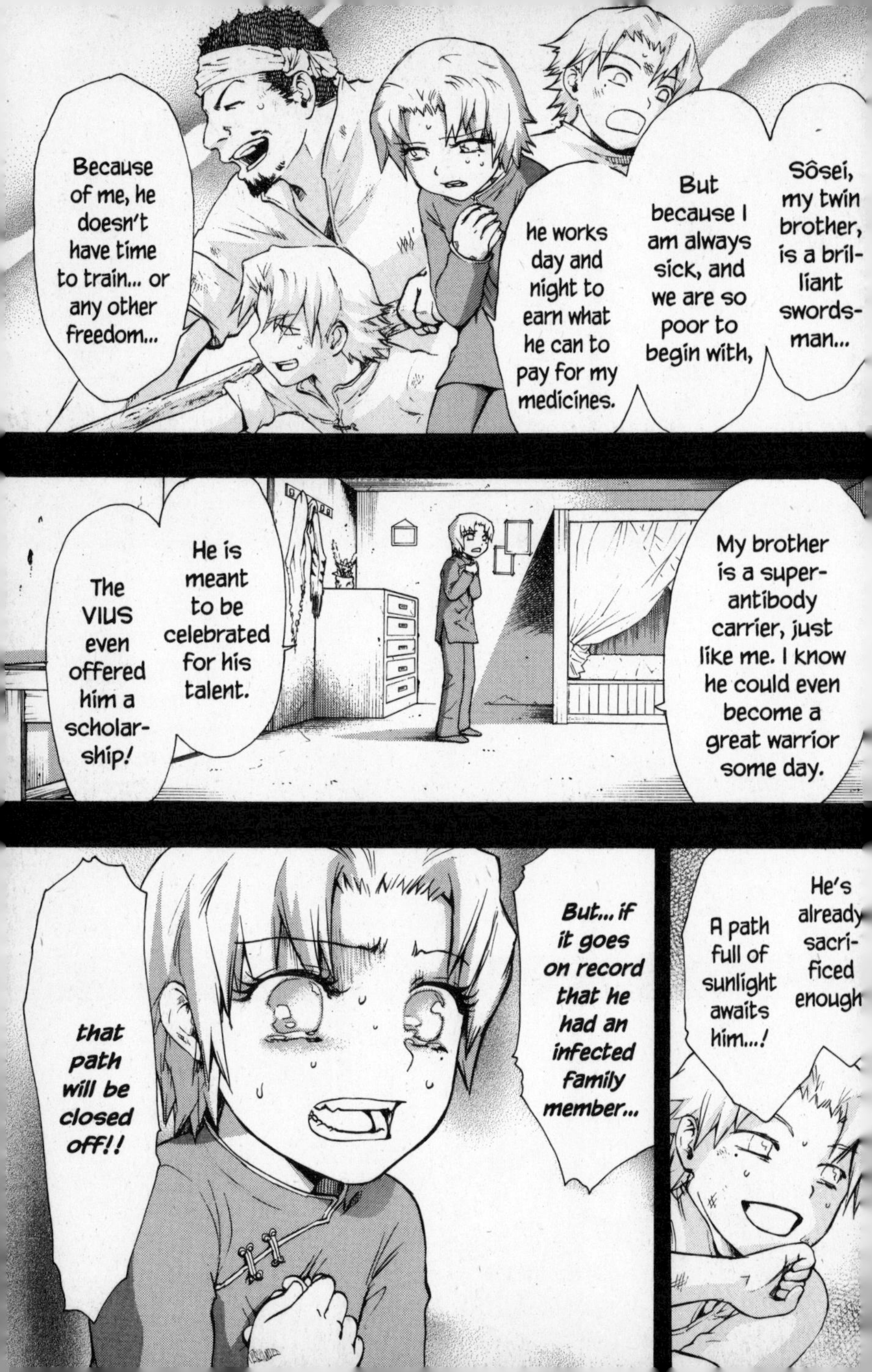
Sôsei, my twin brother, is a brilliant swordsman...
But because I am always sick, and we are so poor to begin with,
he works day and night to earn what he can to pay for my medicines.
Because of me, he doesn't have time to train... or any other freedom...
My brother is a super-antibody carrier, just like me. I know he could even become a great warrior some day.
He is meant to be celebrated for his talent.
The VIUS even offered him a scholarship!
He's already sacrificed enough
A path full of sunlight awaits him...!
But... if it goes on record that he had an infected family member...
that path will be closed off!!

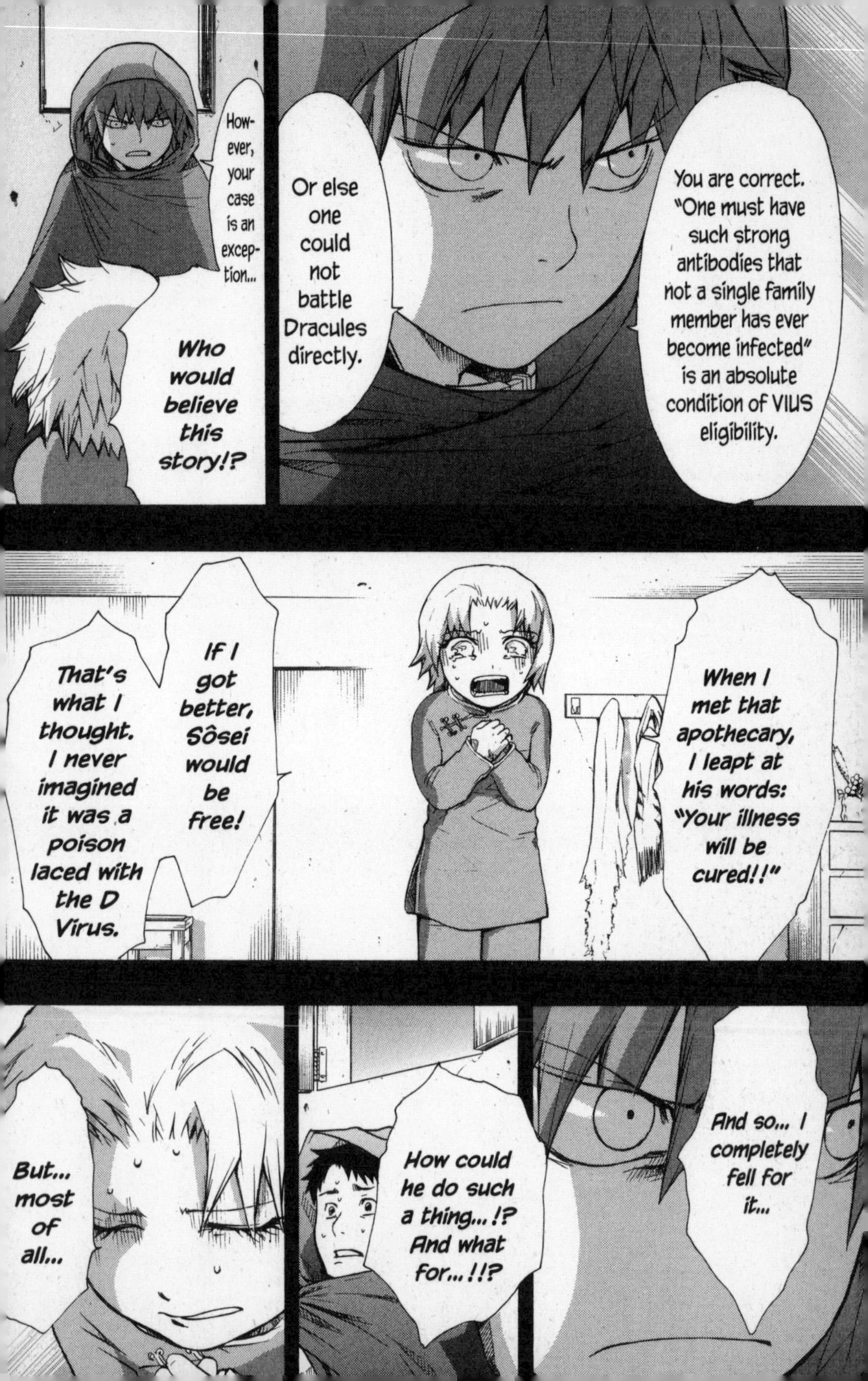
You are correct. "One must have such strong antibodies that not a single family member has ever become infected" is an absolute condition of VIUS eligibility.
Or else one could not battle Dracules directly.
How-ever, your case is an excep-tion...
Who would believe this story!?
When I met that apothecary, I leapt at his words: "Your illness will be cured!!"
If I got better, Sôsei would be free!
That's what I thought. I never imagined it was a poison laced with the D Virus.
And so... I completely fell for it...
How could he do such a thing...!? And what for...!!?
But... most of all...

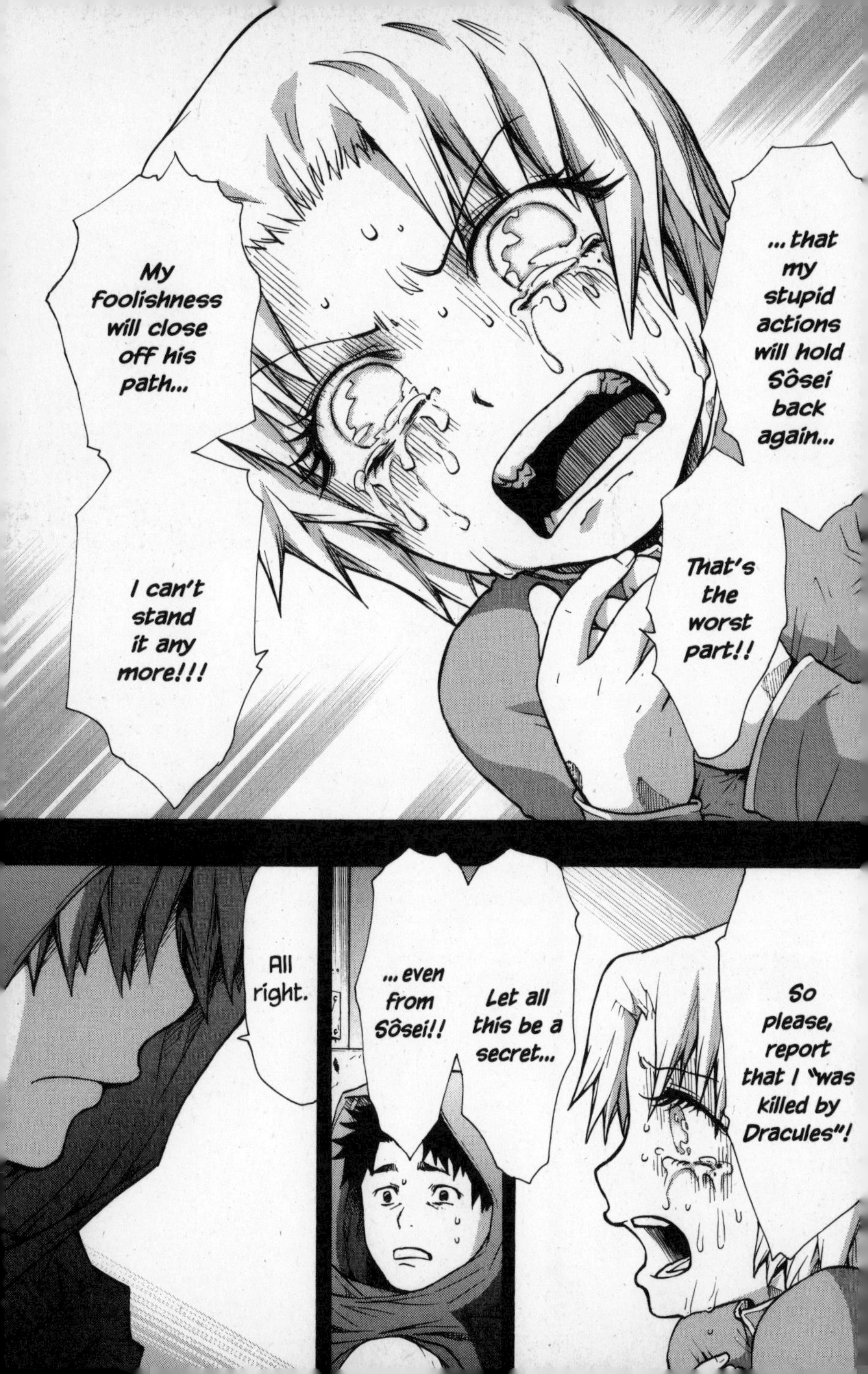
...that my stupid actions will hold Sôsei back again...
That's the worst part!!
My foolishness will close off his path...
I can't stand it any more!!!
So please, report that I "was killed by Dracules"!
Let all this be a secret...
...even from Sôsei!!
All right.

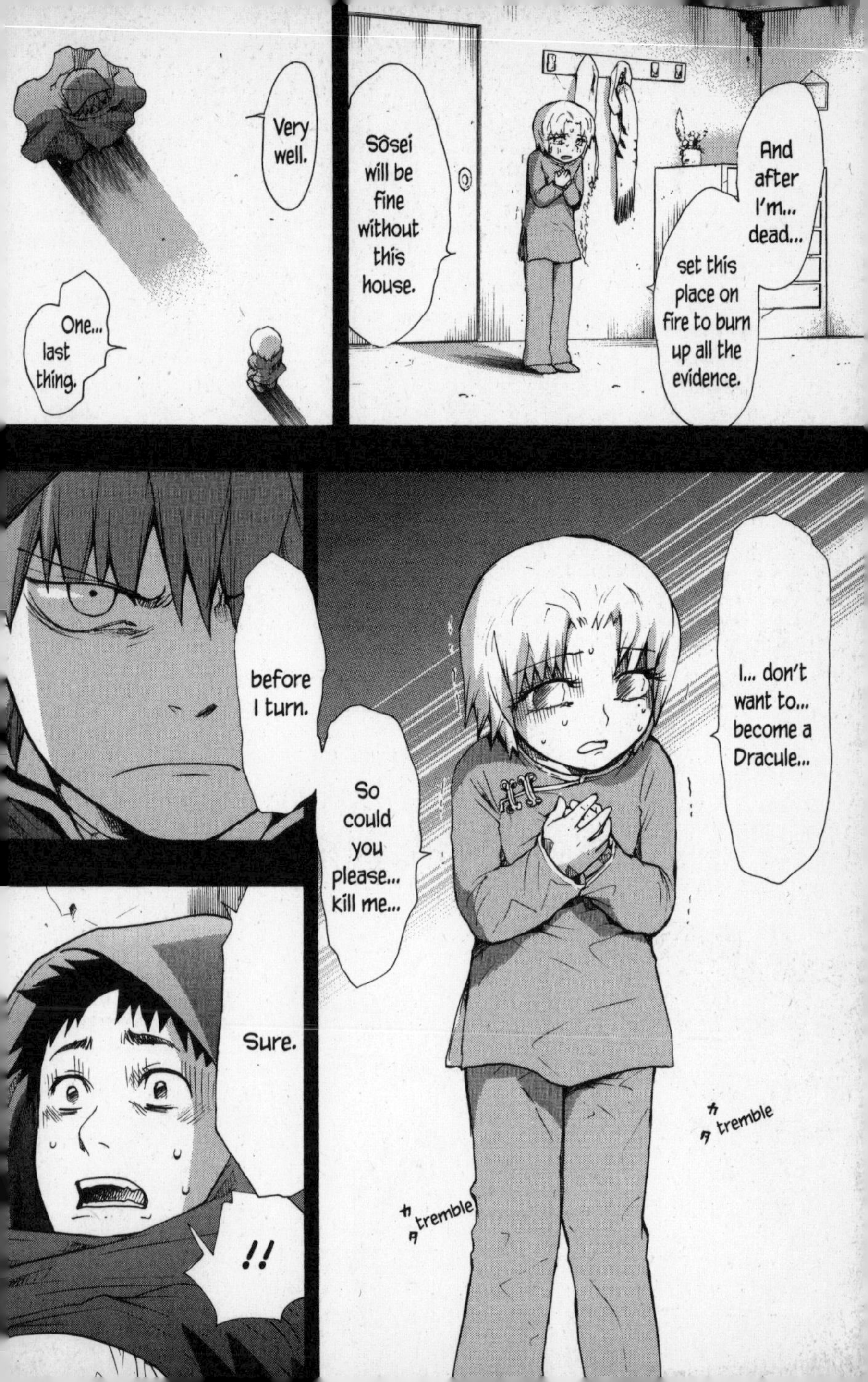

And after I'm... dead...
set this place on fire to burn up all the evidence.
Sôsei will be fine without this house.
Very well.
One... last thing.
I... don't want to... become a Dracule...
before I turn.
So could you please... kill me...
カタ tremble
カタ tremble
Sure.
!!

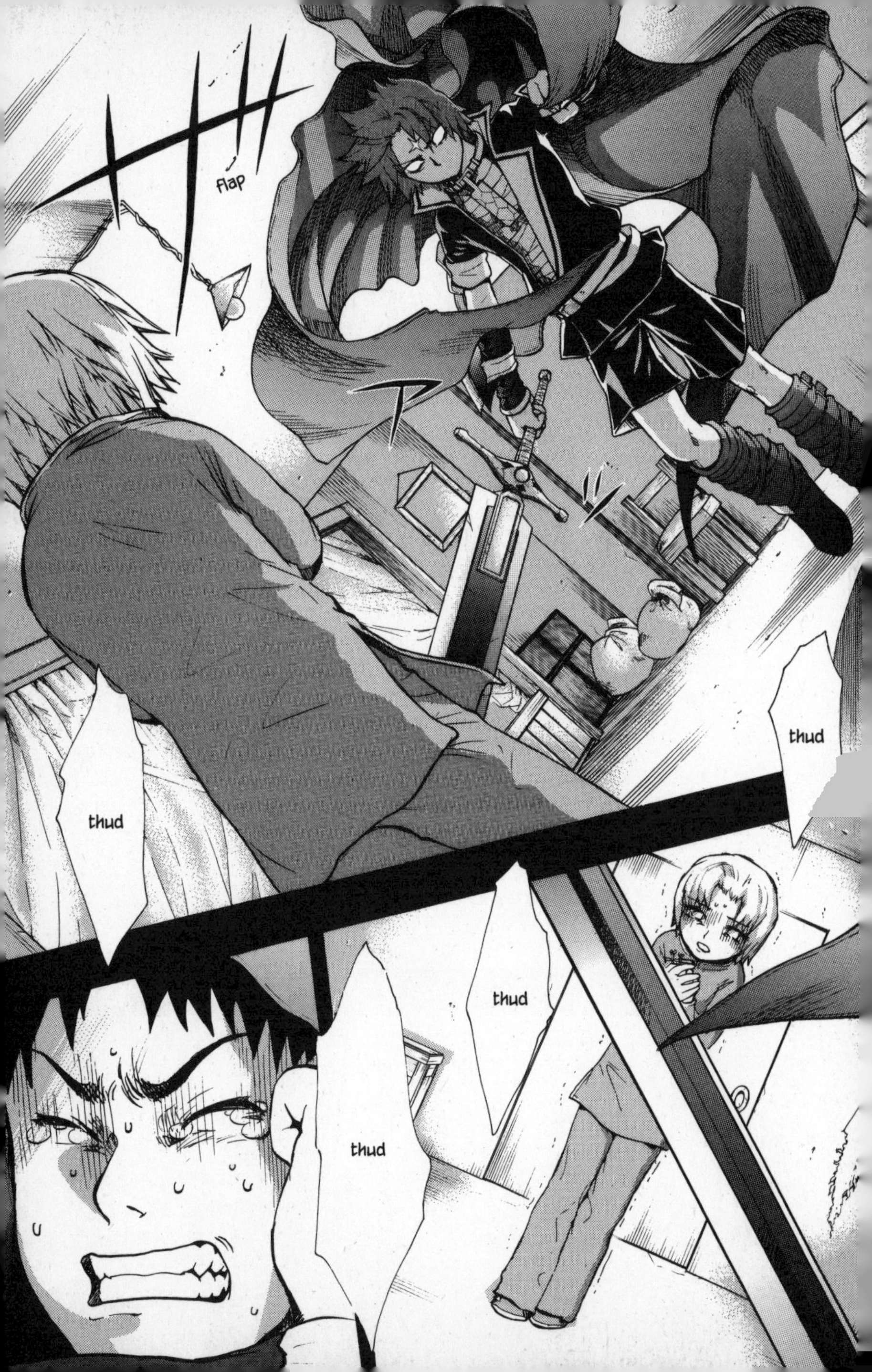
flap
thud
thud
thud
thud

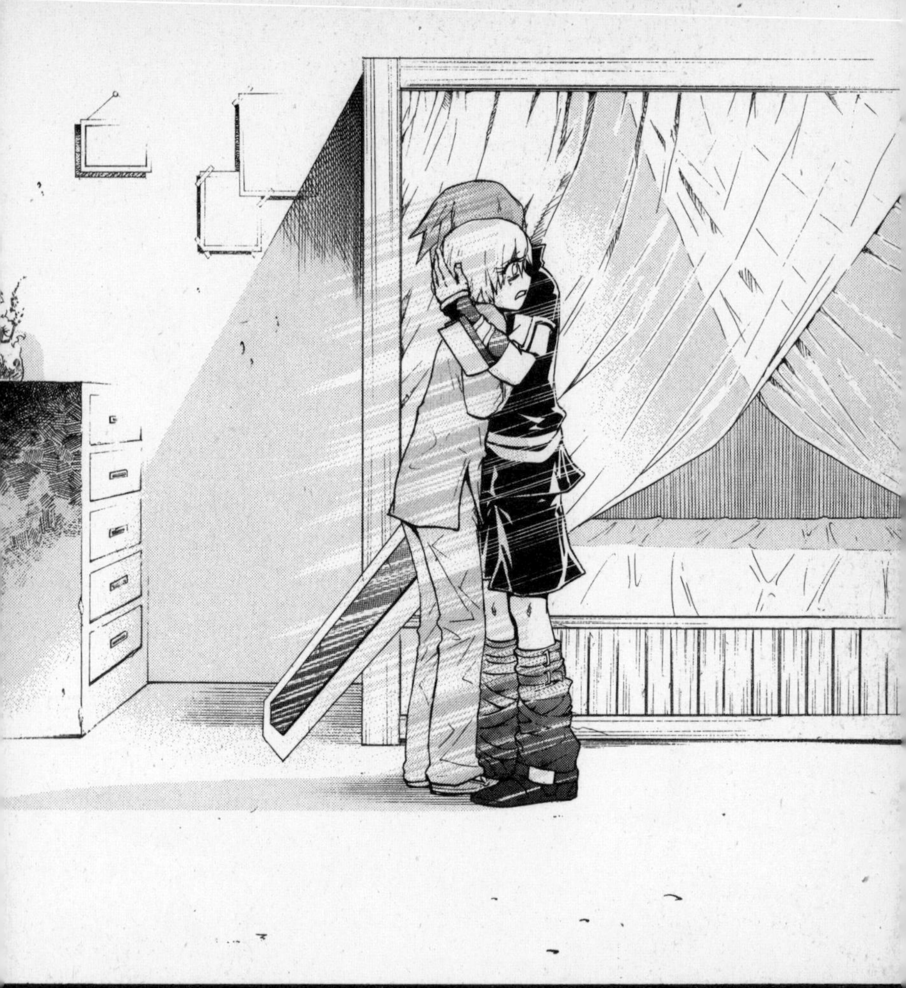
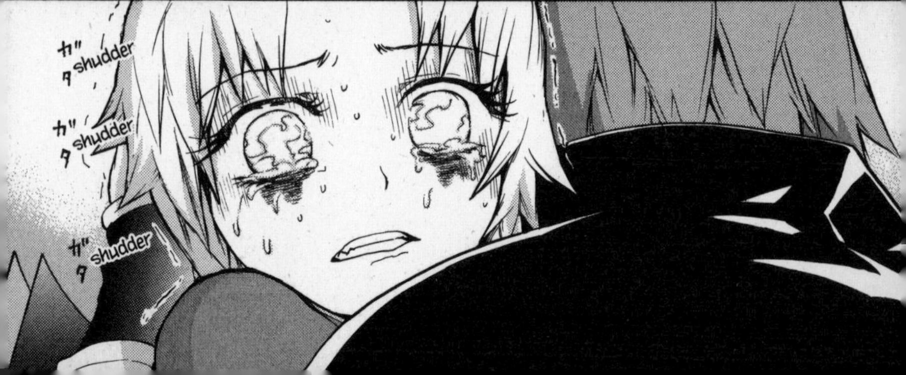
ガタ shudder
ガタ shudder
ガタ shudder

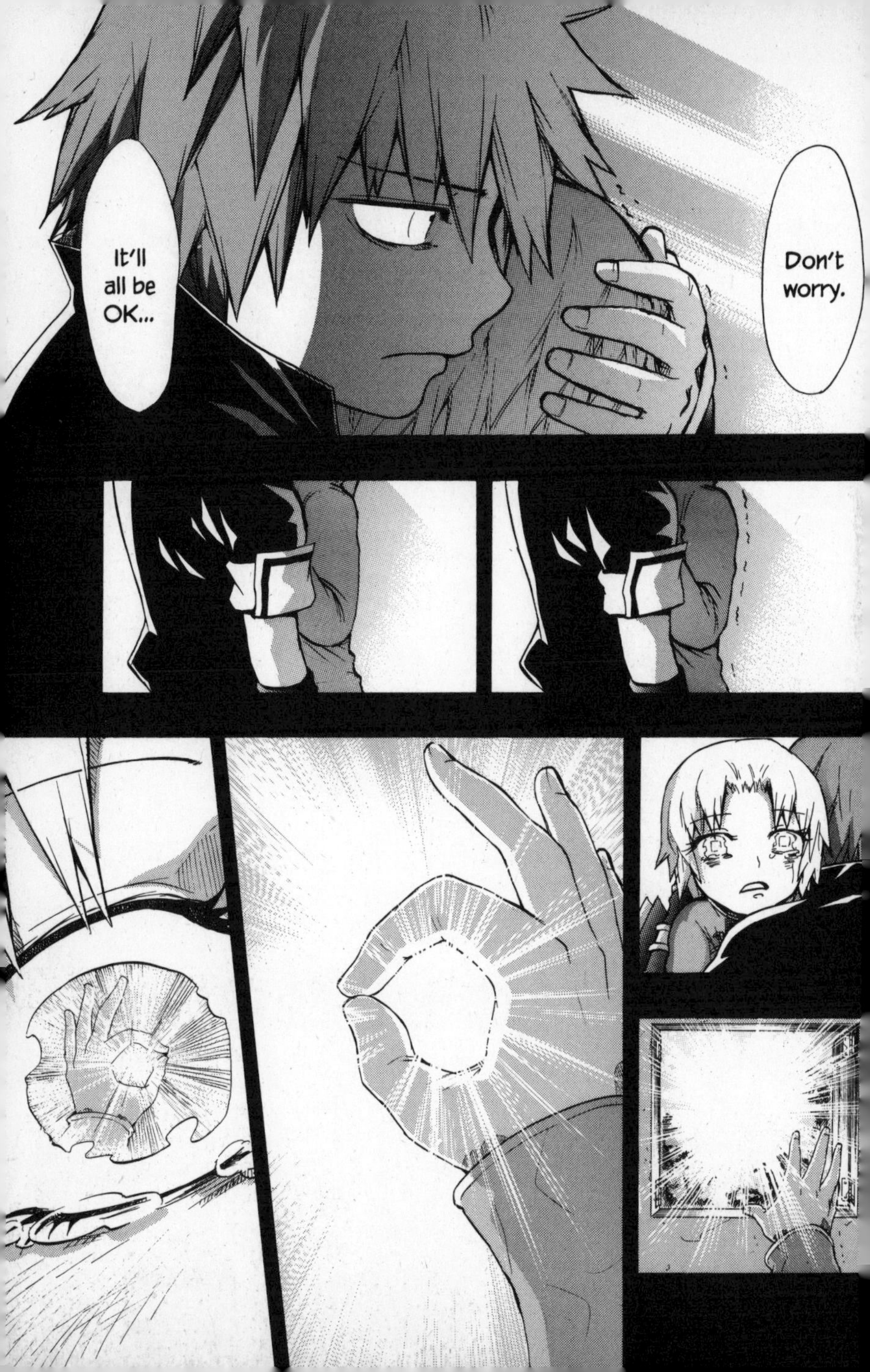
Don't worry.
It'll all be OK...

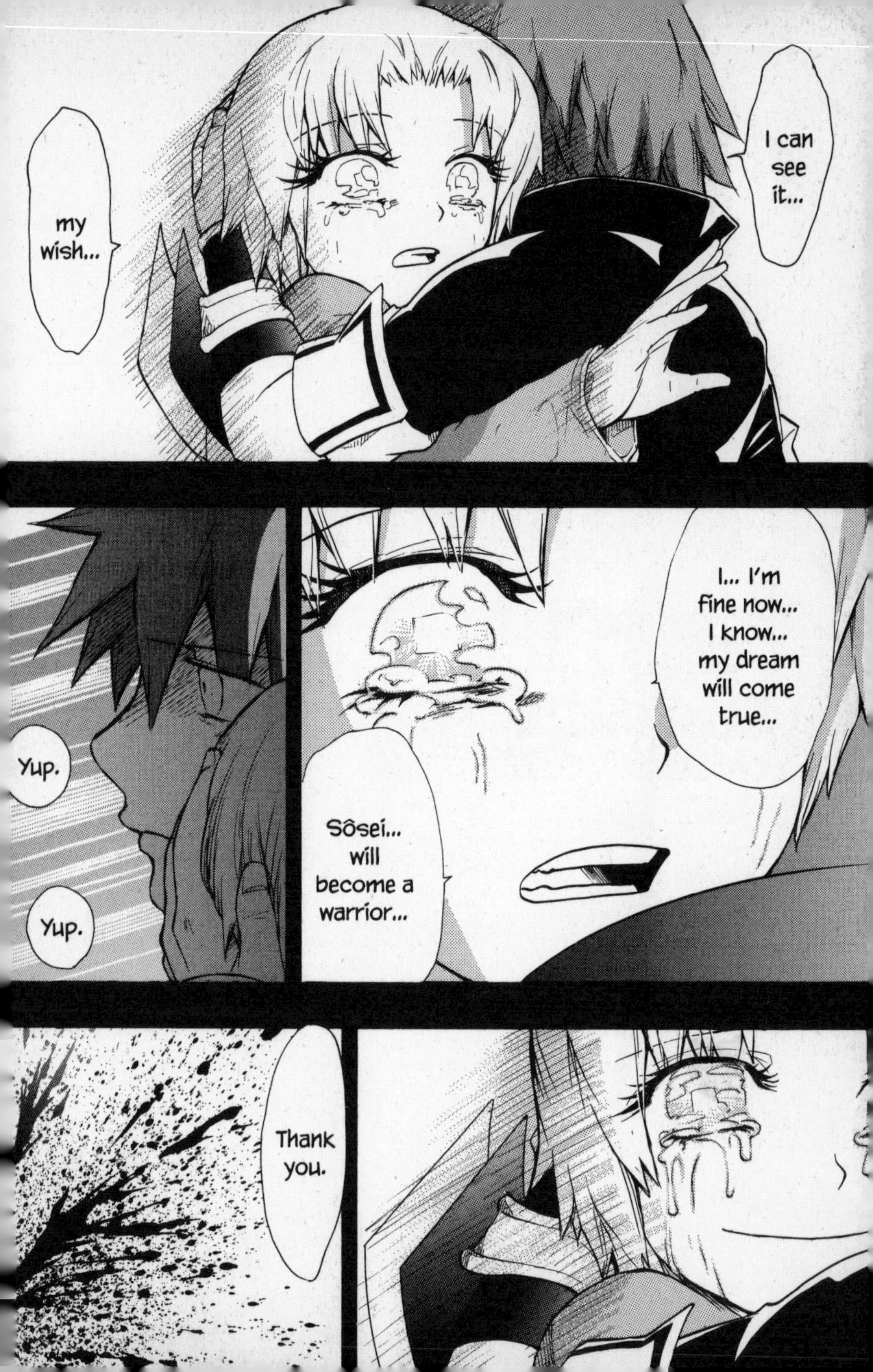
I can see it...
my wish...
I... I'm fine now... I know... my dream will come true...
Sôsei... will become a warrior...
Yup.
Yup.
Thank you.

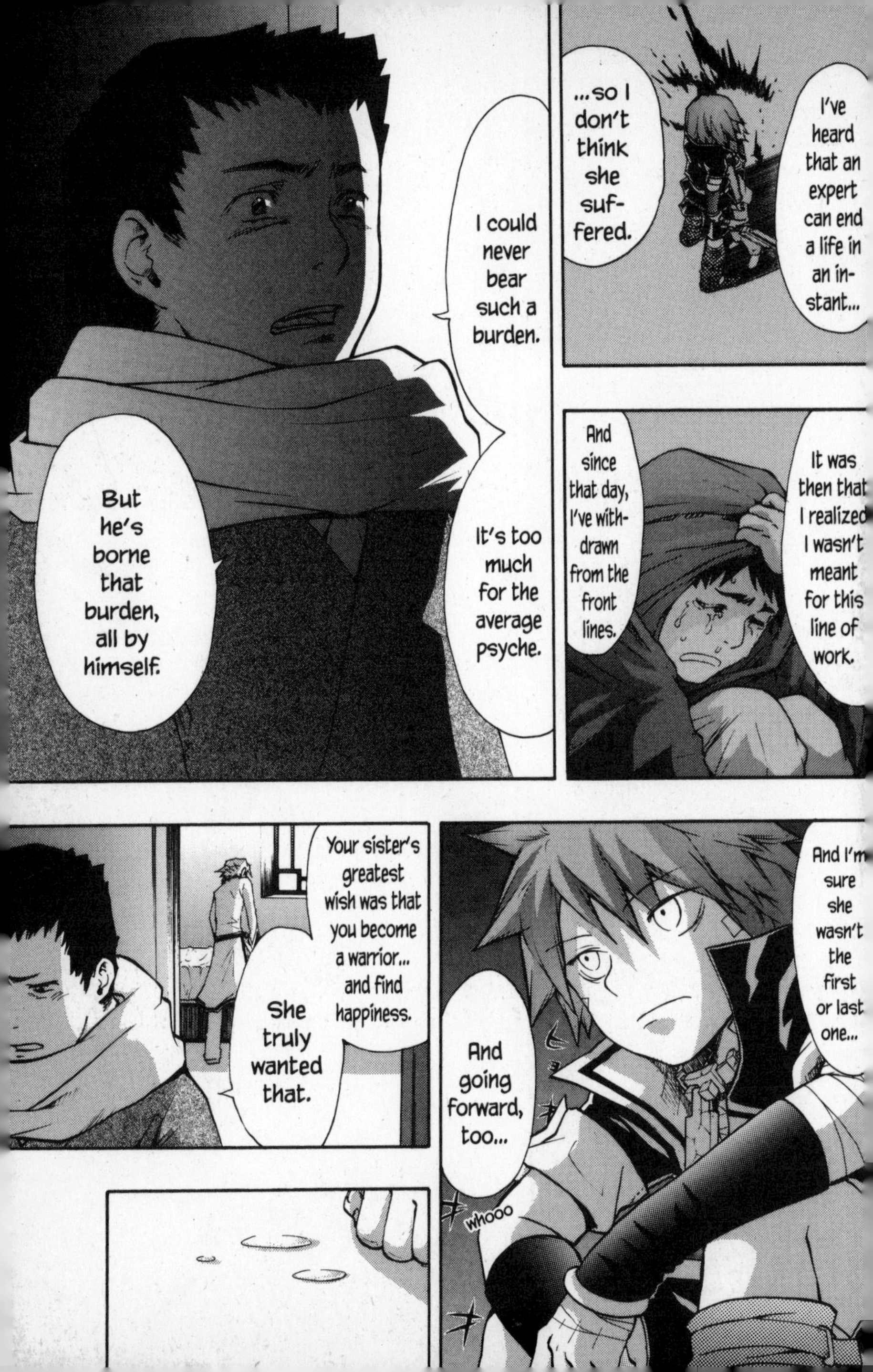
I've heard that an expert can end a life in an instant...
...so I don't think she suffered.
It was then that I realized I wasn't meant for this line of work.
And since that day, I've withdrawn from the front lines.
I could never bear such a burden.
It's too much for the average psyche.
But he's borne that burden, all by himself.
And I'm sure she wasn't the first or last one...
And going forward, too...
whooo
Your sister's greatest wish was that you become a warrior... and find happiness.
She truly wanted that.

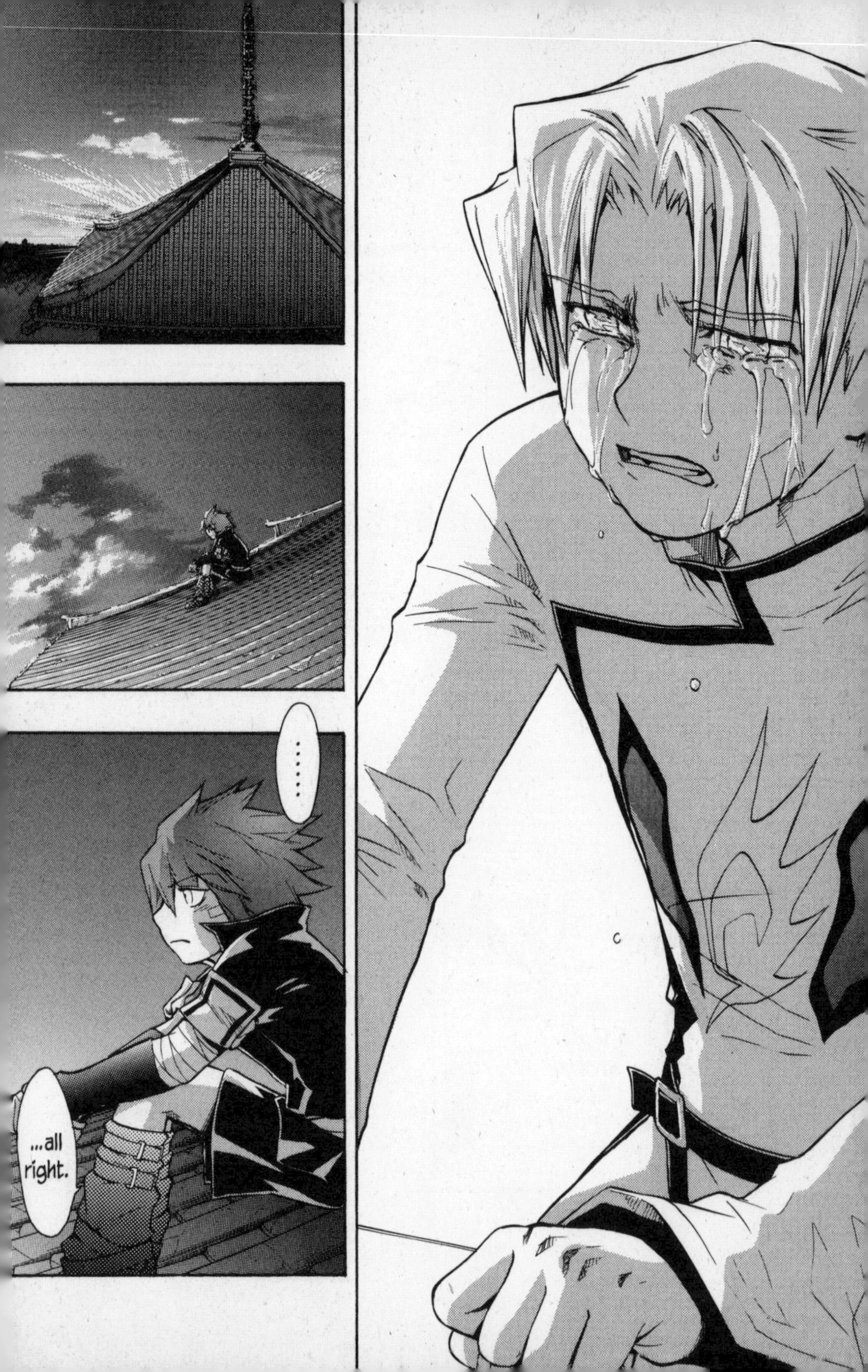
......
...all right.

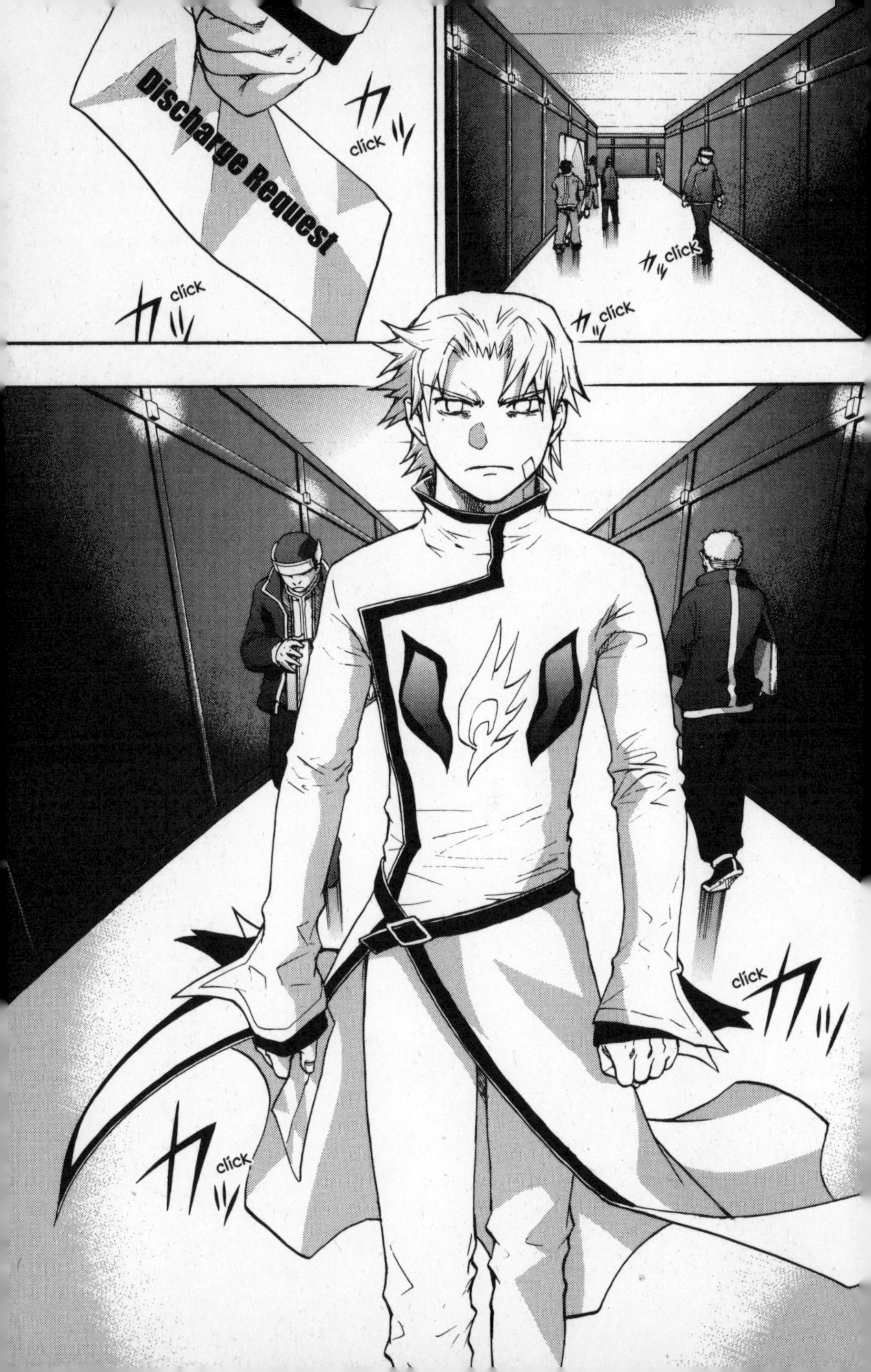

カッ click
カッ click
Discharge Request
カッ click
カッ click
カッ click
カッ click

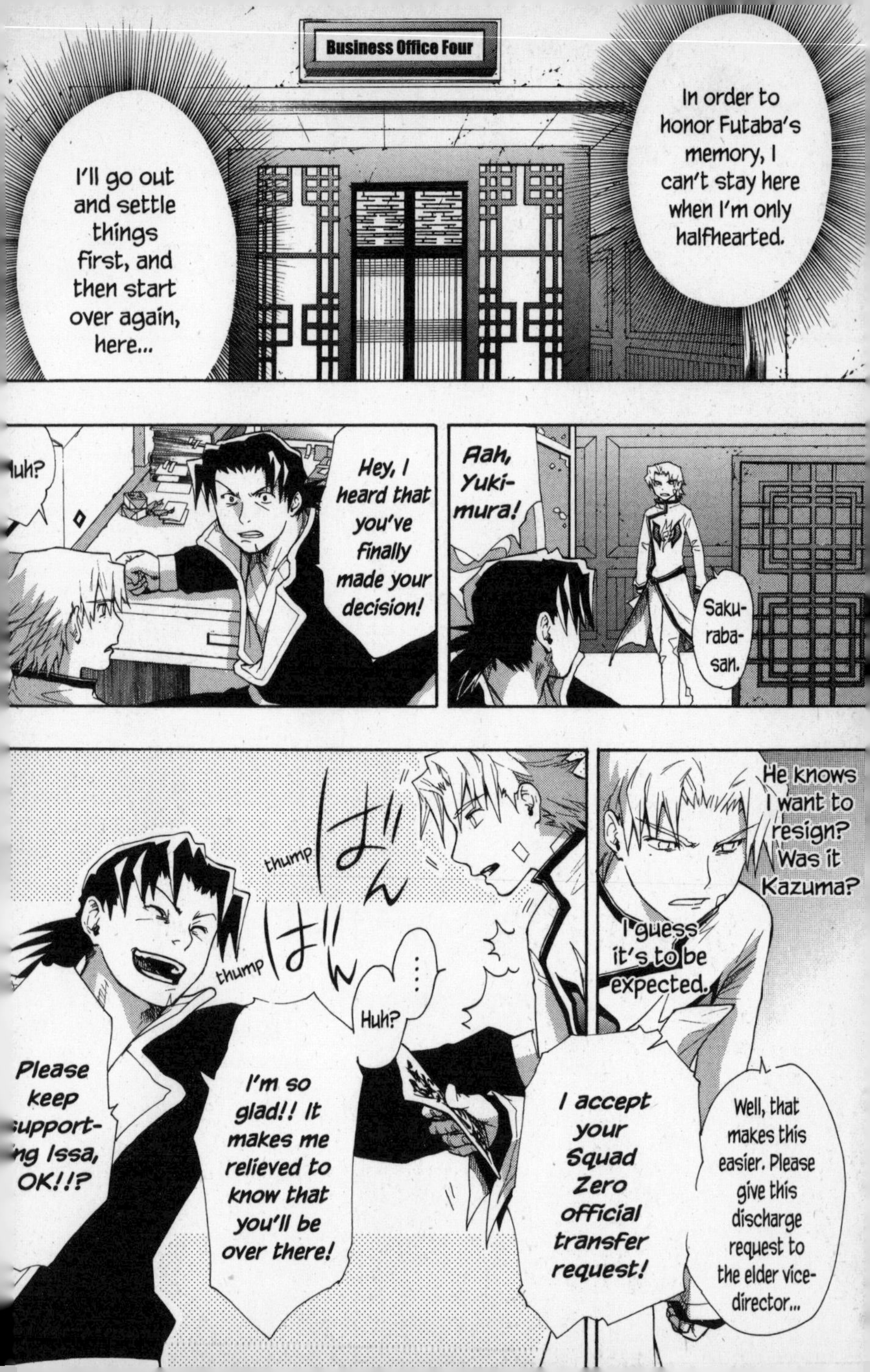
Business Office Four
In order to honor Futaba's memory, I can't stay here when I'm only halfhearted.
I'll go out and settle things first, and then start over again, here...
Aah, Yukimura!
Saku-raba-san.
Hey, I heard that you've finally made your decision!
uh?
He knows I want to resign? Was it Kazuma?
I guess it's to be expected.
Well, that makes this easier. Please give this discharge request to the elder vice-director...
I accept your Squad Zero official transfer request!
thump
thump
...
Huh?
I'm so glad!! It makes me relieved to know that you'll be over there!
Please keep upport-ng Issa, OK!!?

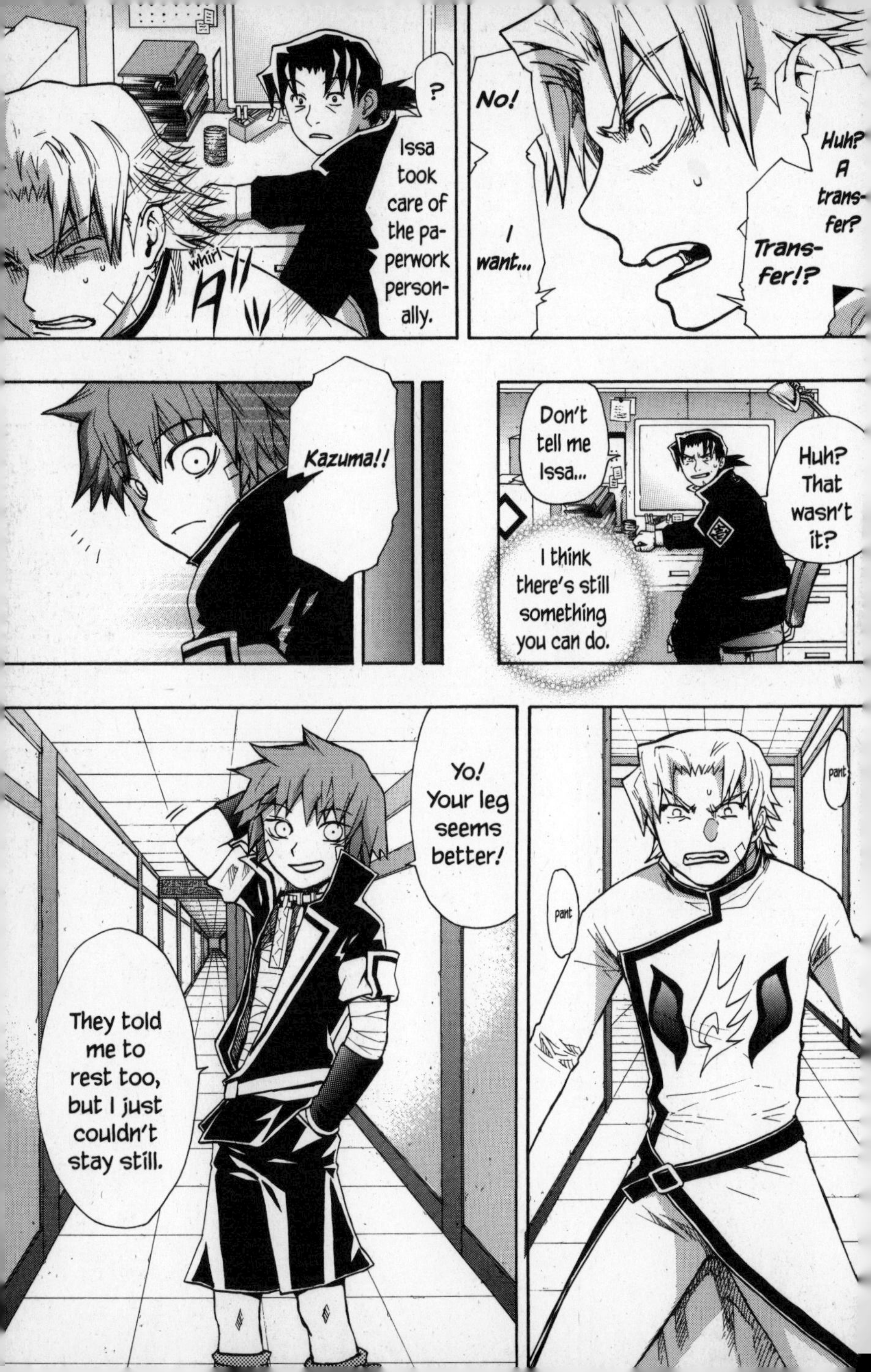
Huh? A transfer?
Transfer!?
No!
I want...
?
Issa took care of the paperwork personally.
whirl
Huh? That wasn't it?
Don't tell me Issa...
I think there's still something you can do.
Kazuma!!
pant
pant
Yo! Your leg seems better!
They told me to rest too, but I just couldn't stay still.

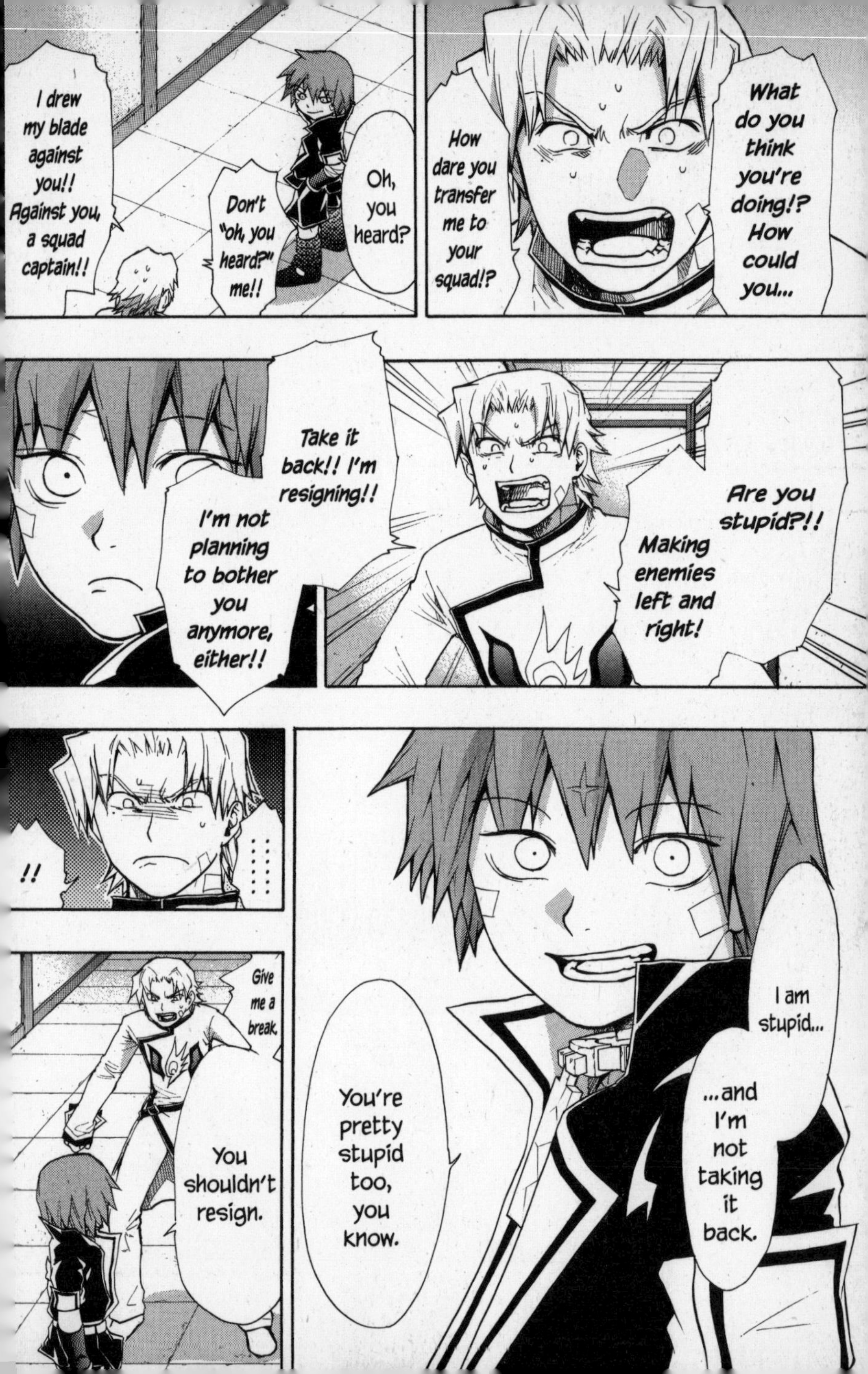
What do you think you're doing!? How could you...
How dare you transfer me to your squad!?
Oh, you heard?
Don't "oh, you heard?" me!!
I drew my blade against you!! Against you, a squad captain!!
Are you stupid?!!
Making enemies left and right!
Take it back!! I'm resigning!!
I'm not planning to bother you anymore, either!!
I am stupid...
...and I'm not taking it back.
You're pretty stupid too, you know.
!!
Give me a break.
You shouldn't resign.

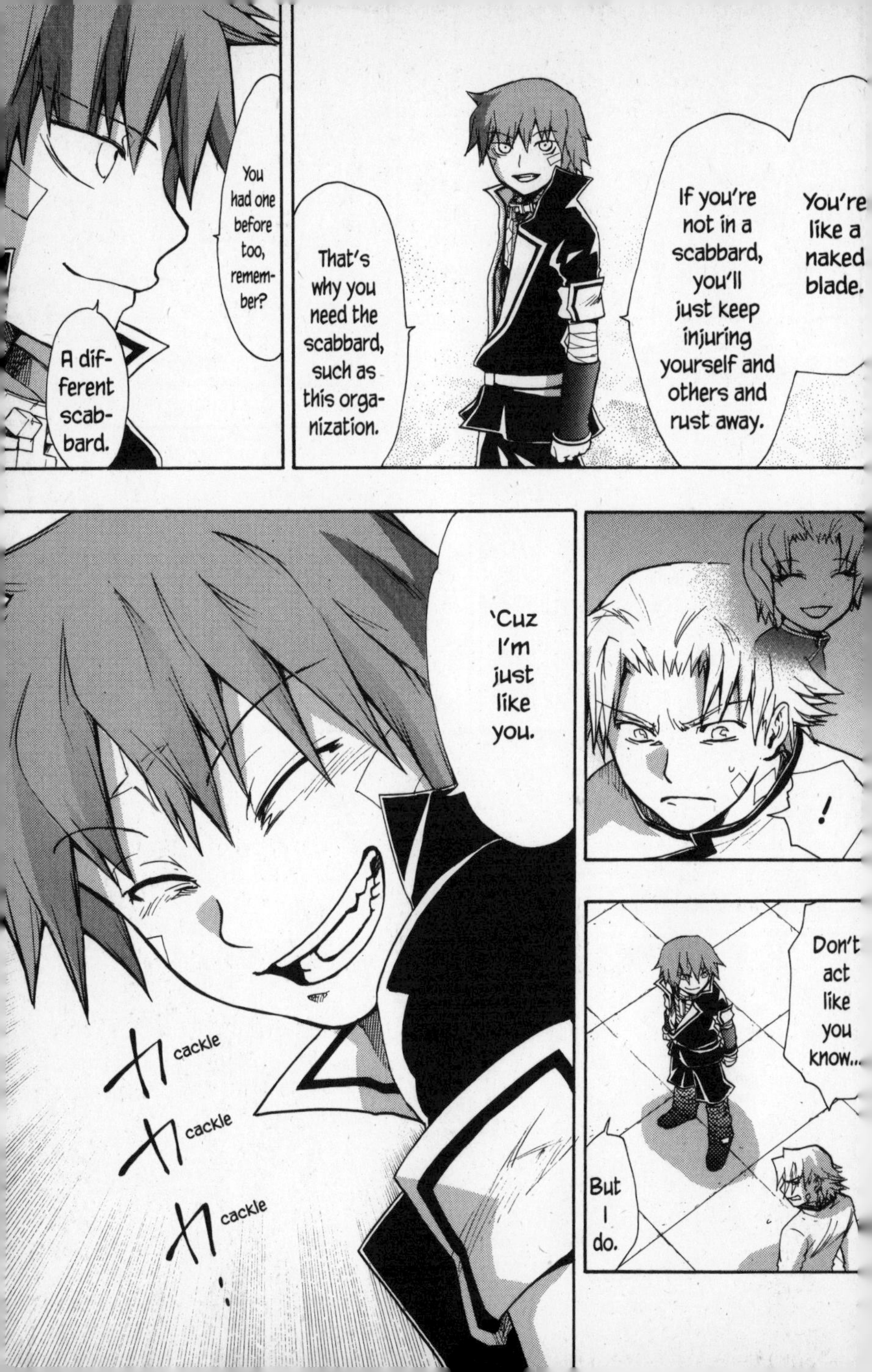
You're like a naked blade.
If you're not in a scabbard, you'll just keep injuring yourself and others and rust away.
That's why you need the scabbard, such as this organization.
You had one before too, remember?
A different scabbard.
!
Don't act like you know...
But I do.
'Cuz I'm just like you.
cackle
cackle
cackle

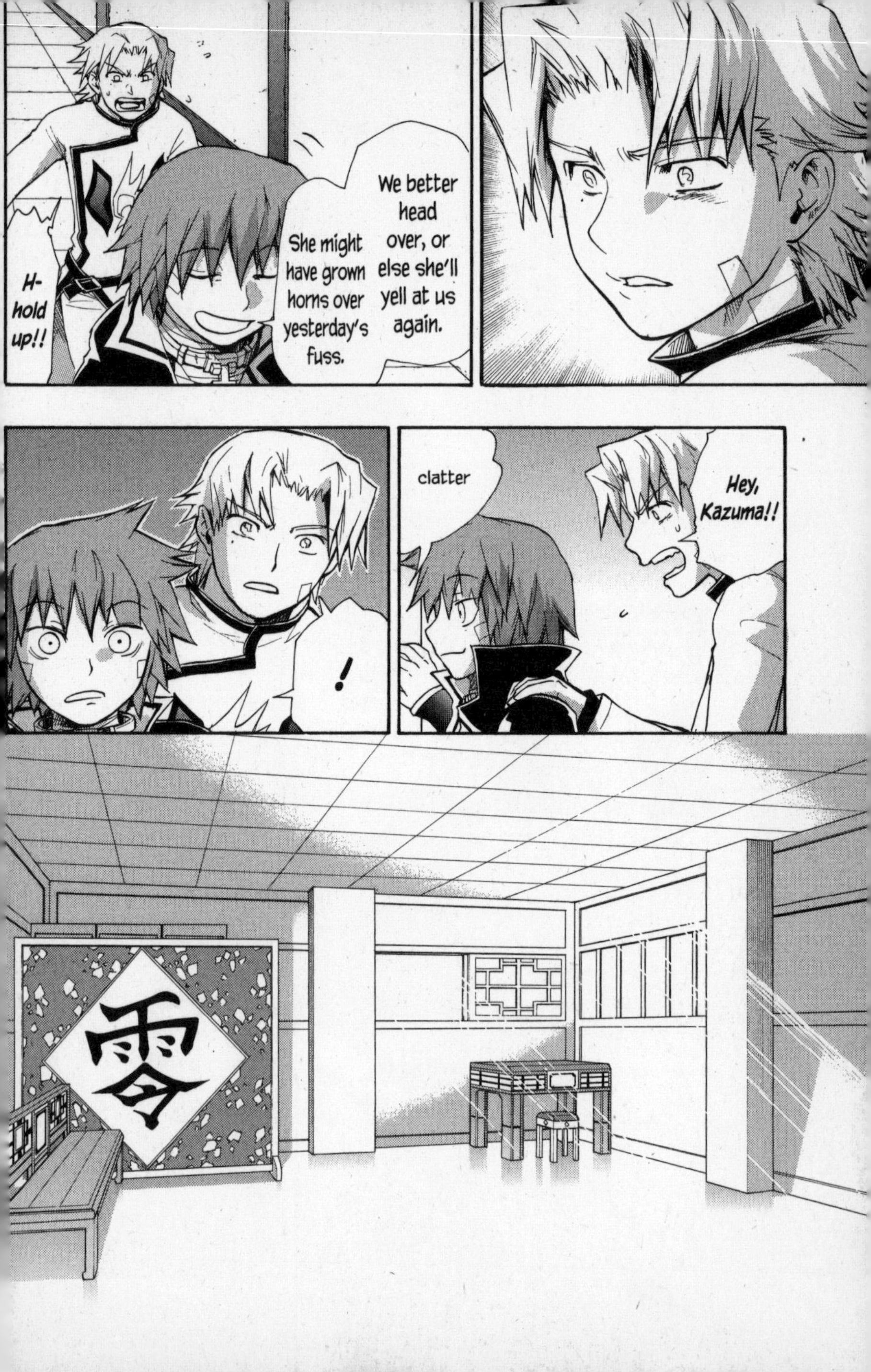
We better head over, or else she'll yell at us again.
She might have grown horns over yesterday's fuss.
H-hold up!!
Hey, Kazuma!!
clatter
!

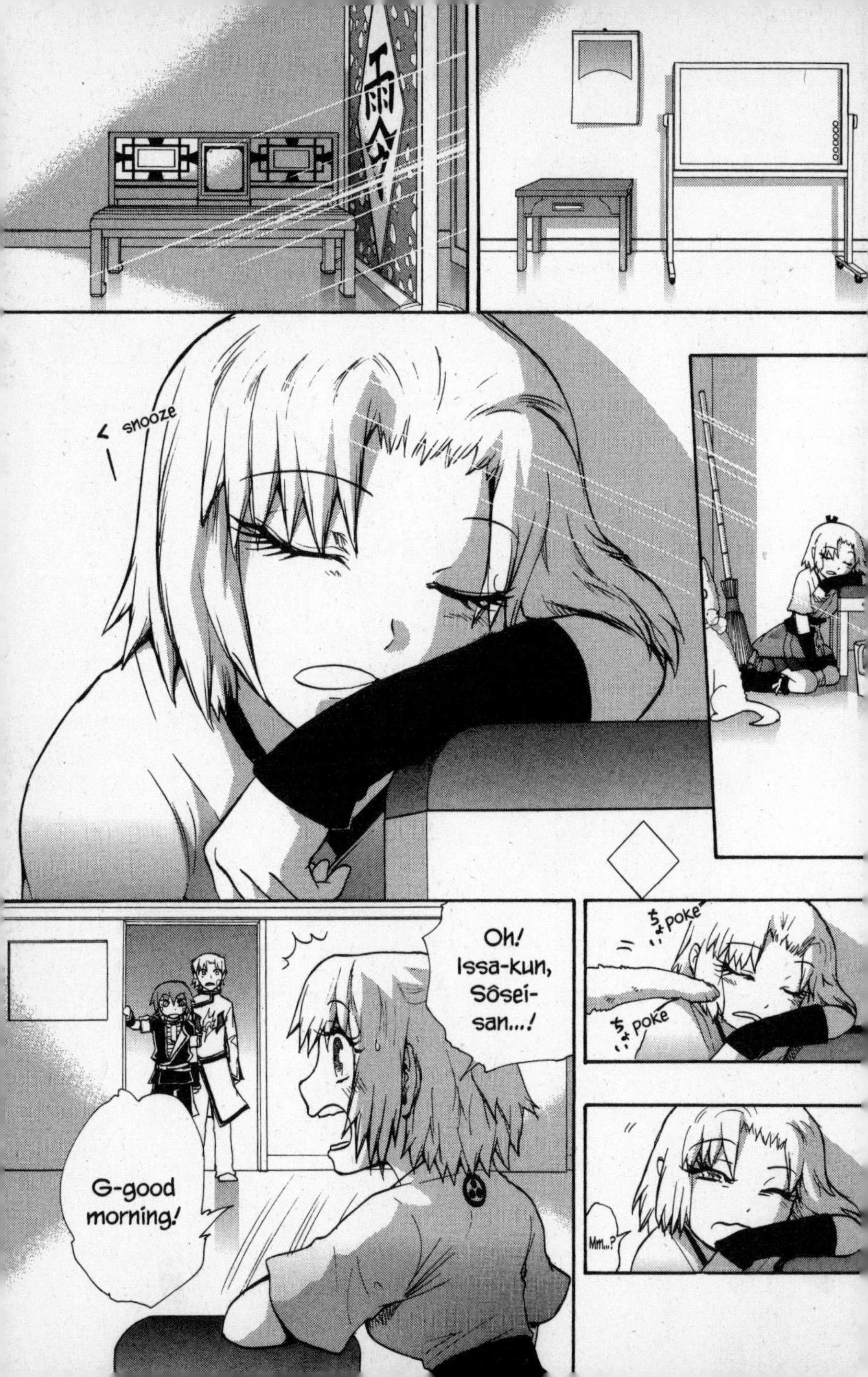
snooze
ちょい poke
ちょい poke
Mm...?
Oh! Issa-kun, Sôsei-san...!
G-good morning!

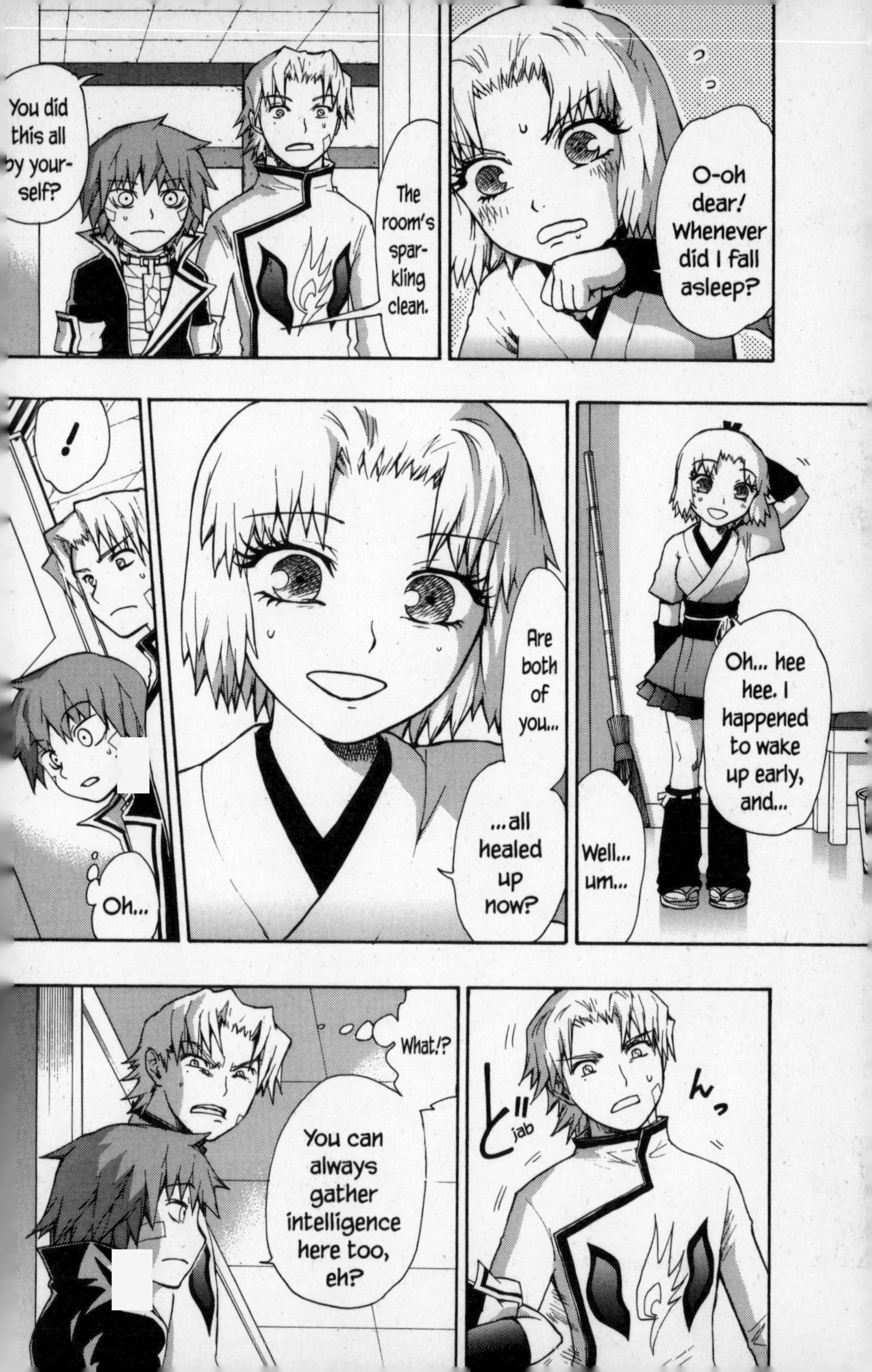
O-oh dear! Whenever did I fall asleep?
The room's spar-kling clean.
You did this all by your-self?
Oh... hee hee. I happened to wake up early, and...
Well... um...
Are both of you...
...all healed up now?
!
Oh...
jab
What!?
You can always gather intelligence here too, eh?

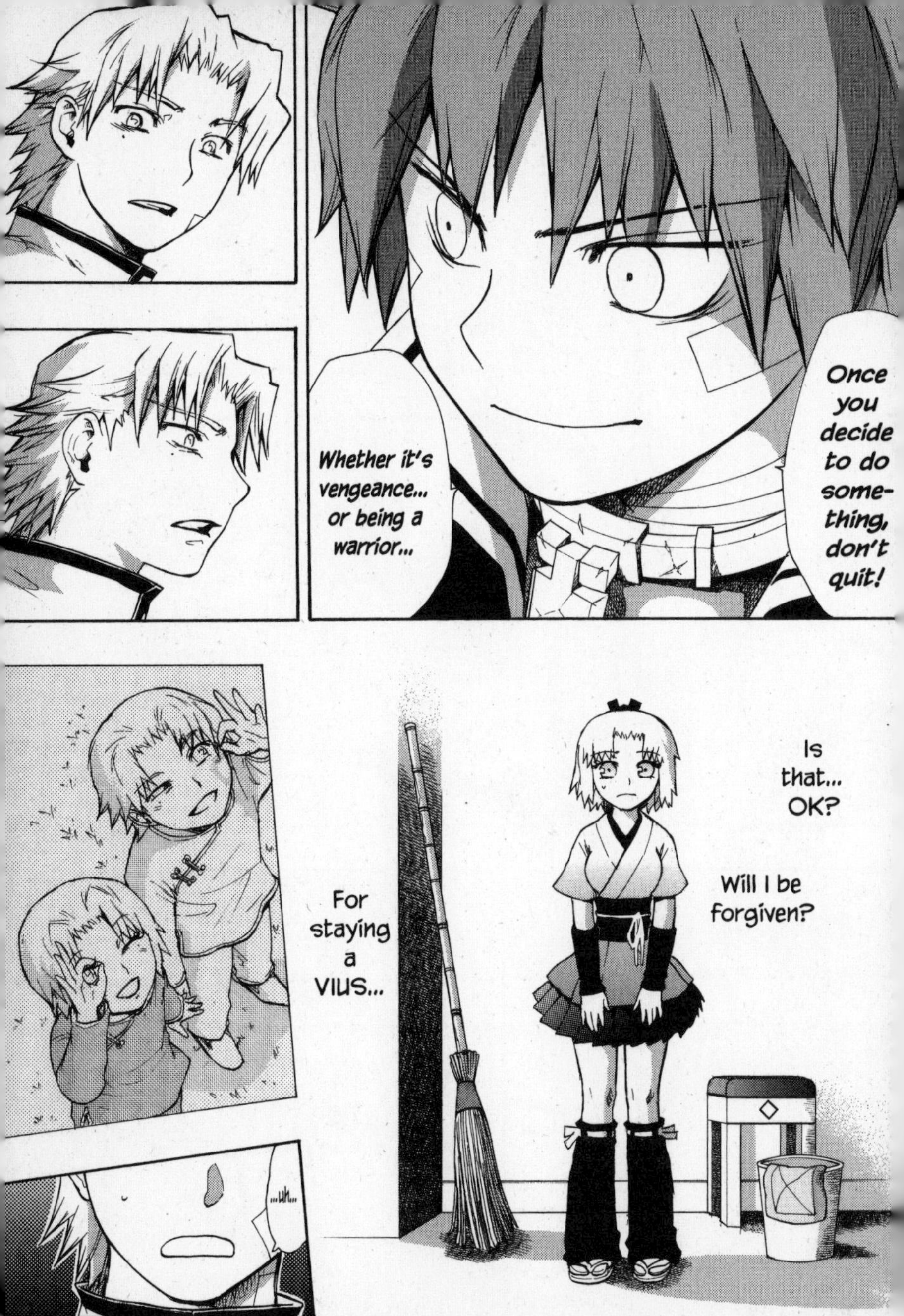
Once you decide to do something, don't quit!
Whether it's vengeance... or being a warrior...
Is that... OK?
Will I be forgiven?
For staying a VIUS...
...uh...

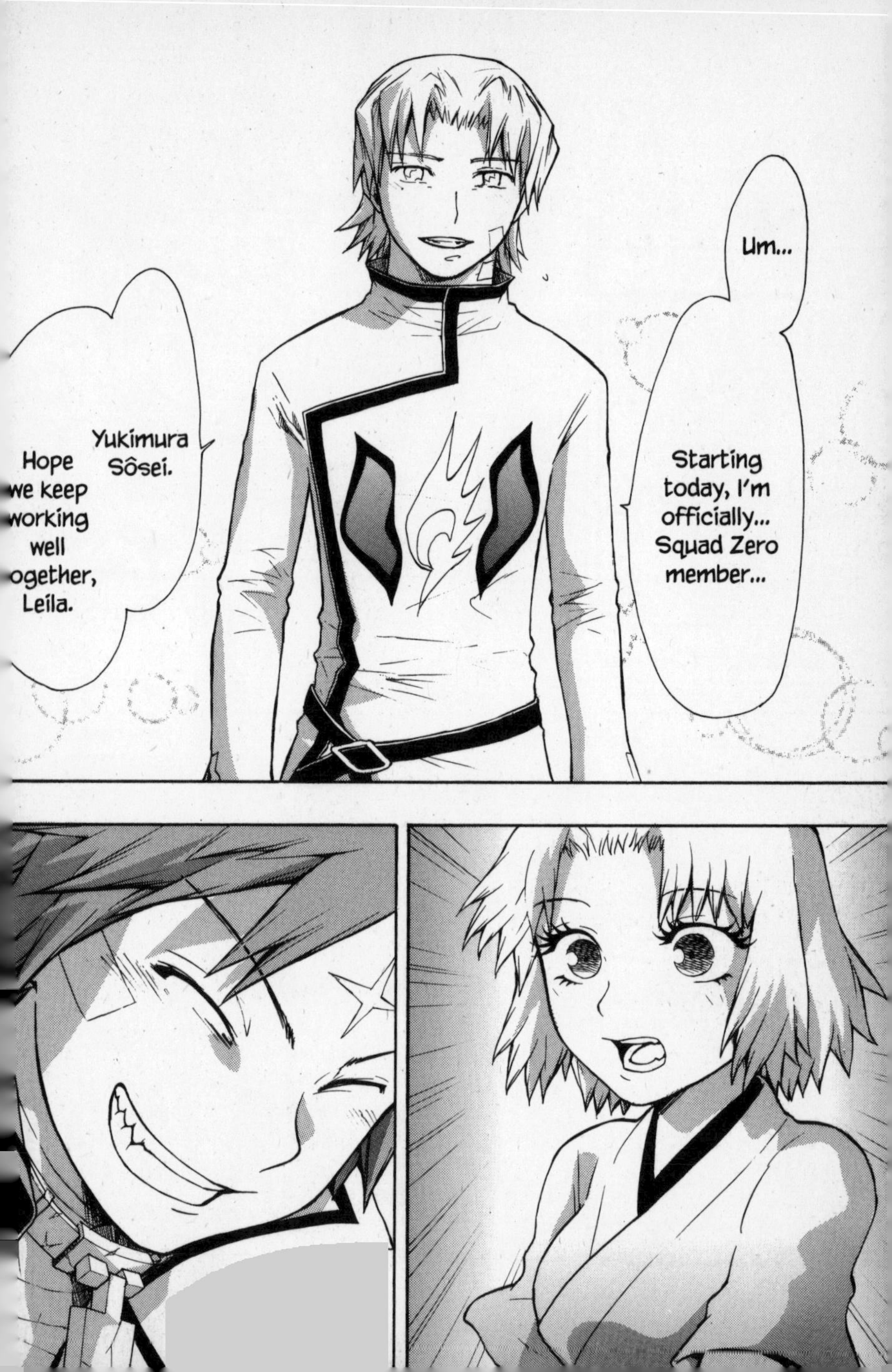
Um...
Starting today, I'm officially... Squad Zero member...
Yukimura Sôsei.
Hope we keep working well ogether, Leila.

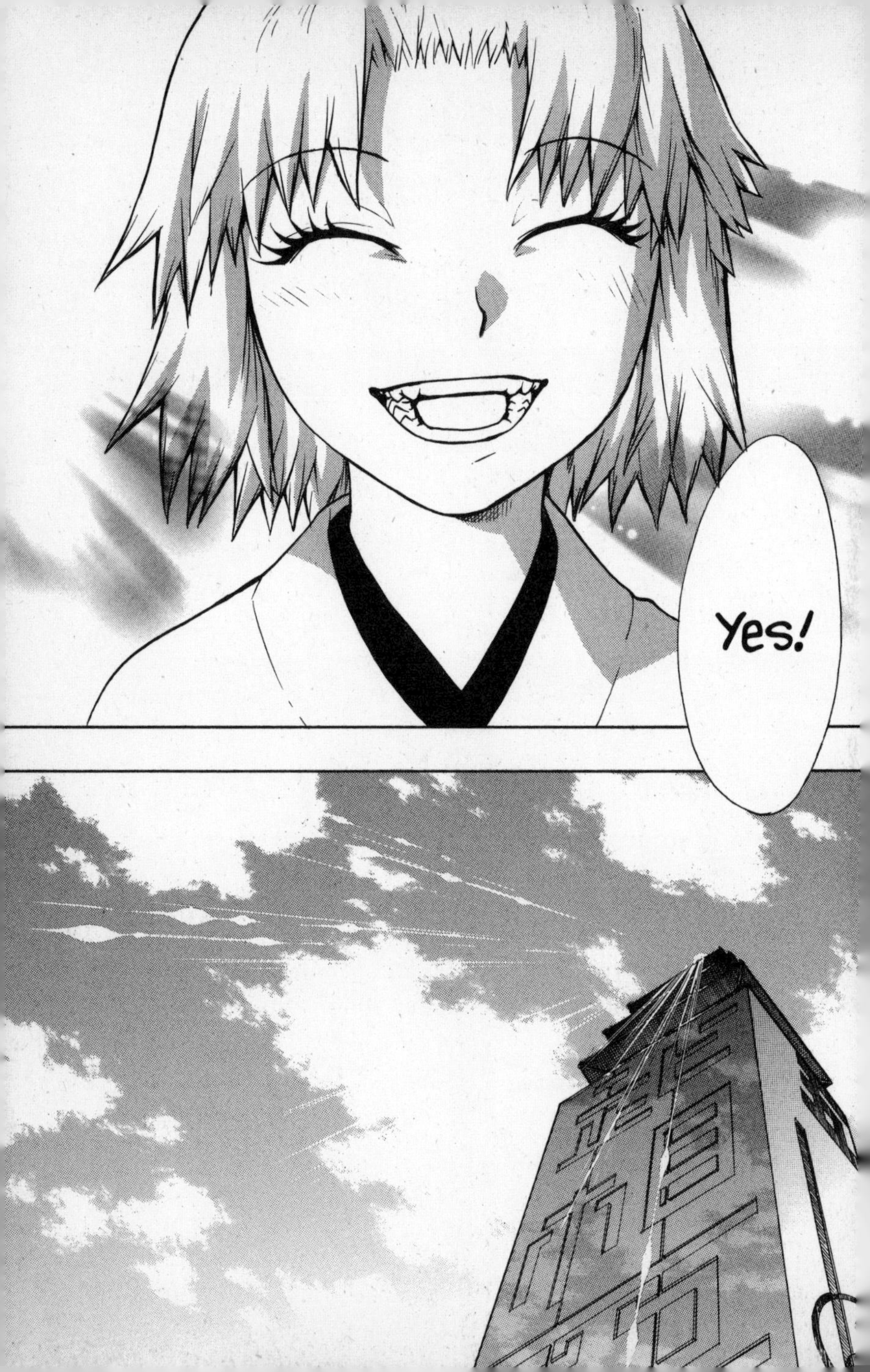
Yes!

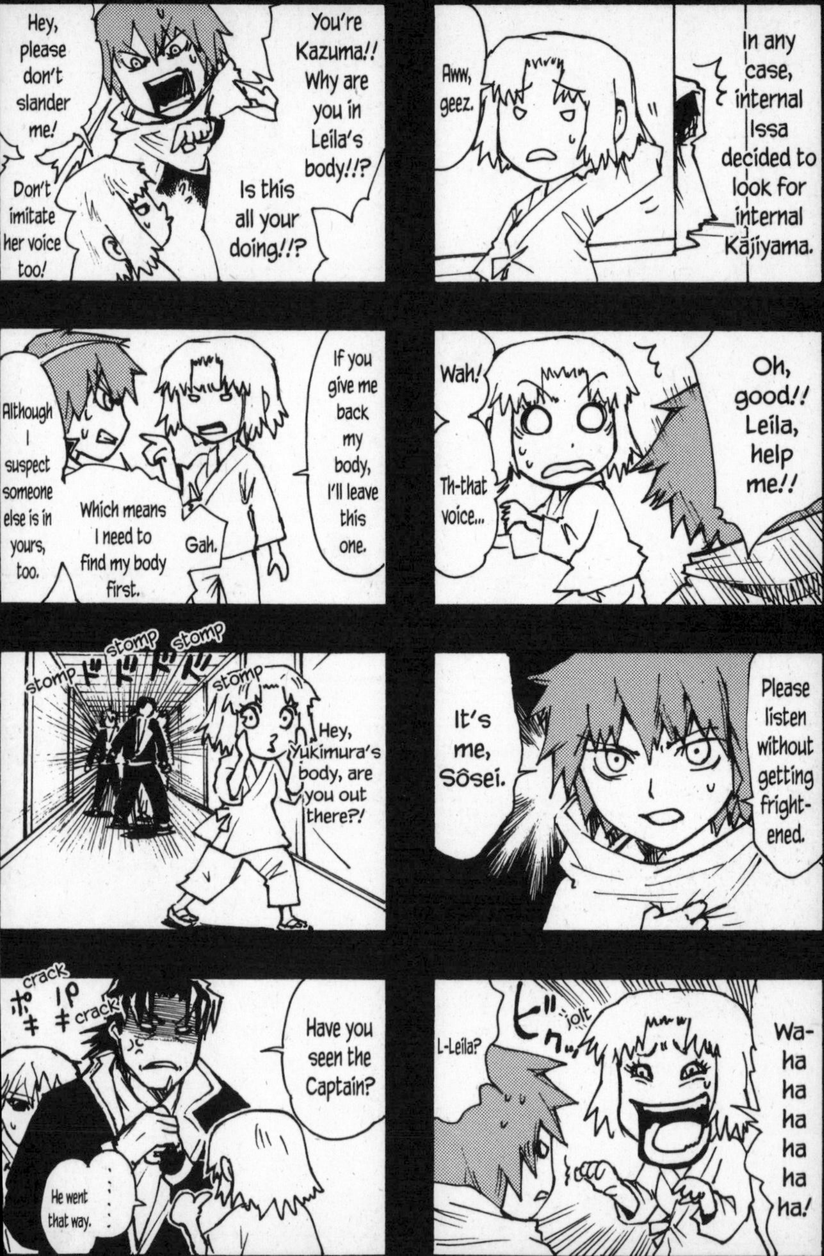
In any case, internal Issa decided to look for internal Kajiyama.
Aww, geez.
You're Kazuma!! Why are you in Leila's body!!?
Is this all your doing!!?
Hey, please don't slander me!
Don't imitate her voice too!
Oh, good!! Leila, help me!!
Wah!
Th-that voice...
If you give me back my body, I'll leave this one.
Although I suspect someone else is in yours, too.
Gah.
Which means I need to find my body first.
Please listen without getting fright-ened.
It's me, Sôsei.
stomp
stomp
stomp
stomp
Hey, Yukimura's body, are you out there?!
Wa-ha ha ha ha ha ha ha!
jolt
L-Leila?
Have you seen the Captain?
crack
crack
He went that way. ......

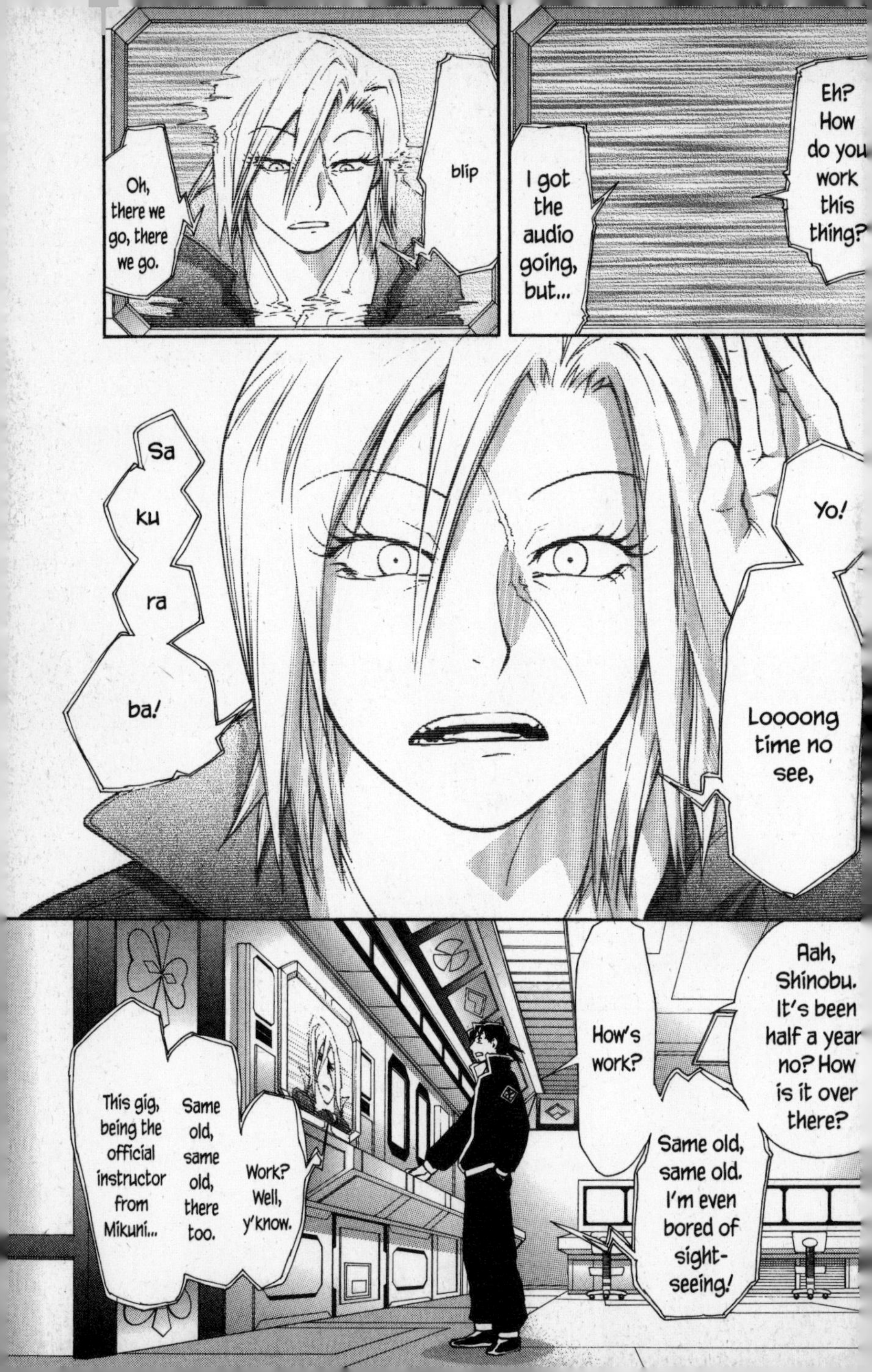
Eh? How do you work this thing?
I got the audio going, but...
blip
Oh, there we go, there we go.
Yo!
Loooong time no see,
Sa ku ra ba!
Aah, Shinobu. It's been half a year no? How is it over there?
How's work?
Same old, same old. I'm even bored of sight-seeing!
Work? Well, y'know.
Same old, same old, there too.
This gig, being the official instructor from Mikuni...

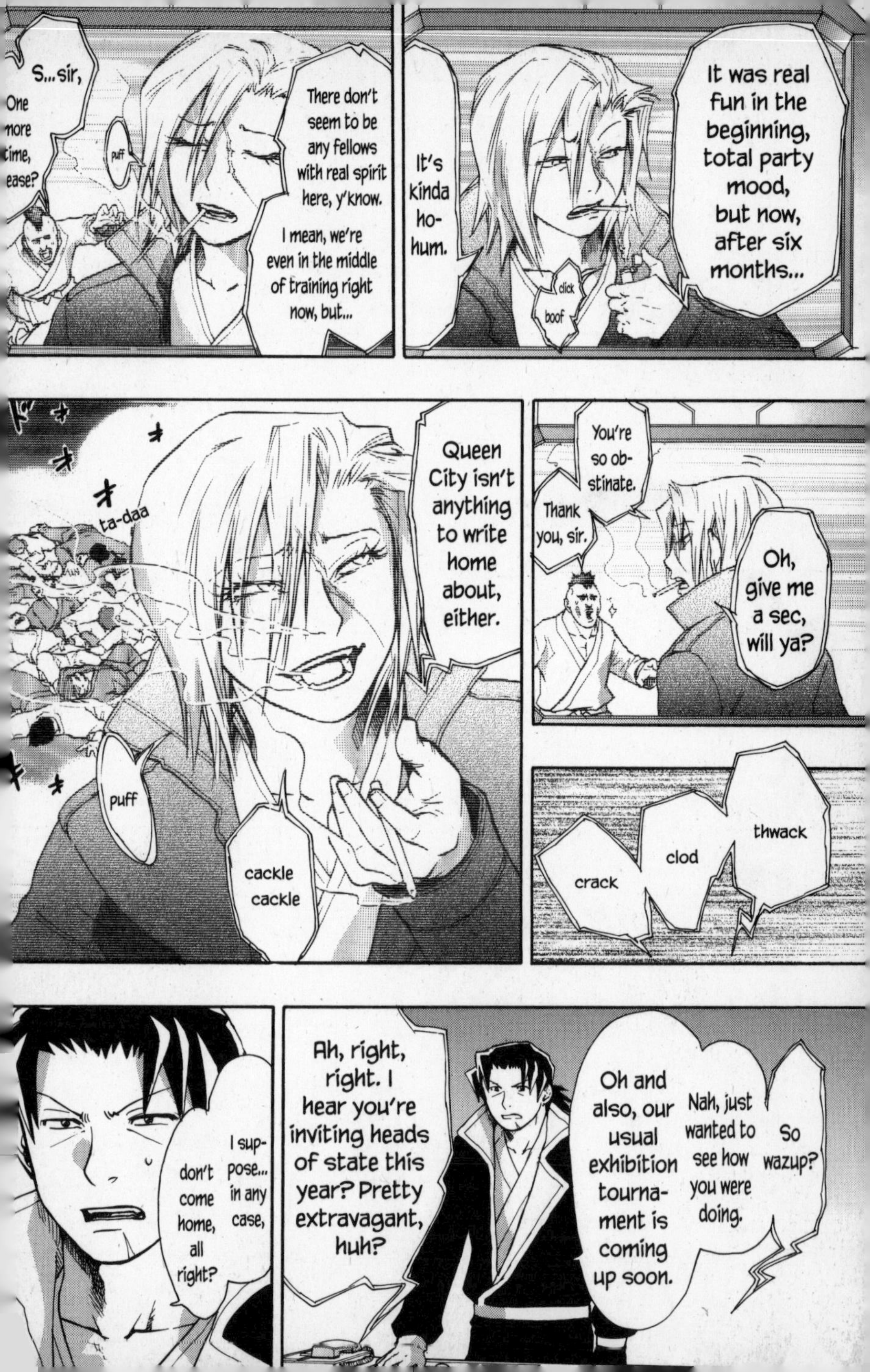
It was real fun in the beginning, total party mood, but now, after six months...
click
boof
It's kinda ho-hum.
There don't seem to be any fellows with real spirit here, y'know.
I mean, we're even in the middle of training right now, but...
puff
S...sir,
One more ime, ease?
You're so ob-stinate.
Thank you, sir.
Oh, give me a sec, will ya?
thwack
clod
crack
Queen City isn't anything to write home about, either.
ta-daa
puff
cackle cackle
So wazup?
Nah, just wanted to see how you were doing.
Oh and also, our usual exhibition tourna-ment is coming up soon.
Ah, right, right. I hear you're inviting heads of state this year? Pretty extravagant, huh?
I sup-pose... in any case,
don't come home, all right?

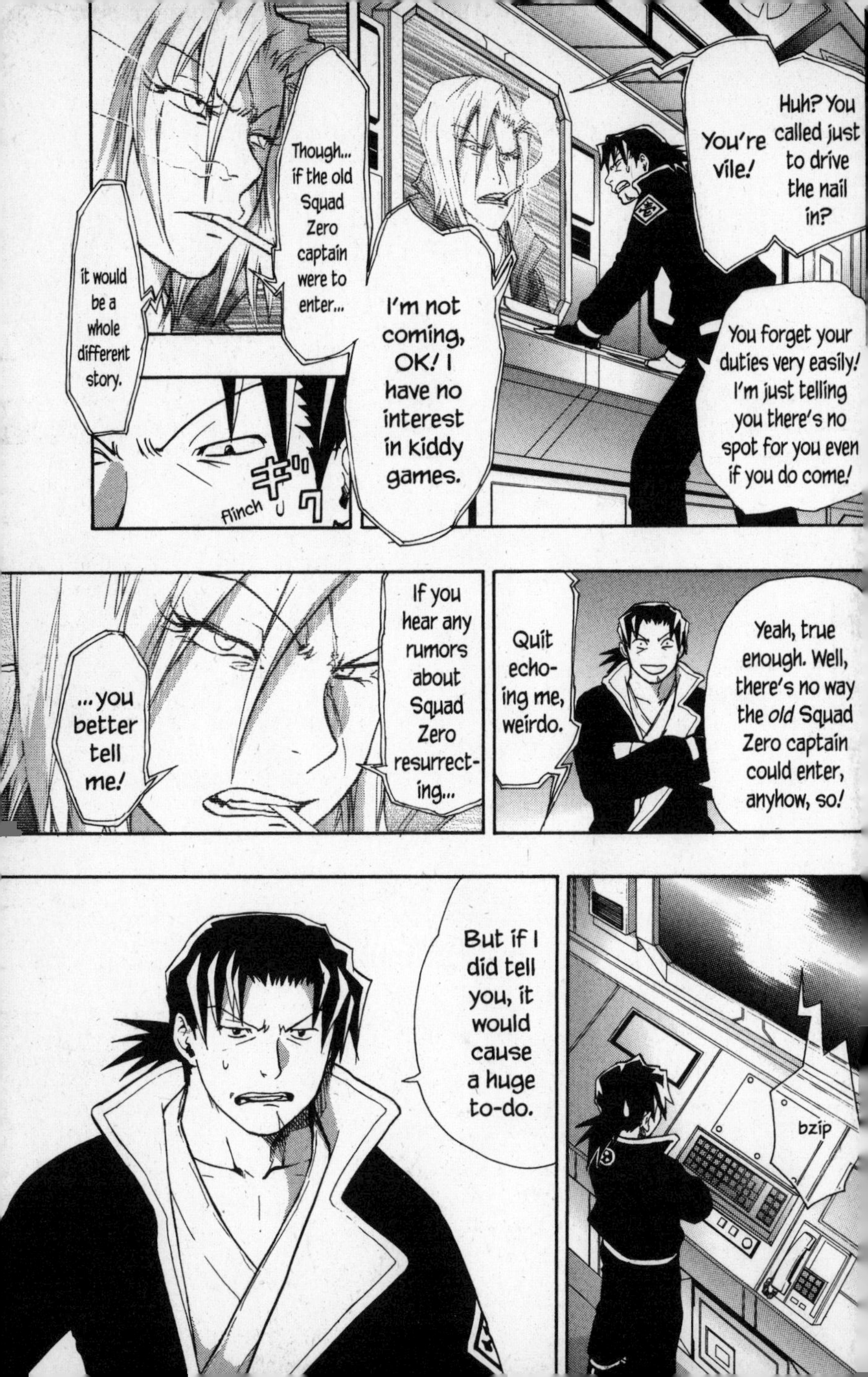
Huh? You called just to drive the nail in?
You're vile!
You forget your duties very easily! I'm just telling you there's no spot for you even if you do come!
I'm not coming, OK! I have no interest in kiddy games.
Though... if the old Squad Zero captain were to enter...
it would be a whole different story.
flinch
Yeah, true enough. Well, there's no way the *old* Squad Zero captain could enter, anyhow, so!
Quit echo-ing me, weirdo.
If you hear any rumors about Squad Zero resurrect-ing...
...you better tell me!
bzip
But if I did tell you, it would cause a huge to-do.

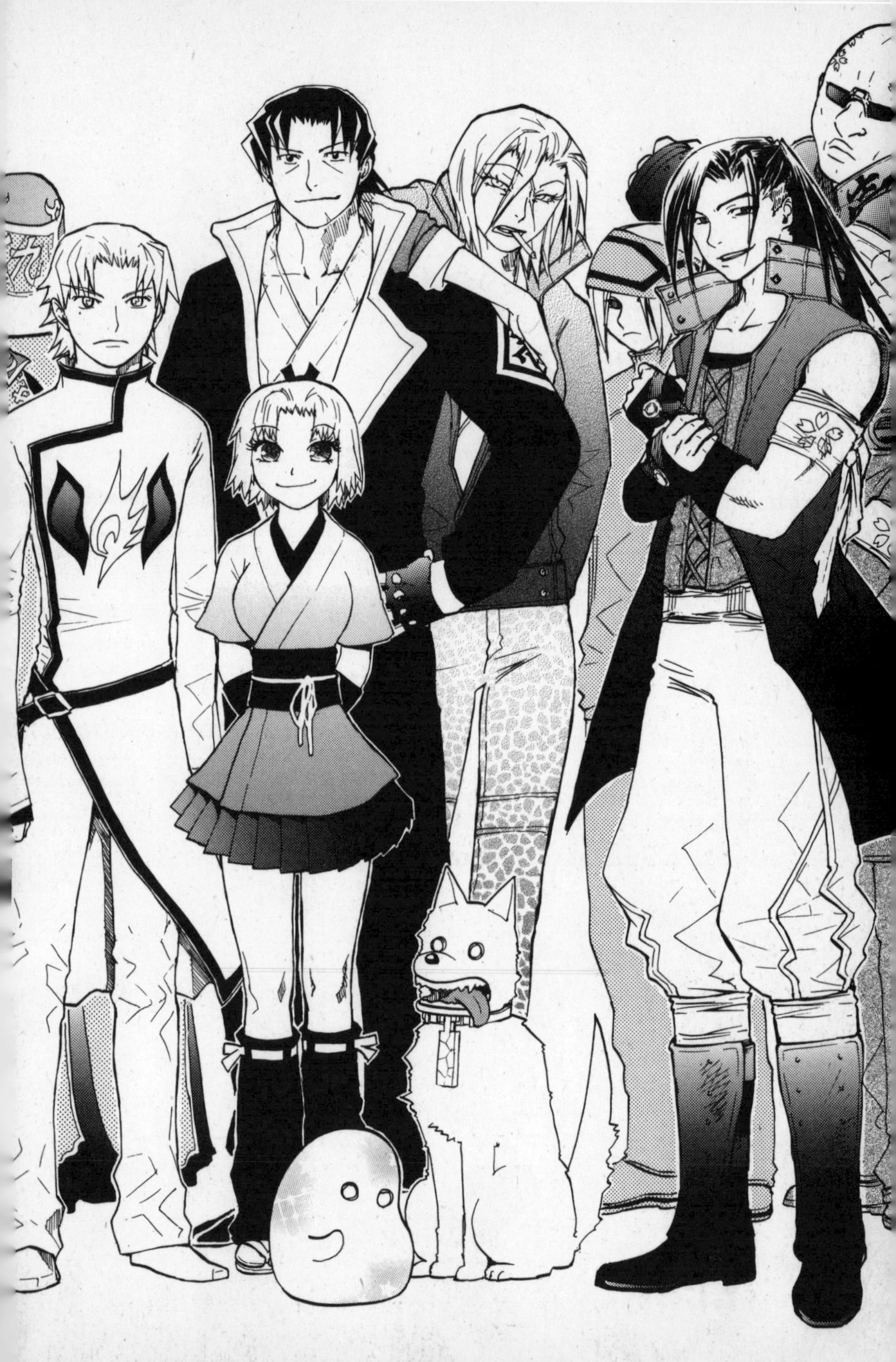

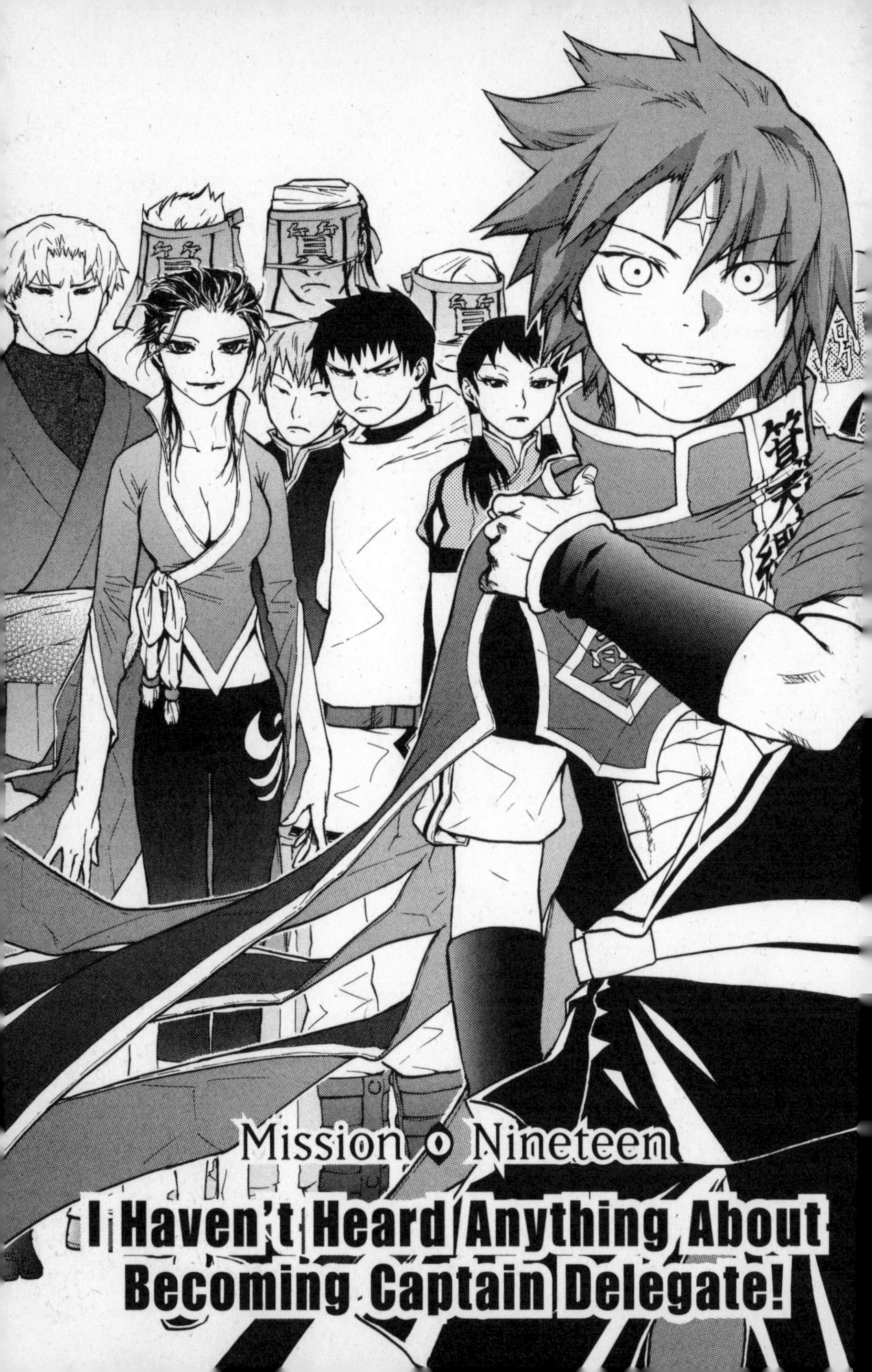
Mission Nineteen
I Haven't Heard Anything About Becoming Captain Delegate!

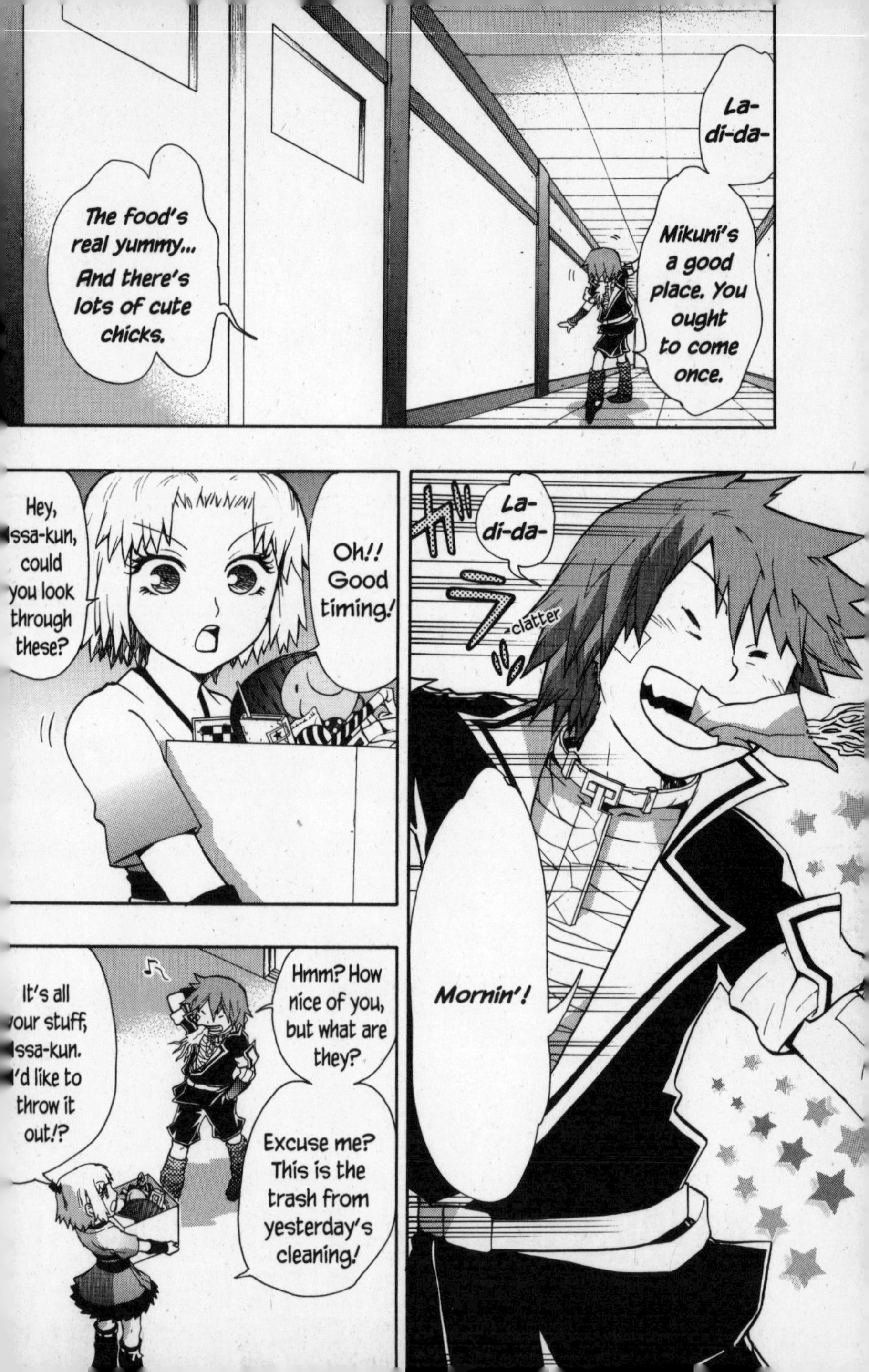
La-di-da-
Mikuni's a good place. You ought to come once.
The food's real yummy... And there's lots of cute chicks.
La-di-da-
clatter
Mornin'!
Oh!! Good timing!
Hey, ssa-kun, could you look through these?
Hmm? How nice of you, but what are they?
Excuse me? This is the trash from yesterday's cleaning!
It's all our stuff, ssa-kun. 'd like to throw it out!?

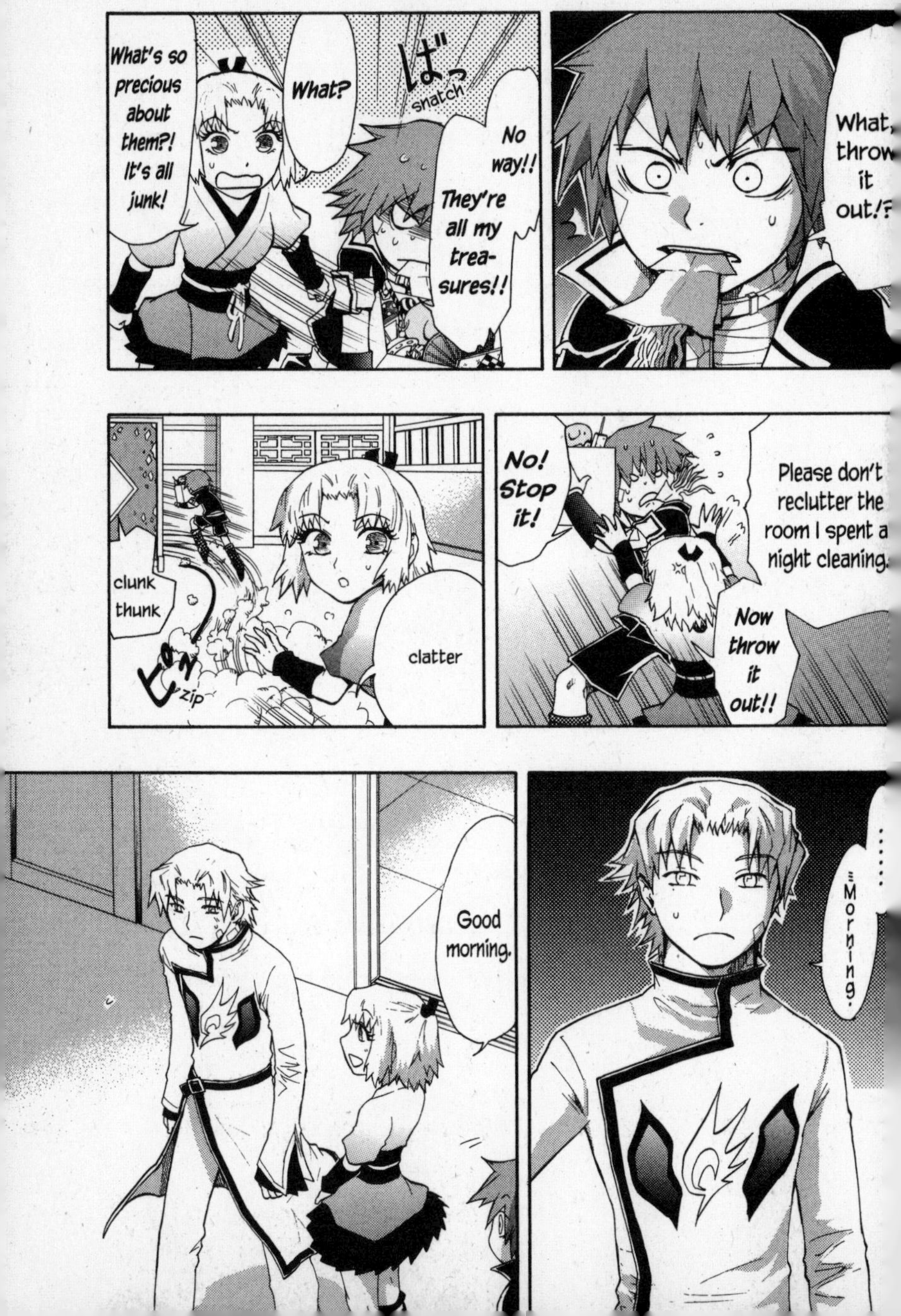
What, throw it out!?
ばっ
snatch
No way!! They're all my treasures!!
What?
What's so precious about them?! It's all junk!
Please don't reclutter the room I spent a night cleaning.
No! Stop it!
Now throw it out!!
clatter
clunk thunk
zip
......
...Morning.
Good morning.

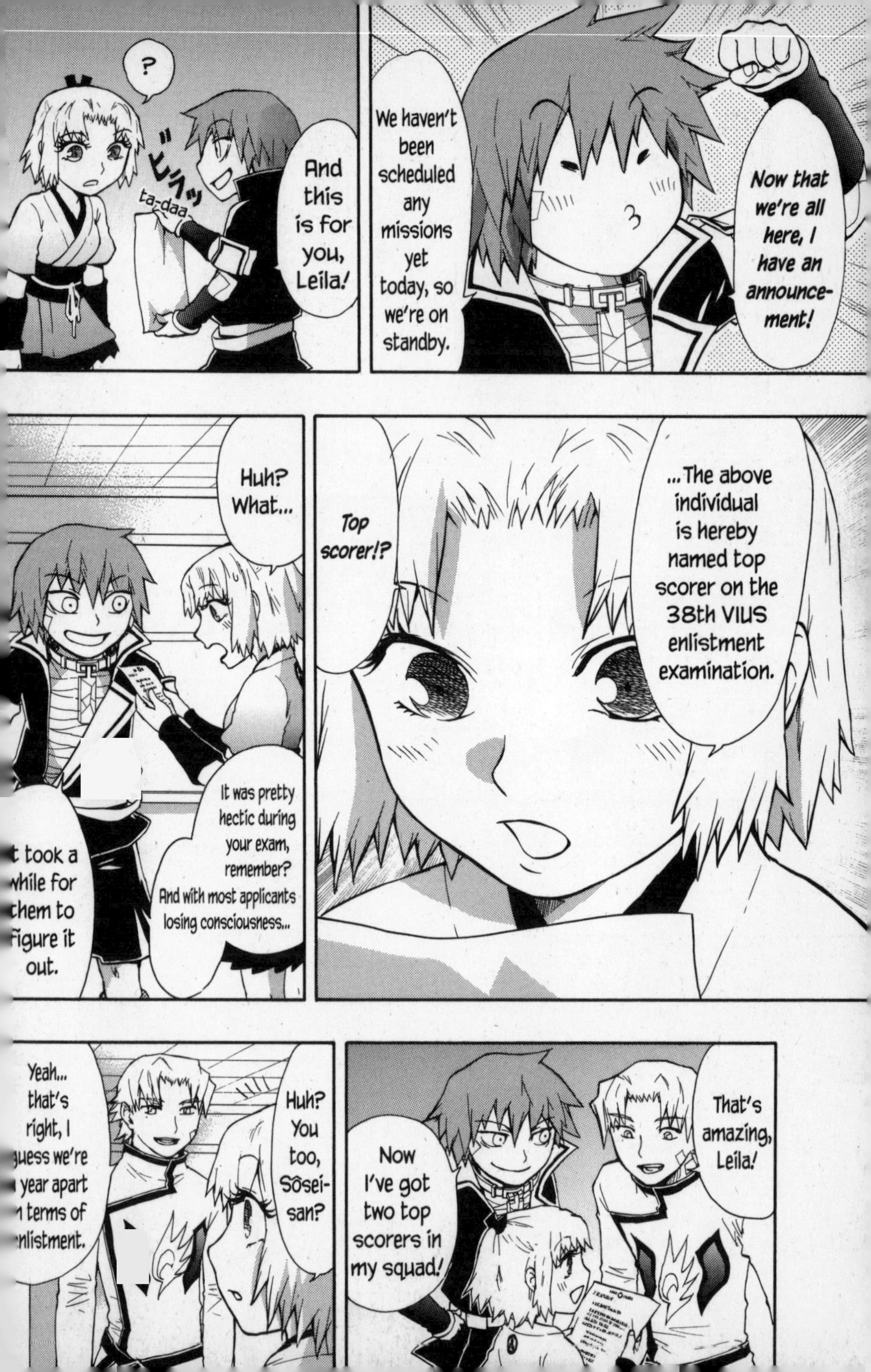
Now that we're all here, I have an announcement!
We haven't been scheduled any missions yet today, so we're on standby.
And this is for you, Leila!
ta-daa
?
...The above individual is hereby named top scorer on the 38th VIUS enlistment examination.
Top scorer!?
Huh? What...
It was pretty hectic during your exam, remember? And with most applicants losing consciousness...
t took a while for them to figure it out.
That's amazing, Leila!
Now I've got two top scorers in my squad!
Huh? You too, Sôsei-san?
Yeah... that's right, I guess we're year apart n terms of nlistment.

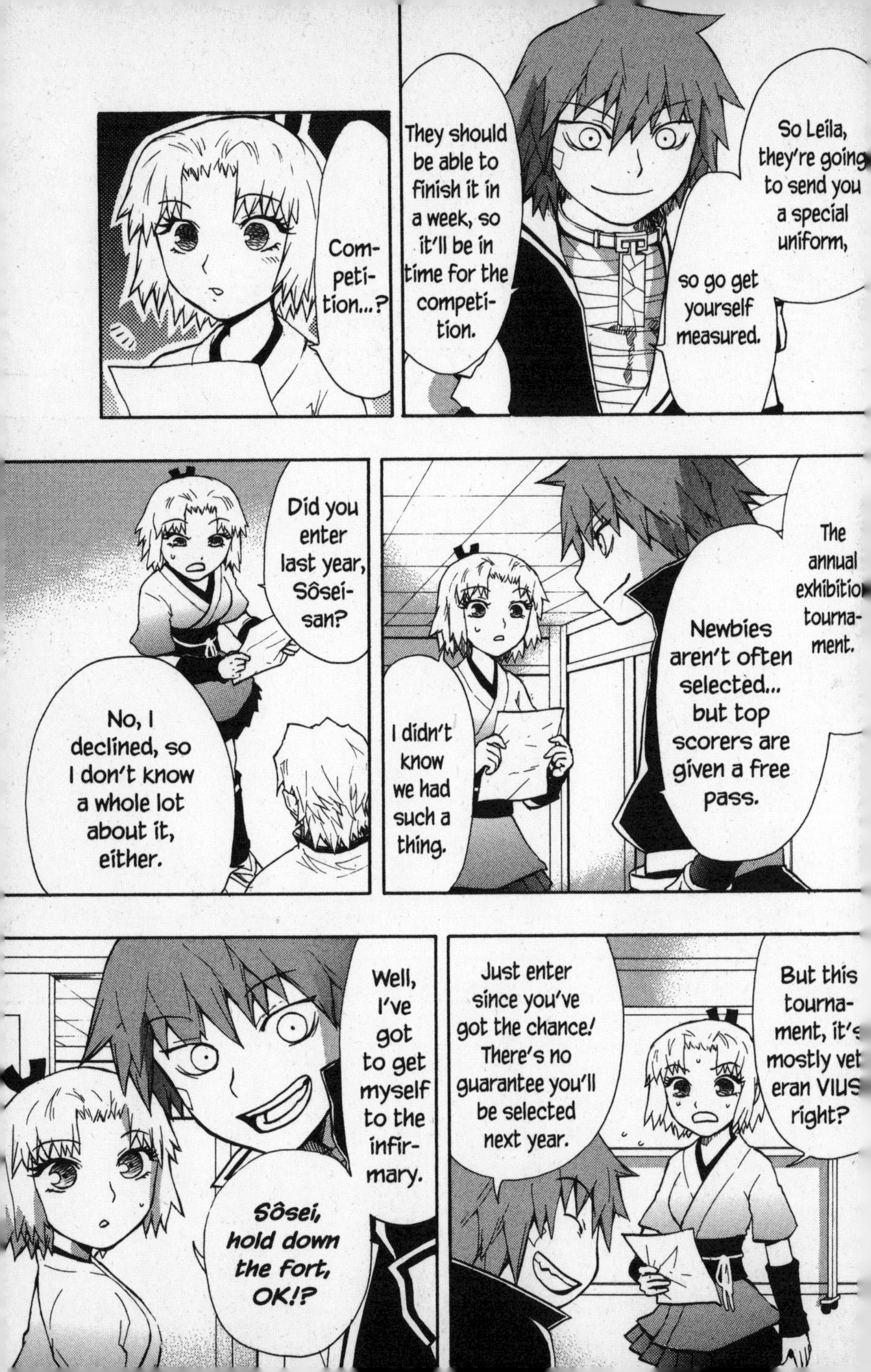
So Leila, they're going to send you a special uniform,
so go get yourself measured.
They should be able to finish it in a week, so it'll be in time for the competition.
Competition...?
The annual exhibitio tournament.
Newbies aren't often selected... but top scorers are given a free pass.
I didn't know we had such a thing.
Did you enter last year, Sôsei-san?
No, I declined, so I don't know a whole lot about it, either.
But this tournament, it' mostly vet eran VIUS right?
Just enter since you've got the chance! There's no guarantee you'll be selected next year.
Well, I've got to get myself to the infirmary.
Sôsei, hold down the fort, OK!?

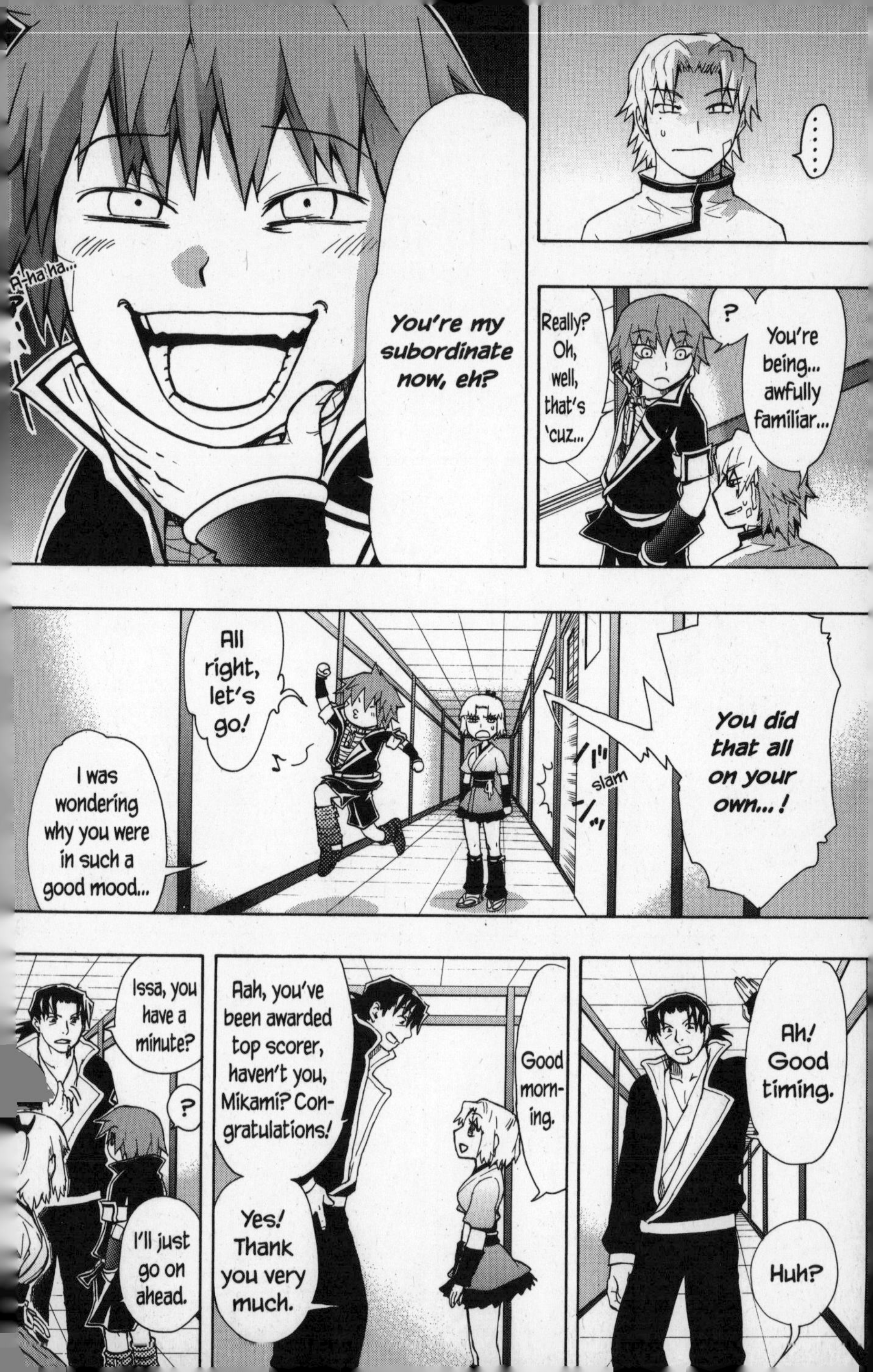
……
?
You're being... awfully familiar...
Really? Oh, well, that's 'cuz...
A-ha ha...
You're my subordinate now, eh?
You did that all on your own...!
slam
All right, let's go!
I was wondering why you were in such a good mood...
Ah! Good timing.
Huh?
Good morning.
Aah, you've been awarded top scorer, haven't you, Mikami? Congratulations!
Yes! Thank you very much.
Issa, you have a minute?
?
I'll just go on ahead.

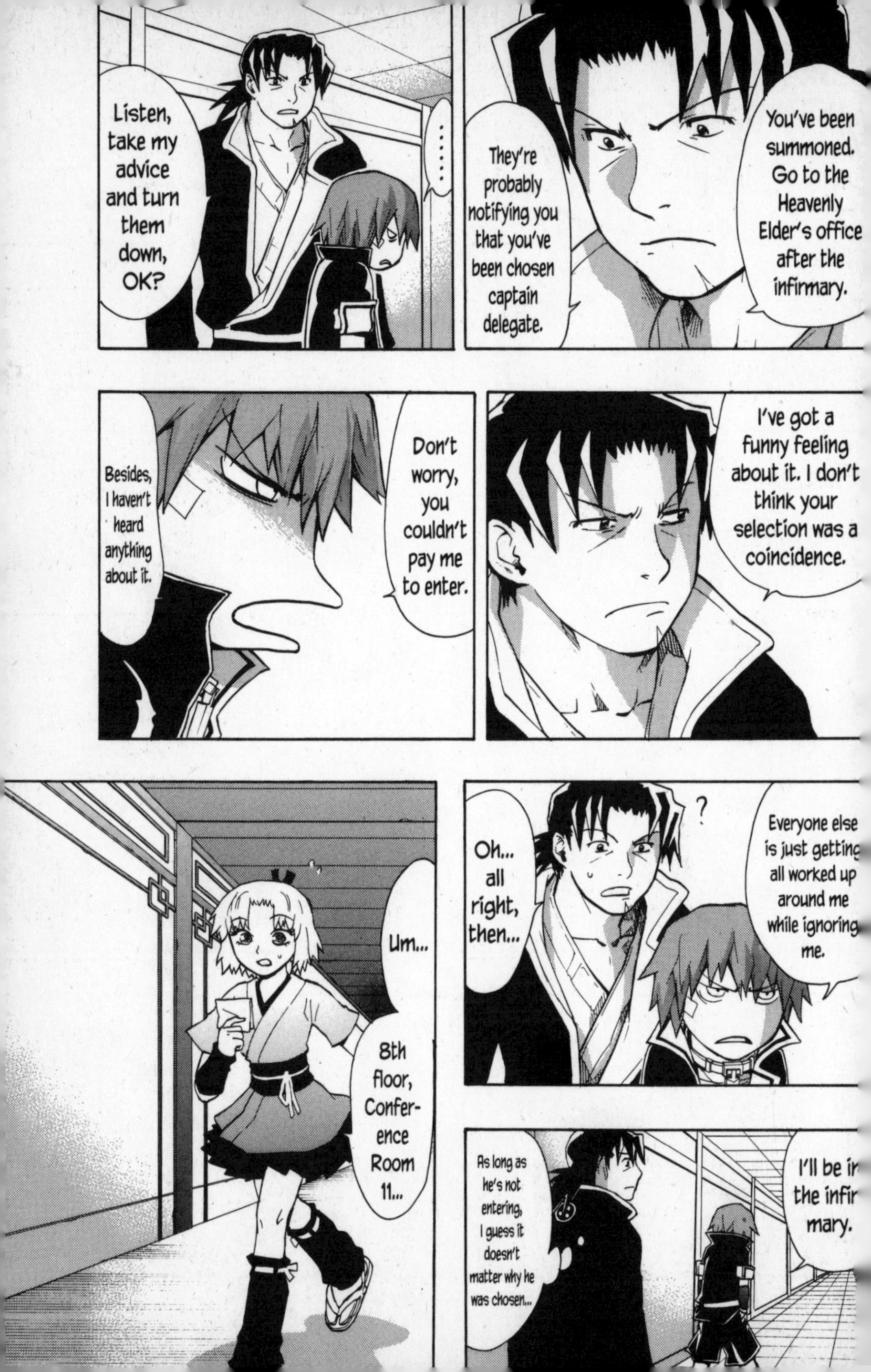
You've been summoned. Go to the Heavenly Elder's office after the infirmary.
They're probably notifying you that you've been chosen captain delegate.
Listen, take my advice and turn them down, OK?
......
I've got a funny feeling about it. I don't think your selection was a coincidence.
Don't worry, you couldn't pay me to enter.
Besides, I haven't heard anything about it.
Everyone else is just gettin all worked up around me while ignorin me.
?
Oh... all right, then...
I'll be i the infir mary.
As long as he's not entering, I guess it doesn't matter why he was chosen...
Um...
8th floor, Confer- ence Room 11...

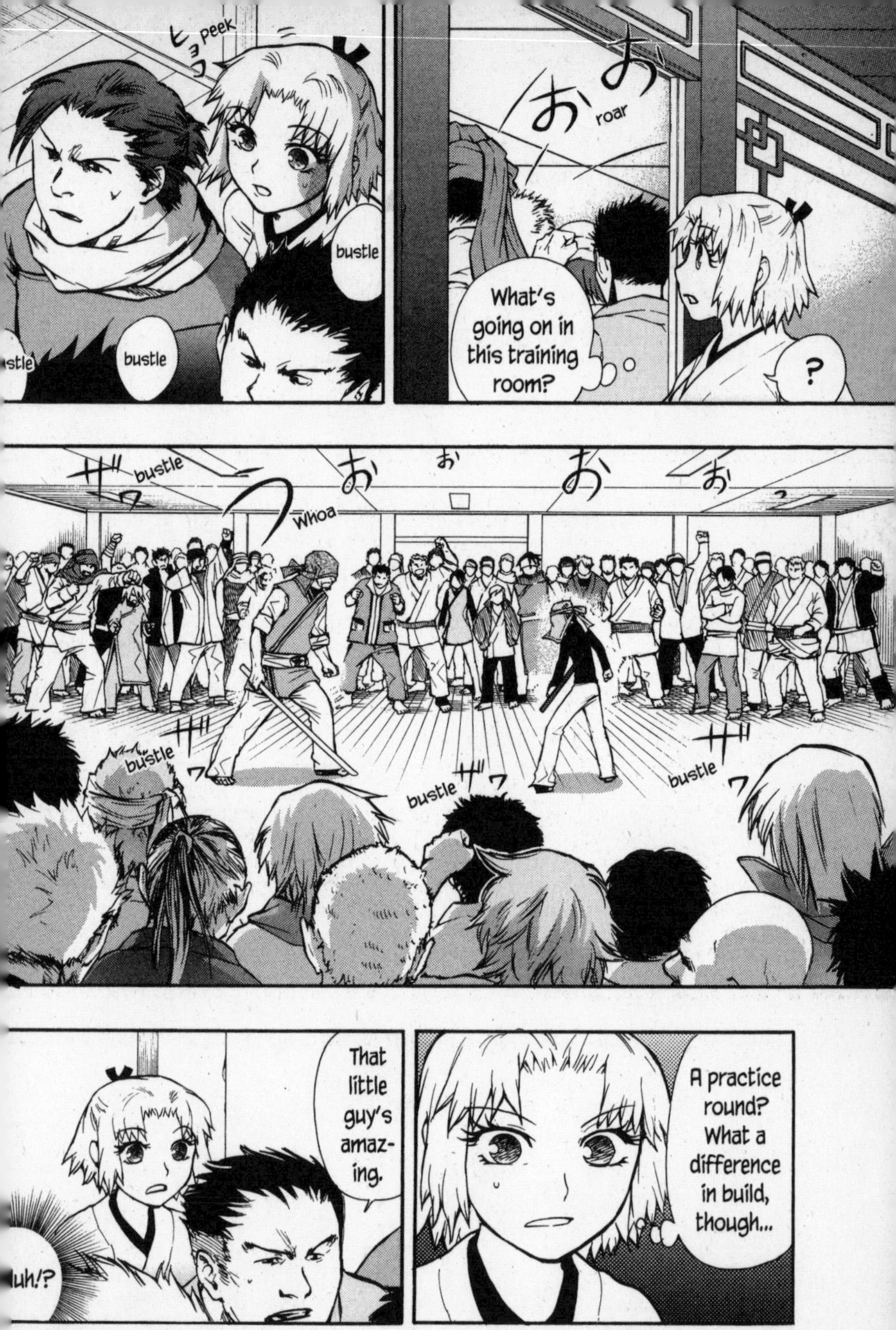

おお
roar
What's going on in this training room?
?
ヒョコ
peek
bustle
bustle
ザワ
bustle
おおおお
Whoa
ザワ
bustle
ザワ
bustle
ザワ
bustle
A practice round? What a difference in build, though...
That little guy's amaz-ing.
uh!?

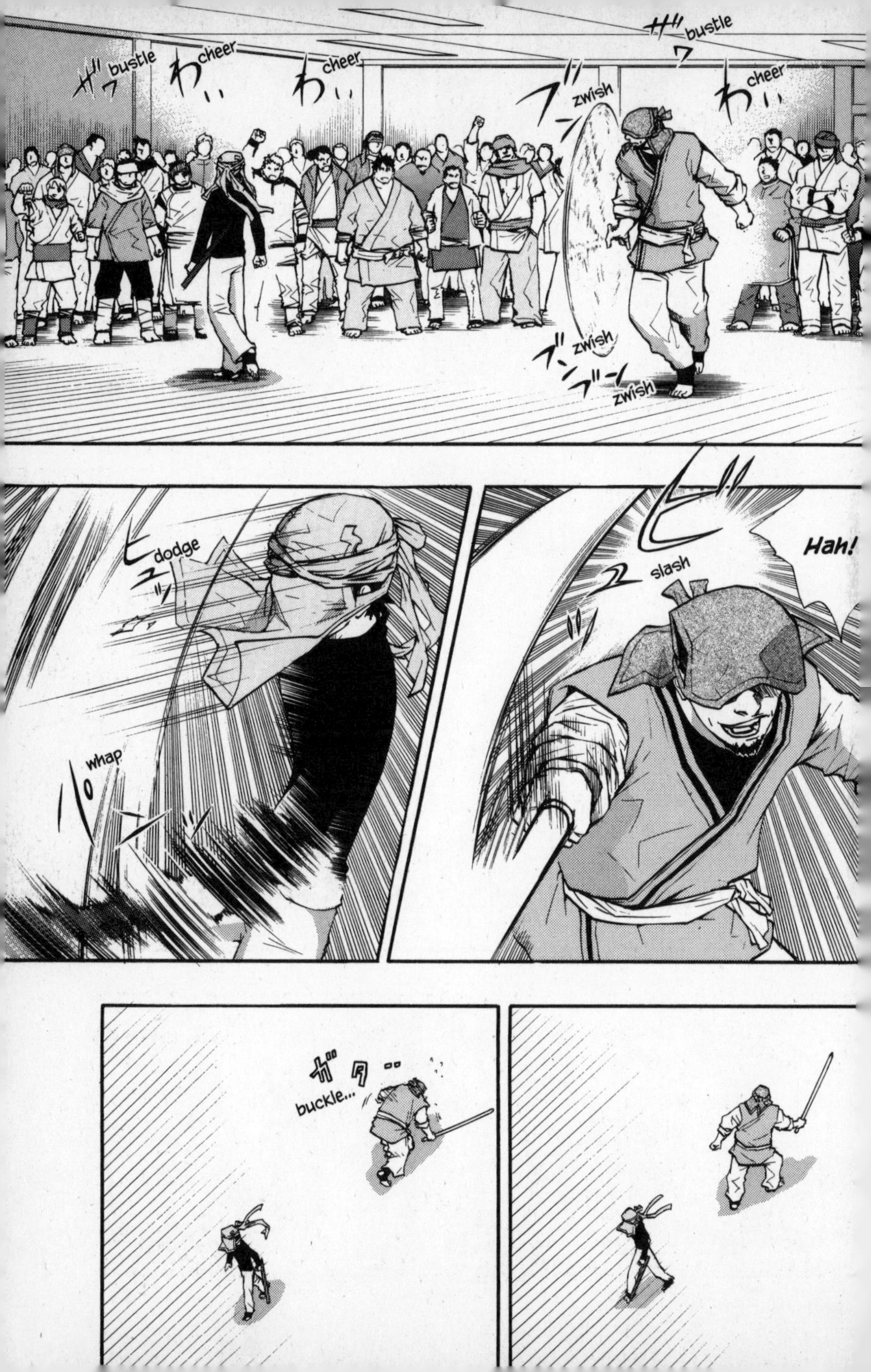
bustle
cheer
zwish
zwish
zwish
cheer
cheer
bustle
Hah!
slash
dodge
whap
buckle...

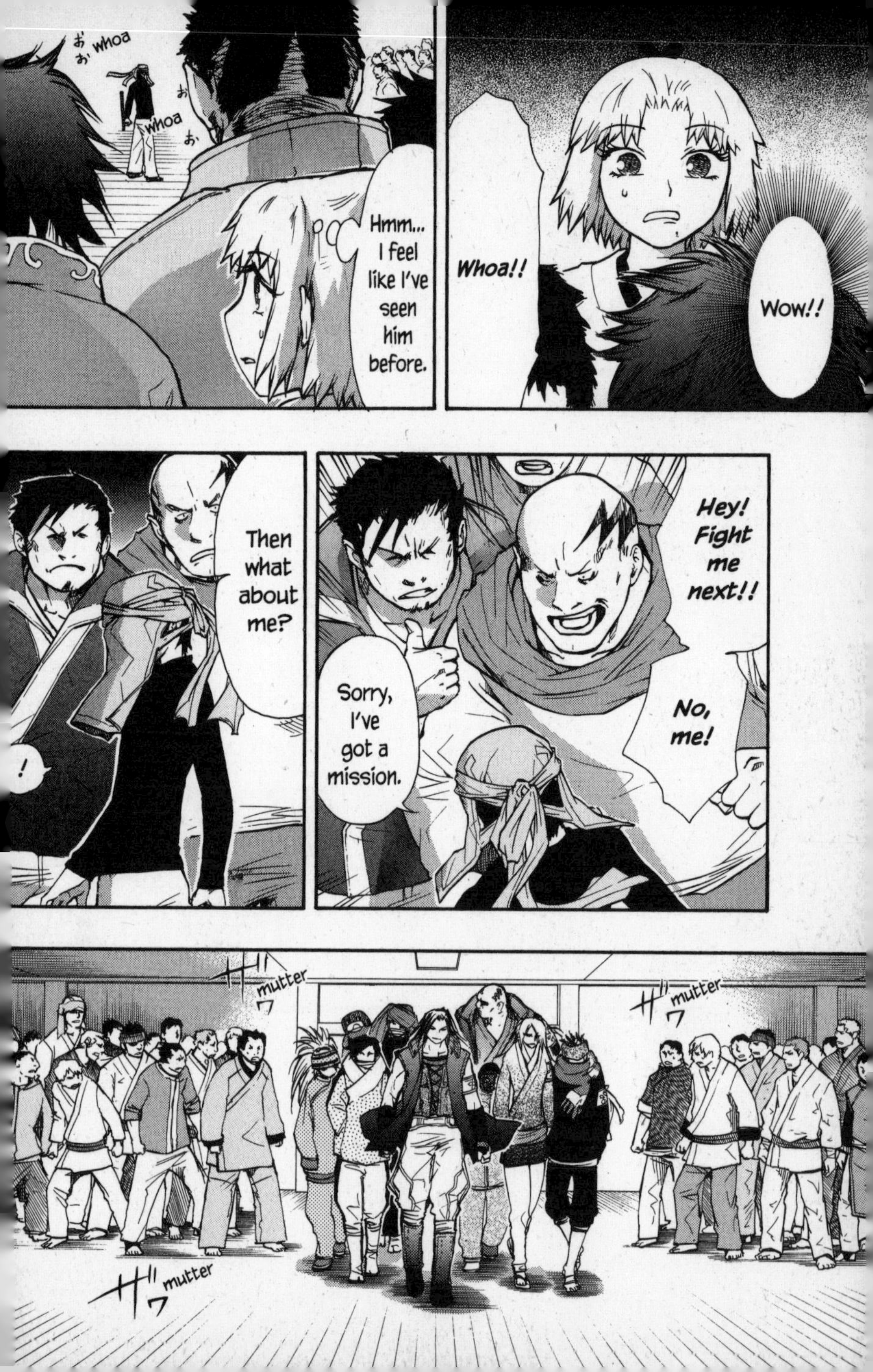
Wow!!
Whoa!!
Hmm... I feel like I've seen him before.
おお whoa
おお whoa
Hey! Fight me next!!
No, me!
Sorry, I've got a mission.
Then what about me?
!
ザワ mutter
ザワ mutter
ザワ mutter

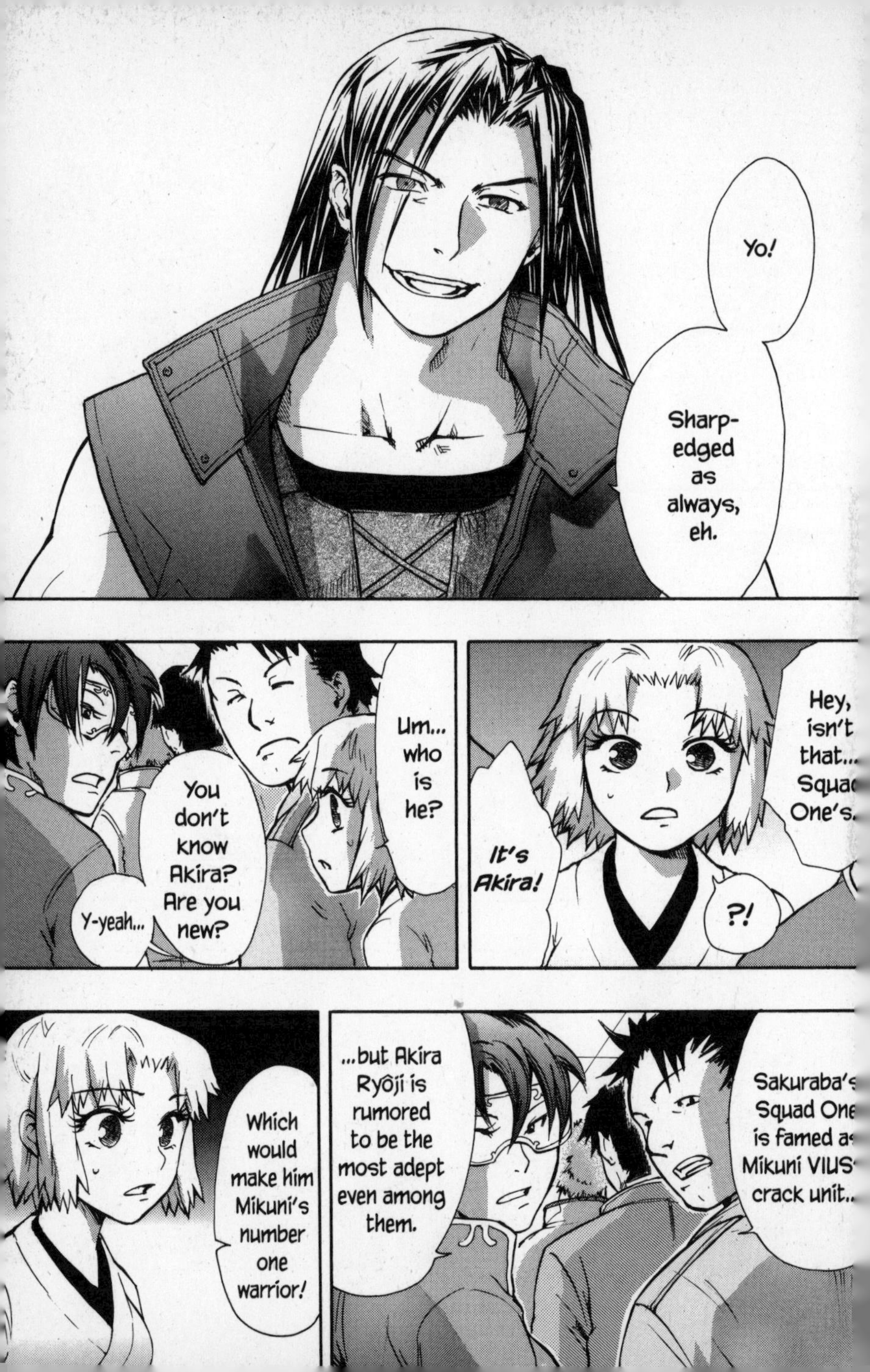
Yo!
Sharp-edged as always, eh.
Hey, isn't that... Squad One's...
?!
It's Akira!
Um... who is he?
You don't know Akira? Are you new?
Y-yeah...
Sakuraba's Squad One is famed as Mikuni VIUS' crack unit...
...but Akira Ryôji is rumored to be the most adept even among them.
Which would make him Mikuni's number one warrior!

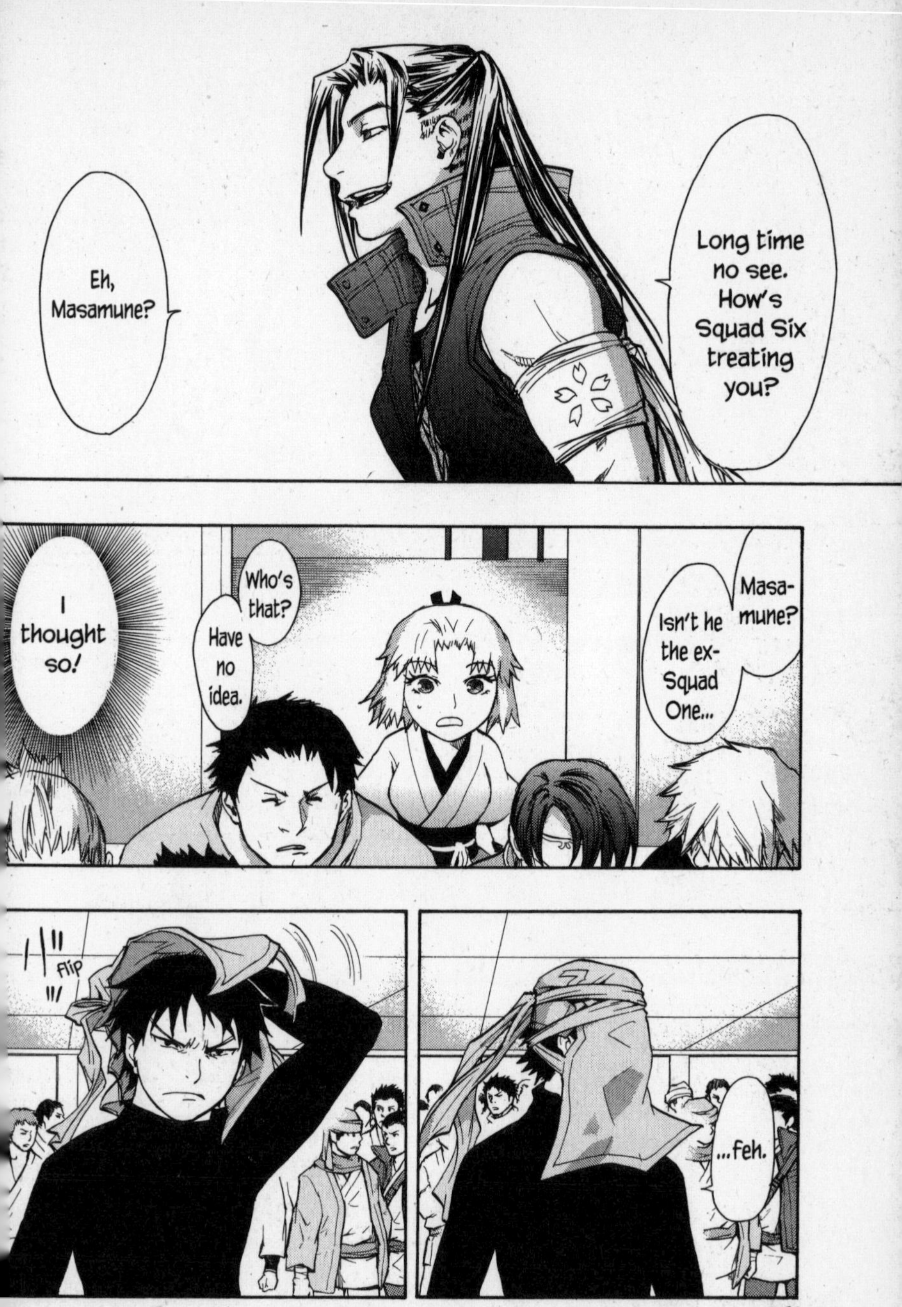
Long time no see. How's Squad Six treating you?
Eh, Masamune?
Masa-mune?
Isn't he the ex-Squad One...
Who's that?
Have no idea.
I thought so!
...feh.
Flip

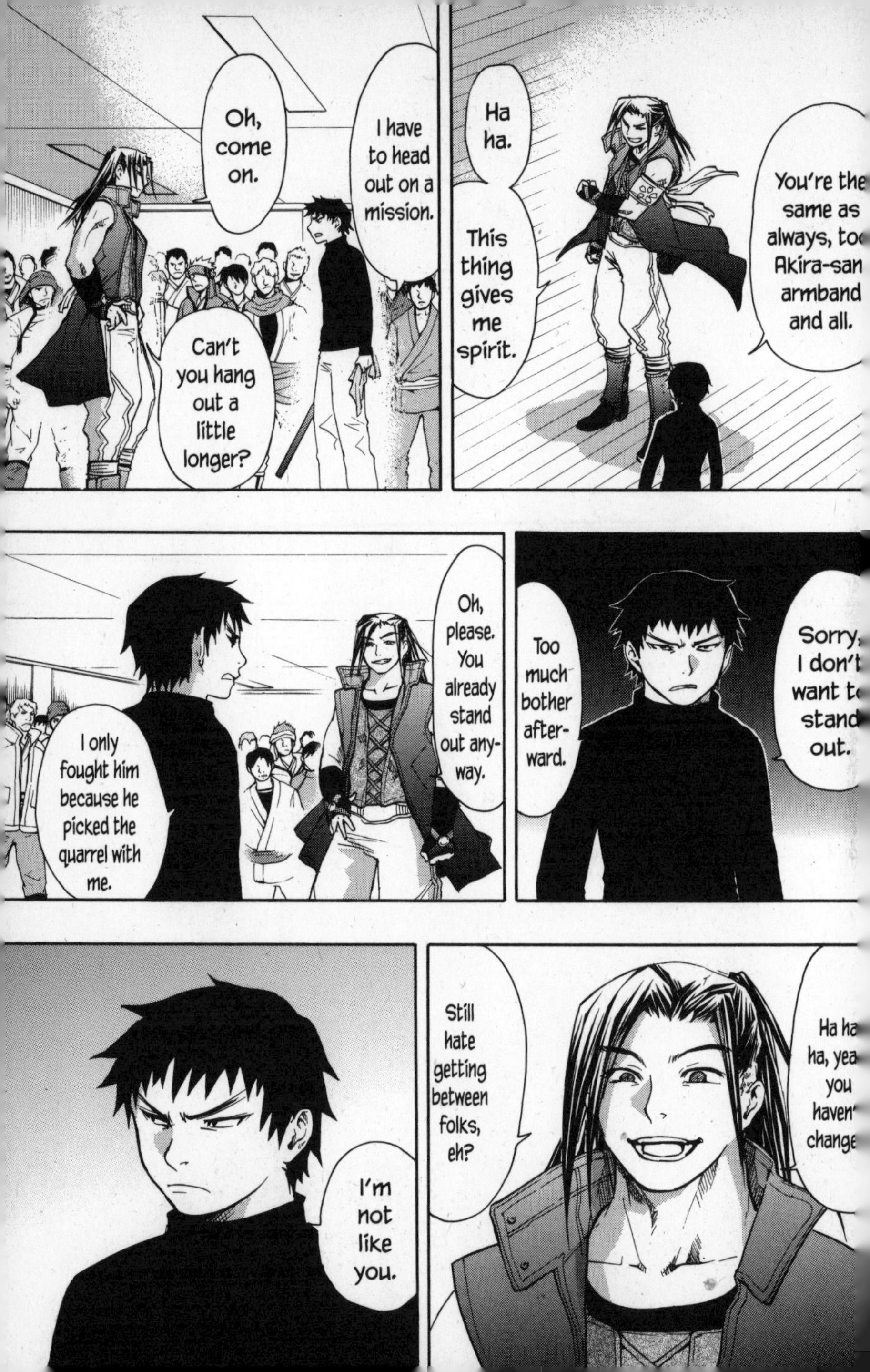

You're the same as always, to Akira-san armband and all.
Ha ha.
This thing gives me spirit.
I have to head out on a mission.
Oh, come on.
Can't you hang out a little longer?
Sorry, I don't want t stand out.
Too much bother after-ward.
Oh, please. You already stand out any-way.
I only fought him because he picked the quarrel with me.
Ha ha ha, yea you haven' change
Still hate getting between folks, eh?
I'm not like you.

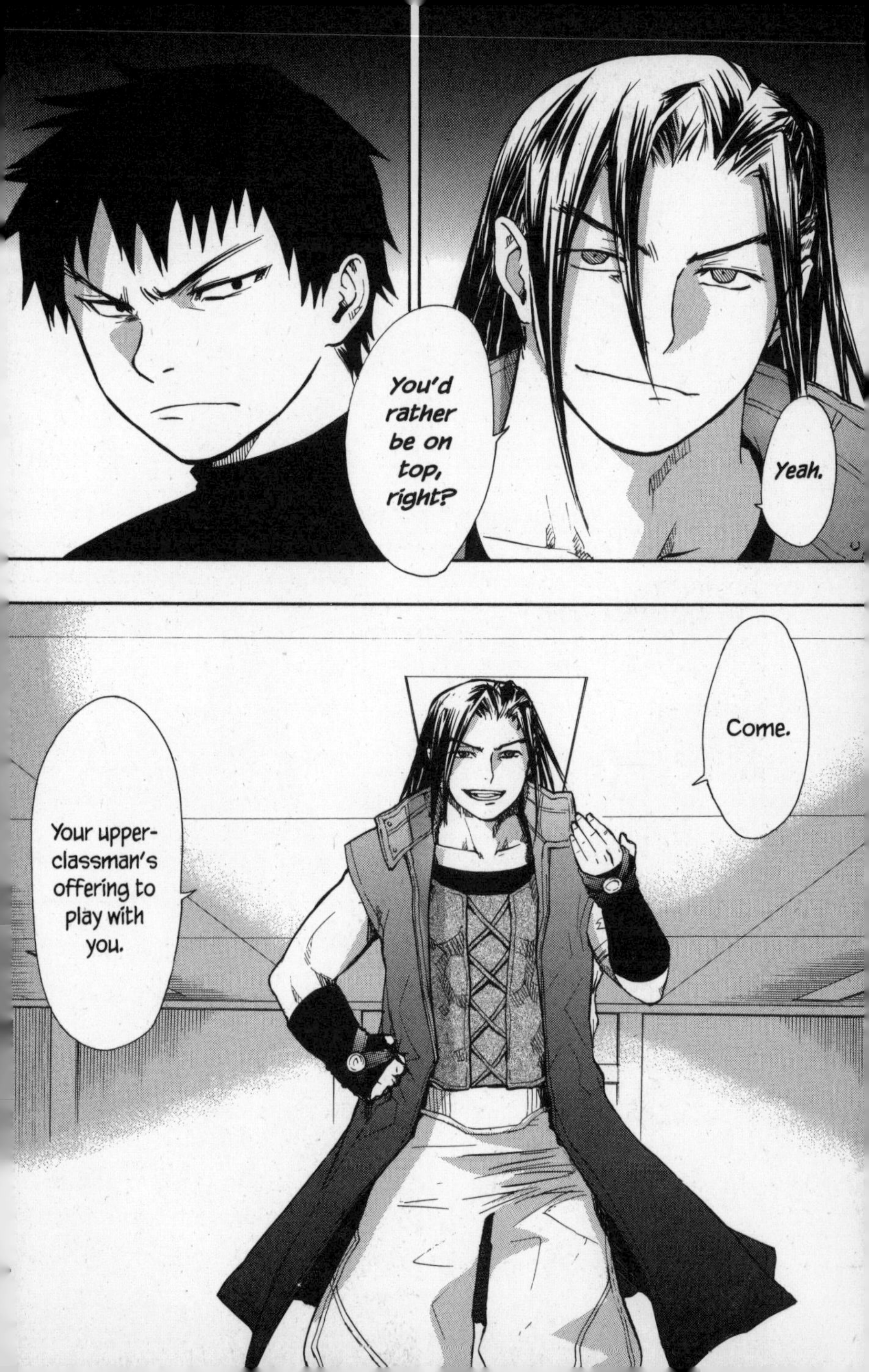

You'd rather be on top, right?
Yeah.
Come.
Your upper-classman's offering to play with you.

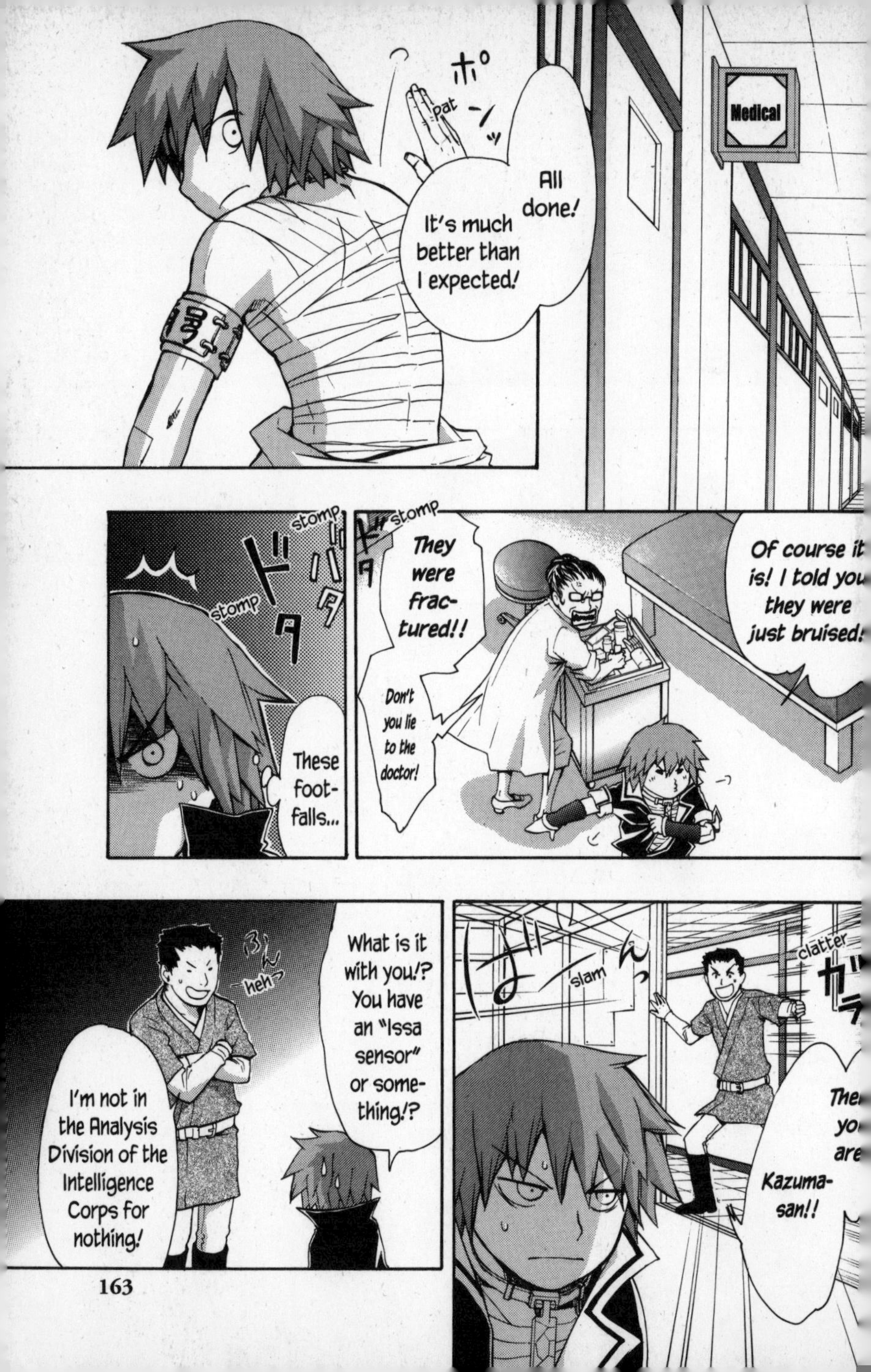
Medical
pat
All done!
It's much better than I expected!
Of course it is! I told you they were just bruised!
stomp
They were frac-tured!!
Don't you lie to the doctor!
stomp
stomp
These foot-falls...
clatter
slam
The yo are Kazuma-san!!
What is it with you!? You have an "Issa sensor" or some-thing!?
heh
I'm not in the Analysis Division of the Intelligence Corps for nothing!

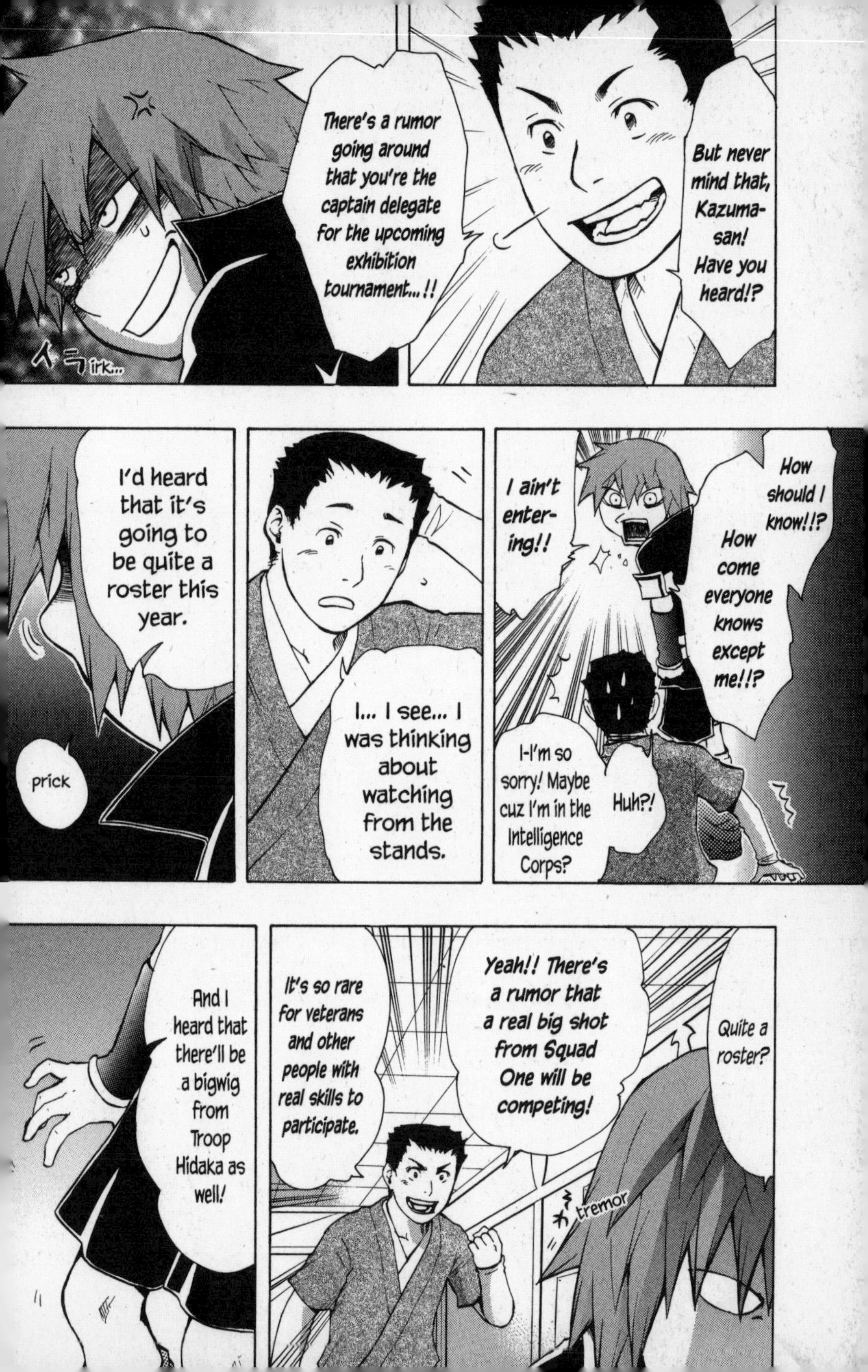
But never mind that, Kazuma-san! Have you heard!?
There's a rumor going around that you're the captain delegate for the upcoming exhibition tournament...!!
イラ irk...
How should I know!!? How come everyone knows except me!!?
I ain't entering!!
Huh?!
I-I'm so sorry! Maybe cuz I'm in the Intelligence Corps?
I... I see... I was thinking about watching from the stands.
I'd heard that it's going to be quite a roster this year.
prick
Quite a roster?
Yeah!! There's a rumor that a real big shot from Squad One will be competing!
It's so rare for veterans and other people with real skills to participate.
ざわ tremor
And I heard that there'll be a bigwig from Troop Hidaka as well!

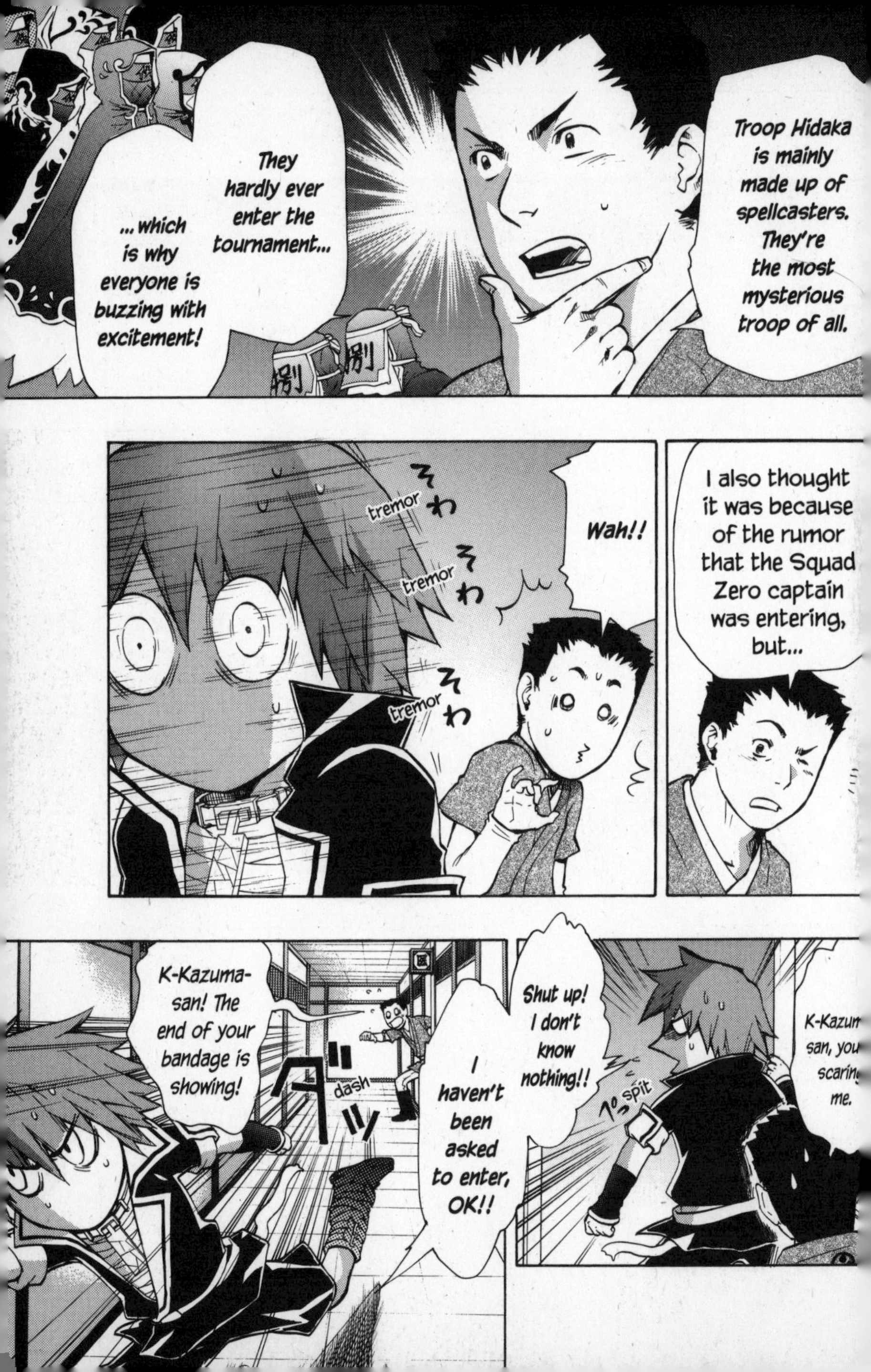
Troop Hidaka is mainly made up of spellcasters. They're the most mysterious troop of all.
They hardly ever enter the tournament...
...which is why everyone is buzzing with excitement!
I also thought it was because of the rumor that the Squad Zero captain was entering, but...
Wah!!
tremor
tremor
tremor
K-Kazum san, you scarin me.
Shut up! I don't know nothing!!
spit
I haven't been asked to enter, OK!!
K-Kazuma-san! The end of your bandage is showing!
dash

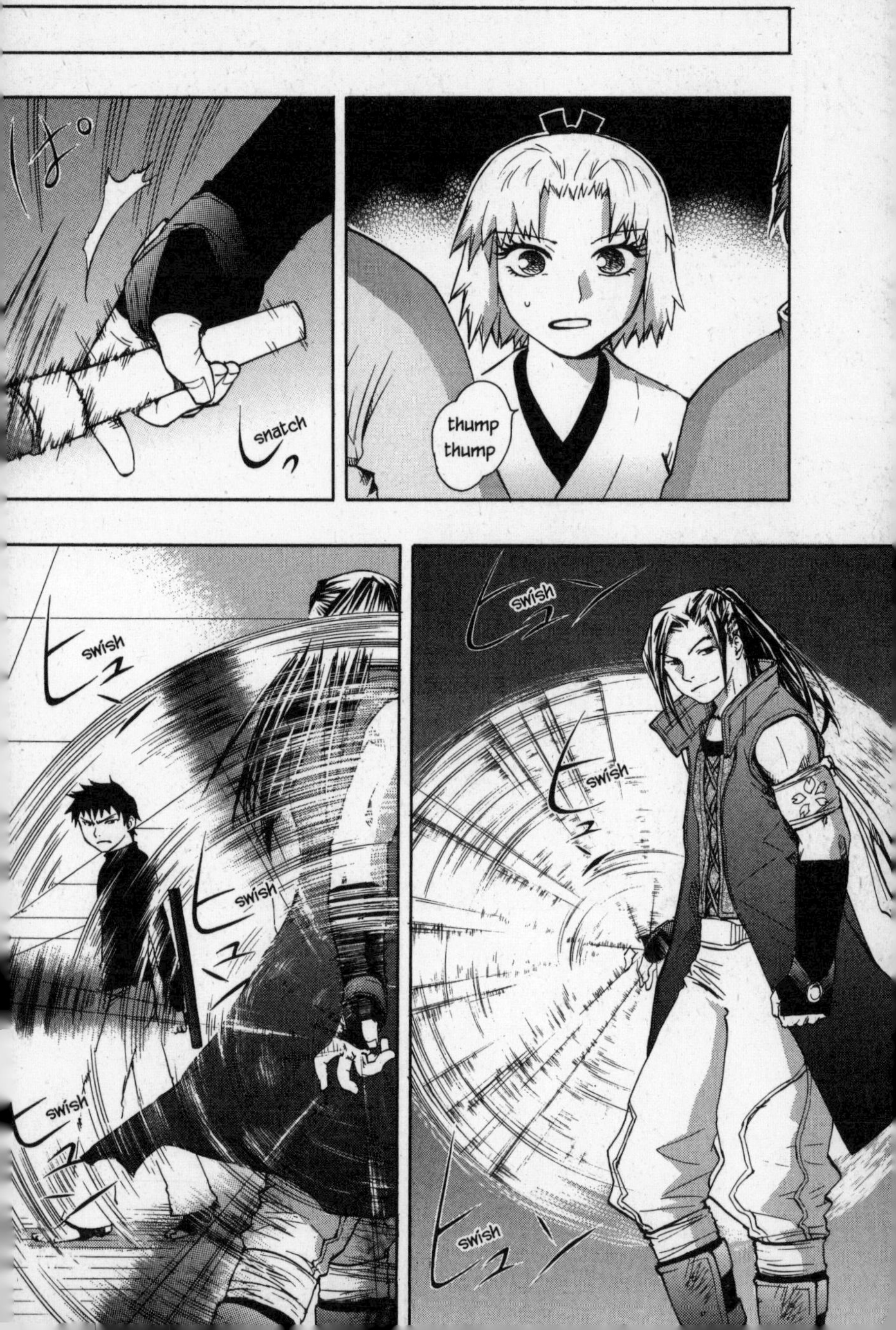
thump thump
snatch
swish
swish
swish
swish
swish
swish

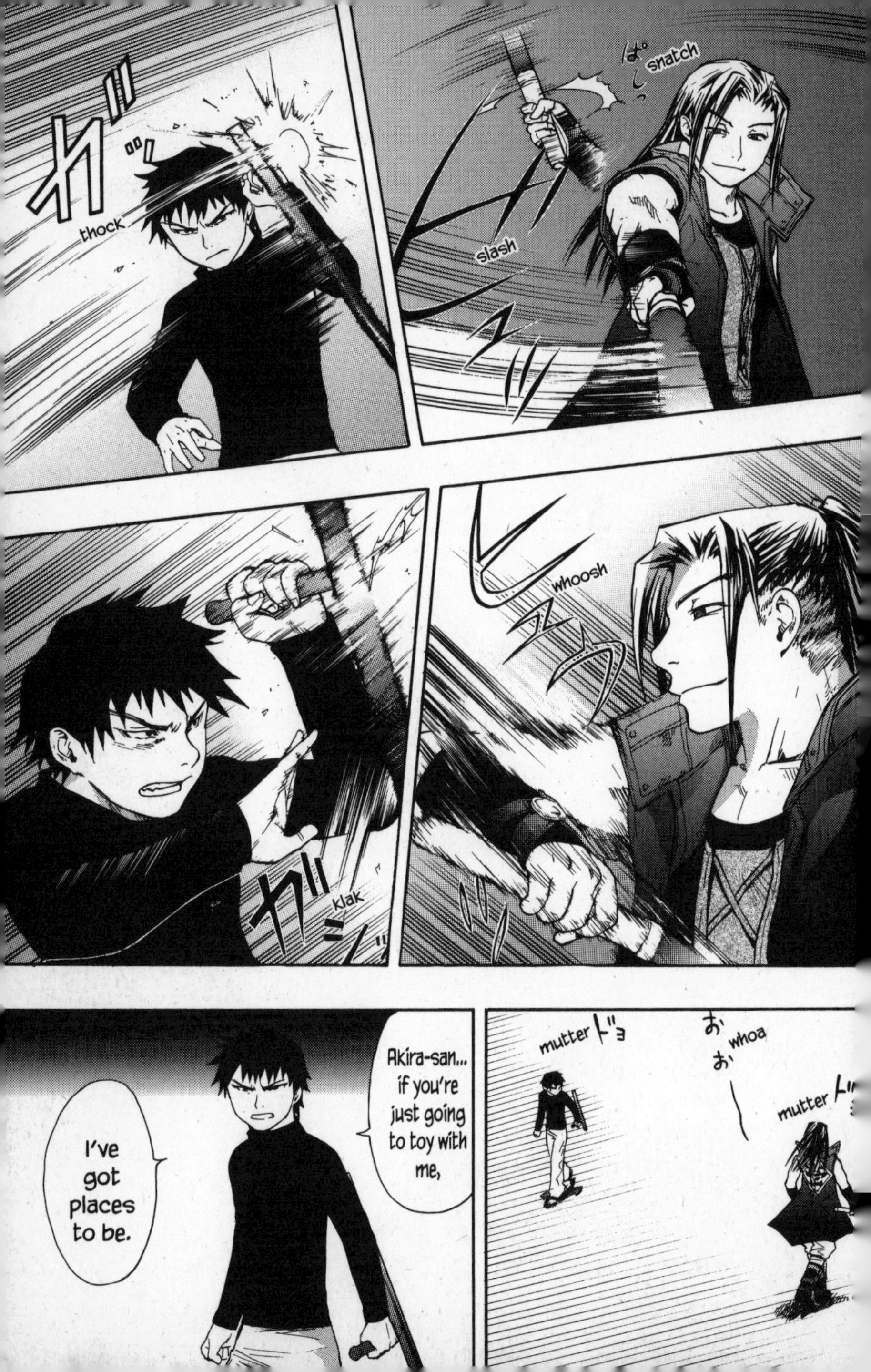
ぱし
snatch
slash
thock
whoosh
klak
mutter ドヨ
おお
whoa
mutter
Akira-san... if you're just going to toy with me,
I've got places to be.

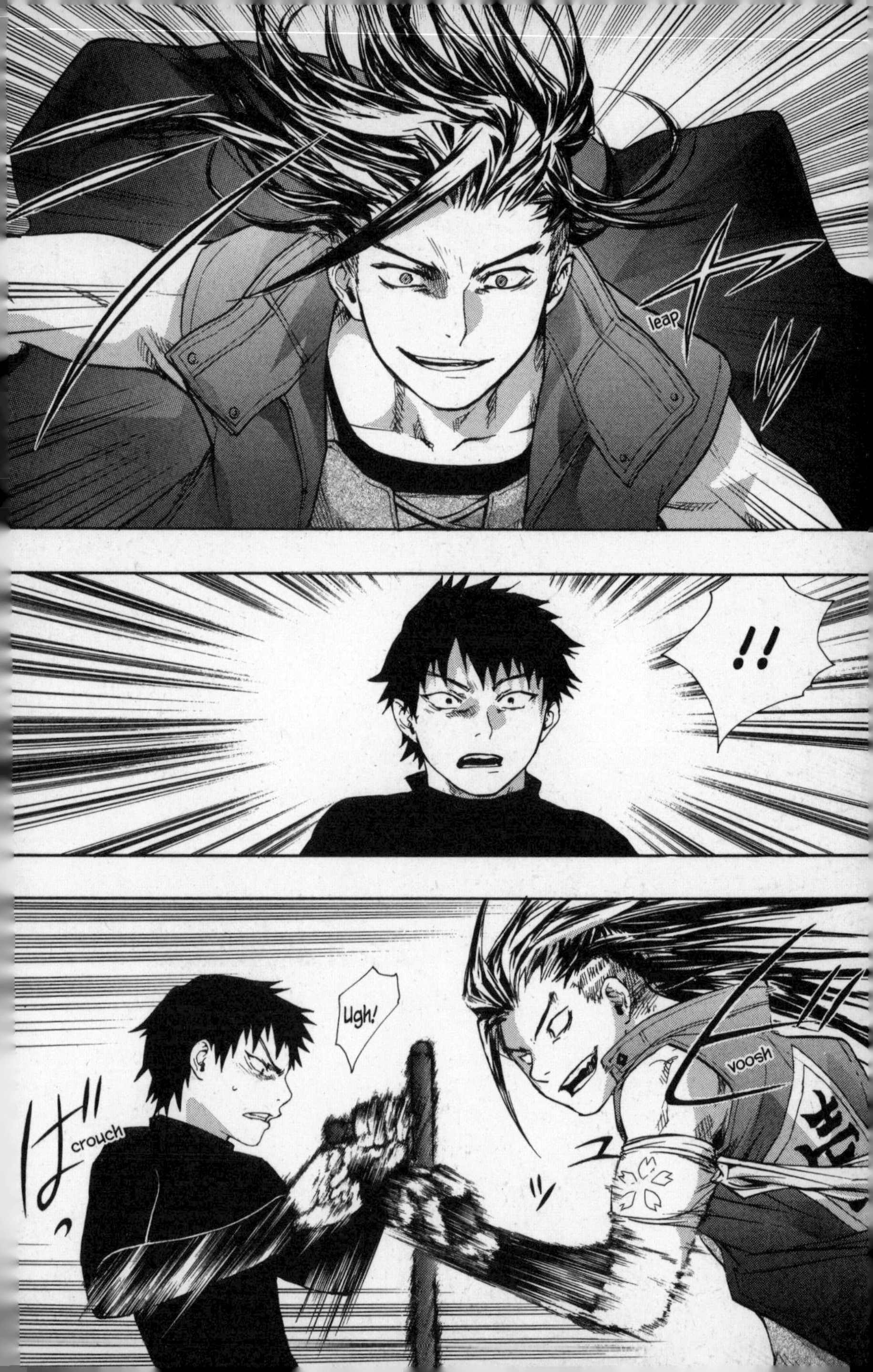
leap
!!
voosh
Ugh!
crouch

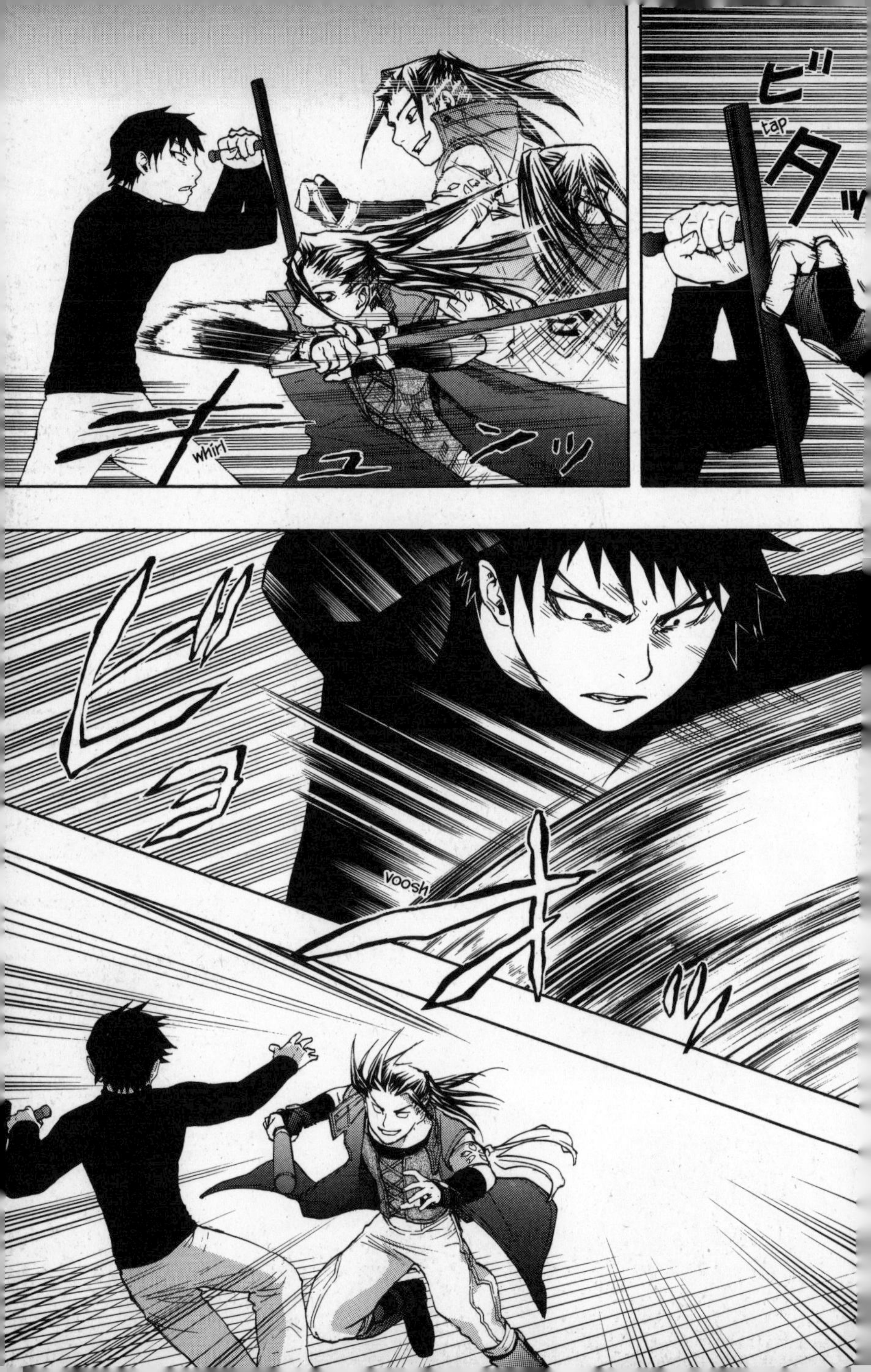
ビダッ
tap
ヒュンッ
whirl
ヒュオッ
voosh

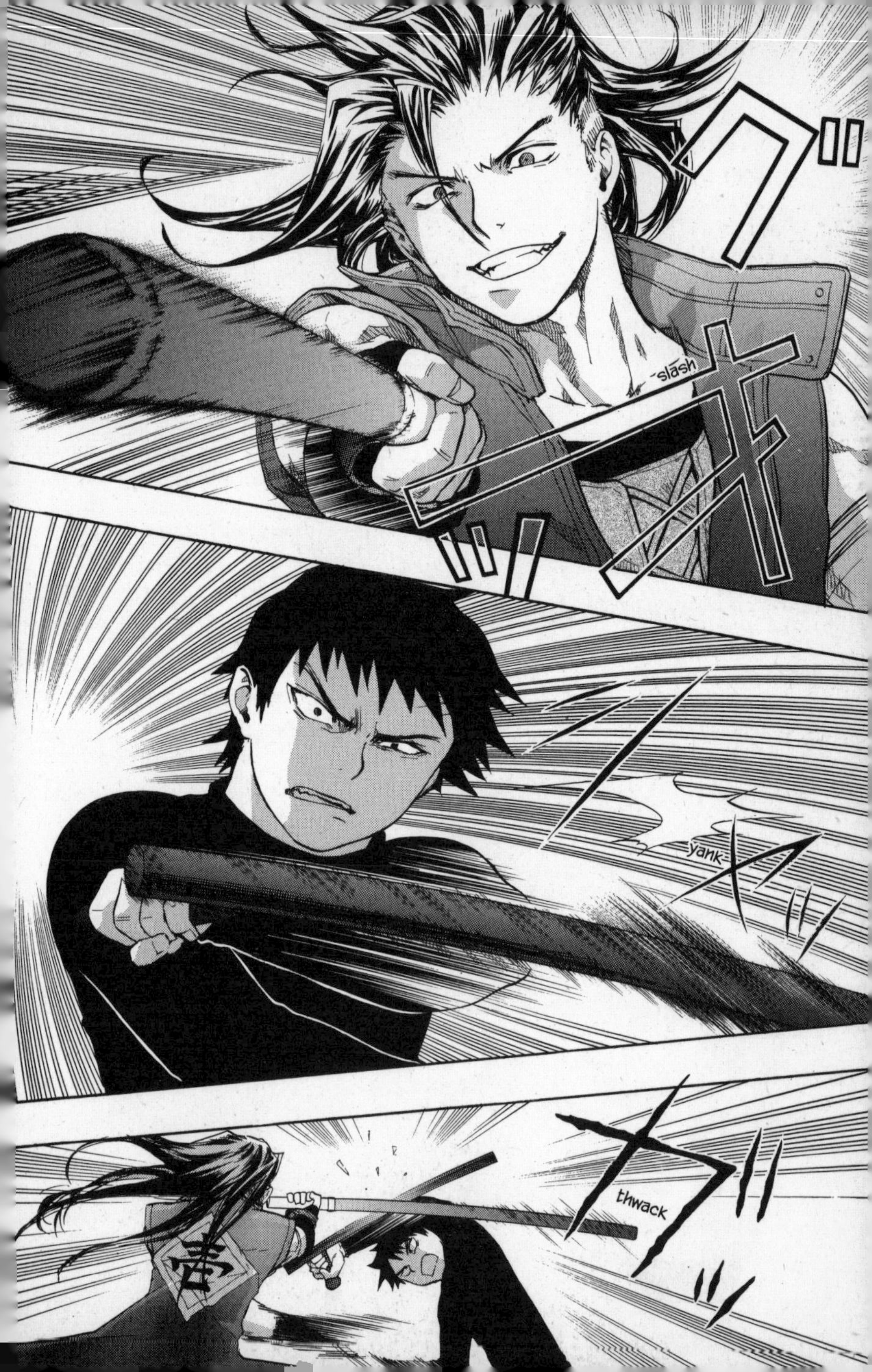
slash
yank
thwack

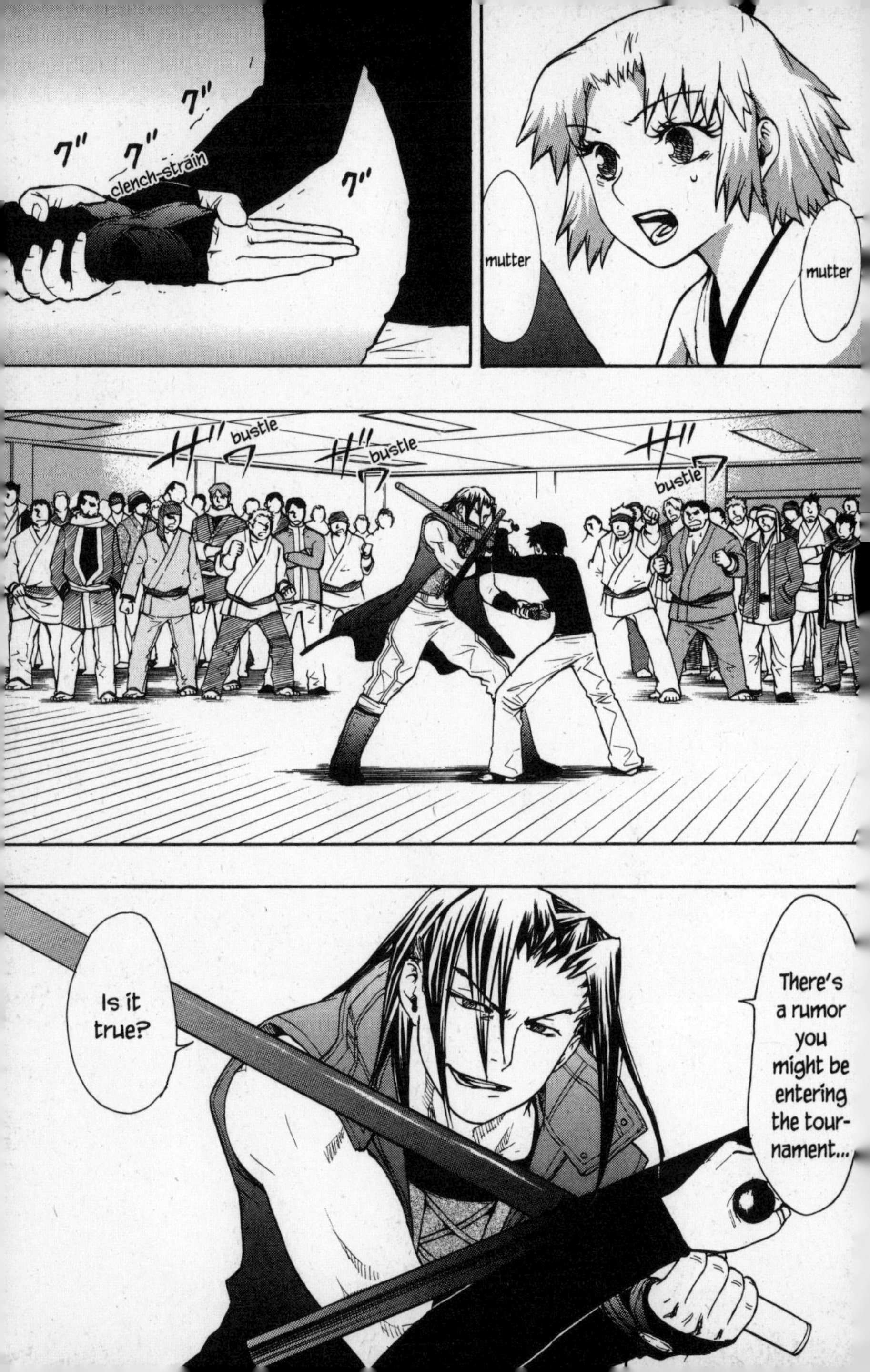
mutter
mutter
グ グ グ グ
clench-strain
ザワ
bustle
ザワ
bustle
ザワ
bustle
There's a rumor you might be entering the tour-nament...
Is it true?

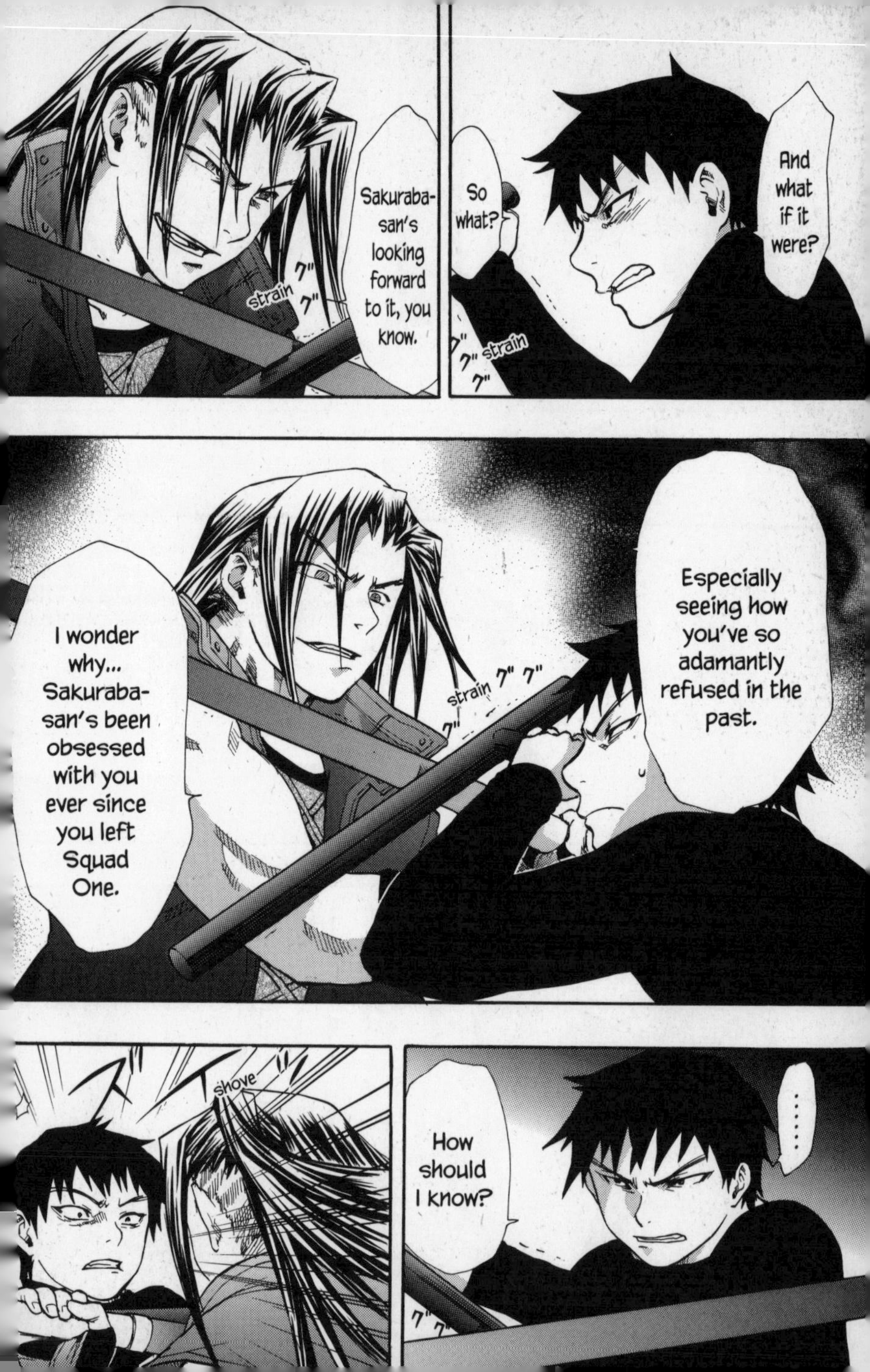
And what if it were?
So what?
strain
Sakuraba-san's looking forward to it, you know.
strain
Especially seeing how you've so adamantly refused in the past.
strain
I wonder why... Sakuraba-san's been obsessed with you ever since you left Squad One.
......
How should I know?
shove

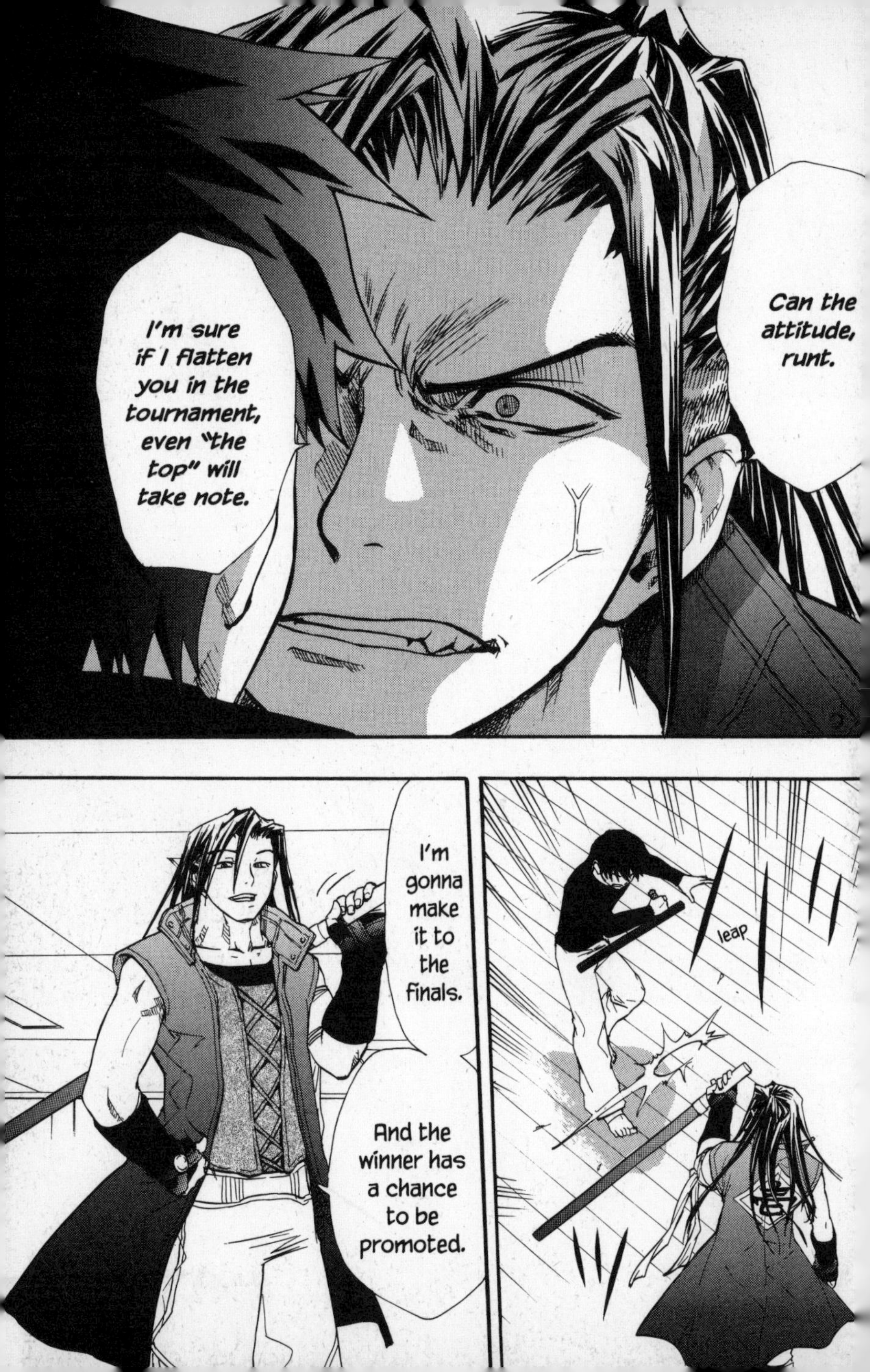
Can the attitude, runt.
I'm sure if I flatten you in the tournament, even "the top" will take note.
leap
I'm gonna make it to the finals.
And the winner has a chance to be promoted.

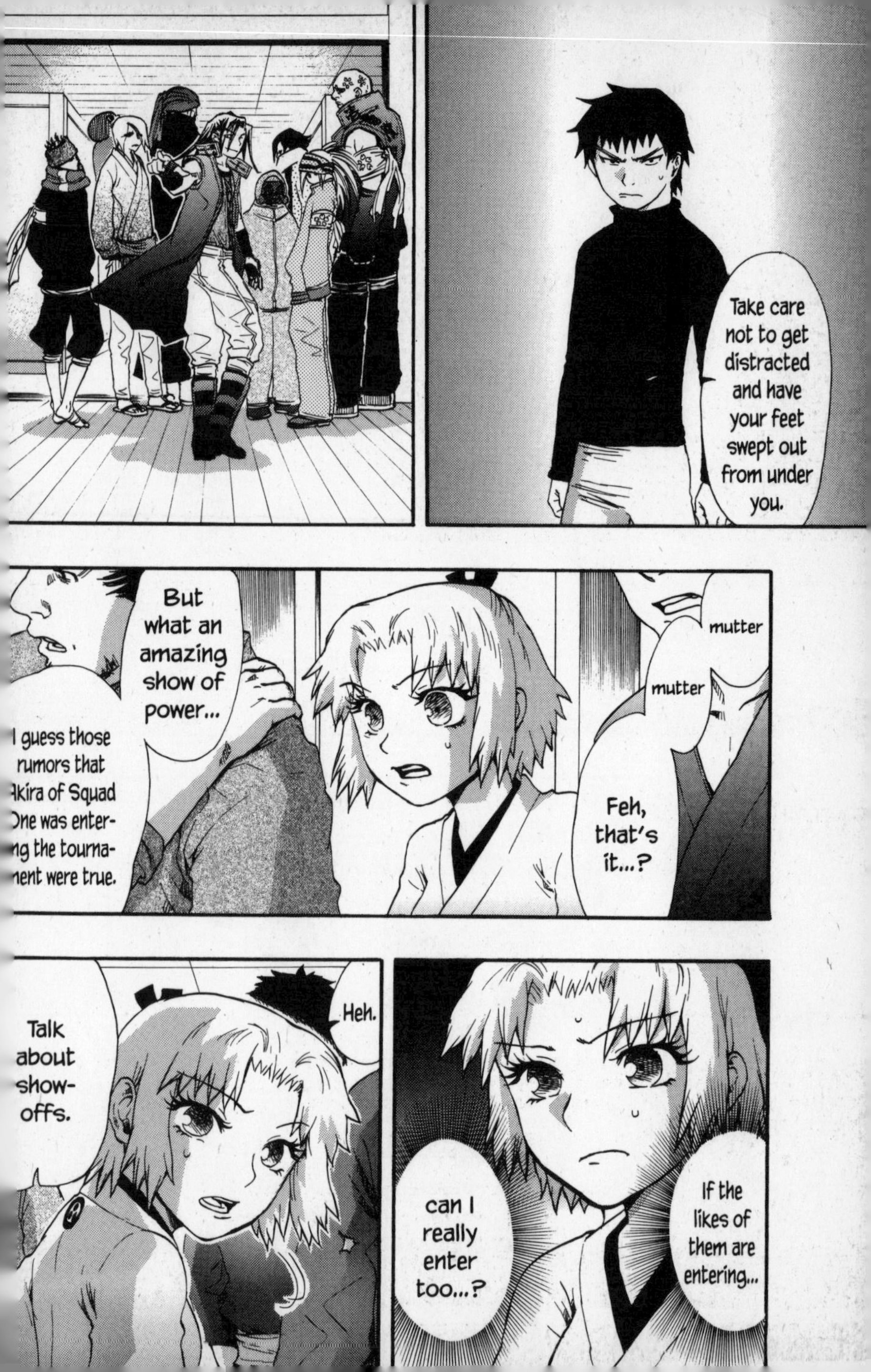
Take care not to get distracted and have your feet swept out from under you.
mutter
mutter
Feh, that's it...?
But what an amazing show of power...
I guess those rumors that Akira of Squad One was entering the tournament were true.
If the likes of them are entering...
can I really enter too...?
Heh.
Talk about show-offs.

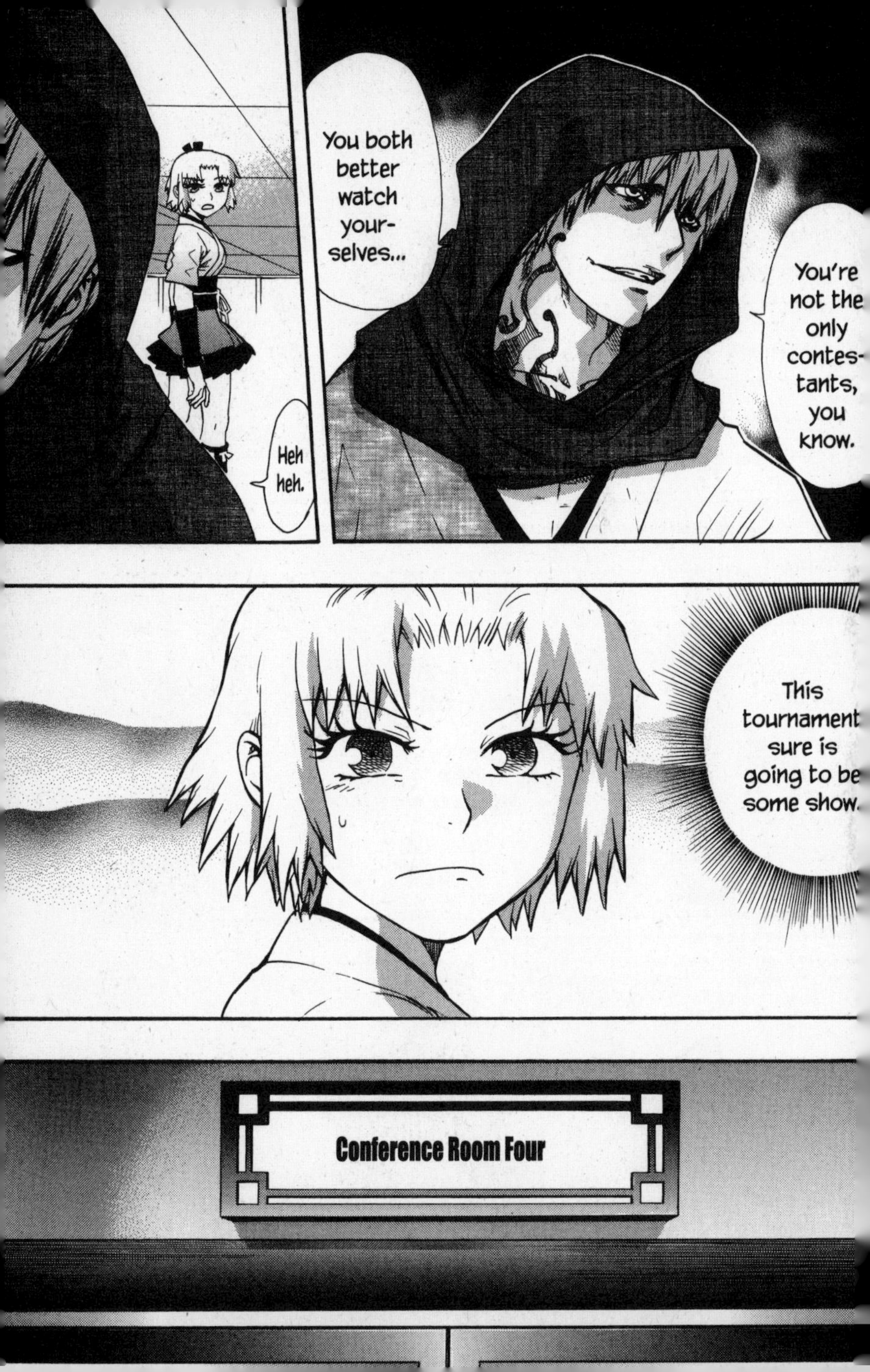
You're not the only contestants, you know.
You both better watch yourselves...
Heh heh.
This tournament sure is going to be some show.
Conference Room Four

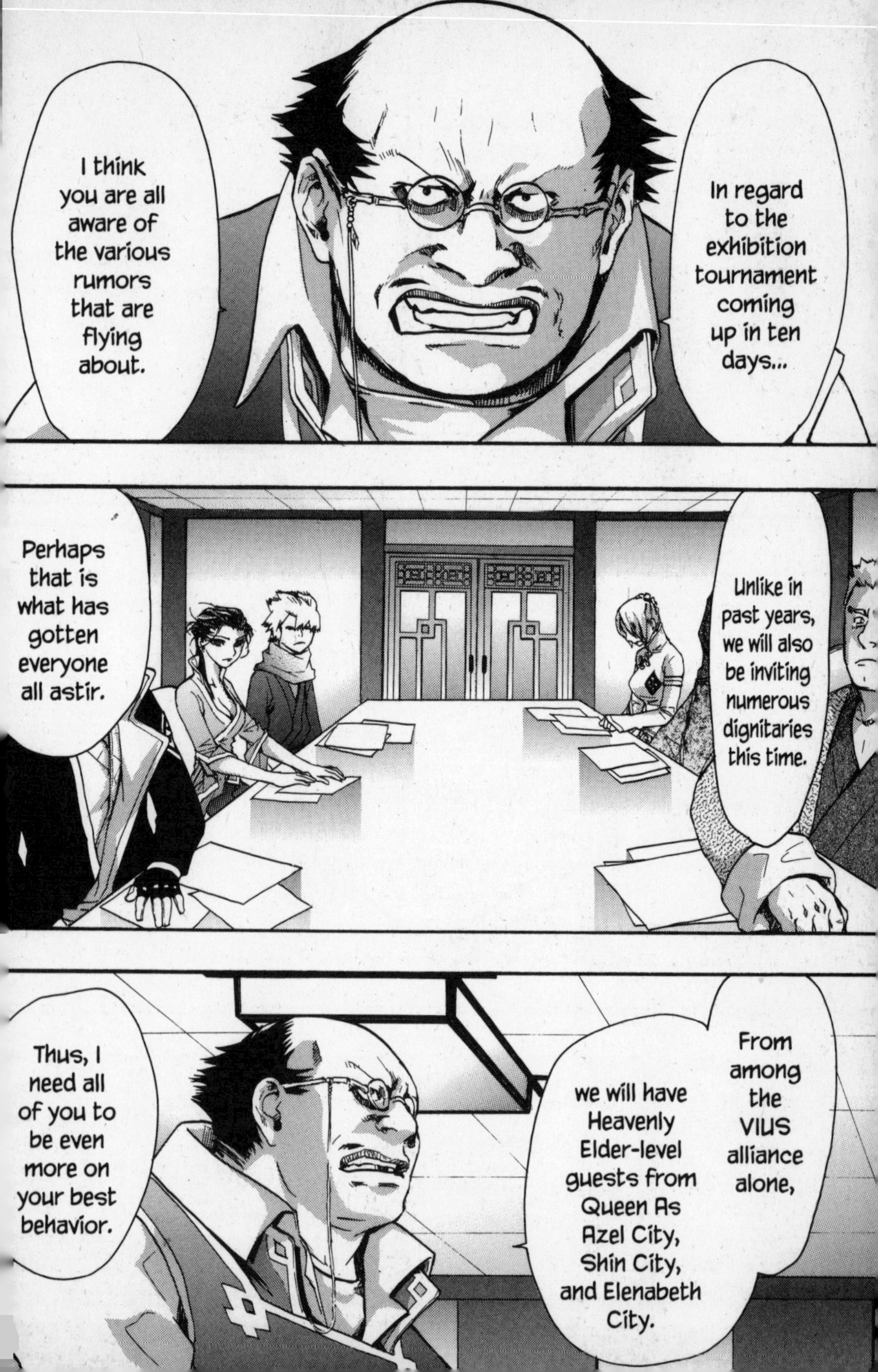
In regard to the exhibition tournament coming up in ten days...
I think you are all aware of the various rumors that are flying about.
Unlike in past years, we will also be inviting numerous dignitaries this time.
Perhaps that is what has gotten everyone all astir.
From among the VIUS alliance alone,
we will have Heavenly Elder-level guests from Queen As Azel City, Shin City, and Elenabeth City.
Thus, I need all of you to be even more on your best behavior.

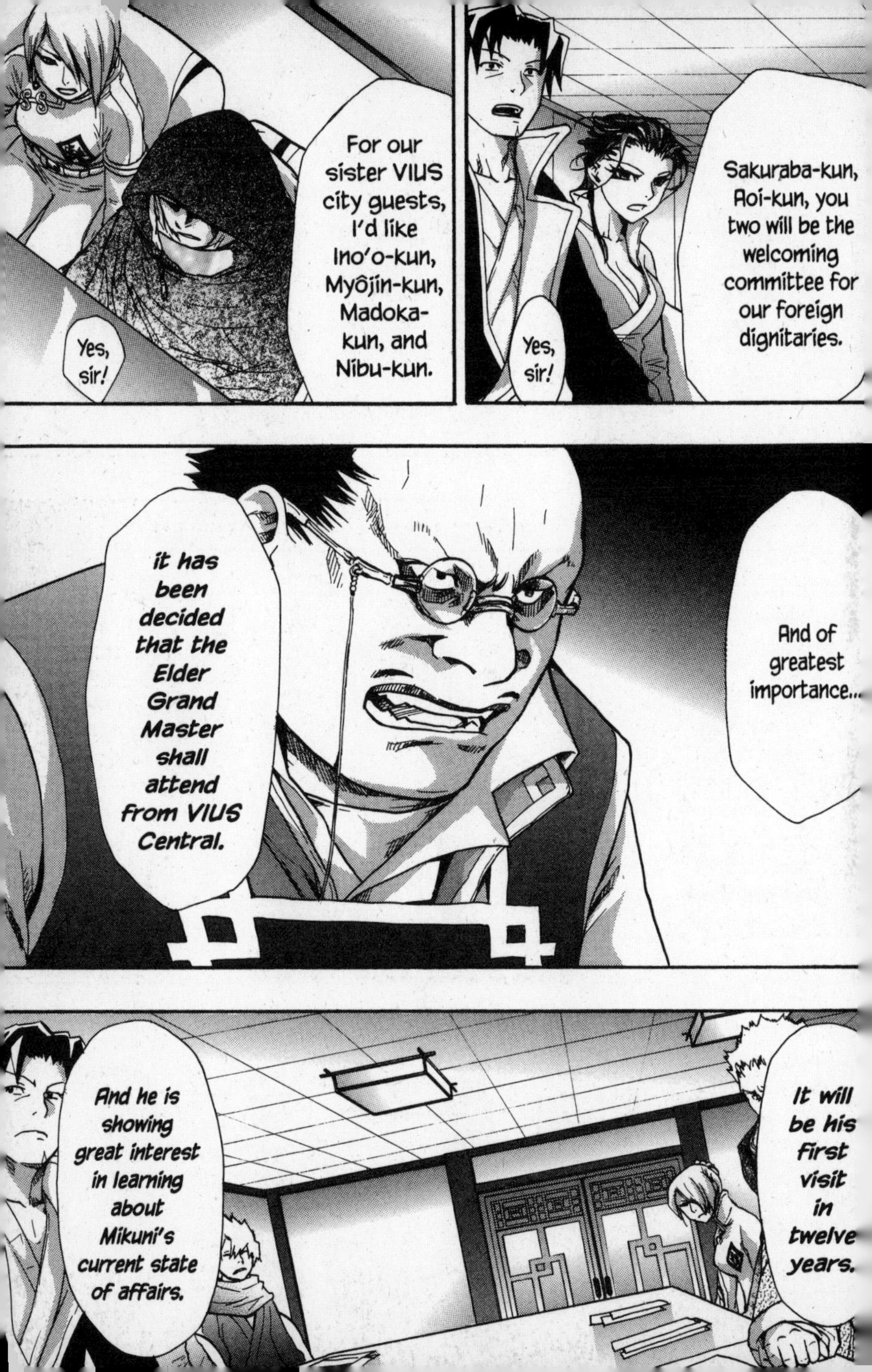
Sakuraba-kun, Aoi-kun, you two will be the welcoming committee for our foreign dignitaries.
Yes, sir!
For our sister VIUS city guests, I'd like Ino'o-kun, Myôjin-kun, Madoka-kun, and Nibu-kun.
Yes, sir!
And of greatest importance...
it has been decided that the Elder Grand Master shall attend from VIUS Central.
It will be his first visit in twelve years.
And he is showing great interest in learning about Mikuni's current state of affairs.

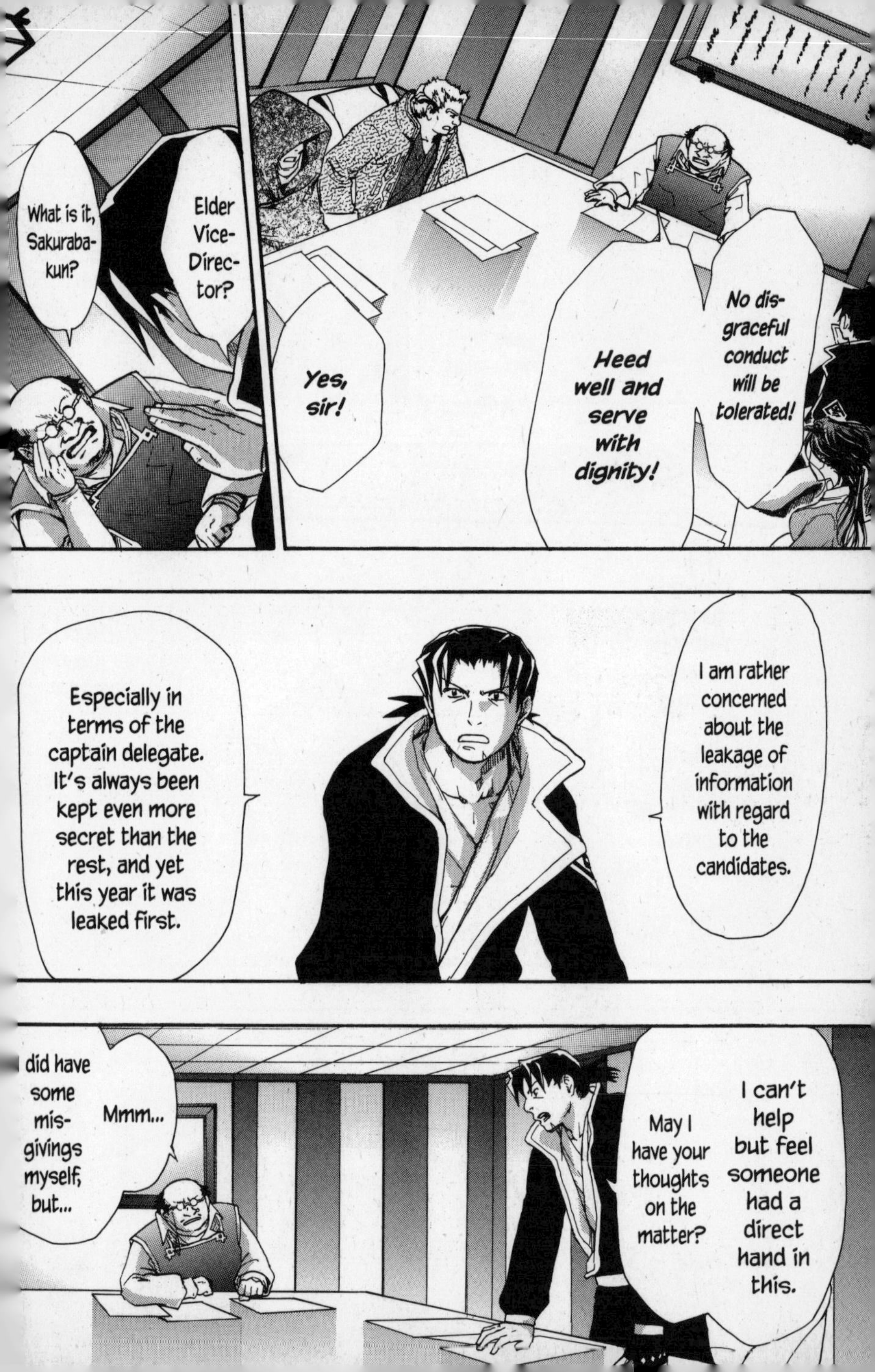
No disgraceful conduct will be tolerated!
Heed well and serve with dignity!
Yes, sir!
Elder Vice-Director?
What is it, Sakuraba-kun?
I am rather concerned about the leakage of information with regard to the candidates.
Especially in terms of the captain delegate. It's always been kept even more secret than the rest, and yet this year it was leaked first.
I can't help but feel someone had a direct hand in this.
May I have your thoughts on the matter?
Mmm...
I did have some misgivings myself, but...

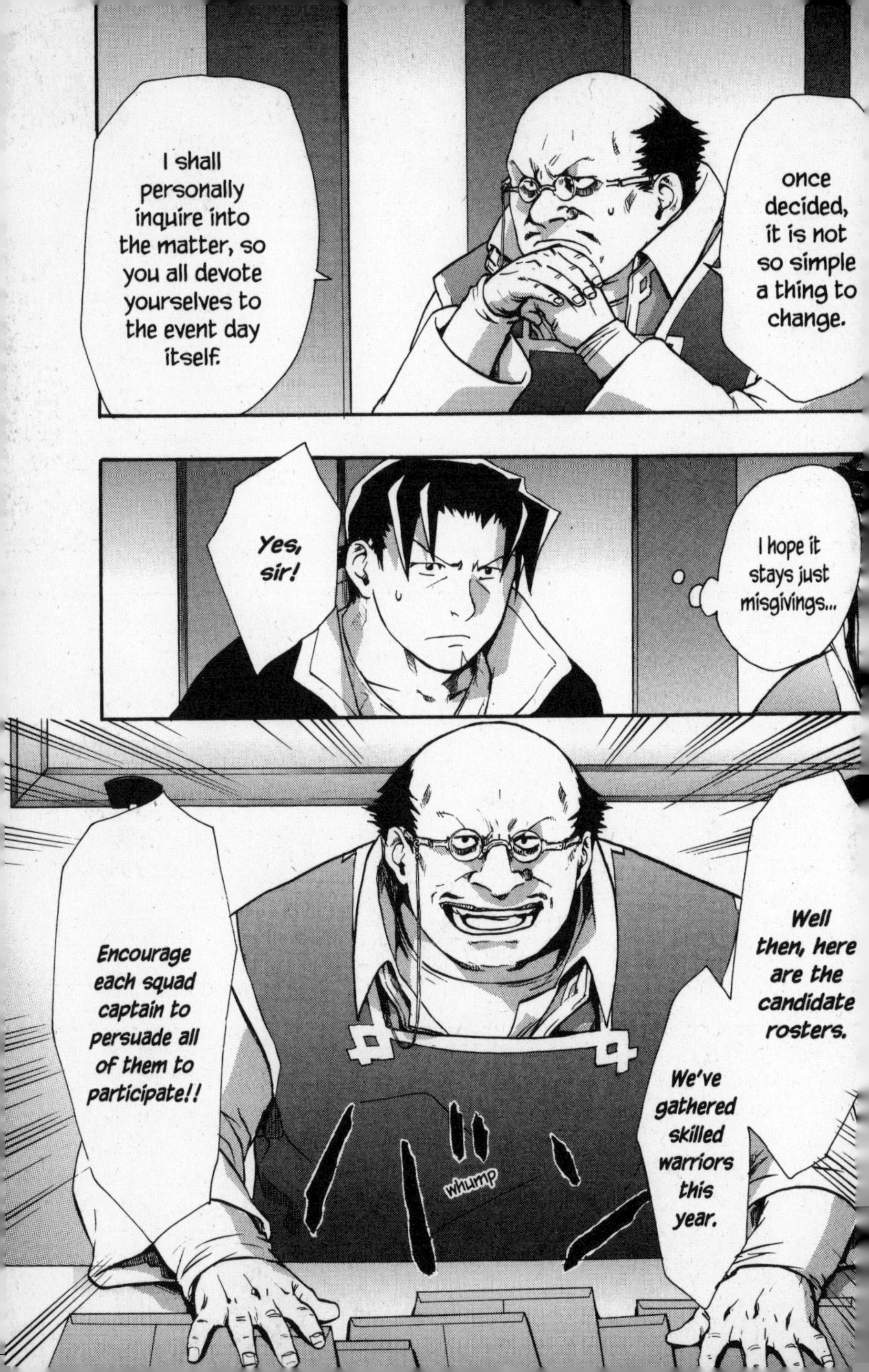
once decided, it is not so simple a thing to change.
I shall personally inquire into the matter, so you all devote yourselves to the event day itself.
I hope it stays just misgivings...
Yes, sir!
Well then, here are the candidate rosters.
We've gathered skilled warriors this year.
whump
Encourage each squad captain to persuade all of them to participate!!

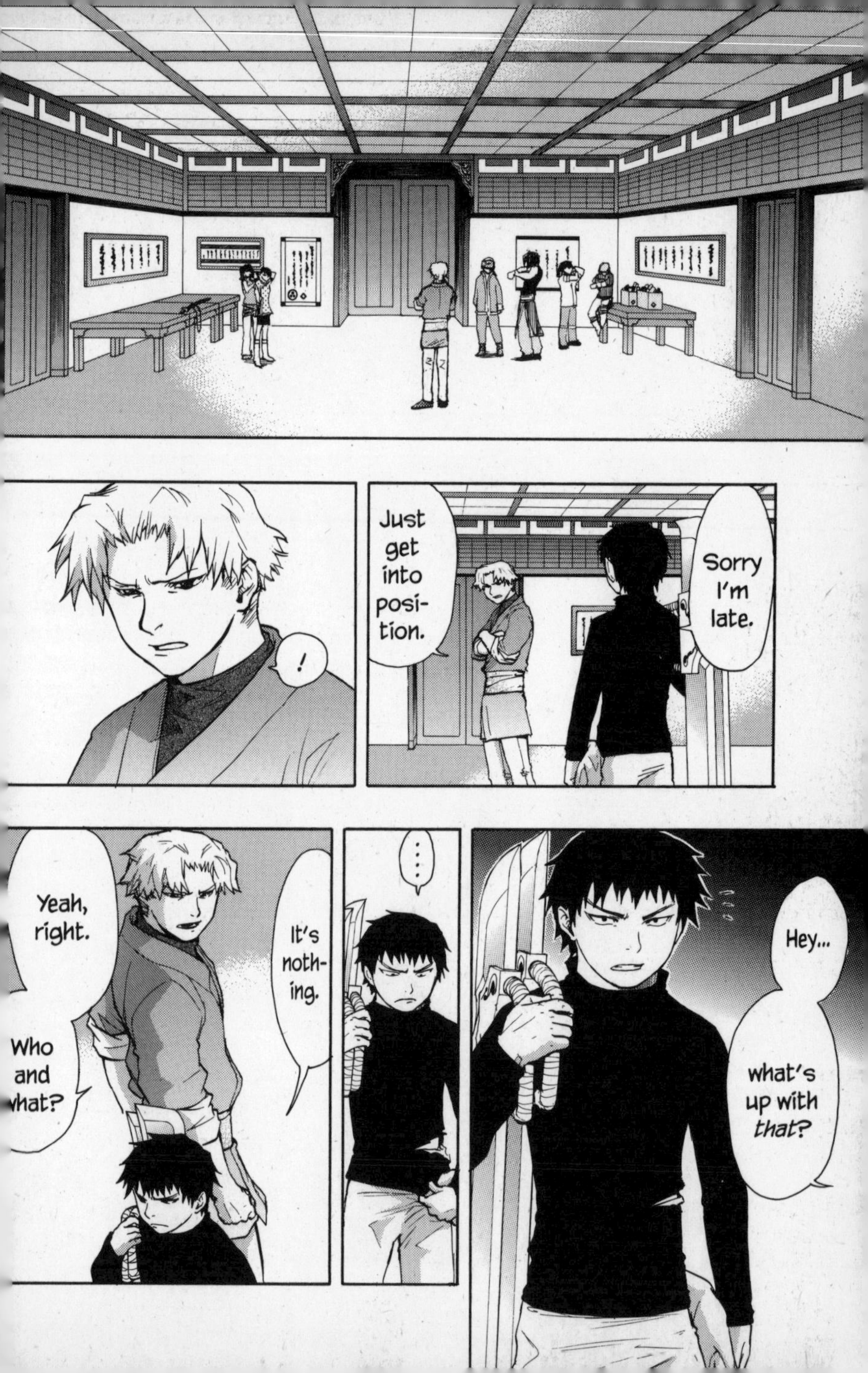

Sorry I'm late.
Just get into posi-tion.
!
Hey...
what's up with *that*?
...
It's noth-ing.
Yeah, right.
Who and what?

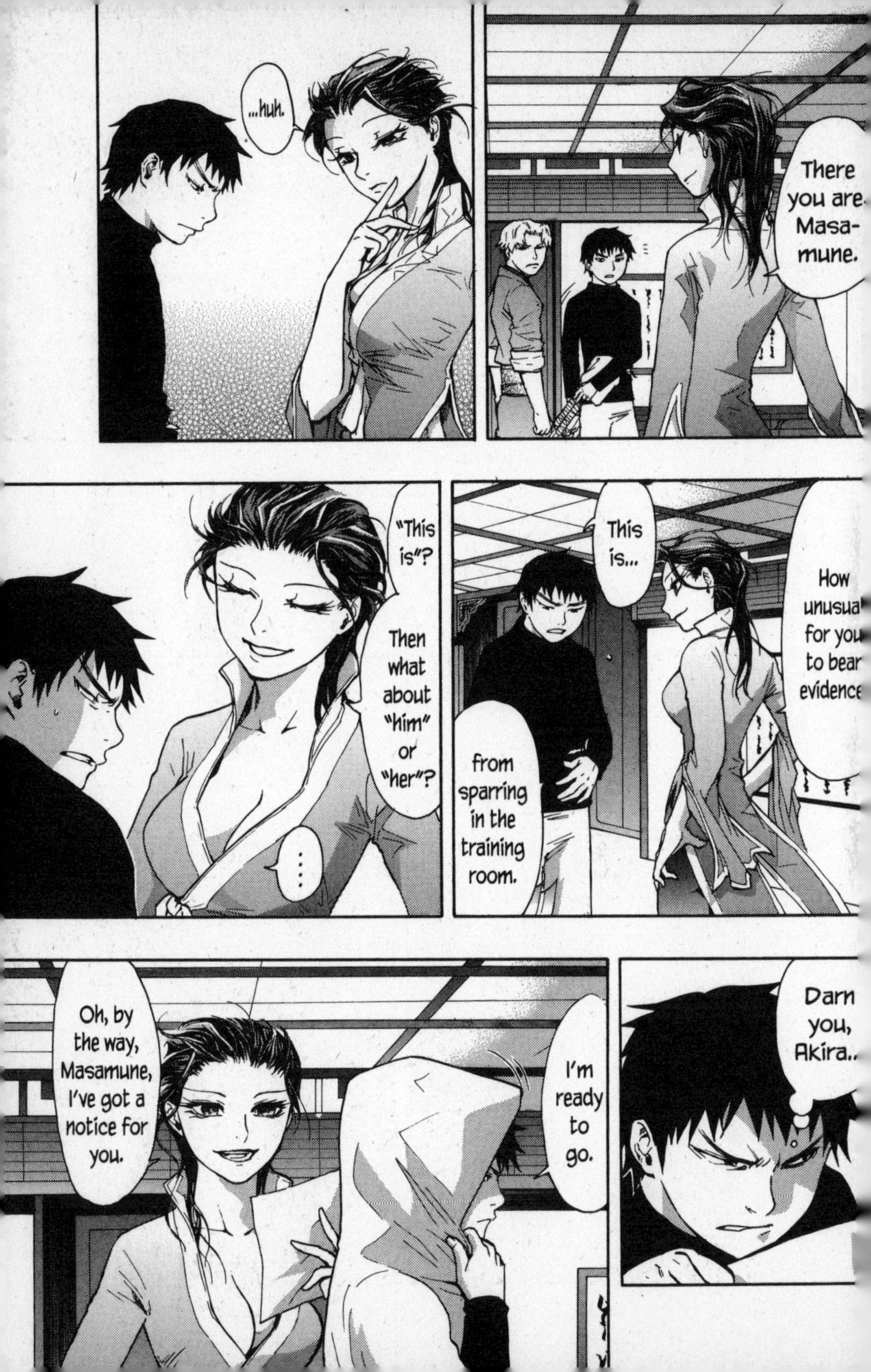

There you are. Masa-mune.
...huh.
How unusua for you to bear evidence
This is...
from sparring in the training room.
"This is"?
Then what about "him" or "her"?
....
Darn you, Akira..
I'm ready to go.
Oh, by the way, Masamune, I've got a notice for you.

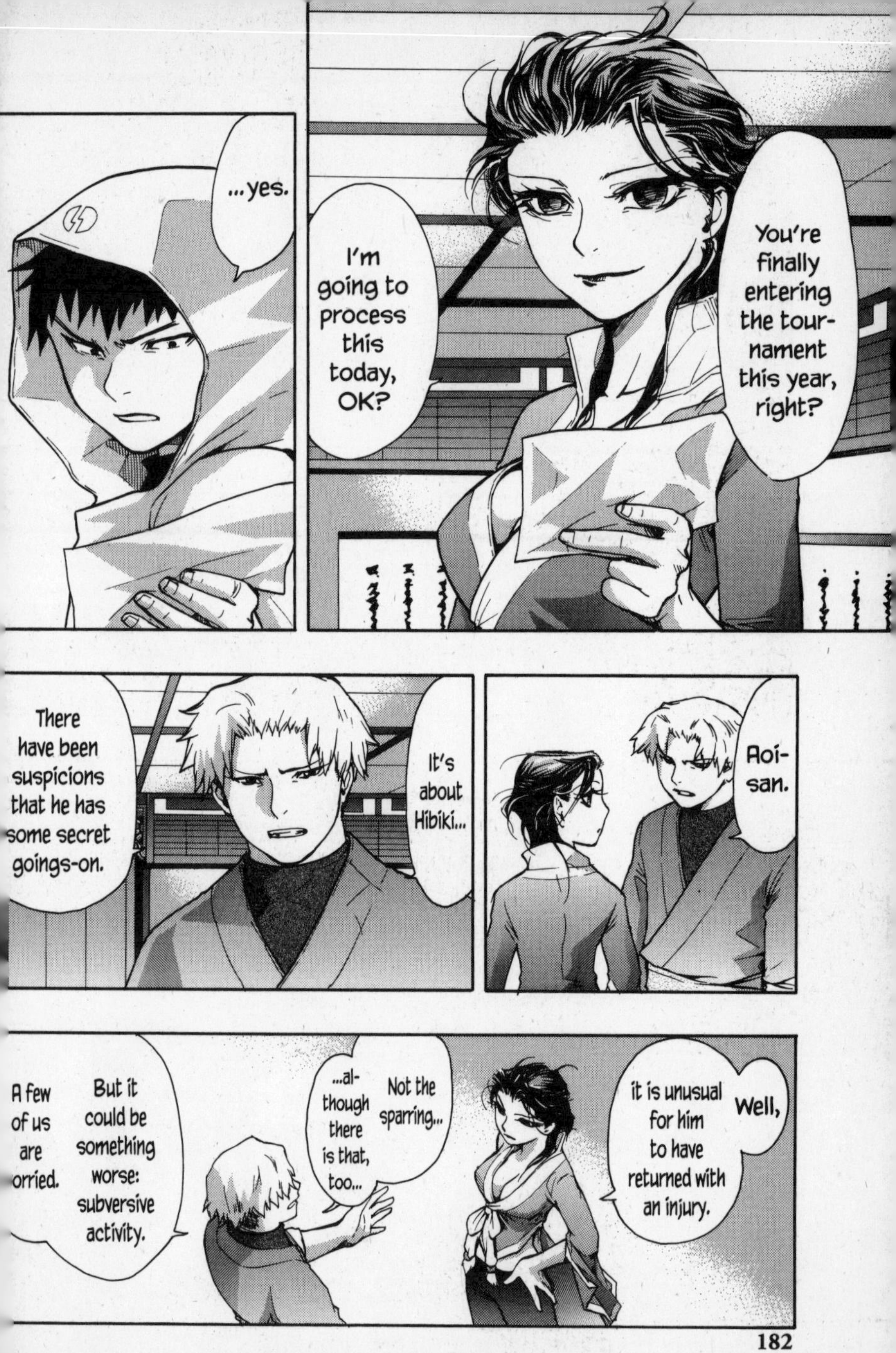
You're finally entering the tour-nament this year, right?
I'm going to process this today, OK?
...yes.
Aoi-san.
It's about Hibiki...
There have been suspicions that he has some secret goings-on.
Well,
it is unusual for him to have returned with an injury.
Not the sparring...
...al-though there is that, too...
But it could be something worse: subversive activity.
A few of us are orried.

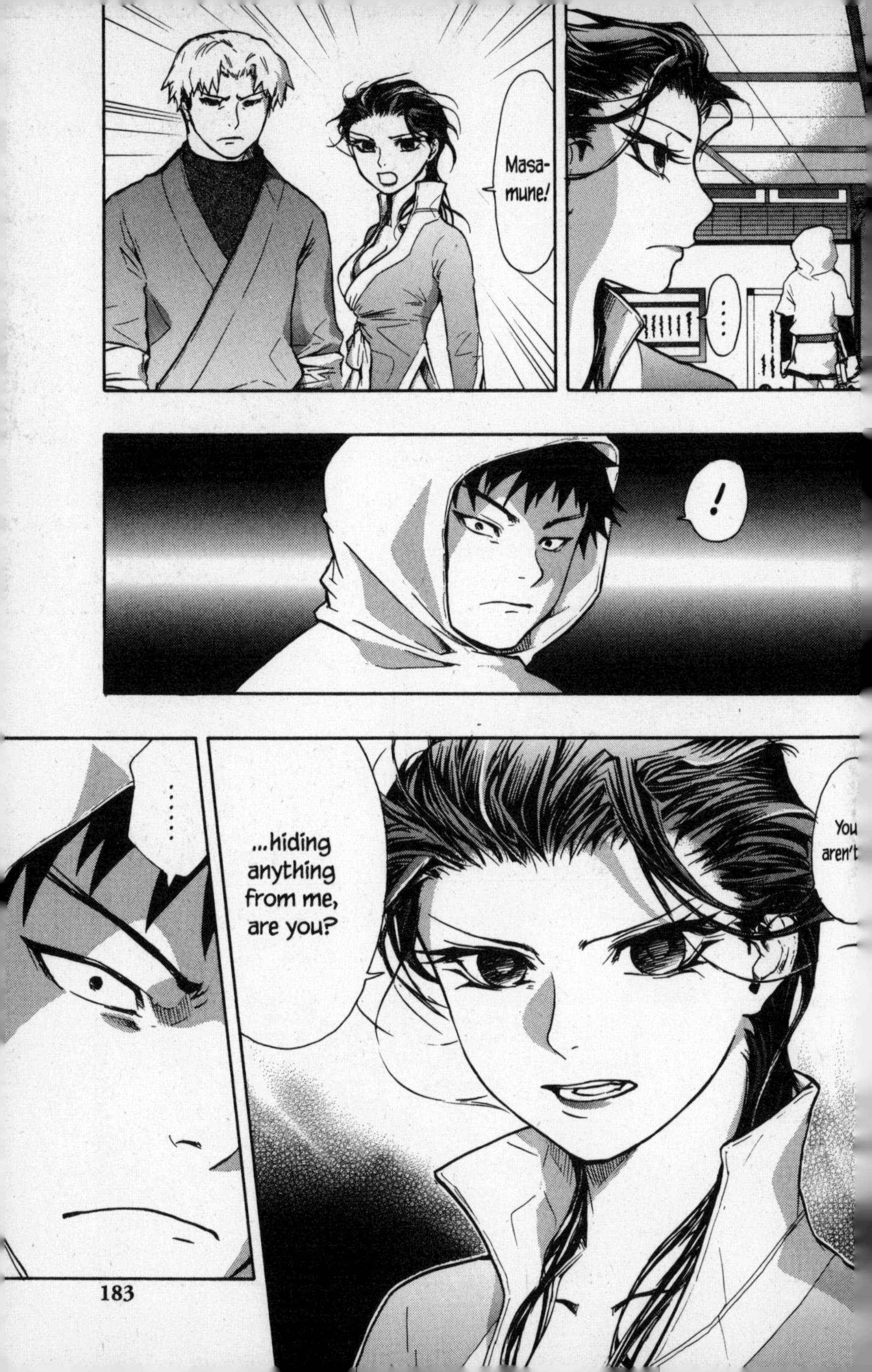
....
Masa-mune!
!
You aren't
...hiding anything from me, are you?
......

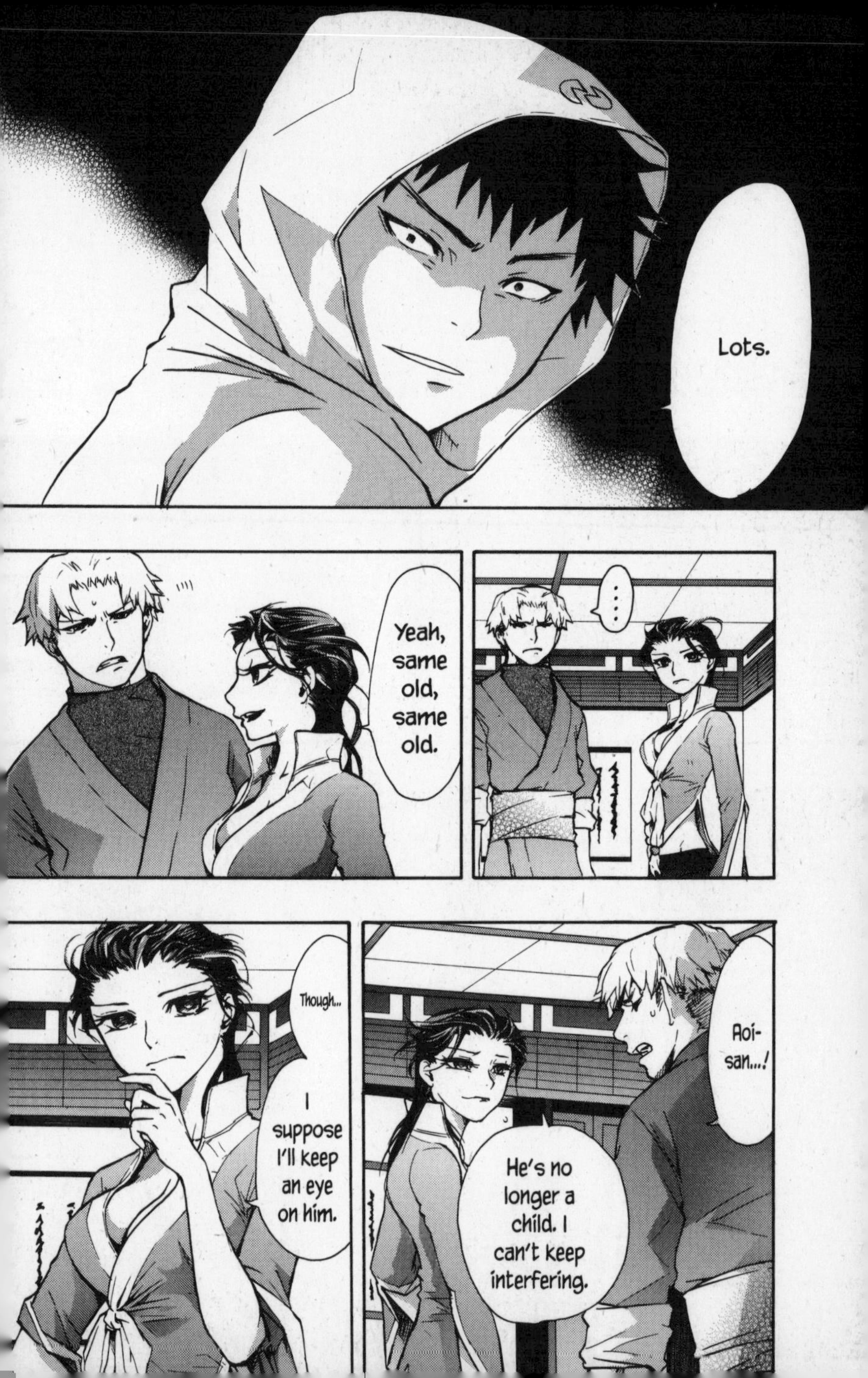
Lots.
. . . .
Yeah, same old, same old.
Aoi-san...!
He's no longer a child. I can't keep interfering.
Though...
I suppose I'll keep an eye on him.

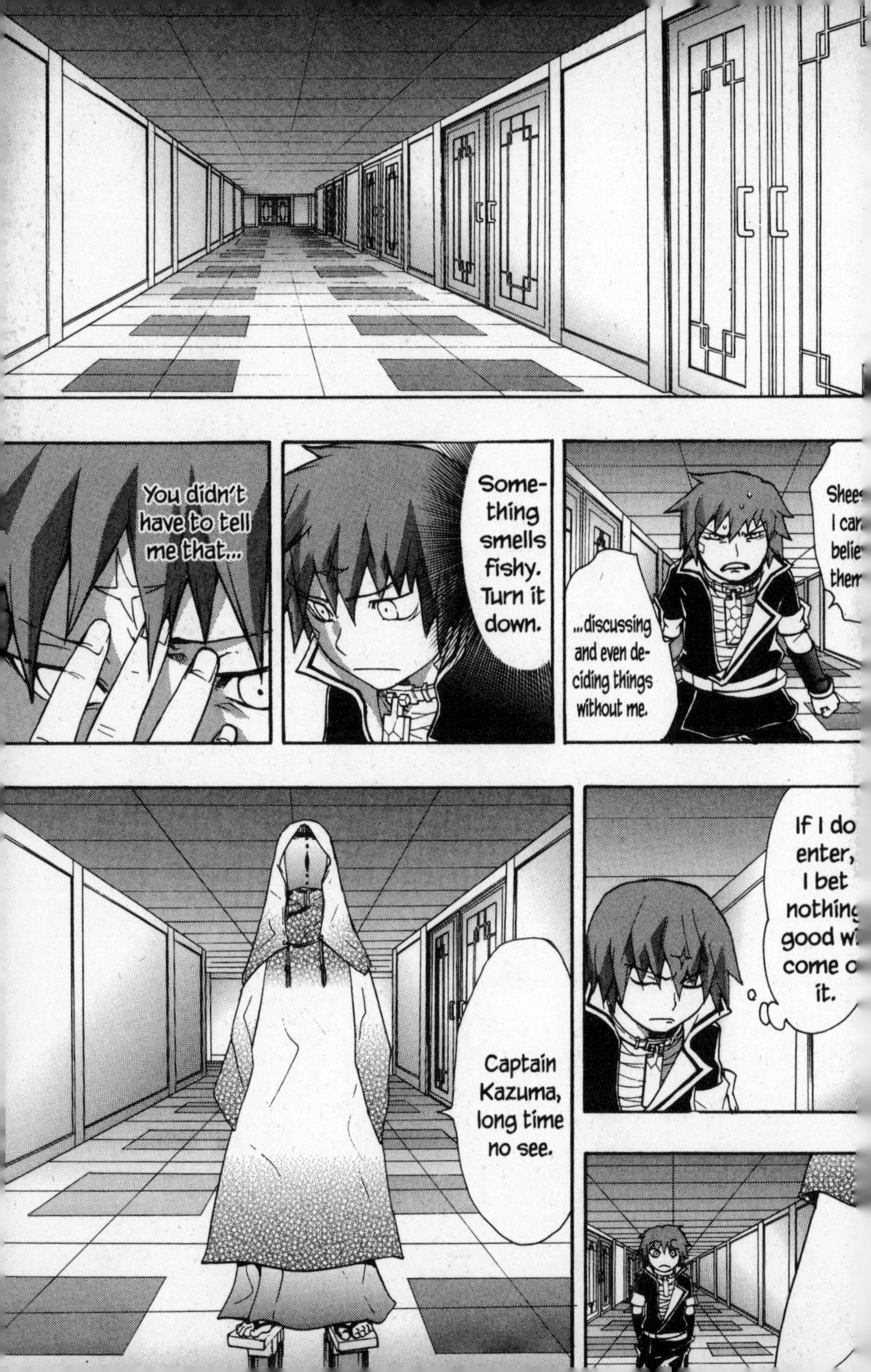
Shees I can belie them
...discussing and even deciding things without me.
Something smells fishy. Turn it down.
You didn't have to tell me that...
If I do enter, I bet nothing good wi come o it.
Captain Kazuma, long time no see.

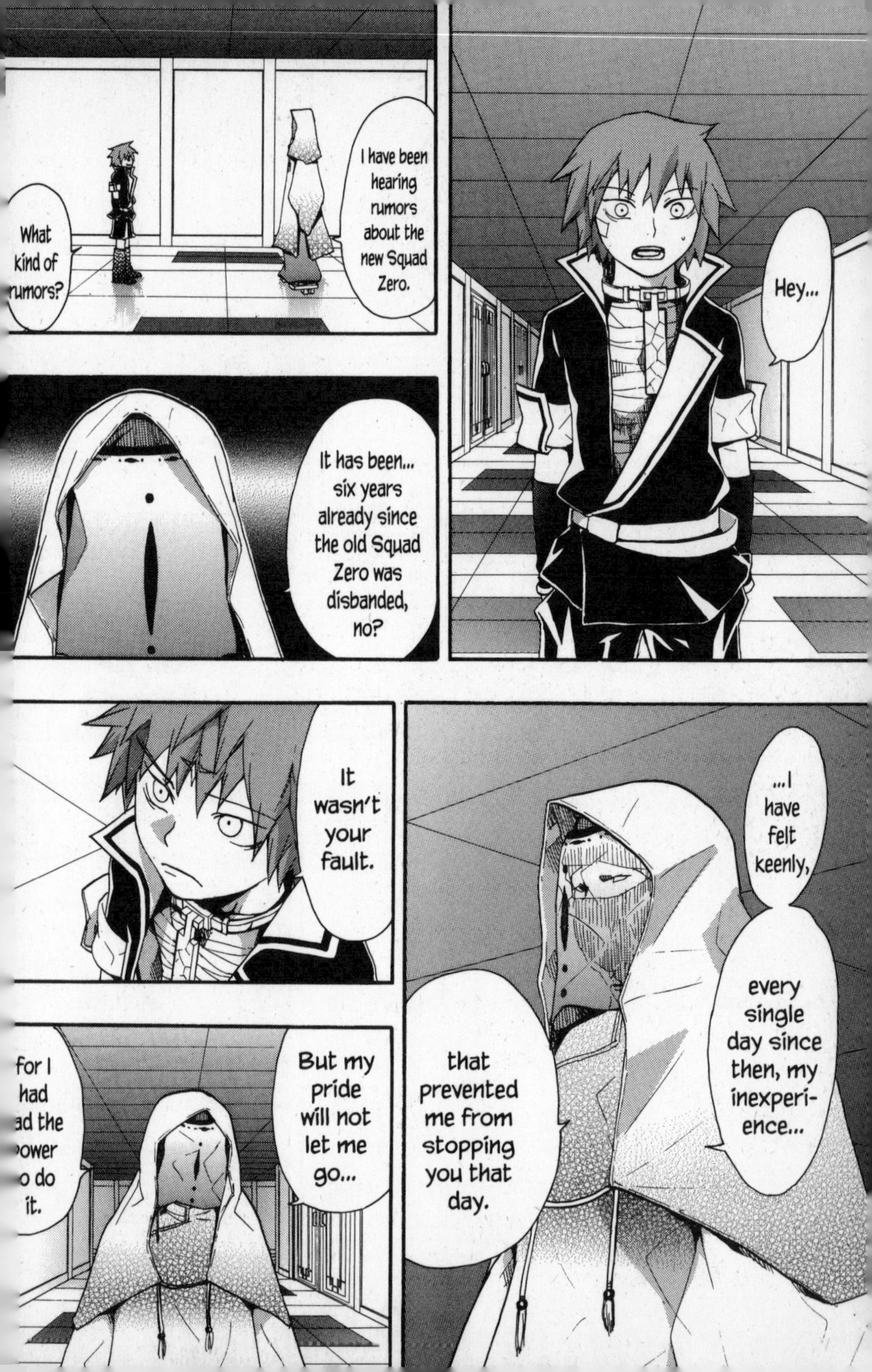
Hey...
I have been hearing rumors about the new Squad Zero.
What kind of rumors?
It has been... six years already since the old Squad Zero was disbanded, no?
...I have felt keenly,
every single day since then, my inexperience...
that prevented me from stopping you that day.
It wasn't your fault.
But my pride will not let me go...
for I had ad the ower o do it.

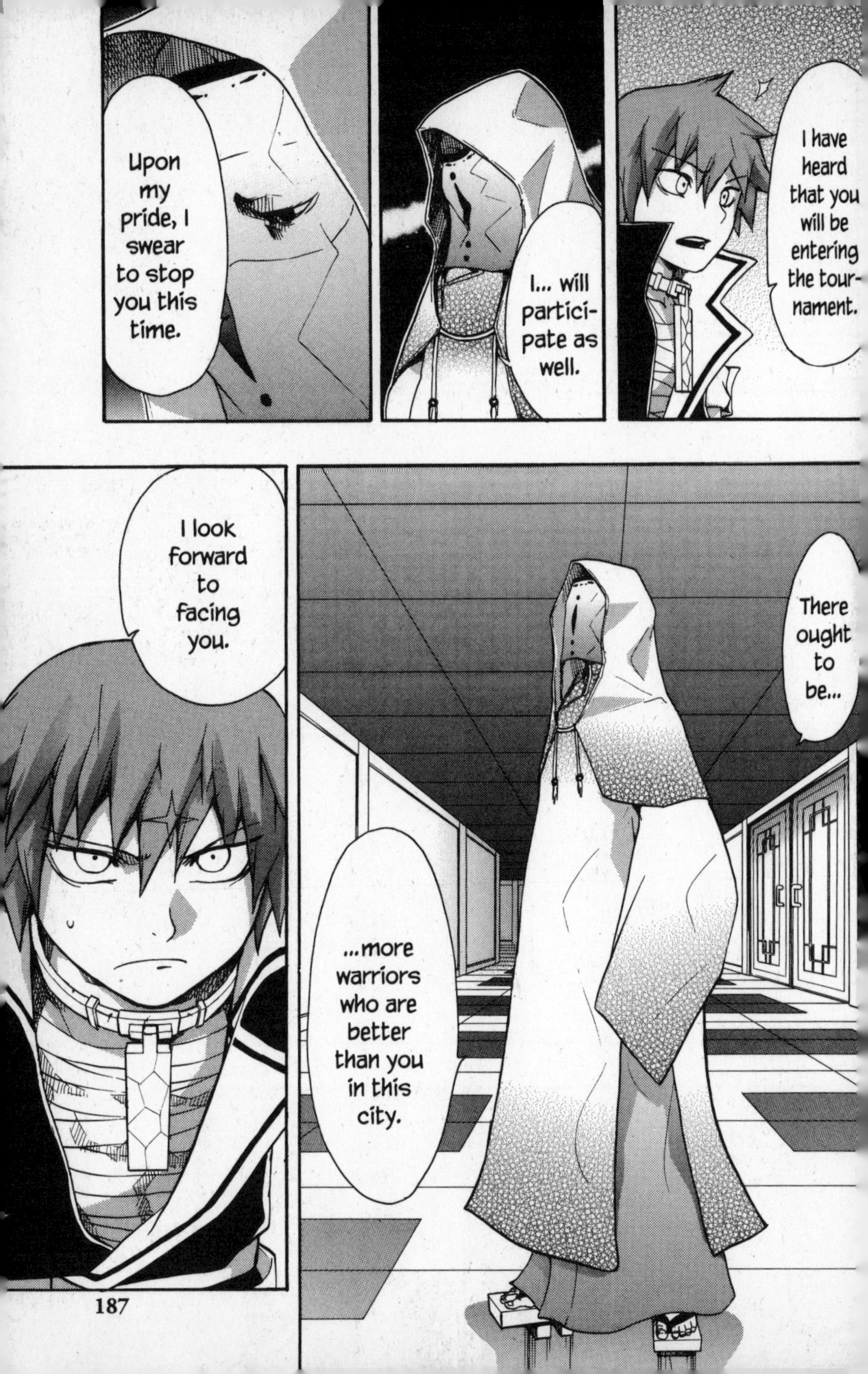
I have heard that you will be entering the tour-nament.
I... will partici-pate as well.
Upon my pride, I swear to stop you this time.
There ought to be...
...more warriors who are better than you in this city.
I look forward to facing you.

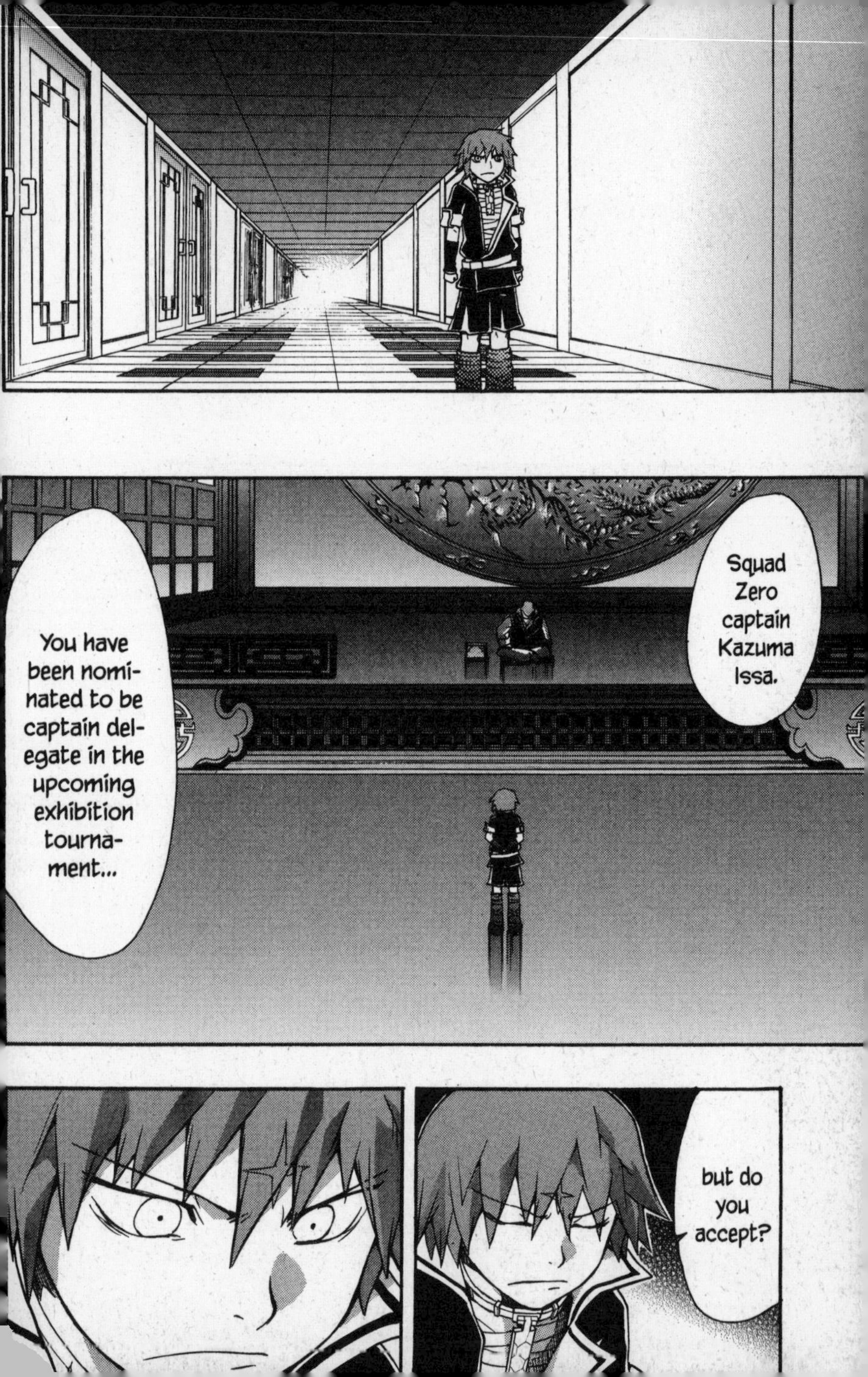
Squad Zero captain Kazuma Issa.
You have been nominated to be captain delegate in the upcoming exhibition tournament...
but do you accept?

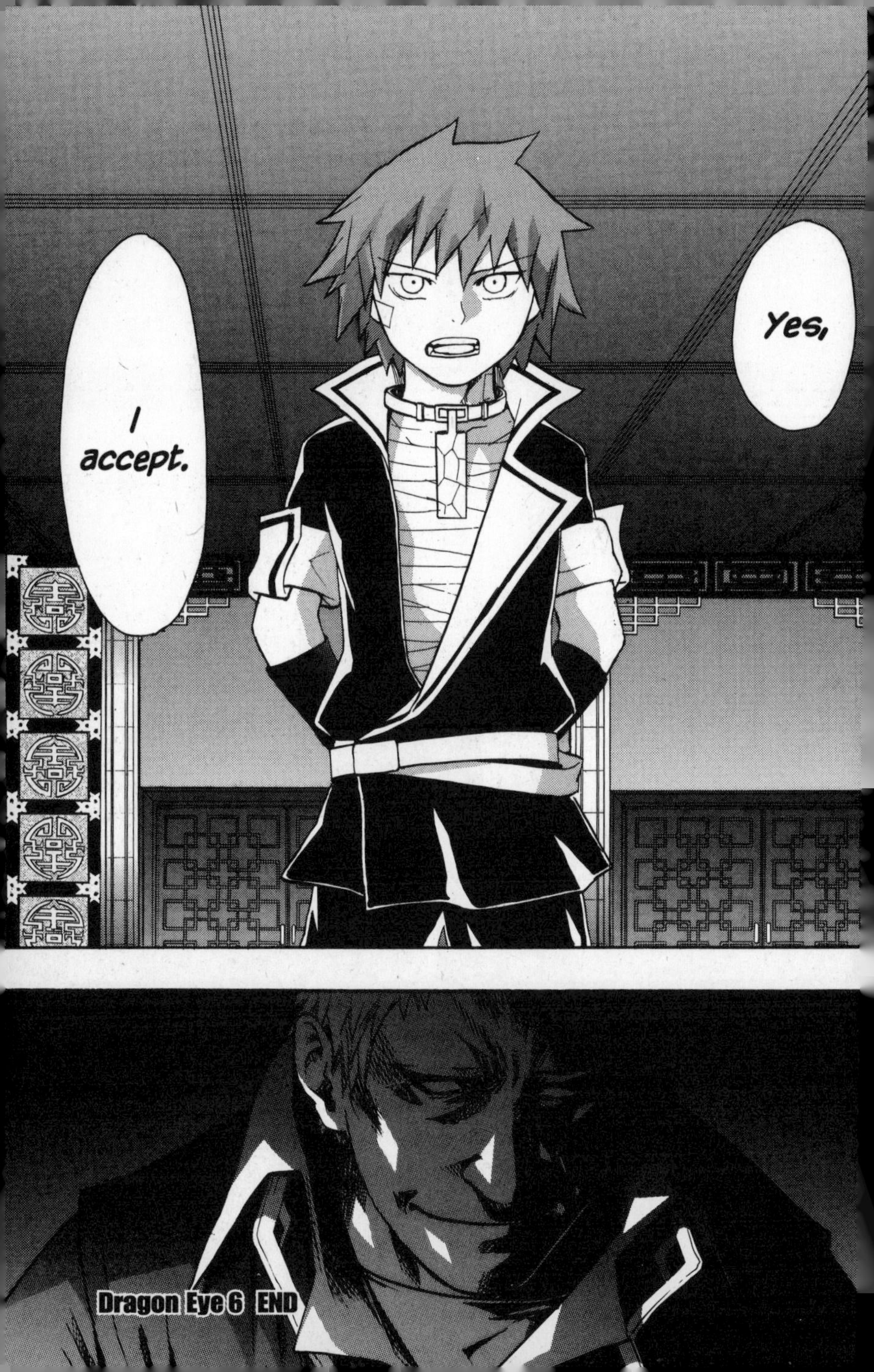
Yes,
I accept.
Dragon Eye 6 END

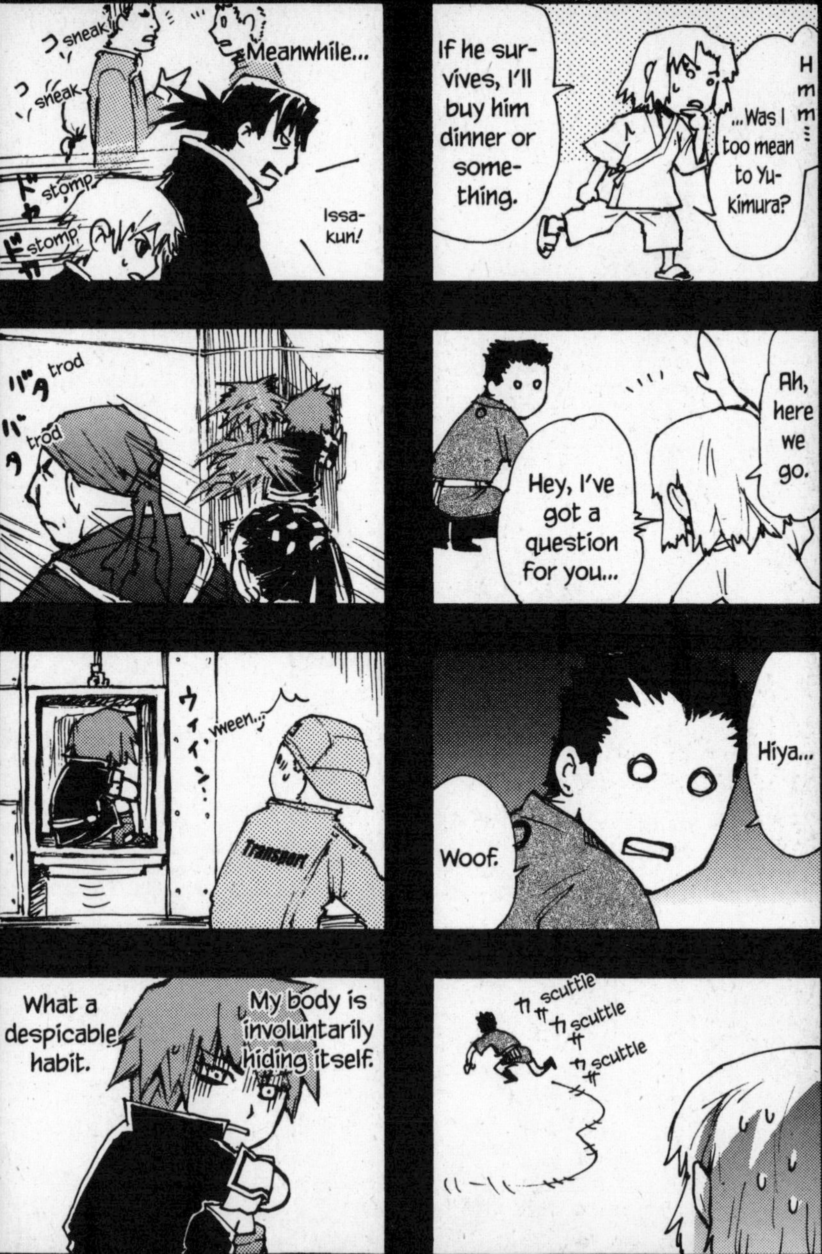
Hmm...
...Was I too mean to Yukimura?
If he survives, I'll buy him dinner or something.
Meanwhile...
sneak
sneak
stomp
stomp
Issa-kun!
Ah, here we go.
Hey, I've got a question for you...
trod
trod
Hiya...
Woof.
vween...
Transport
scuttle
scuttle
scuttle
My body is involuntarily hiding itself.
What a despicable habit.

What Happened One Day 6

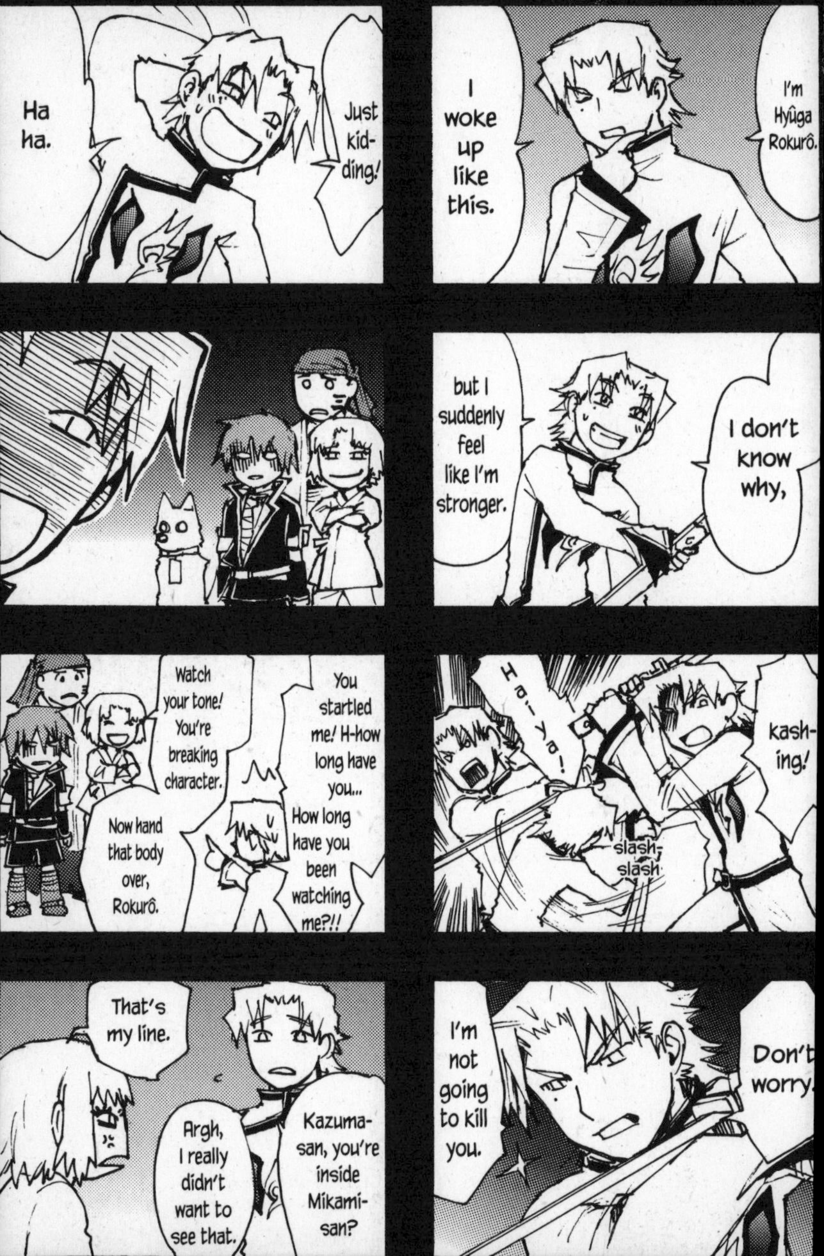
I'm Hyûga Rokurô.
I woke up like this.
I don't know why,
but I suddenly feel like I'm stronger.
kash-ing!
Ha-ya!
slash-slash
Don't worry.
I'm not going to kill you.
Just kid-ding!
Ha ha.
You startled me! H-how long have you... How long have you been watching me?!!
Watch your tone! You're breaking character.
Now hand that body over, Rokurô.
Kazuma-san, you're inside Mikami-san?
That's my line.
Argh, I really didn't want to see that.

What Happened One Day 7

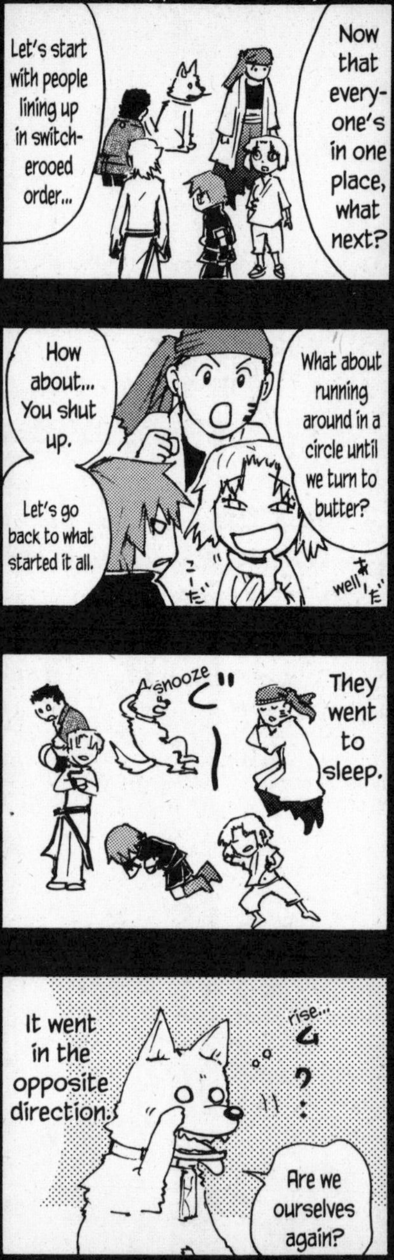
Now that every-one's in one place, what next?
Let's start with people lining up in switch-erooed order...
What about running around in a circle until we turn to butter?
well
How about... You shut up.
Let's go back to what started it all.
They went to sleep.
snooze
rise...
It went in the opposite direction.
Are we ourselves again?

THE END

To everybody who bought Volume 6, thank you very much!
It's Fujiyama here.
Recently, for some unknown reason, I've been in a lot of pain.
But both machinery and human bodies will fall into disrepair if they're not maintained. So I've been trying to take care of myself!

Maintenance Checklist

- Early bedtime: Ongoing battle. Still not achieved.
- Saké: Yet another health benefit of drinking has been proven! But I'll cut back anyway.
- Meals... I'd like to cook my own meals at least seven days out of each month, but it still has not happened. So vexing.

Thanks

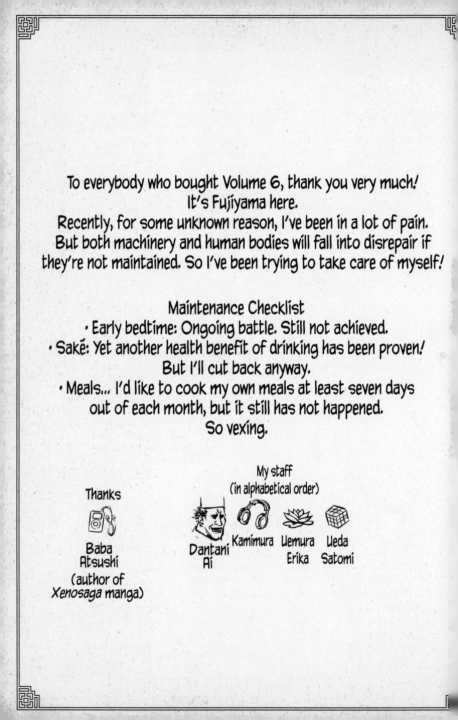

Baba Atsushi
(author of *Xenosaga* manga)

My staff
(in alphabetical order)

Dantani Ai

Kamimura

Uemura Erika

Ueda Satomi

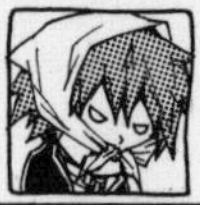

Hiya! As always, we got tons of questions, so I'm real happy! However, I have to do it in secret this time. So please keep your voices down, OK? Here we go (whisper whisper).

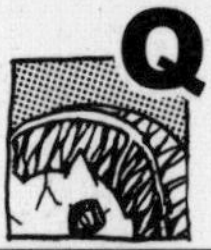
Q

I enjoy reading *Dragon Eye* every month. My question is: Issa and Hibiki's weapons have names, but what about Leila and Sôsei's blades? And if so, who named them, and what is the origin of the names?
Iijima Ken-sa

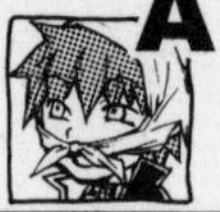
A

Aah, nice question (whisper whisper)! Let me refer to the Author's Notes that I have here for the answer. "Leila's blade... 'Shiraume-maru' ['White Plum Boy'], work of Yoroku Kagome. Was bestowed upon her by her teacher Shimon. Long ago, around the time he founded the Sacred Blade, Shimon School, Shimon commissioned swordsmith Kagome to forge it. Further details unknown."

"Yukimura's blade... 'Musasabi' ['Nightglider']. Was originally a single blade, but Yukimura himself later commissioned a duplicate to make them twin blades. Is an heirloom of his father's, who had been a well-known swordsman."
That's all we seem to know right now. They both seem to be of pretty high quality. Unlike my much-nicked Diamond Sacred Steel...!! (whisper whisper)

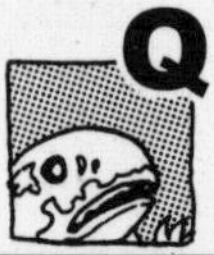
Q

It's really eating at me, but there's that Igunido that's in the shape of a dog!! Does that mean that Igunido can change forms? Or did it always look like that? Please tell me!! Don't-know-where-to-start...san.

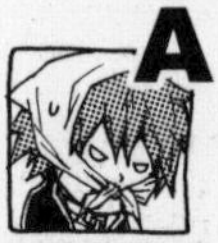
A

Hey, don't shout!! (whisper whisper) Igunido are classified information, so I can't really tell you... but from what I know, I believe he was always that way? I feel like there are all kinds.

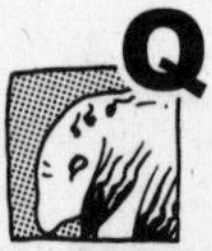
Q

Please tell me more about Natsumi★chan. All the Mikuni women are great beauties, so I keep forgetting about her.
Oda-san

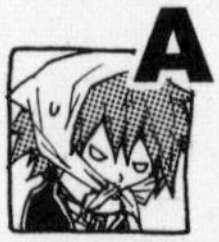
A

Mmm... I've got a bad feeling about this...

tramp tramp tramp

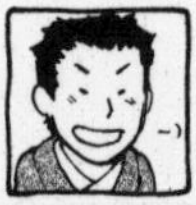

There you are! I finally found you, Kazuma-san!! What are you doing in such a dark, cramped space?!!

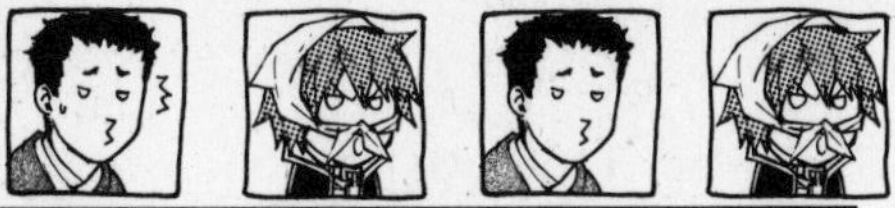

Shoot, he tracked me down... I was trying so hard to hide from him...

You're so mean. I told you I'd support you for the next Q&A session!

But it's such a pain when you join in.

H-how could you!!

Then let me prove to you how helpful my vast knowledge can be!! What's this... it's like this next query was sent in with me in mind!! Well, here's my data, as proud Fan Club Member Number 18!! "Having suddenly rocketed to superstardom through her role in the hit drama *The Little Devils Series*, Natsumi ★ is a much-adored fashion idol to little girls, and she lives right here in Mikuni City. The songs released by this singing and fighting little devil Emilin are all chart-topping hits, and related merchandise is perpetually sold out..."

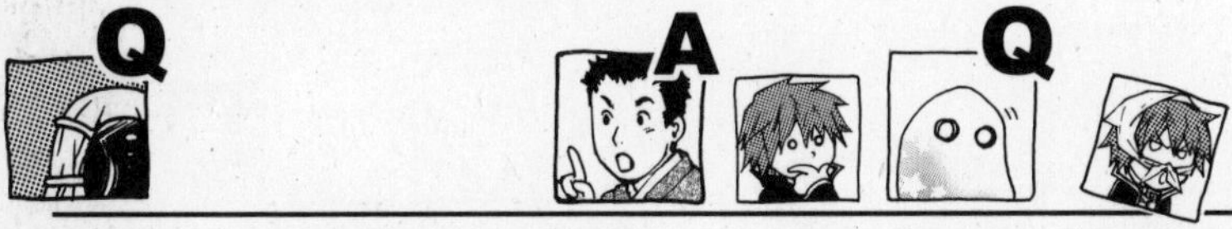

Q
A
Q

All right, that's enough!

How young can one apply to take the VIUS enlistment examination? Also, is there a retirement age?
Saeki Nozomi-san

OK, assistant! You answer this one!

(Don't tell me you don't know, Kazuma-san!) Yes, yes... here we go. There is technically no minimum or maximum age limit to VIUS membership. Merely "as long as you can fulfill the duties of a warrior," so it seems the average is to start applying around 13 years old. By the way, I successfully enlisted when I was 14!

Kajiyama-san mentioned he was from a large family, but how many siblings does he have?
Sala-san

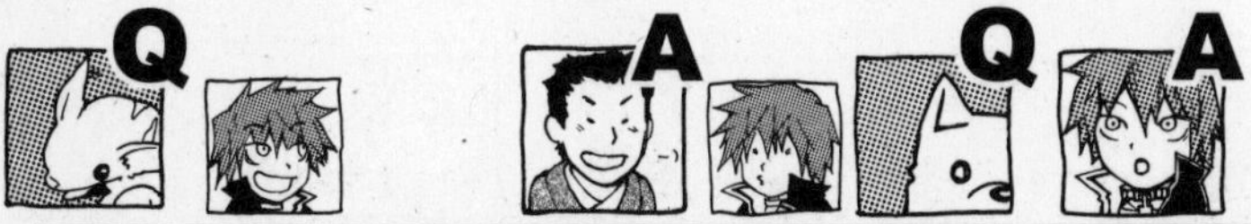

Q
A
Q
A

Yeah, I believe Kanikama has eight siblings. I think he's the third oldest? It's a huge family!

How many Skyway vehicles are there in Mikuni?
Taketomi Jin-san

All right! Assistant, look it up!!

Yes, sir. Click-click-click (acquiring data). Here it is. There are currently 18 Skyway vehicles in operation throughout Mikuni. Including those off-line for maintenance, 21.

And for some reason, they've apparently all got different designs!?

In Mikuni, are there any police-like jobs other than the VIUS??

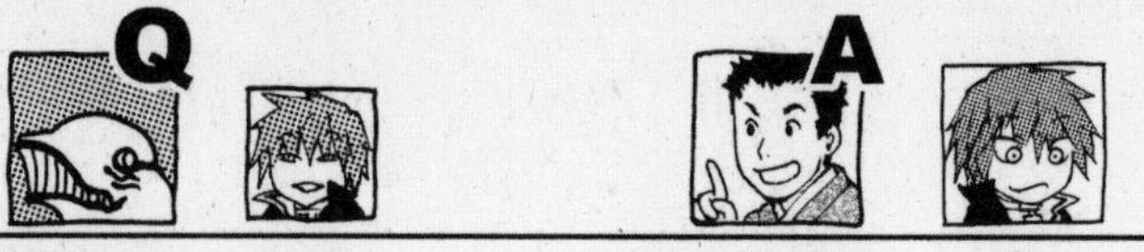

And incidents other than those involving Dracules? Are the VIUS employed for any and all incidents that occur in Mikuni?? Kitsune-san [Fox-san]

Nice question! Actually, there is a separate police force. I'll let my assistant go into detail.

Yes, yes! In Mikuni City, the VIUS are troops that only respond to situations involving Dracules or the D Virus. All other incidents or crimes fall under the jurisdiction of the Civil Defense Unit. They correspond to your "police force."

When one eats and runs, the Civil Defense officers are the ones who will chase you!

Does Hibiki-san have a thing for Aoi-san? ^^;
It bothers me so much I can't sleep at night. Also, I want to know what kind of woman is everyone's type! I-love-Hibiki-san

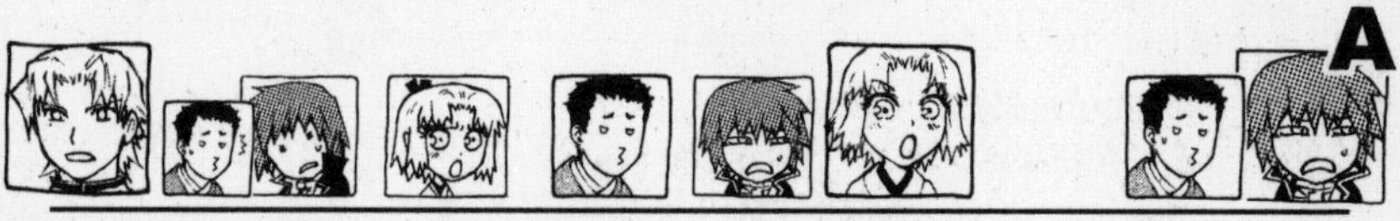

How should I know! Just sleep, will you!

Kazuma-san, we must answer more politely.

stomp
stomp
stomp

Oh! There you are! Why didn't you let me know?!

(Wah! More trouble!)

Mmm. I'm not giving up the assistant's seat even for you, Mikami-san!

Unh! But as a Squad Zero member, I can't give way, either.

Hyûga, back off a bit, will you?

Waah...

Why don't we all do it together?

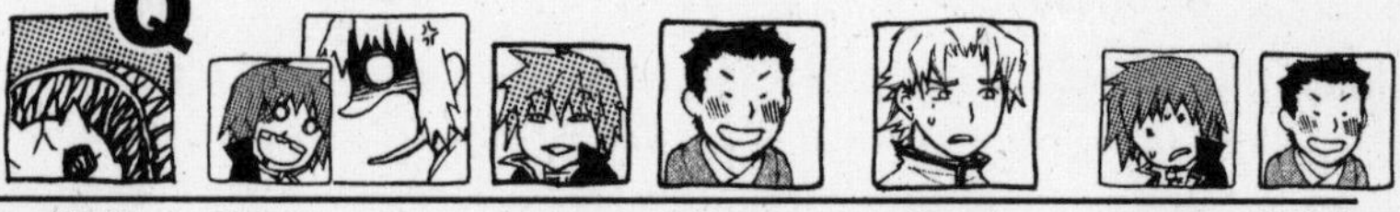

Y-Yukimura-kun...

Waah, it's getting mighty complicated! All right then, answer in order!!

Wh-what, starting with me?! Mm... I like feminine women... I suppose?

Oh! I know, I know! I like kind, generous, soft...

You mean not all violent like Leila?! Wa-ha ha.

Grrr (strangle)

That's why I didn't want to do this together!

Please give me the bios of all of the Squad Zero members. Also, who is the dumbest person and who is the smartest person who appeared in Volume 4? Nameko [Mushroom] Dracule-san

A

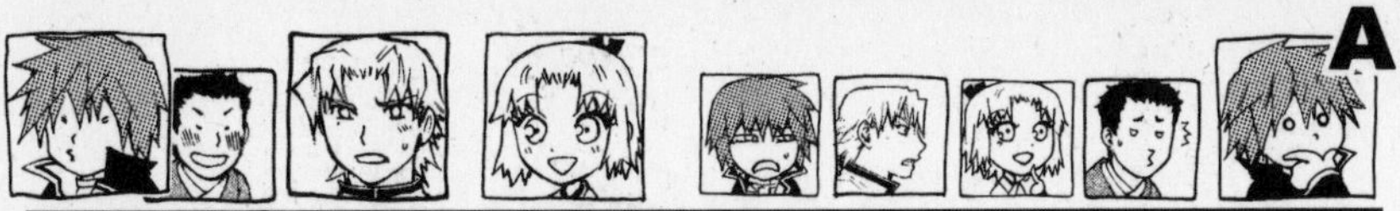

That's quite a perilous question. Of course, the dumbest one is Hyûga Rokurô...
K-Kazuma-san!!
I think the smartest is Captain Aoi...
The dumbest has got to be you, Kazuma.
What?!!
Hey! Just introduce yourselves one by one!!
Huh? Oh, uh... I am Mikami Leila, 14 years old... my forte is shiritori word games and cleaning, I guess.
Self-introduction? ...I'm Yukimura Sôsei, 17 years old... my forte is memorization, I guess.
I'm Hyûga Rokurô, 20 years old!!
Whoops, we're out of space! Well then, see you next time!

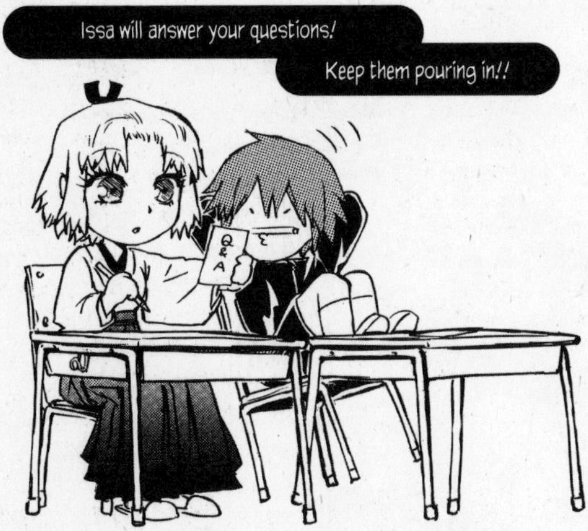

Issa will answer your questions!
Keep them pouring in!!
Q&A

Seeking all questions and concerns about Dragon Eye!

Seeking Correspondence!

*Furthermore, please be aware that all submissions, including your personal information, will be handed over to the author, so send us your questions at your own risk.

What to submit

Please send us, in addition to your question(s), your address, name (and a pen name, if you have one), age, school year (or type of work), and phone number or e-mail address. If your submission is printed, we will send you a small present.

Address to:

112-8001 Tokyo City Bunkyô District Otowa
2-12-21 Kôdansha Monthly Shônen Sirius
Attn: "*Dragon Eye* Q&A Corner"

Email:

sirius@kodansha.co.jp

(if you are e-mailing us your question(s), please write the Q&A corner name in the subject line)

TRANSLATION NOTES

Japanese is a tricky language for most Westerners, and translation is often more art than science. For your edification and reading pleasure, here are notes on some of the places where we could have gone in a different direction in our translation of the work, or where a Japanese cultural reference is used.

Troop designation symbols, various pages

Most VIUS members wear their troop designations somewhere on their uniforms, and equipment and objects sometimes bear stamps as well. For example, on page 1, the iron-on patch on Leila's right shoulder has the character for zero emblazoned on it, and the back of Issa's jacket reads "Squad Zero in the house." On pages 148-49, one veil depicts the older way of writing the number nine, while two in the center (along the page fold) depict the number eight and three on the far left depict the number seven.

She might have grown horns, page 138

In Japan, saying that someone has "grown horns" means they're in a rage. The "horns" refer to the horns that Oni ogres sport—ogres, of course, being known for their fearsome tempers.

H-hold up!!

She might have grown horns over yesterday's fuss.

We better head over, or else she'll yell at us again.

Dried squid, page 150

A common pub appetizer, *surume* are squid or cuttlefish that are gutted, dried, boiled (with or without seasoning), pressed flat, and then dried once more. Sold either whole, as seen here hanging from Issa's mouth, or pre-shredded into strips, they are a chewy, leathery snack that exercises one's jaw.

La-di-da-

clatter

Mornin'!

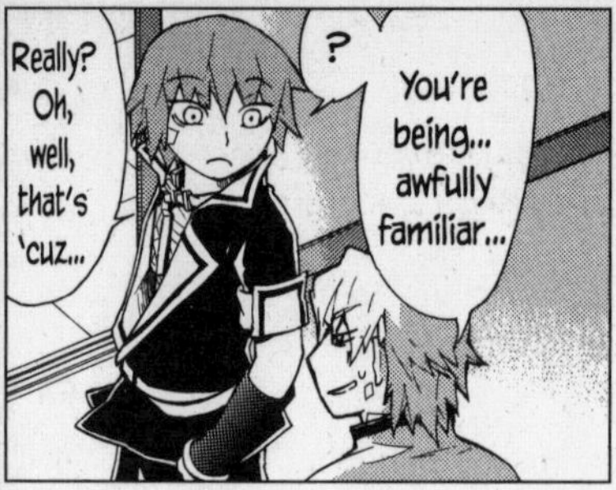
?
You're being... awfully familiar...
Really? Oh, well, that's 'cuz...

"You're being... awfully familiar," page 154

Sôsei bristles because Issa has suddenly called him by his first name, rather than his last, as Issa always has before. In Japan, the way in which you address someone—by first or last name, or with or without honorifics, is often a sign of how close you are to them. It's considered to be a sign of unusual intimacy to refer to someone by their first name, without honorifics. Issa often shows his rebellious temperament by seldom using honorifics, even with his fellow captains, and tends to address those he's particularly close to by first name only.

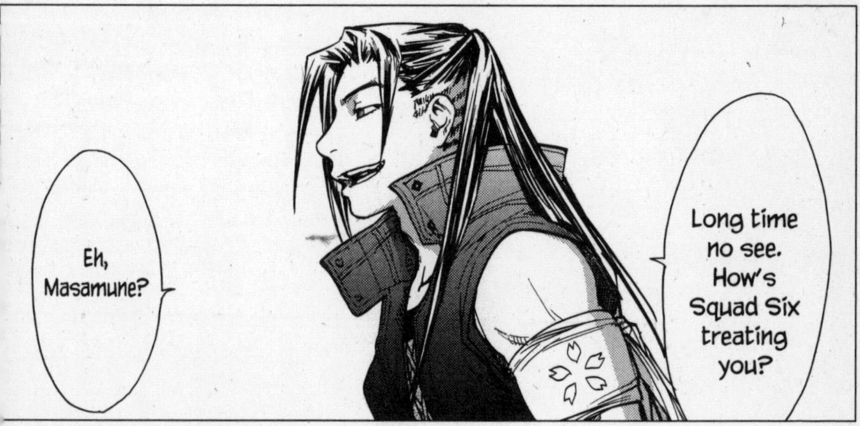
Long time no see. How's Squad Six treating you?
Eh, Masamune?

Akira's armband, page 160

The flower symbol on Akira's armband is a pictorial depiction of the sakura or cherry blossom. It is probably because his squad captain is Sakuraba, whose name is made up of the *kanji* for "cherry blossom" and "yard."

Emilin, page 195

"Emilin" is the name of the little devil character the idol Natsumi plays on TV. The popularity of this character, and the series it appears in, helped launch her career.

Shiritori, page 197

A popular children's word game and educational tool where two or more players must go around (in order) in a circle saying a word that begins with the same syllable the previous person's word ended in. For example, "*miso*" could be followed with "*Sôsei.*" The name *Shiritori* literally means "take the bottom," since Japanese is traditionally written vertically. The game ends when someone either repeats a word or uses a word ending in the syllable "*n*" or "*un,*" because there are no words that begin with that syllable. Some play with additional rules such as no proper nouns, no foreign words, or the use of only words of a certain genre or a certain number of syllables.

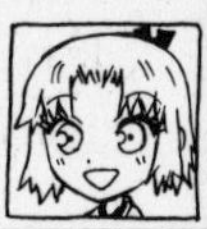

Huh? Oh, uh... I am Mikami Leila, 14 years old... my forte is shiritori word games and cleaning, I guess.

TOMARE!

止まれ

[STOP!]

You're going the wrong way!

Manga is a completely different type of reading experience.

To start at the beginning, go to the end!

That's right! Authentic manga is read the traditional Japanese way—from right to left. Exactly the opposite of how American books are read. It's easy to follow: Just go to the other end of the book, and read each page—and each panel—from right side to left side, starting at the top right. Now you're experiencing manga as it was meant to be!